Data-Driven Governance Through AI, Digital Marketing, and the Privacy Interplay

José Ramón Saura
Rey Juan Carlos University, Spain

IGI Global
Scientific Publishing
Publishing Tomorrow's Research Today

Vice President of Editorial — Melissa Wagner
Managing Editor of Acquisitions — Mikaela Felty
Managing Editor of Book Development — Jocelynn Hessler
Production Manager — Mike Brehm
Cover Design — Phillip Shickler

Published in the United States of America by
IGI Global Scientific Publishing
701 East Chocolate Avenue
Hershey, PA, 17033, USA
Tel: 717-533-8845
Fax: 717-533-8661
Website: https://www.igi-global.com E-mail: cust@igi-global.com

Library of Congress Cataloging-in-Publication Data

Names: Saura, José Ramón, 1992- editor.
Title: Data-driven governance through AI, digital marketing, and the privacy interplay / edited by: Jose Ramon Saura.
Description: Hershey PA : IGI Global Scientific Publishing, [2025] | Includes bibliographical references. | Summary: "The primary aim of this book is to provide a comprehensive understanding of how artificial intelligence (AI) and digital marketing are being utilized in the sphere of public or professional (industry) governance and to critically examine the implications these technologies have on privacy and public policy"-- Provided by publisher.
Identifiers: LCCN 2024048772 (print) | LCCN 2024048773 (ebook) | ISBN 9798369369456 (hardcover) | ISBN 9798369369463 (paperback) | ISBN 9798369369470 (ebook)
Subjects: LCSH: Artificial intelligence--Industrial applications. | Internet marketing. | Data privacy.
Classification: LCC TA347.A78 D37 2025 (print) | LCC TA347.A78 (ebook) | DDC 381/.142--dc23/eng/20250108
LC record available at https://lccn.loc.gov/2024048772
LC ebook record available at https://lccn.loc.gov/2024048773

British Cataloguing in Publication Data
A Cataloguing in Publication record for this book is available from the British Library.

Table of Contents

Detailed Table of Contents

This study explores the transformative role of artificial intelligence (AI) in digital governance by examining four diverse case studies: Saudi Arabia, Estonia, Singapore, and Spain. Using a case study methodology, the research investigates how AI has been integrated into public administration to enhance efficiencyand address societal challenges. Findings reveal significant variations in approaches to AI integration, influenced by each country's socio-economic contexts and governance priorities. Key theoretical implications include the need to balance technological innovation with socio-political considerations, while practical insights emphasize the scalability of interoperable systems and the critical role of transparency in fostering public trust. Despite notable advancements, challenges such as ensuring inclusivity, addressing algorithmic bias, and safeguarding data privacy persist, underscoring the need for ongoing policy adaptation and citizen engagement.

Data is considered the new oil of the current world economy. Therefore, it is necessary to analyze the quality of the data as a preliminary phase in the interaction processes with algorithms and artificial intelligence. This chapter explores the critical importance of data quality within the surveillance economy and its implications for digital governance. It addresses the challenges of ensuring accurate, reliable data in an era of pervasive data collection and usage. The discussion highlights strategies for improving data governance practices to enhance privacy and accountability in AI-driven environments.

Scholars who have studied big data in Small and Medium Enterprises (SMEs) often focus on the technicalities/applicability and factors that encourage or inhibit its use. Therefore, the question of "how could SMEs leverage big data in view of their limited resources as compared to large firms?" remains unanswered. This chapter assesses the realities concerning SMEs adoption of big data and proposes guiding measures to help SMEs overcome the impeding challenges and optimize their use, particularly for better decision making. While SMEs limited adoption of big data is attributed to the limited resources, complexity and/or underestimation of their benefits, the main challenges are often cost, data privacy and security, lack of in-house capabilities, lack of IT skills and analytic expertise, and lack of a supportive culture. We argue that a successful big data system must encompass key budgets, IT infrastructure, data architecture, management/governance, security/privacy, data analytics and skilled workforce. Measures of big data's effective application and implications are discussed.

In an increasingly digitalized world, social media has transformed communication and information consumption, but it has also raised ethical concerns regarding privacy and mental health, particularly among young people. The study of TikTok, one of the most popular platforms, offers an opportunity to examine how addictive design captures users' attention, while surveillance capitalism commodifies their data. This analysis highlights the need for ethical design, promoting practices that prioritize transparency and user well-being.

Textile companies have gradually realized that data is essential for improving sales and revenue margins because clothing brands and retailers must develop manufacturing and sale styles that resonate with customers. In recent decades, with advancements in various categories of data analytics and artificial intelligence techniques (e.g., machine learning), the value of data-driven applications has been well acknowledged by textile clothing retailers as they use these predictive software outputs for regular

in educational management. This hybrid approach highlights how AI tools can complement traditional methods, opening new possibilities for academic planning and educational research.

This study presents an innovative Convolutional Neural Network (CNN) framework designed to improve fingerprint classification, particularly distinguishing between authentic and counterfeit prints. Fingerprint authentication is crucial in biometric security, but advanced techniques for creating fake fingerprints demand ongoing improvements in classification methods. We propose a CNN architecture that effectively captures the intricate features of fingerprint images using convolutional and pooling layers, enhanced by dropout regularization to prevent overfitting. Our approach employs a diverse, meticulously curated dataset, divided into training, validation, and test sets for robust model training and performance evaluation. Rigorous testing, including cross-validation and extensive metrics analysis, demonstrates our CNN model's exceptional accuracy and reliability in discerning genuine from fraudulent prints. This research enhances fingerprint authentication systems by addressing the challenges of sophisticated manipulation techniques.

Digital transformation has driven the use of tools like Power BI in education, offering advanced data analysis and visualization capabilities. This study examines the feasibility of designing a dashboard to analyze key indicators for master's program graduates in Spanish universities. The main goal was to identify, structure, and visualize metrics to uncover trends and patterns. Four phases guided the methodology: data collection and validation of 14 files with variables like gender, modality, branches, and regions; definition of generic KPIs to outline broad metrics on graduates by type of university and location; creation of specific KPIs for in-depth analysis and chart configuration; and defining the steps to set up an interactive Power BI dashboard. Conclusions emphasize Power BI's value in democratizing data access and fostering data-driven decision-making. Limitations include reliance on high-quality data and technical training. This study offers a replicable approach, key indicators, and adaptable dashboards to enhance university management and higher education effectiveness.

Preface

In the rapidly evolving landscape of public administration and private corporations, the integration of artificial intelligence (AI) and digital marketing has redefined traditional governance models (Birkstedt et al., 2023). Public institutions across the globe are increasingly adopting data-driven approaches to enhance operational efficiency, deliver personalized services, and address pressing societal challenges (Saura et al., 222). This transformation marks a shift in the relationship between governments and citizens, introducing opportunities for greater transparency, accessibility, and inclusivity in governance. At the same time, these technological advancements pose significant ethical, legal, and social challenges, particularly concerning privacy (Zhang et al., 2021) and data protection (Lyulyov et al., 2024).

The central theme of this edited book is the connection between data-driven governance, AI, and digital marketing, with a specific emphasis on their impact on privacy. While AI offers unparalleled capabilities in processing large datasets and deriving actionable insights, its deployment in public administration raises profound questions about data ownership, algorithmic bias, and the protection of individual freedoms. Similarly, digital marketing strategies traditionally associated with private-sector innovation are being repurposed within the public sphere to foster citizen engagement and promote public policies (Bovaird, 2007). This dual use of AI and digital marketing requires a nuanced understanding of their benefits and limitations within the governance context (Saura et al., 2024).

The edited book takes an interdisciplinary approach, drawing from fields such as public administration, data science, law, and ethics to provide a comprehensive perspective on the subject matter. Through an analytical lens, it explores how governments can leverage AI and digital marketing to achieve policy goals while ensuring accountability and fairness. The text does not merely celebrate the potential of these technologies but also critically examines the risks they pose, particularly in societies where regulatory frameworks are either weak or nonexistent (Willems et al., 2023). To ground these discussions, the edited book includes a range of case studies from diverse geopolitical and socio-economic contexts. These examples illustrate both the successes and pitfalls of implementing data-driven governance strategies, offering valuable lessons for policymakers and practitioners alike.

Likewise, the edited book aims to foster a balanced and pragmatic understanding of how AI and digital marketing can be harnessed to improve public sector outcomes by juxtaposing innovative applications with cautionary tales. Also, the ethical implications of AI in governance form a core focus of the edited book. As public institutions increasingly rely on AI-driven systems, issues such as algorithmic accountability, transparency, and inclusivity have come to the forefront. For instance, AI algorithms, while efficient, can inadvertently reinforce existing inequalities or marginalize vulnerable populations if not carefully designed and monitored. The edited book emphasizes the importance of establishing robust ethical guidelines and regulatory mechanisms to mitigate these risks and ensure that AI serves as a tool for equitable governance.

Another dimension explored in this edited book is privacy's role in the data-driven governance age. The collection and analysis of vast amounts of personal data, while enabling governments to anticipate and address citizen needs more effectively, also heighten the risk of surveillance and data misuse. This paradox (Saura, 2024), the need for data to improve governance and the imperative to protect individual privacy, forms a recurring theme throughout the text. The edited book advocates for a rights-based approach to data governance that prioritizes citizen trust and empowerment over short-term efficiency gains.

In addition to examining the technological and ethical dimensions of the topic, the edited book also considers the political and economic implications of data-driven governance. It discusses how new tools of AI and digital marketing reshape power dynamics within society, influence public opinion, and alter the nature of democratic engagement. While these technologies have the potential to enhance participatory governance, they can also be weaponized to manipulate citizen behavior or entrench authoritarian control. The text urges readers to critically evaluate the broader societal impacts of these technologies beyond their immediate applications. Therefore, the overarching goal of this edited book is to bridge the gap between academic research and practical implementation in the field of data-driven governance. Synthesizing insights from theory and practice provides a roadmap for policymakers, researchers, and practitioners seeking to navigate the complexities of AI and digital marketing in public administration. The edited book contributes to the academic discourse and also offers actionable recommendations for designing and implementing governance strategies that are both innovative and ethical. This overview serves as the foundation for the subsequent chapters, which delve deeper into specific aspects of data-driven governance, from the challenges of data quality (Nzeako et al, 2024) and the role of behavioral economics (Rasetti, 2020) to the ethical dilemmas (Brough et al., 2021; Saura et al., 2021) posed by surveillance capitalism and the transformative potential of AI in smart cities (Zuboff, 2023). Together, these chapters provide a holistic view of the opportunities and challenges associated with the integration of AI and digital marketing in governance.

The subject of data-driven governance and data privacy holds a relevant position in the contemporary world. At a time when digital transformation is reshaping every aspect of human activity, from economic interactions to social connections and political engagement, public administration stands at the crossroads of unprecedented change (Dwivedi et al., 2023). In this context, governments worldwide are increasingly embracing AI technologies and data analytics to modernize public services, enhance decision-making, and foster greater citizen engagement. This paradigm shift, however, occurs in a context characterized by complex challenges and conflicting priorities.

At the same time, the ubiquity of digital technology has rendered data the lifeblood of modern economies and governance systems (Einav and Levin, 2014). Now, governments are better equipped to collect, analyze, and utilize data at a scale and speed unimaginable in previous decades. Whether it is predicting health crises (Lee, 2009), optimizing urban transportation (Hernández-Tamurejo et al., 2024), or tailoring public services to individual needs, the potential applications of AI and data-driven solutions are vast. Countries such as Singapore, Estonia, and the United Arab Emirates are often cited as leaders in this space, having developed comprehensive digital governance strategies that integrate AI to streamline bureaucratic processes and improve quality of life and are analized in the edited book.

However, as governments increasingly rely on data-centric models, the world has also witnessed a growing awareness of these technologies' ethical and societal risks. The Cambridge Analytica scandal (Hinds et al., 2020), for instance, exposed how data could be weaponized to manipulate public opinion, raising concerns about surveillance and the erosion of democratic values. Similarly, reports of algorithmic bias in public service delivery have underscored the need for transparency and accountability in AI systems. These incidents highlight the dual-edged nature of data-driven governance: while it promises efficiency and innovation, it also poses risks to individual freedoms and social equity if left unchecked.

Likewise, the rapid advancements in AI have also amplified the importance of privacy as a fundamental human right. In many countries, data protection regulations such as the General Data Protection Regulation (GDPR) in Europe (Hoofnagle et al., 2019) have emerged as critical tools for safeguarding individual privacy. Yet, even these frameworks are often inadequate to address the complexities of AI and digital marketing in public administration. The constant tension between the need for data to improve governance and the imperative to protect citizens from surveillance underscores the pressing need for innovative solutions that reconcile these objectives. The global nature of digital technology has also introduced new dimensions to governance. Cross-border data flows (Meltzer, 2015), international collaborations in AI development, and the influence of multinational tech corporations have blurred the lines between national and global governance. For example, cities like Dubai and Singapore have positioned themselves as global hubs for smart city technologies, leveraging AI to attract investment and talent while addressing urban challenges (Herath et al., 2022). At the same time, disparities in digital infrastructure and resources between developed and developing nations have created a digital divide that risks exacerbating global inequalities. This edited book situates the discussion within these global dynamics, recognizing the interconnectedness of governance, technology, and socio-economic contexts.

Also, in the wake of the COVID-19 pandemic, the relevance of data-driven governance has grown even more pronounced (González-Padilla et al., 2024). Governments worldwide relied on AI-powered systems to track infections, manage vaccine distribution, and disseminate public health information. While these efforts showcased the potential of technology to address global crises, they also revealed significant gaps in preparedness, coordination, and ethical oversight. The pandemic served as a stress test for digital governance systems, exposing both their strengths and vulnerabilities. This context reinforces the urgency of developing resilient, inclusive, and ethical governance models that can adapt to future challenges (Hernández-Tamurejo et al., 2024a).

The integration of digital marketing strategies into public governance is another facet that reflects broader societal trends. Traditionally the domain of private enterprises, digital marketing techniques are now being employed by governments to foster citizen engagement and promote public policies. From social media campaigns that encourage civic participation (González-Padilla et al., 2022) to targeted advertisements that disseminate public health messages, these strategies have become integral to modern governance. However, their use also raises questions about transparency, manipulation, and the ethical boundaries of state influence over individual behavior (Saura et al., 2023). Furthermore, the rise of surveillance capitalism (Zuboff, 2023) has shifted the focus of data governance debates to the role of private tech giants in shaping public life. Platforms like TikTok, Faceedited book, and Google collect and process vast amounts of data, often in ways that blur the lines between public and private interests. Governments must navigate this complex terrain, balancing collaboration with private entities to harness technological innovation while ensuring that public interest and citizen rights remain paramount.

In today's world, the subject of this edited book intersects with numerous pressing global issues, including climate change, economic inequality, and social justice. For instance, AI-driven systems are increasingly being used to promote sustainability, from optimizing energy use in smart cities to monitoring deforestation and pollution. At the same time, these technologies can perpetuate existing inequalities if their deployment fails to account for diverse socio-economic contexts. Similarly, the use of AI in law enforcement and border control has sparked debates about systemic bias and human rights, highlighting the need for rigorous ethical oversight. Therefore, this edited book positions itself as a critical contribution to these ongoing discussions. Thus, examining the interplay of AI, digital marketing, and privacy in governance, the edited book aims to provide a roadmap for navigating the complexities of digital transformation. It addresses the technical and operational aspects of these technologies and their broader implications for society, ethics, and public policy.

Relating the target audience

The topic of data-driven governance through AI, digital marketing, and its interaction with privacy has broad implications, making this edited book relevant to a diverse range of readers. Each segment of the target audience engages with the subject matter from unique perspectives, reflecting their specific interests, expertise, and responsibilities. This edited book has been designed to cater to the following key groups.

One of the primary audiences for this edited book consists of researchers and students specializing in governance, information technology, ethics, political science, and related disciplines. For academics, the edited book offers a rich source of case studies, theoretical frameworks, and analytical insights that contribute to the broader body of knowledge on digital governance. The interdisciplinary nature of the edited book bridges gaps between fields, providing a comprehensive resource that can serve as a foundation for scholarly discussions and further research. Students, particularly those pursuing advanced degrees, will find the edited book valuable for understanding the complexities of AI integration in governance. Its structured approach to analyzing both opportunities and challenges will help them navigate the intricate relationship between technology, policy, and society. Additionally, the edited book's emphasis on ethical considerations and regulatory frameworks offers students a practical understanding of the responsibilities and implications of deploying AI and digital marketing in public administration.

Also, policymakers and government officials represent another significant segment of the target audience. As the custodians of public trust and the architects of regulatory frameworks, they play a critical role in shaping the trajectory of digital governance. This edited book provides them with actionable insights into the successful integration of AI and data-driven strategies in governance, informed by real-world case studies from diverse contexts. For policymakers, the chapters on surveillance capitalism, algorithmic bias, and privacy frameworks offer practical guidance on navigating the ethical dilemmas associated with data-driven technologies. The edited book emphasizes the importance of transparency and citizen engagement in fostering public trust, equipping policymakers with the tools to design inclusive and equitable governance strategies. Moreover, government officials at various levels of administration will benefit from the edited book's exploration of operational challenges, such as data quality, resource constraints, and the need for inter-agency collaboration.

Next, professionals working at the intersection of technology and public sector management are another key audience for this edited book. This includes IT managers, data scientists, project coordinators, and consultants involved in designing and implementing AI systems for public administration. The edited book's detailed analysis of topics such as data governance, ethical AI design, and big data applications provides practical knowledge that can inform their daily work. For instance, chapters that address data quality challenges and propose frameworks for effective data analytics in public sector contexts are particularly relevant to IT professionals tasked with developing scalable and secure solutions. Similarly, the discussion on the role of AI in smart cities and sustainability offers practical insights for professionals working in urban planning and environmental management. The edited book's emphasis on balancing technological innovation with ethical considerations will resonate with those seeking to implement responsible AI practices.

Also, privacy advocates and civil society organizations focused on data protection and digital rights will find the edited book's examination of privacy issues highly relevant. As governments and private entities increasingly rely on data-driven technologies, these groups hold them accountable and ensure that citizen rights are protected. The edited book equips privacy advocates with evidence-based arguments and case studies that highlight both the benefits and risks of data-driven governance. Therefore, addressing themes such as surveillance capitalism, algorithmic transparency, and regulatory gaps, the edited book empowers civil society organizations to engage in informed advocacy. It also provides a platform for discussing alternative governance models that prioritize citizen empowerment and participatory decision-making. Although primarily focused on public administration, the edited book also holds relevance for industry leaders and innovators in the private sector. Technology companies, particularly those involved in AI development and data analytics, are increasingly collaborating with governments to provide digital solutions. This partnership necessitates a deep understanding of public sector needs, challenges, and ethical considerations, which this edited book seeks to address. For industry leaders, the edited book's analysis of the ethical design of digital platforms offers valuable insights into aligning business practices with societal values.

Lastly, educators and trainers involved in teaching public administration, technology ethics, or data science will find this edited book an indispensable resource. Its well-rounded exploration of theory and practice, supported by real-world examples, makes it an ideal text for developing curricula or training programs. The edited book's focus on interdisciplinary learning ensures that it can be integrated into a variety of educational settings, from technical workshops to policy seminars.

Chapters included in this edited book

Each chapter of this edited book has been curated to address specific aspects of data-driven governance, AI, digital marketing, and their implications for privacy. Together, they create a comprehensive narrative that bridges theoretical insights with practical applications, providing the reader with a holistic understanding of the subject. The book's first section lays the theoretical foundations and thematic approaches to digital governance driven by AI, offering a comprehensive exploration of its conceptual underpinnings and emerging frameworks. The second section shifts focus to practical applications, presenting case studies that illustrate the integration of AI to enhance governance in both public and private sectors, highlighting innovative strategies and addressing challenges in digital marketing, social media marketing or data analytics. Below is a detailed exploration of the importance of each chapter and its contribution to the overall discourse:

Chapter 1: Digital Governance Across Continents: Cases from Diverse National Strategies

This chapter analyzes how countries with varying socio-economic contexts and governance structures integrate AI into public administration. Examining the cases of Saudi Arabia, Estonia, Singapore, and Spain highlights the diversity of approaches to digital governance. Each nation's unique strategy underscores critical scalability, inclusivity, and transparency lessons. For instance, Estonia's success in e-governance reflects the benefits of early adoption and citizen-centric design, while Singapore's emphasis on smart city initiatives demonstrates how AI can address urban challenges. This chapter presents successes and challenges and lays the foundation for understanding the global landscape of AI-driven governance.

Chapter 2: Data Quality in the Surveillance Economy: Challenges of Digital Governance in the Paradox of Data Decontextualization

In an era where data is often described as the "new oil" this chapter delves into the critical importance of data quality for effective digital governance. It explores the paradox of data decontextualization, where the sheer volume of data often obscures its accuracy and reliability. The chapter emphasizes that poor data quality can undermine the efficacy of AI systems, leading to flawed policy decisions and eroding public trust. This chapter addresses a foundational issue in AI deployment by discussing strategies for improving data governance, ensuring that subsequent analyses and applications rest on a robust data framework.

Chapter 3: Reassessing the Jurisprudential Foundation of Intellectual Property Laws in the Age of Artificial Intelligence

The rapid advancement of AI has raised profound questions about the nature of intellectual property (IP) laws, particularly concerning AI-generated works. This chapter critically examines the limitations of existing IP frameworks, which were designed with human authorship in mind. It explores scenarios where AI systems create content, designs, or inventions, challenging traditional notions of originality and ownership. By proposing new legal paradigms, the chapter contributes to the ongoing debate about how to adapt IP laws to the realities of the AI age, ensuring that innovation is encouraged while safeguarding the rights of creators.

Chapter 4: Liberal Democracy, Behavioral Governance, and Communication: Risks and Opportunities

This chapter examines how behavioral economics has influenced public policy through the lens of governance and communication. Analyzing the rise of behavioral governance units worldwide highlights the opportunities and risks associated with using behavioral insights to optimize citizen behavior. For example, public health and environmental sustainability interventions have demonstrated the potential of such approaches to drive positive societal change. However, the chapter also warns of the ethical implications of manipulating citizen behavior, particularly in ways that may infringe upon autonomy or exacerbate inequalities. Its focus on regulatory frameworks and ethical safeguards is particularly relevant to liberal democracies navigating the complexities of behavioral governance.

Chapter 5: Leveraging Big Data in SMEs: Pathways to Effective Application

Small and Medium Enterprises (SMEs) often face unique challenges in adopting big data technologies due to limited resources and expertise. This chapter explores how SMEs can overcome these barriers to leverage big data for better decision-making and competitiveness. It provides a practical framework for implementing data-driven strategies, addressing issues such as cost, data privacy, and the development of a supportive organizational culture. After focusing on the specific needs of SMEs, the chapter broadens the scope of the edited book, demonstrating how data-driven governance principles can be adapted to diverse organizational contexts.

Chapter 6: Unethical Design in TikTok and Its Connection to Surveillance Capitalism and Collective Intelligence

This chapter critically examines TikTok, a social media platform emblematic of the broader phenomenon of surveillance capitalism. It investigates how addictive design features capture user attention while commodifying personal data for profit. The chapter explores how platforms like TikTok influence societal behaviors and perceptions by connecting these practices to collective intelligence. This analysis underscores the urgent need for ethical design principles that prioritize user well-being and data protection. The chapter serves as a case study in balancing innovation with responsibility, offering lessons for both policymakers and technology developers.

Chapter 7: Role of Data Analytics in Sustainability in Apparel Supply Chain Management

This chapter demonstrates the transformative potential of data analytics in promoting sustainability within the apparel industry. By analyzing real-world applications, it highlights how advanced analytics can optimize supply chain operations, reduce waste, and improve environmental outcomes. The chapter also discusses the role of technologies like the Internet of Things (IoT) in capturing and processing real-time data, enabling faster and more effective decision-making. This case study underscores the broader applicability of data-driven strategies beyond governance, illustrating their potential to address global challenges such as sustainability.

Chapter 8: Exploring a Smart City and the Epicenter of Megatrends in Innovation with Artificial Intelligence: The Case of Dubai

Dubai serves as a leading example of how Artificial Intelligence (AI) can revolutionize urban development, making this chapter a focal point for discussions on smart cities. By examining Dubai's integration of AI into public services, healthcare, transportation, and environmental management, the chapter demonstrates how strategic planning and investment in AI can transform cities into global innovation hubs. It highlights the city's evolution from a regional leader to a global trendsetter in urban technology, providing a scalable model for other cities seeking to adopt AI-driven solutions. Additionally, this chapter emphasizes the importance of sustainability and inclusivity in smart city planning, advocating for governance frameworks that ensure equitable access to technological advancements.

Chapter 9: Artificial Intelligence in Data Visualization: Enhancing Research Through Generative Graphs

The transformative potential of generative AI in data visualization is explored in this chapter, using educational data from Madrid as a case study. By integrating traditional statistical tools with advanced AI capabilities, the chapter demonstrates how AI can streamline the analysis and visualization of complex datasets, uncovering trends and patterns that might otherwise remain hidden. It emphasizes the value of AI in enhancing evidence-based decision-making, particularly in fields like academic planning and policy formulation. The chapter also addresses challenges such as inconsistencies in AI-generated outputs, highlighting the need for human oversight to ensure accuracy and reliability. Its hybrid approach exemplifies how AI can complement traditional methodologies, opening new possibilities for data-driven research.

Chapter 10: A Proficient Fake Fingerprint Identification System Based on CNN to Ensure Human Security

This chapter delves into biometric security, focusing on the development of a Convolutional Neural Network (CNN)-based system for distinguishing authentic fingerprints from counterfeit ones. It addresses the growing sophistication of fingerprint forgery techniques, presenting an innovative solution to enhance the reliability of biometric authentication systems. By detailing the system's architecture, including convolutional and pooling layers, and the application of dropout regularization to prevent overfitting, the chapter offers valuable technical insights for researchers and practitioners in security and AI fields. It also underscores the importance of rigorous testing and performance evaluation, contributing to the broader discourse on the role of AI in enhancing human security.

Chapter 11: Digital Transformation in Spanish Universities: Key Indicator Design and Data Visualization with Power BI

The final chapter explores the role of digital tools like Power BI in advancing the digital transformation of higher education institutions. Focusing on Spanish universities examines how key performance indicators (KPIs) can be designed and visualized to improve decision-making processes. The chapter outlines a methodology for collecting, validating, and analyzing data, offering practical guidance for educators and administrators seeking to leverage data analytics in institutional management. Its emphasis on democratizing data access and fostering a culture of data-driven decision-making aligns with the broader goals of digital governance.

The replicable nature of the framework presented in this chapter makes it a valuable resource for higher education institutions worldwide.

After presenting the chapters included in this edited book, it is clear that it aims to provide an interdisciplinary perspective on the evolving landscape of data-driven governance, AI, and digital marketing, with a focus on privacy concerns. The edited book contributes significantly to academic research, policy development, and professional practice by bridging theoretical discussions with practical applications. One of the key contributions of the edited book is its emphasis on ethical considerations and regulatory frameworks. As governments and organizations increasingly adopt AI-driven solutions, the importance of balancing innovation with accountability and fairness cannot be overstated. The chapters collectively advocate for transparency, inclusivity, and citizen empowerment as foundational principles of data-driven governance. The edited book also serves to showcase global best practices, drawing lessons from diverse contexts to inform future governance strategies. Whether it is the innovative approaches of smart cities like Dubai, the challenges of integrating AI into small and medium enterprises, or the ethical dilemmas of behavioral governance, the case studies presented in this edited book offer valuable insights for stakeholders across sectors. Moreover, the edited book contributes to the broader discourse on the societal implications of AI and digital marketing.

Finally, the edited book shapes the future of digital governance by fostering a deeper understanding of the interplay between technology, policy, and ethics. Its comprehensive approach ensures that it remains a vital resource for those seeking to harness the potential of AI and data-driven strategies while safeguarding the principles of democracy, privacy, and social justice.

REFERENCES

Birkstedt, T., Minkkinen, M., Tandon, A., & Mäntymäki, M. (2023). AI governance: Themes, knowledge gaps and future agendas. *Internet Research*, 33(7), 133–167. DOI: 10.1108/INTR-01-2022-0042

Bovaird, T. (2007). Beyond engagement and participation: User and community coproduction of public services. *Public Administration Review*, 67(5), 846–860. DOI: 10.1111/j.1540-6210.2007.00773.x

Brough, M., Literat, I., & Ikin, A. (2020). "Good social media?": Underrepresented youth perspectives on the ethical and equitable design of social media platforms. *Social Media + Society*, 6(2), 2056305120928488. DOI: 10.1177/2056305120928488

Dwivedi, Y. K., Sharma, A., Rana, N. P., Giannakis, M., Goel, P., & Dutot, V. (2023). Evolution of artificial intelligence research in Technological Forecasting and Social Change: Research topics, trends, and future directions. *Technological Forecasting and Social Change*, 192, 122579. DOI: 10.1016/j.techfore.2023.122579

Einav, L., & Levin, J. (2014). The data revolution and economic analysis. *Innovation Policy and the Economy*, 14(1), 1–24. DOI: 10.1086/674019

González-Padilla, P., López, A. F., & Lacárcel, F. J. (2022). Main government-related data extraction techniques: a review. *Handbook of research on artificial intelligence in government practices and processes*, 142-160. https://doi.org/DOI: 10.4018/978-1-7998-9609-8.ch009

González-Padilla, P., Navalpotro, F. D., & Saura, J. R. (2024). Managing entrepreneurs' behavior personalities in digital environments: A review. *The International Entrepreneurship and Management Journal*, 20(1), 89–113. DOI: 10.1007/s11365-022-00823-4

Herath, H. M. K. K. M. B., & Mittal, M. (2022). Adoption of artificial intelligence in smart cities: A comprehensive review. *International Journal of Information Management Data Insights*, 2(1), 100076. DOI: 10.1016/j.jjimei.2022.100076

Hernández-Tamurejo, Á., Lacárcel, F. J. S., & Corvello, V. (2024a). Exploring smart workers' willingness to sacrifice and its managerial entrepreneurship implications towards a new mobility paradigm. *The International Entrepreneurship and Management Journal*, 20(3), 2047–2074. DOI: 10.1007/s11365-024-01004-1

Hernández-Tamurejo, Á., Sáiz-Sepúlveda, Á., Herráez, B. R., & Saura, J. R. (2024). Exploring consumer perceptions of engine technology in vehicle purchase decision-making. *ESIC Market.Economic & Business Journal*, 55(1), e336. Advance online publication. DOI: 10.7200/esicm.55.336

Hinds, J., Williams, E. J., & Joinson, A. N. (2020). "It wouldn't happen to me": Privacy concerns and perspectives following the Cambridge Analytica scandal. *International Journal of Human-Computer Studies*, 143, 102498. DOI: 10.1016/j.ijhcs.2020.102498

Hoofnagle, C. J., Van Der Sloot, B., & Borgesius, F. Z. (2019). The European Union general data protection regulation: What it is and what it means. *Information & Communications Technology Law*, 28(1), 65–98. DOI: 10.1080/13600834.2019.1573501

Lee, K. (2009). How the Hong Kong government lost the public trust in SARS: Insights for government communication in a health crisis. *Public Relations Review*, 35(1), 74–76. DOI: 10.1016/j.pubrev.2008.06.003 PMID: 32288049

Lyulyov, O., Pimonenko, T., Saura, J. R., & Barbosa, B. (2024). How do e-governance and e-business drive sustainable development goals? *Technological Forecasting and Social Change*, 199, 123082. DOI: 10.1016/j.techfore.2023.123082

Meltzer, J. P. (2015). The I nternet, Cross-Border Data Flows and International Trade. *Asia & the Pacific Policy Studies*, 2(1), 90–102. DOI: 10.1002/app5.60

Nzeako, G., Akinsanya, M. O., Popoola, O. A., Chukwurah, E. G., & Okeke, C. D. (2024). The role of AI-Driven predictive analytics in optimizing IT industry supply chains. *International Journal of Management & Entrepreneurship Research*, 6(5), 1489–1497. DOI: 10.51594/ijmer.v6i5.1096

Rasetti, M. (2020). The new frontiers of AI in the arena of behavioral economics. *Mind & Society*, 19(1), 5–9. DOI: 10.1007/s11299-020-00226-4

Saura, J. R. (2024). Algorithms in Digital Marketing: Does Smart Personalization Promote a Privacy Paradox? *FIIB Business Review*, 13(5), 499–502. DOI: 10.1177/23197145241276898

Saura, J. R., Palacios-Marqués, D., & Iturricha-Fernández, A. (2021). Ethical design in social media: Assessing the main performance measurements of user online behavior modification. *Journal of Business Research*, 129, 271–281. DOI: 10.1016/j.jbusres.2021.03.001

Saura, J. R., Palacios-Marqués, D., & Ribeiro-Soriano, D. (2023). Privacy concerns in social media UGC communities: Understanding user behavior sentiments in complex networks. *Information Systems and e-Business Management*, •••, 1–21. DOI: 10.1007/s10257-023-00631-5

Saura, J. R., Ribeiro-Soriano, D., & Palacios-Marqués, D. (2022). Assessing behavioral data science privacy issues in government artificial intelligence deployment. *Government Information Quarterly*, 39(4), 101679. DOI: 10.1016/j.giq.2022.101679

Saura, J. R., Škare, V., & Dosen, D. O. (2024). Is AI-based digital marketing ethical? Assessing a new data privacy paradox. *Journal of Innovation & Knowledge*, 9(4), 100597. DOI: 10.1016/j.jik.2024.100597

Willems, J., Schmid, M. J., Vanderelst, D., Vogel, D., & Ebinger, F. (2023). AI-driven public services and the privacy paradox: Do citizens really care about their privacy? *Public Management Review*, 25(11), 2116–2134. DOI: 10.1080/14719037.2022.2063934

Zhang, Y., Wu, M., Tian, G. Y., Zhang, G., & Lu, J. (2021). Ethics and privacy of artificial intelligence: Understandings from bibliometrics. *Knowledge-Based Systems*, 222, 106994. DOI: 10.1016/j.knosys.2021.106994

Zuboff, S. (2023). The age of surveillance capitalism. In *Social theory re-wired* (pp. 203–213). Routledge. DOI: 10.4324/9781003320609-27

Chapter 1
Digital Governance Across Continents:
Cases From Diverse National Strategies

Eliana Bejarano-Murillo
https://orcid.org/0009-0005-1114-8128
Rey Juan Carlos University, Spain

ABSTRACT

This study explores the transformative role of artificial intelligence (AI) in digital governance by examining four diverse case studies: Saudi Arabia, Estonia, Singapore, and Spain. Using a case study methodology, the research investigates how AI has been integrated into public administration to enhance efficiencyand address societal challenges. Findings reveal significant variations in approaches to AI integration, influenced by each country's socio-economic contexts and governance priorities. Key theoretical implications include the need to balance technological innovation with socio-political considerations, while practical insights emphasize the scalability of interoperable systems and the critical role of transparency in fostering public trust. Despite notable advancements, challenges such as ensuring inclusivity, addressing algorithmic bias, and safeguarding data privacy persist, underscoring the need for ongoing policy adaptation and citizen engagement.

INTRODUCTION

In an increasingly globalized society, the integration of AI into digital governance represents one of the most disruptive transformations in public administration in recent decades (Milakovich, 2012). As governments worldwide strive to meet the

DOI: 10.4018/979-8-3693-6945-6.ch001

demands of a more interconnected citizenry, AI has emerged as a powerful solution to enhance both the internal efficiency of administrative processes and the quality and speed of public services. Through advanced machine-learning algorithms and the processing of vast volumes of data, AI enables governments to achieve greater precision and predictability in decision-making, optimizing resource allocation and improving strategic planning. This, in turn, contributes to more agile and proactive public administration, capable of anticipating problems and addressing them effectively within increasingly shorter timeframes (Attard-Frost et al., 2024).

In this context, one of the most significant benefits of AI in digital governance is its ability to automate routine and repetitive tasks that typically consume substantial time and human resources. When automation strategies are developed, governments can enhance procedural accuracy while freeing employees to focus on more strategically and creatively valuable activities. For example, AI-driven systems can manage repetitive administrative tasks such as document classification, file management, database organization, and real-time document verification (Saura, 2022). This reduces error margins and improves operational efficiency. Not only does this benefit the administration, but it also positively impacts the citizen experience by providing quicker and more effective responses to their requests and needs. However, in the long term, it may also have profound implications for employability (Pagani et al., 2023).

Simultaneously, AI in digital governance enables large-scale data analysis, which facilitates the development of evidence-based public policies. Through data mining and predictive analytics, governments can detect patterns in areas such as public health, education, public safety, and economic development. This allows policies to be designed with greater precision, tailored to the specific needs of regions or population groups. For instance, AI predictive models can also anticipate surges in demand for healthcare services, enabling hospitals and health centers to prepare in advance and avoid overcrowding (Saraswat et al., 2022). Similarly, in the context of traffic management, predictive analytics can help optimize urban mobility. In terms of public safety, AI can also predict crime patterns in urban areas, enabling security resources to be allocated to key locations and times, thereby increasing the effectiveness and efficiency of protecting citizens.

Likewise, another relevant aspect of AI in the context of digital governance is its application to direct interactions between the state and citizens. AI has revolutionized the way citizens engage with the state, fostering a more dynamic, accessible, and personalized relationship. AI-powered citizen service systems have transformed traditional communication channels, providing continuous access to public services and information 24/7. This not only improves the user (citizen) experience by reducing wait times and offering immediate responses but also optimizes the work of public administrations, allowing officials to focus on more complex and significant tasks (Floridi et al., 2021).

Additionally, these systems are designed to learn from every interaction, which means their responsiveness and understanding of citizens' needs improve over time, delivering more efficient and personalized services. AI is also playing a crucial role in identifying needs and detecting emerging social problems, enabling governments to act with greater speed and precision (Kulal et al., 2024). Through advanced data processing techniques, AI can analyze feedback, social media trends, and demographic data to identify socially significant issues such as rising gender-based violence cases, disease outbreaks, or challenges in accessing basic services. These capabilities provide the necessary information to develop strategies and policies that effectively respond to social demands before they escalate into crises. Furthermore, this type of analysis helps identify underserved or vulnerable population sectors, aiding governments in prioritizing resource distribution and ensuring services reach those who need them most (Sanina et al., 2023).

In this way, one of the most critical challenges in this context is the integration of secure automated decision-making systems that uphold principles of fairness and avoid discrimination against certain population groups (Kuziemski and Misuraca, 2020). Since many AI algorithms are trained using historical data, there is a risk of perpetuating previous biases or inequalities, potentially leading to unfair decisions. To mitigate these issues, it is essential for governments to implement AI governance policies that ensure transparency and auditability of the algorithms used in administrative processes. This involves developing interpretable algorithms and establishing ethical and regulatory frameworks to guide the use of AI in a way that respects the rights of all citizens and maintains public trust in these systems (Makridakis, 2017). Furthermore, transparency in the use of AI is essential to fostering public trust in digital government services. Citizens must have access to clear and precise information regarding how their data is used and how decisions that directly affect them are made. Potential solutions include the establishment of ethics committees, the involvement of external auditors, and mechanisms for citizens to question or appeal automated decisions. As AI becomes a cornerstone of public administration, citizen trust will hinge on their perception of these systems as fair, secure, and oriented toward the common good.

In this context, this chapter investigates four prominent cases of AI-driven digital governance in Saudi Arabia, Estonia, Singapore, and Spain. Each country has adopted unique approaches and faced distinct challenges on its path to state digitalization. These cases demonstrate how AI can enhance operational efficiency, optimize infrastructure, promote technological innovation, personalize citizen engagement, and strengthen government responsiveness. They highlight the positive impacts that advanced digital governance can have on society and sustainable economic development. The central research question guiding this study is: *How can the adoption of AI in digital governance promote public trust while enhancing efficiency, innovation, and societal well-being?* To address this question, the study pursues the following secondary objectives:

- Analyze the distinct approaches Saudi Arabia, Estonia, Singapore, and Spain took in implementing AI-driven digital governance.
- Identify the challenges faced by each country and the strategies employed to overcome them.
- Explore the implications of AI-driven governance for sustainable development and innovation.
- Provide a comparative analysis to derive best practices and lessons applicable across different governance contexts.

To achieve the objectives outlined earlier, this study adopts the case study methodology, a robust approach particularly suited for investigating complex, real-world phenomena in their specific contexts. This methodology allows for an in-depth examination of how each country integrates AI into digital governance, addressing unique challenges and leveraging distinct opportunities. The case study method provides a framework for analyzing the intricate interplay between policy, technology, and societal impacts, facilitating a comprehensive understanding of both the successes and limitations of AI-driven governance. This approach not only enables the identification of context-specific strategies but also supports the derivation of broader insights and best practices that may inform the development of digital governance in other settings. Finally, the present chapter is structured as follows: the next section outlines the Case Study methodology employed in this research. Subsequently, each of the selected cases is analyzed in detail. Finally, the chapter concludes with a comparative discussion of the findings and their theoretical and practical implications.

The Case Study Methodology: Analyzing Saudi Arabia, Estonia, Singapore, and Spain

This study employs the case study methodology as its primary approach to analyze and compare the strategies and policies implemented in five countries and regions: Saudi Arabia, Estonia, Dubai, Singapore, and Spain. The selection of this methodology stems from its capacity to provide an in-depth understanding of complex phenomena within their real-life contexts, offering a detailed examination of the connection between specific policies and their socio-economic, political, and cultural environments.

Thus, the case study methodology is a qualitative research approach widely recognized for its ability to investigate intricate issues in depth (Meyer, 2001). It focuses on exploring a particular phenomenon, organization, or policy within its specific setting, enabling the researcher to capture the nuances and contextual factors that influence outcomes. Unlike methodologies that aim for broad generalizations, case studies prioritize the detailed and holistic understanding of a limited number of cases, making it particularly valuable for exploratory, explanatory, or evaluative research (Njie and Asimiran, 2014). In this way, the roots of case study research can be traced back to the early 20th century in disciplines such as sociology and anthropology, where it was initially used as a descriptive tool. Over time, the methodology evolved to incorporate more analytical and comparative dimensions, enabling it to test theories, uncover causal relationships, and generate practical insights. Its flexibility allows researchers to use diverse data collection techniques, including qualitative interviews, document analysis, and quantitative metrics, to triangulate findings and enhance validity (Schlunegger et al., 2024).

In contemporary research, case studies are increasingly recognized for their role in bridging theory and practice. They not only illuminate specific instances but also offer broader implications by identifying patterns, developing frameworks, and proposing scalable solutions. This makes them particularly suitable for interdisciplinary studies that address multifaceted problems in fields like public policy, economics, and governance (Bennett and Elman, 2006). Therefore, the case study methodology holds significant importance in addressing research questions that require an understanding of how and why phenomena occur. Furthermore, it allows for the examination of dynamic and context-sensitive processes, such as policy implementation and institutional transformation, which may be overlooked by methods relying solely on aggregated data or theoretical modeling. For this research, the case study approach was particularly appropriate due to the diversity and complexity of the contexts under investigation. Saudi Arabia, Estonia, Dubai, Singapore, and Spain each represent unique developmental trajectories characterized by distinct socio-political structures, economic priorities, and technological advancements. Analyzing these cases individually and comparatively enables the identification of transferable insights, as well as an appreciation of the contextual factors that influence their applicability.

Case Studies Selection and its Link to AI Governance

The research process involved the selection of these cases based on their relevance to the study's objectives (Hartley, 2004). First, Saudi Arabia was chosen for its ambitious Vision 2030 reform agenda aimed at economic diversification. Secondly, Estonia serves as a benchmark for digital innovation and governance. Thirdly, Dubai exemplifies a transformative approach to economic modernization and urban development. Fourth, Singapore stands out for its efficiency-driven policies and high developmental achievements, while fifthly, Spain offers a European perspective on sustainability and innovation in public policy.

Data collection was conducted through secondary sources, including governmental reports, academic publications, and global databases. The analysis employed a comparative framework to explore similarities and differences across the selected cases, with a focus on identifying best practices, challenges, and context-specific dynamics. Therefore, this research contributes to a nuanced understanding of how diverse strategies and policies shape developmental outcomes in varying contexts. It also highlights the importance of adaptability and context-awareness in formulating effective governance and policy frameworks.

Analysis of Results

The Case of Saudi Arabia

Saudi Arabia has emerged as a leader in integrating advanced technologies into digital governance, leveraging AI and digitalization across multiple facets of its administrative processes. This transformation is a central component of its ambitious national plan, "Vision 2030" (Bakry et al., 2021), launched in 2016 to diversify the Saudi economy and reduce its dependence on oil. Vision 2030 aims to establish Saudi Arabia as a global hub for technology and innovation, transforming both the public and private sectors through the adoption of advanced technologies, with a particular emphasis on digitalization and AI as engines of development and sustainability (Basri et al., 2020; Memish et al., 2021).

Saudi Arabia's commitment to technology is embodied in various initiatives designed not only to enhance the efficiency of public services but also to improve transparency, accessibility, and user experience. At the heart of this transformation is the Saudi Data and Artificial Intelligence Authority (SDAIA) (Memish et al., 2021), established in 2019 to spearhead the country's AI and big data strategies. SDAIA is tasked with formulating policies, setting standards, and ensuring the ethical use of data and AI in both public and private sectors. This organization serves as the cornerstone of the national AI strategy and has overseen the development of digital platforms that revolutionize citizen-government interactions, improving services in critical areas such as health, education, and security (Allmnakrah and Evers, 2020).

In this way, under the Vision 2030 framework, Saudi Arabia has adopted a "Digital Government" approach that incorporates AI technologies to enhance efficiency in public administration. This strategy focuses on three pillars: (i) creating a vibrant society, (ii) fostering a thriving economy, and (iii) building an ambitious nation. Digitalization acts as a cross-cutting tool influencing these pillars to improve citizens' quality of life and stimulate sustainable economic growth based on knowledge (Khan and Khan, 2020). To this end, the Saudi government has invested heavily in digital infrastructure and launched various platforms that facilitate access to public services. These platforms not only digitize processes but also integrate AI to proactively anticipate and meet citizens' needs. Through this digital ecosystem, the country aims not only to modernize its institutions but also to position itself as a pioneer in using AI and digitalization in public administration.

One notable example of digital governance in Saudi Arabia is the Absher platform, launched in 2010 by the Ministry of Interior. Absher is a public service portal that allows citizens and residents to complete a wide range of government transactions online. Offering more than 160 services, from passport renewals to fine payments and personal data updates, the platform has drastically reduced the need for in-person transactions, enhancing accessibility and efficiency. Absher also stands out for integrating AI and big data to personalize user experiences and predict their needs. By analyzing user data, the platform can provide tailored services and recommendations based on interaction history. Furthermore, Absher employs advanced security measures such as facial recognition and biometric authentication, reinforcing privacy and data security for citizens. It has become a regional model and an inspiration for other digital government initiatives using AI in public administration.

In the healthcare sector, Saudi Arabia has implemented advanced AI tools to improve medical care and expand access to services in remote areas. The Ministry of Health has promoted telemedicine and AI-assisted diagnostics to optimize resources and ensure citizens receive quality healthcare regardless of their geographic location. These tools enable remote consultations and provide patients with rapid and accurate diagnoses, a critical advancement in a country with vast geographic distances.

AI systems have also been employed in monitoring patients with chronic diseases. Using IoT devices, doctors can track patients' vital signs in real time, enabling early intervention when anomalies are detected. Additionally, AI algorithms help anticipate disease patterns and forecast healthcare system demands, facilitating better resource allocation and emergency planning.

During the COVID-19 pandemic (Alsmadi et al., 2021), the Saudi government launched applications such as "Tabaud" (Shml et al., 2022) and "Tawakkalna" (Andejany et al., 2022), which use AI to track infections, identify close contacts, and provide real-time updates on the public health situation. These tools enabled a swift and effective response to the outbreak, aiding in medical resource management and controlling virus spread. The success of these applications underscores AI's potential in emergency management and public health administration.

AI has also transformed public safety management in Saudi Arabia. Authorities have implemented advanced surveillance and data analysis systems to enhance urban safety and security during large-scale events. For instance, during the annual pilgrimage to Mecca (Owais et al., 2024), the government uses AI to manage crowd flows, prevent security incidents, and coordinate emergency teams. Real-time data analysis enables AI systems to anticipate and mitigate risks, allowing authorities to act promptly and prevent dangerous situations in large gatherings. Urban surveillance systems also include cameras with facial recognition and behavior pattern analysis capabilities, alerting authorities to suspicious activities. These technologies have optimized public safety and enabled faster, more precise interventions during emergencies. Additionally, during events like the pilgrimage, these systems effectively manage the movement of millions of people, contributing to attendees' safety and the event's efficient organization.

In the digital era, cybersecurity is essential to maintaining trust in government platforms. Saudi Arabia has implemented a robust cybersecurity framework to protect its digital infrastructure and citizens' data. The National Cybersecurity Center, in coordination with SDAIA (Alotaibi et al., 2022), uses AI to identify and mitigate cyber threats in real time, enhancing the resilience of government platforms against potential attacks. These systems detect anomalous patterns and adapt their responses to counter new threats, ensuring the security of personal data and the continuity of digital public services.

In addition to protecting citizens' data, the Saudi government has enacted strict regulations to ensure the ethical and secure use of AI. These policies reinforce user privacy and establish standards for data management, critical for maintaining public trust in a digitized context. Furthermore, Saudi Arabia's cyber infrastructure is designed to protect system integrity and minimize the risk of critical information loss through AI use. The country continues to expand its digital governance ecosystem through AI, aiming to establish itself as a global leader in technological innovation and efficient public administration. However, Saudi Arabia must address ongoing AI regulation to prevent biases in decision-making and ensure the equitable use of these systems. As the country advances in service digitalization, cybersecurity and privacy will remain critical areas for investment and development (Alogaiel and Alrwais, 2023).

Saudi Arabia's experience offers valuable lessons for other countries seeking to adopt AI in their governance strategies. The creation of specialized institutions, such as SDAIA, and the implementation of robust cybersecurity policies have been critical to the success of its digital transformation. These elements demonstrate that the effective use of AI in government requires not only advanced technology but also solid regulation and ethical commitment to citizens.

It should be highlighted that the case of Saudi Arabia is an inspiring example of how AI and digitalization can transform the relationship between government and citizens. From accessible public service platforms and optimized security to a strong focus on cybersecurity, Saudi Arabia has shown that it is possible to build a government that is more efficient, secure, and aligned with the needs of a modern society. These efforts reinforce AI's role in public administration and serve as a model for other countries aiming to improve their governmental structures through cutting-edge technologies (Ibrahim, 2024). Saudi Arabia's experience highlights the transformative potential of AI and the importance of a long-term vision, such as Vision 2030, to guide this transformation. The country has made significant strides toward robust digital governance, laying the groundwork for a future where AI and digital technologies not only enhance public service efficiency but also drive economic growth and foster a more connected and informed society.

Saudi Arabia's experience demonstrates how a well-defined digital governance strategy can overcome complex challenges and adapt to a rapidly evolving global environment. By addressing key issues such as data protection (Kanojia, 2023), cybersecurity, and AI transparency, Saudi Arabia positions itself as not only a technological leader but also an example of comprehensive digital transformation. Through its commitment to innovation and sustainable development, Saudi Arabia continues advancing its goal of creating a state that, through digitalization, responds more agilely and effectively to citizen demands, setting a model for integrating technology into modern governance.

Estonia and Digital Governance

Estonia is globally recognized as a leader in digital governance and one of the most digitalized societies in the world (Kerikmäe and Pärn-Lee, 2021). Since gaining independence from the Soviet Union in 1991, Estonia has built an advanced technological infrastructure that has enabled it to digitize nearly all its government services, fundamentally transforming the relationship between the state and its citizens. Aiming to overcome geographic and economic limitations, Estonia has developed an innovative "digital state" model that facilitates quick, secure, and efficient access to public services (Joamets and Chochia, 2020). This model has laid the foundation for a digital governance ecosystem that integrates AI and continues to evolve toward new forms of public management and efficiency.

The implementation of AI in Estonia's governance framework is a natural progression in its digitalization journey. The Estonian government has adopted an AI strategy that spans multiple sectors, including healthcare, education, transportation, and public services, aiming to increase efficiency, reduce costs, and enhance citizens' quality of life (Masso et al., 2023). AI is used both for decision-making and personalizing public services, positioning Estonia as an exemplar of how governments can maximize advanced technologies to optimize their operations.

One of the cornerstones of Estonia's digital infrastructure is the X-Road system (Hardy, 2024), a data exchange platform that enables the interoperability of all public and private systems in the country while integrating AI. X-Road is a secure network connecting databases from various institutions, allowing efficient and secure data sharing among government and private entities. Through X-Road, citizens can perform a wide range of activities, from online voting to document signing and payments, without needing to visit physical offices (Saputro et al., 2020). This has created a more agile, efficient, and citizen-centric administration. The integration of AI within X-Road has facilitated the automation of administrative processes, making government services faster and more accessible. For instance, AI is used to analyze real-time data and provide predictive assessments, helping the government anticipate service demands and proactively address population needs. AI also identifies usage patterns, enabling the design of personalized services and the optimization of resources (Kerikmäe and Pärn-Lee, 2021).

Another notable innovation in Estonia is its e-Residency program, which allows anyone worldwide to become an "e-resident" and access Estonia's digital services without residing in the country. This program uses AI for identity verification and security, enabling e-residents to establish and manage businesses in Estonia remotely (Jermalavičius, 2024). The e-Residency program has facilitated the creation of international businesses, establishing Estonia as a digital hub for entrepreneurs worldwide. For Estonia, e-Residency generates significant revenue and extends its digital governance model beyond its borders. Leveraging AI and digitalization, the e-Residency program has demonstrated a model of economic inclusion and accessibility that other countries are considering replicating. AI plays a critical role in managing the platform by quickly and securely analyzing and authenticating applications, enhancing system trust and efficiency (Heller, 2017).

Estonia has also pioneered AI use in its judicial system. The country has implemented a virtual judge powered by AI to resolve minor cases, such as low-value commercial disputes. This virtual judge (Kerikmäe and Pärn-Lee, 2021) reduces the workload of human courts and expedites the resolution of minor conflicts, ensuring quick and efficient access to justice. While significant cases are still resolved by human judges, the virtual judge exemplifies how AI can improve the justice system, making legal services more accessible and efficient (Bodul, 2023).

In other public services, Estonia employs AI to personalize citizen experiences and optimize resource management. For example, AI systems prioritize requests and automatically distribute cases to appropriate departments based on urgency and complexity. This capability allows the Estonian government to respond swiftly to citizens' needs, improving service quality and reducing waiting times (Gavrilova and Gurvitsh-Suits, 2020).

In the healthcare sector, Estonia uses AI to enhance telemedicine services and manage medical data. Leveraging X-Road's interoperability, Estonian doctors can access patient medical histories instantly and securely, enabling faster and more personalized care. AI analyzes these data to create predictive models that identify potential health risks, improving disease prevention and treatment. Digitalization in healthcare also involves AI-assisted resource planning and management, allowing the system to forecast service demand and allocate personnel and medical equipment efficiently. This has been particularly useful in managing emergencies and responding to disease outbreaks, such as during the COVID-19 pandemic, when Estonia employed AI to track contacts and monitor virus spread (Annus and Merimaa, 2024).

Likewise, Estonia has prioritized the security of its digital systems, implementing advanced cybersecurity measures that use AI to monitor, detect, and mitigate threats. As a digitally advanced nation, Estonia is acutely aware of cybersecurity risks and has adopted a proactive approach to protect its infrastructure and citizens' data (Sarapuu and Saarniit, 2020). The government employs AI systems to detect unusual patterns in network traffic and anticipate cyberattacks, enabling rapid responses to potential threats (Robinson et al., 2021). Estonia's commitment to protecting personal data is evident in its legislation, which ensures that all collected data are securely stored and ethically used (Kerikmäe and Pärn-Lee, 2021). AI technologies, such as advanced encryption and biometric verification, are integrated into government security systems to safeguard information privacy. Additionally, Estonia's data audit system allows citizens to see who has accessed their personal information, reinforcing transparency and trust in digital services (Paes, 2023).

Recognizing that sustaining a digital governance system requires digitally skilled citizens, Estonia has focused on education and capacity building. The government has implemented specific programs to teach programming and AI from early school levels, ensuring that future generations are equipped to actively participate in the digital economy. Public sector employees are also trained in AI and big data tools to ensure they are prepared to manage the state's digital infrastructure. Moreover, Estonia promotes AI research and development through dedicated innovation programs and funding. Universities and research centers collaborate closely with the government to explore AI applications that can be integrated into digital governance.

This collaborative approach among academia, government, and the private sector is a hallmark of Estonia's digital ecosystem.

The case of Estonia provides key lessons for countries aiming to implement a digital governance model. Estonia's commitment to building interconnected and secure digital infrastructure, such as X-Road, highlights the importance of developing user-centered and interoperable systems that facilitate access to public services (Ebers and Tupay, 2023). The integration of AI across various sectors has optimized government efficiency and improved service quality. Estonia's success lies in its holistic approach to digital transformation, encompassing infrastructure, cybersecurity, education, and talent development in AI.

Looking ahead, Estonia plans to expand the use of AI in public services while ensuring that digital governance advances remain accessible to all citizens and uphold high standards of ethics and transparency. The country also aims to maintain its leadership in cybersecurity by enhancing its detection and response capabilities and exploring emerging technologies such as blockchain to improve data security and transparency.

Estonia represents an exemplary model of digital governance that combines AI and advanced technologies to transform the relationship between the state and its citizens. From accessible public services to state-of-the-art cybersecurity and a commitment to transparency, Estonia has created a unique digital ecosystem setting a global benchmark. Estonia's experience underscores the importance of interoperability, digital skills development, and ethical AI use—key elements for any country aspiring to implement a successful digital governance strategy.

Singapore as a Model of Digital Governance

Singapore is widely recognized as one of the most advanced countries in digital governance and the adoption of AI in public administration (Huiling and Goh, 2017). As Asia's financial and technological hub, Singapore has heavily invested in digital transformation and the development of a smart government, where AI and emerging technologies play a central role in optimizing public services and facilitating interactions between the government and its citizens. Through its "Smart Nation" initiative (Hoe, 2016), launched in 2014, Singapore has implemented a digital governance model aimed at enhancing citizens' lives through data-driven, connected, and advanced digital services.

The Smart Nation initiative (Chang and Das, 2020) emphasizes integrating AI across multiple sectors, including healthcare, transportation, education, and security, with the goal of building a more efficient, sustainable, and citizen-centric nation. To achieve this, Singapore has developed robust digital infrastructure and promoted policies that regulate and encourage the ethical use of AI, striking a balance between technological innovation and protecting citizens' privacy and rights (Chia, 2016).

A cornerstone of Singapore's digital governance is Singpass, introduced in 2003 (Sipahi and Saayi, 2024). This digital identity system serves as a key platform in the country's governance infrastructure, enabling citizens and residents to access over 1,400 public and private services through a unified digital portal. Singpass uses AI-powered biometric technology, such as facial recognition and fingerprint scanning, to authenticate users securely, ensuring a high level of security in accessing services (Goggin and Zhuang, 2023). AI also plays an important role in personalizing services offered via Singpass. The system analyzes user data to provide recommendations and streamline access to relevant services. Through this platform, citizens can efficiently perform tasks such as renewing passports, paying taxes, applying for public housing, and accessing healthcare services. Singpass exemplifies efficiency in managing digital identity and demonstrates how AI can optimize government-citizen interactions (Bonsay et al., 2021).

In the healthcare sector, Singapore has employed AI to enhance the management and distribution of medical resources and optimize population health services. During the COVID-19 pandemic, Singapore utilized AI tools to conduct contact tracing, predict virus spread, and manage hospital resources. These tools enabled a swift and effective response, mitigating the pandemic's impact on the healthcare system (Liu et al., 2020). Additionally, AI has been used for predictive health data analysis, anticipating disease outbreaks, and adjusting public health policies accordingly. This predictive capability is especially critical in a densely populated country where outbreaks can spread rapidly (Chik and Sugumaran, 2024). AI also supports hospitals in managing medical supply inventories and allocating staff more efficiently, optimizing resource utilization and improving patient care quality.

In transportation, Singapore has adopted AI to manage its urban mobility system (Seltenrijch, 2024), which is essential for maintaining a smooth and safe flow of traffic in a highly urbanized city. AI-powered intelligent traffic systems analyze real-time data from sensors, cameras, and connected devices across the city to adjust traffic signals, identify congestion hotspots, and suggest alternative routes to improve urban mobility. Public transport also benefits from AI by forecasting peak demand, adjusting schedules, and optimizing the frequency of trains and buses. These measures improve transportation efficiency and reduce carbon emissions by minimizing congestion and energy consumption. AI is also employed for predictive maintenance of transportation systems, ensuring vehicles and infrastructure remain in optimal condition and minimizing downtime (Aloupogianni et al., 2024).

Singapore leverages AI in public safety infrastructure to maintain order and security for its citizens. With a network of strategically distributed cameras and sensors, AI enables real-time monitoring of public spaces and the detection of suspicious activities. These AI systems can identify risks and notify authorities immediately, allowing for rapid and efficient responses (Neyazi et al., 2023). During large-scale events or emergencies, Singapore's AI-enhanced surveillance systems analyze behavior patterns and anticipate potential security incidents, contributing to effective crowd management and coordinated emergency responses to ensure public safety (Neyazi et al., 2023).

The financial sector in Singapore has been a major beneficiary of digital transformation and AI adoption. The Monetary Authority of Singapore (MAS) (Fan, 2018) has fostered a regulatory environment that supports financial innovation, enabling banks and fintech companies to develop services using AI and blockchain technologies. AI detects fraud and analyzes real-time risks, preventing illicit activities and ensuring transaction security. AI systems also analyze customer behavior patterns, offering personalized recommendations and enhancing user experiences in banking.

Blockchain has also been explored to facilitate transparency and traceability in financial transactions. Combined with AI, blockchain improves efficiency and security in asset management, promotes financial inclusion, and delivers high-quality services to citizens and businesses. The government ensures that the development of AI and blockchain in the financial sector adheres to high ethical and transparency standards, strengthening trust in the country's financial systems.

Singapore has adopted an ethical approach to implementing AI in digital governance. Aware of the challenges AI poses regarding privacy and transparency, the government has established clear guidelines and regulatory frameworks. In 2020, Singapore released the "Model AI Governance Framework" (Goode et al., 2023), providing organizations with guidance for developing and using AI responsibly, ensuring transparency, and respecting user rights. These policies address algorithmic bias and protect personal data, critical in a context where technology is widely used in public services.

Singapore's commitment to ethical AI governance ensures that emerging technologies are used to maximize benefits while minimizing risks to society. This regulatory structure fosters innovation while ensuring AI developments are secure, inclusive, and aligned with human rights principles. Ethical AI practices strengthen public trust in government digital systems, reinforcing Singapore's reputation as a leader in digital governance (Óhéigeartaigh et al., 2020).

Despite its significant advancements, Singapore faces challenges on its path to fully integrated digital governance. Key issues include adapting its infrastructure to support the growth of AI and other emerging technologies and ensuring all citizens are included in digital transformation by providing access to technology and training to bridge the digital divide. Singapore remains committed to addressing these challenges through digital education policies and technological inclusion programs, ensuring all citizens benefit from AI and digitalization advancements.

Looking ahead, Singapore plans to expand its use of AI in areas such as education, sustainability, and urban development. With a long-term vision, the government aims to position Singapore as a "Smart Nation" (Leong et al., 2021), a global leader in integrating AI into public administration. Future initiatives include exploring new applications in smart cities and sustainability, leveraging AI to monitor and reduce resource consumption, better manage energy, and minimize environmental impact.

Singapore's case illustrates how a nation can harness AI and advanced technologies to transform its governance system and improve citizens' quality of life. Through its Smart Nation initiative and its ethical approach to technology use, Singapore has built an efficient, secure, and accessible digital governance model that serves as a global example. From healthcare and transportation to the financial sector, AI has optimized processes and facilitated the creation of a well-managed, interconnected society.

Singapore's experience underscores the importance of strategic vision and robust infrastructure in effectively implementing AI in public services. Its focus on ethical and responsible AI regulation builds public trust in technology and ensures that the benefits of digitalization are accessible to all. Looking to the future, Singapore continues to pursue its goal of becoming one of the world's first fully digitalized and sustainable nations, integrating AI into its governance to address the challenges of the 21st century.

Initiatives and Case Study of Spain

Spain has undergone a significant digital transformation in recent decades, with AI and other emerging technologies playing a key role in modernizing public services and improving administrative efficiency in certain areas (Lozano et al., 2021). The Spanish government has prioritized digitalization as a tool to enhance the interaction between the state and its citizens while ensuring a more transparent and accessible administration. This transformation aligns with the European Union's strategic framework, which aims to promote digitalization across member states to create a single digital market (Guevara-Gómez et al., 2021).

The National Artificial Intelligence Strategy (Sánchez Bravo, 2022), unveiled in 2020, outlines specific objectives for integrating AI into public governance and fostering this technology's ethical and responsible use. This strategy focuses on key areas such as economic development, sustainability, and digital education, with a vision of improving citizens' quality of life through technological advancement. At the same time, the Spanish government has implemented policies to balance innovation with data protection and privacy, ensuring that the use of AI in public administration complies with established ethical and legal standards.

Spain has made progress in developing a unified digital services portal, a centralized access point where citizens can efficiently carry out procedures and access public services. This portal enables direct and personalized interaction with public administration and employs AI to optimize citizen services. Through AI, the system can anticipate users' needs and provide relevant information and services, reducing wait times and enhancing the user experience.

The digitalization of citizen services includes the implementation of AI-driven chatbots and virtual assistants, which have been deployed across various public agencies to respond quickly and accurately to citizen inquiries. These AI systems proved especially useful during the COVID-19 pandemic, as they handled a high volume of questions and requests in a short period, providing up-to-date information on health and public services (Prieto et al., 2020). AI has facilitated the automation of processes, enabling the government to maintain seamless communication with citizens in administrative or consultative tasks, thereby optimizing available resources.

Spain has also applied AI in urban mobility management and public transportation, particularly in major cities like Madrid and Barcelona (Mozos-Blanco et al., 2018). Using sensors, cameras, and real-time data analytics platforms, AI improves traffic planning and control, reduces congestion, and minimizes environmental impact. These intelligent transportation systems optimize traffic flow and contribute to sustainability by lowering carbon emissions. Public transportation in Spanish cities also leverages AI to manage service frequency and adapt to real-time demand. This capability is particularly valuable during special events or peak hours, where AI helps predict traffic patterns and adjust schedules and frequencies for public transport. The efficient management of urban mobility through AI represents a significant step toward creating smart cities in Spain, enhancing both the efficiency and sustainability of transportation services (Orejon-Sanchez et al., 2022).

In the healthcare sector, Spain has experienced a transformation driven by digitalization and the use of AI in specific contexts. Telemedicine, accelerated by the COVID-19 pandemic, has become an essential tool for providing remote medical care, particularly for minor cases (Torres-Penalva and Moreno-Izquierdo, 2023). Through digital platforms and applications, citizens can access medical consultations without traveling, improving healthcare accessibility and reducing the strain on medical centers and hospitals (Ortega-Calvo et al., 2023). Additionally, AI is used for predictive health data analysis to anticipate service demand, manage resources, and foresee disease outbreaks. By integrating AI into healthcare systems, patterns can be identified, and predictions can be made using historical data—essential for planning healthcare services and informed decision-making. This approach has been particularly effective in managing chronic diseases, enabling continuous and personalized patient monitoring and improving their quality of life.

Spain has also adopted AI in its efforts toward sustainability and energy efficiency, which are national priorities given its commitments under the European Green Deal (Wendler, 2022). In energy management, AI optimizes consumption in public buildings by controlling lighting, heating, and other systems based on occupancy and environmental conditions. These practices not only conserve energy resources but also reduce the carbon footprint of government buildings, contributing to national and international sustainability goals. Moreover, AI analyzes energy consumption patterns to design public policies that promote energy savings and the use of renewable sources. For instance, in autonomous communities like Andalusia and Catalonia (García-López et al., 2024), AI is used to optimize energy distribution networks and enhance the integration of renewable energy into the power grid. Through these technologies, the Spanish government aims to secure a sustainable energy future by maximizing renewable resources and minimizing environmental impact.

In education (Galindo-Domínguez et al., 2024), Spain has promoted digital competency training to prepare the population for the challenges of the digital era. AI has been implemented in educational programs to deliver personalized learning, tailoring content and teaching methods to individual student needs, particularly at the master's level. This approach is especially useful in Spain's diverse educational system, where AI helps reduce dropout rates and improves the inclusion of students with special educational needs. The government has also launched initiatives to promote digital literacy among citizens, ensuring that everyone can benefit from digital services and reducing the digital divide. Through training programs, the state not only prepares the population for employment in emerging sectors but also aims to strengthen the development of an innovation and technology ecosystem that drives economic growth and fosters social cohesion.

Likewise, Spain has emphasized the importance of ethics and transparency in the use of AI in public administration. The National Artificial Intelligence Strategy includes ethical principles to guide the development and implementation of AI, ensuring that its use respects human rights and complies with data protection regulations. This ethical approach is reinforced by Spain's commitment to the GDPR (Floridi et al., 2021), which safeguards citizen privacy within the EU. Transparency is a key component of state digitalization, allowing citizens to understand how and why decisions are made through automated systems. Ethical AI use in governance strengthens public trust and ensures that citizens can safely and fairly benefit from technology.

Finally, Spain's case demonstrates how a country can leverage AI and digitalization to enhance governance and deliver more efficient and accessible public services. From healthcare to energy management and urban mobility, AI has optimized processes and improved service delivery to citizens. Spain's commitment to ethics and transparency in technology use highlights the importance of responsible governance in the digital age. As Spain continues its digital transformation, the use of AI is expected to expand into new sectors, such as justice and natural resource management, positioning Spain as a leader in digital governance within the European Union.

Discussion

The cases of Saudi Arabia, Estonia, Singapore, and Spain provide a compelling comparative analysis of how AI can be integrated into digital governance, with each country illustrating diverse approaches shaped by its socio-economic context, governance priorities, and technological capabilities. While all four nations have made significant strides in their digital transformation, their strategies reflect distinct emphases on infrastructure, public services, ethical governance, and citizen-centric innovations. These differences underscore the importance of context-specific approaches, as suggested by adaptive governance theories (Karpouzoglou et al., 2016), which emphasize the alignment of technological solutions with societal needs and institutional frameworks (Van Assche et al., 2022).

A key shared feature across these countries is the prioritization of robust digital infrastructure, which serves as the key for AI integration. For example, Estonia's X-Road platform exemplifies an interoperable system seamlessly connecting public and private sectors, enabling secure data sharing and personalized services. Similarly, Singapore's Singpass acts as a centralized digital identity gateway, leveraging biometric AI technologies to provide secure access to a wide array of services. These systems align with theories of digital governance that prioritize efficiency and scalability through interoperability. Saudi Arabia's Absher system, by contrast, combines centralization with advanced AI for user personalization, emphasizing trust and security in its design. Spain, while moving toward a unified portal for public services, has yet to achieve the interoperability seen in Estonia or the biometrics-driven sophistication of Singapore and Saudi Arabia. These variations highlight the link between infrastructural maturity and national priorities. For instance, Estonia and Singapore focus on interoperability and scalability, while Saudi Arabia prioritizes citizen trust through high-security measures. At the same time, Spain adopts a more gradual approach, emphasizing accessibility and inclusivity to drive adoption, particularly in alignment with EU standards on digitalization.

Thus, AI-driven personalization is another shared priority among these nations, yet its implementation varies significantly. In the case of Singapore, AI systems are particularly advanced in optimizing public services across transportation, healthcare, and public safety, leveraging predictive analytics to manage demand and allocate resources effectively. Estonia, with its focus on administrative automation, integrates AI into sectors like the judiciary, as seen in its virtual judge for minor disputes. Saudi Arabia employs AI extensively in healthcare, where telemedicine and chronic disease monitoring have transformed service delivery, particularly in alignment with its Vision 2030 goals. Spain, while incorporating AI in public health resource planning and telemedicine, lags in implementing the predictive and proactive functionalities evident in other cases. These differences align with innovation diffusion theory (Wonglimpiyarat and Yuberk, 2005), which highlights how technological adoption is shaped by institutional capacities and societal readiness.

Likewise, transportation and urban mobility further demonstrate how AI's application reflects each country's priorities. Singapore and Estonia effectively use AI to manage real-time traffic data and optimize public transportation schedules, aligning with smart city frameworks that emphasize efficiency and sustainability. Spain employs similar techniques but places greater emphasis on reducing carbon emissions and aligning with the European Green Deal. In contrast, Saudi Arabia's focus on transportation is less pronounced, with greater attention directed toward healthcare and administrative efficiency. These variations illustrate how AI can be leveraged to address context-specific challenges, from urban density in Singapore to environmental sustainability in Spain.

In the same context, ethical governance emerges as a cornerstone of digital transformation in all four countries, though the emphasis and approach differ. Singapore's AI Governance Framework exemplifies proactive regulation, providing clear guidelines for responsible AI use across sectors. Estonia leads in fostering public trust through transparency, allowing citizens to audit data access. Spain aligns its governance with EU-wide GDPR standards, ensuring compliance with stringent data protection regulations, while Saudi Arabia emphasizes trust-building through the oversight of the SDAIA. These approaches resonate with governance theories that stress the importance of legitimacy and accountability in technological adoption, underscoring how cultural and institutional factors influence ethical frameworks.

Also, citizen engagement and user-centric services are focal points for all four nations, though their strategies reflect different governance models. Estonia and Singapore excel at leveraging real-time data to personalize services and improve user experience, while Saudi Arabia prioritizes trust-building through secure, AI-enhanced platforms like Absher, facilitating a wide range of administrative tasks. Spain emphasizes inclusivity, focusing on reducing the digital divide and improving accessibility for underserved populations. These strategies highlight how each country's approach aligns with societal priorities, such as fostering trust, promoting inclusivity, or ensuring efficiency (Kulal et al., 2024).

Finally, sustainability emerges as a more explicit priority in Singapore and Spain than in Estonia and Saudi Arabia. Singapore integrates AI into urban planning and energy management, aligning with smart city and sustainability frameworks, while Spain emphasizes renewable energy and efficient resource utilization as part of its commitments under the European Green Deal. Estonia, while not explicitly prioritizing sustainability, benefits from a digital-first approach that inherently reduces resource consumption. Saudi Arabia's efforts in this domain are less prominent, focusing instead on healthcare and service efficiency. These distinctions underscore how different governance priorities shape the application of AI to broader societal challenges, such as environmental sustainability and urban management.

The analyzed cases illustrate the importance of tailoring digital governance strategies to national contexts, as adaptive governance theory suggests while ensuring that AI serves citizens ethically, inclusively, and sustainably. It could be highlighted that Estonia and Singapore demonstrate the potential of deeply integrated systems to achieve efficiency and scalability, while Saudi Arabia and Spain adopt more specialized approaches, focusing on sectors such as healthcare and mobility. Transparency and ethical oversight are universally critical, with Estonia leading in data access transparency, Singapore in regulatory frameworks, Saudi Arabia in platform security, and Spain in aligning with EU standards. Spain's focus on sustainability adds an important dimension, demonstrating how digital governance can support broader environmental objectives. These experiences collectively provide actionable insights for countries seeking to harness AI's transformative potential, emphasizing the need for strategic vision, robust infrastructure, and citizen-centered innovation to ensure that technology aligns with societal needs and values.

CONCLUSIONS

This study employed a case study methodology to analyze the integration of AI in digital governance across four diverse contexts: Saudi Arabia, Estonia, Singapore, and Spain. The methodology allowed for an in-depth exploration of each country's strategies, challenges, and innovations, providing a nuanced understanding of how AI is transforming public administration. After examining these cases, the study sought to address the research question: *How can the adoption of AI in digital governance promote public trust while enhancing efficiency, innovation, and societal well-being?* The comparative analysis also pursued secondary objectives, including the identification of unique approaches, challenges, and best practices in each case and the role of transparency and ethical oversight in fostering trust and efficiency. The findings reveal that each country has tailored its AI and digital governance strategies to its unique socio-economic and political contexts. Saudi Arabia's initiatives, framed within its Vision 2030 agenda, focus on centralizing public services and building citizen trust through secure, AI-driven platforms like Absher, with a particular emphasis on healthcare and administrative efficiency. Estonia, often seen as a pioneer in digital governance, excels in interoperability and transparency through platforms like X-Road, integrating AI into sectors such as public administration and the judiciary. Singapore's Smart Nation initiative demonstrates a holistic approach to AI integration, leveraging predictive analytics and advanced digital identity systems like Singpass to optimize transportation, healthcare, and public safety. Spain's efforts, aligned with the European Union's digitalization goals, emphasize inclusivity, sustainability, and adherence to ethical standards, with notable progress in telemedicine, energy efficiency, and urban mobility.

The comparative analysis highlights commonalities and divergences across the cases. All four countries leverage AI to enhance efficiency and personalization in public services, yet their implementation varies significantly. Estonia and Singapore excel in deeply integrated systems, while Saudi Arabia and Spain focus on sector-specific innovations. Ethical governance and transparency emerge as critical pillars, with Estonia and Singapore leading in proactive regulatory frameworks and citizen-centric features. Spain emphasizes alignment with EU standards, while Saudi Arabia prioritizes trust-building through strict oversight. Therefore, the study finds that the adoption of AI in digital governance can enhance public trust and societal well-being when grounded in ethical principles, transparency, and inclusivity. Meeting the secondary objectives, the analysis identifies transferable lessons: the importance of interoperable infrastructure (as demonstrated by Estonia), the role of secure digital identity systems (Singapore), the value of strategic alignment with national and international goals (Spain), and the need for culturally adapted trust-building measures (Saudi Arabia).

As AI continues to evolve, these cases underscore the necessity of balancing innovation with ethical considerations, ensuring that the benefits of digital governance are accessible to all citizens while safeguarding their rights and privacy. The findings offer a roadmap for other nations seeking to harness AI's transformative potential in public administration, highlighting the critical role of strategic vision, robust infrastructure, and citizen engagement in achieving sustainable and inclusive digital governance.

Theoretical Implications

This study contributes to the theoretical understanding of AI's role in digital governance by emphasizing its potential to reshape government and citizens' relationships. It highlights how AI can enhance public trust through transparency, ethical governance, and personalized service delivery, aligning with existing theories on technology adoption and trust in public institutions. The case study methodology provides empirical evidence supporting the argument that AI's integration into public administration requires a nuanced balance between technological innovation and socio-political considerations. After comparing diverse governance models, this research offers a framework for analyzing how contextual factors such as cultural values, regulatory environments, and technological infrastructure influence the adoption and success of AI in governance. Furthermore, the study underscores the relevance of governance theories that prioritize inclusivity, efficiency, and sustainability. For instance, the findings align with the concept of adaptive governance (Karpouzoglou et al., 2016), where technology is not merely a tool for efficiency but a means to foster citizen engagement and address societal challenges, such as sustainability and equitable access to services. This theoretical lens can guide future research on the evolving role of AI in governance systems globally.

Practical Implications

The findings of this study provide actionable insights for policymakers, public administrators, and technology developers. First, the importance of creating robust, interoperable digital infrastructures, as demonstrated by Estonia and Singapore, serves as a blueprint for countries aiming to integrate AI into public governance. These systems enable efficient data sharing, service personalization, and streamlined administrative processes, improving public trust and operational efficiency. Second, the study highlights the necessity of ethical AI frameworks and transparent governance mechanisms to address concerns around data privacy, algorithmic bias, and inclusivity. Estonia's citizen-accessible data audit system and Singapore's proactive AI Governance Framework exemplify best practices that can be adapted to different contexts. Spain's alignment with GDPR also underscores the importance of harmonizing national and international regulatory standards. Third, the integration of AI in sector-specific applications, such as healthcare, transportation, and public safety, offers insights into how governments can tailor technological solutions to address local challenges. Saudi Arabia's focus on secure, centralized services and Spain's emphasis on sustainability demonstrate the versatility of AI in addressing diverse governance priorities.

Limitations and Future Research

While the case study methodology provides in-depth insights, the study's findings are context-specific and may not be universally generalizable. The selection of countries limits the scope of comparison to a subset of governance models, leaving room for future research to explore other regions or less-developed nations to identify broader trends and challenges. Additionally, the study relies primarily on secondary data, which may not fully capture the on-ground realities or citizen perspectives on AI-driven governance. Future research could incorporate primary data collection, such as interviews or surveys with policymakers and citizens, to provide a more comprehensive understanding of the impacts of AI integration. Lastly, the study focuses on current initiatives and outcomes, but the long-term societal and ethical implications of AI in governance remain uncertain. Future research could examine the evolution of these systems over time, particularly how they adapt to emerging technologies, changing regulatory landscapes, and evolving citizen expectations. Specific attention should also be given to areas like AI in justice systems, the intersection of AI and sustainability, and the potential risks of over-reliance on automated decision-making in governance.

REFERENCES

Allmnakrah, A., & Evers, C. (2020). The need for a fundamental shift in the Saudi education system: Implementing the Saudi Arabian economic vision 2030. *Research in Education*, 106(1), 22–40. DOI: 10.1177/0034523719851534

Alogaiel, N. F., & Alrwais, O. A. (2023). An assessment of the quality of open government data in Saudi Arabia. *IEEE Access : Practical Innovations, Open Solutions*, 11, 61560–61599. DOI: 10.1109/ACCESS.2023.3285611

Alotaibi, A., Alsubaie, D., Alaskar, H., Alhumaid, L., Thuwayni, R. B., Alkhalifah, R., & Alhumoud, S. (2022, January). Kingdom of Saudi Arabia: Era of Smart Cities. In *2022 2nd International Conference on Computing and Information Technology (ICCIT)* (pp. 285-292). IEEE.

Aloupogianni, E., Doctor, F., Karyotis, C., Maniak, T., Tang, R., & Iqbal, R. (2024, July). An AI-Based Digital Twin Framework for Intelligent Traffic Management in Singapore. In *2024 International Conference on Electrical, Computer and Energy Technologies (ICECET)* (pp. 1-6). IEEE. DOI: 10.1109/ICECET61485.2024.10698642

Alsmadi, M. K., Al-Marashdeh, I., Alzaqebah, M., Jaradat, G., Alghamdi, F. A., Mohammad, R. M. A., & Tayfour, M. (2021). Digitalization of learning in Saudi Arabia during the COVID-19 outbreak: A survey. *Informatics in Medicine Unlocked*, 25, 100632. DOI: 10.1016/j.imu.2021.100632 PMID: 34150983

Andejany, M., Sounni, I., Akbar, A., & Alsubaie, F. (2022). Critical success factors addressing Covid-19 pandemic: Case of Tawakkalna application in Saudi Arabia. *IEOM,* 1520-1535.

Annus, T., & Merimaa, K. (2024). The role of government in leading the pandemic response: The Estonian experience. In *Resilient Health* (pp. 433–443). Academic Press. DOI: 10.1016/B978-0-443-18529-8.00035-4

Attard-Frost, B., Brandusescu, A., & Lyons, K. (2024). The governance of artificial intelligence in Canada: Findings and opportunities from a review of 84 AI governance initiatives. *Government Information Quarterly*, 41(2), 101929. DOI: 10.1016/j.giq.2024.101929

Bakry, S. H., & Saud, B. A. A. (2021). A roadmap to AI: An insight from the Saudi Vision 2030. *Artificial Intelligence and Its Contexts: Security, Business and Governance,* 201-223.

Basri, W. (2020). Examining the impact of artificial intelligence (AI)-assisted social media marketing on the performance of small and medium enterprises: Toward effective business management in the Saudi Arabian context. *International Journal of Computational Intelligence Systems*, 13(1), 142–152. DOI: 10.2991/ijcis.d.200127.002

Bennett, A., & Elman, C. (2006). Qualitative research: Recent developments in case study methods. *Annual Review of Political Science*, 9(1), 455–476. DOI: 10.1146/annurev.polisci.8.082103.104918

Bodul, D. (2023). Can artificial intelligence (AI) replace the judge?. *Harmonius: J. Legal & Soc. Stud. Se. Eur., 15.*

Bonsay, J. O., Cruz, A. P., Firozi, H. C., & Camaro, P. J. C. (2021). Artificial intelligence and labor productivity paradox: The economic impact of AI in China, India, Japan, and Singapore. *Journal of Economics. Finance and Accounting Studies*, 3(2), 120–139. DOI: 10.32996/jefas.2021.3.2.13

Chang, F., & Das, D. (2020). Smart nation Singapore: Developing policies for a citizen-oriented smart city initiative. *Developing National Urban Policies: Ways Forward to Green and Smart Cities,* 425-440.

Chia, E. S. (2016, June). Singapore's smart nation program—Enablers and challenges. In *2016 11th System of Systems Engineering Conference (SoSE)* (pp. 1-5). IEEE.

Chik, W. B., & Sugumaran, H. (2024). Legal governance of artificial intelligence in healthcare devices and services in Singapore. In *Research Handbook on Health, AI and the Law* (pp. 373-391). Edward Elgar Publishing. DOI: 10.4337/9781802205657.00030

Ebers, M., & Tupay, P. K. (2023). *Artificial intelligence and machine learning powered public service delivery in Estonia: Opportunities and legal challenges.* Springer. DOI: 10.1007/978-3-031-19667-6

Éigeartaigh, S. S., Whittlestone, J., Liu, Y., Zeng, Y., & Liu, Z. (2020). Overcoming barriers to cross-cultural cooperation in AI ethics and governance. *Philosophy & Technology*, 33(4), 571–593. DOI: 10.1007/s13347-020-00402-x

Fan, P. S. (2018). Singapore approach to develop and regulate FinTech. In *Handbook of Blockchain, Digital Finance, and Inclusion, Volume 1* (pp. 347-357). Academic Press. DOI: 10.1016/B978-0-12-810441-5.00015-4

Floridi, L., Cowls, J., King, T. C., & Taddeo, M. (2021). How to design AI for social good: Seven essential factors. *Ethics, Governance, and Policies in Artificial Intelligence,* 125-151.

Galindo-Domínguez, H., Delgado, N., Losada, D., & Etxabe, J. M. (2024). An analysis of the use of artificial intelligence in education in Spain: The in-service teacher's perspective. *Journal of Digital Learning in Teacher Education*, 40(1), 41–56. DOI: 10.1080/21532974.2023.2284726

García-López, J., Domínguez-Amarillo, S., & Sendra, J. J. (2024). Clustering open data for predictive modeling of residential energy consumption across variable scales: A case study in Andalusia, Spain. *Buildings*, 14(8), 2335. DOI: 10.3390/buildings14082335

Gavrilova, V., & Gurvitsh-Suits, N. A. (2020). Contemporary innovation challenges–Future of adoption artificial intelligence: Case of Estonia. *European Integration Studies*, 14(14), 217–225. DOI: 10.5755/j01.eis.1.14.26143

Goggin, G., & Zhuang, K. V. (2023). Apps, mobilities, and migration in the Covid-19 pandemic: Covid technology and the control of migrant workers in Singapore. *International Journal of Cultural Studies*, 26(6), 636–654. DOI: 10.1177/13678779231160802

Goode, K., Kim, H. M., & Deng, M. (2023). Examining Singapore's AI progress. *Center for Security and Emerging Technology,* 19.

Guevara-Gómez, A., de Zárate-Alcarazo, L. O., & Criado, J. I. (2021). Feminist perspectives to artificial intelligence: Comparing the policy frames of the European Union and Spain. *Information Polity*, 26(2), 173–192. DOI: 10.3233/IP-200299

Hardy, A. (2024). Estonia's digital diplomacy: Nordic interoperability and the challenges of cross-border e-governance. *Internet Policy Review*, 13(3), 1–31. DOI: 10.14763/2024.3.1785

Hartley, J. (2004). What is a case study. *Essential guide to qualitative methods in organizational research, 323.*

Heller, N. (2017). Estonia, the digital republic. *The New Yorker, 18,* 12.

Hoe, S. L. (2016). Defining a smart nation: The case of Singapore. *Journal of Information. Communication and Ethics in Society*, 14(4), 323–333. DOI: 10.1108/JICES-02-2016-0005

Huiling, E., & Goh, B. (2017). AI, robotics and mobility as a service: The case of Singapore. *Field Actions Science Reports. The Journal of Field Actions, (Special Issue 17),* 26-29.

Ibrahim, N. M. H. (2024). Artificial intelligence (AI) and Saudi Arabia's governance. *Journal of Developing Societies*, 0169796X(4), 241288590. DOI: 10.1177/0169796X241288590

Jermalavičius, T. (2024). Caught between today and tomorrow: Defence AI in Estonia. In *The Very Long Game: 25 Case Studies on the Global State of Defense AI* (pp. 149–171). Springer Nature Switzerland. DOI: 10.1007/978-3-031-58649-1_7

Joamets, K., & Chochia, A. (2020). Artificial intelligence and its impact on labour relations in Estonia. *Slovak Journal of Political Sciences*, 20(2), 255–277. DOI: 10.34135/sjps.200204

Kanojia, S. (2023). Ensuring privacy of personal data: A panoramic view of legal developments in personal data protection law in Saudi Arabia. *Manchester Journal of Transnational Islamic Law and Practice*, 19(3), 270–276.

Karpouzoglou, T., Dewulf, A., & Clark, J. (2016). Advancing adaptive governance of social-ecological systems through theoretical multiplicity. *Environmental Science & Policy*, 57, 1–9. DOI: 10.1016/j.envsci.2015.11.011

Kerikmäe, T., & Pärn-Lee, E. (2021). Legal dilemmas of Estonian artificial intelligence strategy: In between of e-society and global race. *AI & Society*, 36(2), 561–572. DOI: 10.1007/s00146-020-01009-8

Khan, M. K., & Khan, M. B. (Eds.). (2020). *Research, innovation and entrepreneurship in Saudi Arabia: Vision 2030*. Routledge. DOI: 10.4324/9781351040020

Kulal, A., Rahiman, H. U., Suvarna, H., Abhishek, N., & Dinesh, S. (2024). Enhancing public service delivery efficiency: Exploring the impact of AI. *Journal of Open Innovation*, 10(3), 100329. DOI: 10.1016/j.joitmc.2024.100329

Kuziemski, M., & Misuraca, G. (2020). AI governance in the public sector: Three tales from the frontiers of automated decision-making in democratic settings. *Telecommunications Policy*, 44(6), 101976. DOI: 10.1016/j.telpol.2020.101976 PMID: 32313360

Leong, S., Lee, T., Leong, S., & Lee, T. (2021). The internet in Singapore: From 'intelligent island' to 'smart nation.' *Global Internet Governance: Influences from Malaysia and Singapore,* 31-49.

Liu, S., Ko, Q. S., Heng, K. Q. A., Ngiam, K. Y., & Feng, M. (2020). Healthcare transformation in Singapore with artificial intelligence. *Frontiers in Digital Health*, 2, 592121. DOI: 10.3389/fdgth.2020.592121 PMID: 34713061

Lozano, I. A., Molina, J. M., & Gijón, C. (2021). Perception of artificial intelligence in Spain. *Telematics and Informatics*, 63, 101672. DOI: 10.1016/j.tele.2021.101672

Makridakis, S. (2017). The forthcoming artificial intelligence (AI) revolution: Its impact on society and firms. *Futures*, 90, 46–60. DOI: 10.1016/j.futures.2017.03.006

Masso, A., Kaun, A., & Van Noordt, C. (2023). Basic values in artificial intelligence: Comparative factor analysis in Estonia, Germany, and Sweden. *AI & Society*, •••, 1–16.

Memish, Z. A., Altuwaijri, M. M., Almoeen, A. H., & Enani, S. M. (2021). The Saudi Data & Artificial Intelligence Authority (SDAIA) vision: Leading the kingdom's journey toward global leadership. *Journal of Epidemiology and Global Health*, 11(2), 140–142. DOI: 10.2991/jegh.k.210405.001 PMID: 33876596

Meyer, C. B. (2001). A case in case study methodology. *Field Methods*, 13(4), 329–352. DOI: 10.1177/1525822X0101300402

Milakovich, M. E. (2012). *Digital governance: New technologies for improving public service and participation*. Routledge., DOI: 10.4324/9780203815991

Mozos-Blanco, M. Á., Pozo-Menéndez, E., Arce-Ruiz, R., & Baucells-Aletà, N. (2018). The way to sustainable mobility: A comparative analysis of sustainable mobility plans in Spain. *Transport Policy*, 72, 45–54. DOI: 10.1016/j.tranpol.2018.07.001

Neyazi, T. A., Ng, S. W. T., Hobbs, M., & Yue, A. (2023). Understanding user interactions and perceptions of AI risk in Singapore. *Big Data & Society*, 10(2), 20539517231213823. DOI: 10.1177/20539517231213823

Njie, B., & Asimiran, S. (2014). Case study as a choice in qualitative methodology. *Journal of research & method in Education, 4*(3), 35-40.

Orejón-Sanchez, R. D., Crespo-Garcia, D., Andres-Diaz, J. R., & Gago-Calderon, A. (2022). Smart cities' development in Spain: A comparison of technical and social indicators with reference to European cities. *Sustainable Cities and Society*, 81, 103828. DOI: 10.1016/j.scs.2022.103828

Ortega-Calvo, A. S., Morcillo-Jimenez, R., Fernandez-Basso, C., Gutiérrez-Batista, K., Vila, M. A., & Martin-Bautista, M. J. (2023). Aimdp: An artificial intelligence modern data platform. Use case for Spanish national health service data silo. *Future Generation Computer Systems*, 143, 248–264. DOI: 10.1016/j.future.2023.02.002

Owais, M., & Alshehri, A. (•••). Perspectives on intelligent transportation systems future in Mecca area. [Paes, S. Centric AI: From ethics to action: A study of human-centric AI implementation in public services, comparing the Estonian approach with approaches used in other countries.]. *International Journal of Computer Applications*, 975, 8887.

Pagani, R. N., de Sá, C. P., Corsi, A., & de Souza, F. F. (2023). AI and Employability: Challenges and Solutions from this Technology Transfer. In *Smart Cities and Digital Transformation: Empowering Communities, Limitless Innovation, Sustainable Development and the Next Generation* (pp. 253-284). Emerald Publishing Limited. DOI: 10.1108/978-1-80455-994-920231012

Prieto, F. A., Baltas, N. G., Rios-Pena, L., & Rodriguez, P. (2020). COVID-19 impact estimation on ICU capacity at Andalusia, Spain, using artificial intelligence.

Robinson, N., Hardy, A., & Ertan, A. (2021). *A curious and cautious approach to artificial intelligence and national security*. DOI: 10.2139/ssrn.4105328

Sánchez Bravo, Á. (2022). España digital 2025. Estrategia nacional de inteligencia artificial. *Inteligencia artificial y filosofía del derecho*.

Sanina, A., Balashov, A., & Rubtcova, M. (2023). The socio-economic efficiency of digital government transformation. *International Journal of Public Administration*, 46(1), 85–96. DOI: 10.1080/01900692.2021.1988637

Saputro, R., Pappel, I., Vainsalu, H., Lips, S., & Draheim, D. (2020, April). Prerequisites for the adoption of the X-Road interoperability and data exchange framework: A comparative study. In *2020 Seventh International Conference on eDemocracy & eGovernment (ICEDEG)* (pp. 216-222). IEEE. DOI: 10.1109/ICEDEG48599.2020.9096704

Sarapuu, K., & Saarniit, L. (2020). Public administration in Estonia: A search for identity. *European Perspec,* 317.

Saraswat, D., Bhattacharya, P., Verma, A., Prasad, V. K., Tanwar, S., Sharma, G., Bokoro, P. N., & Sharma, R. (2022). Explainable AI for healthcare 5.0: Opportunities and challenges. *IEEE Access : Practical Innovations, Open Solutions*, 10, 84486–84517. DOI: 10.1109/ACCESS.2022.3197671

Saura, J. R. (2022). Using predictive algorithm in local governance administrative decision making: a bibliometric analysis of current practices. *Smart cities and law, e-governance and rights, 178*(121561), 91.

Schlunegger, M. C., Zumstein-Shaha, M., & Palm, R. (2024). Methodologic and Data-Analysis Triangulation in Case Studies: A Scoping Review. *Western Journal of Nursing Research*, 46(8), 611–622. DOI: 10.1177/01939459241263011 PMID: 39076135

Seltenrijch, F. (2024). How can smart transportation systems contribute to the reduction of carbon emissions in Singapore?: A scoping review (Bachelor's thesis, University of Twente).

Shml, E. M. A., & Aris, S. A. (2022). A review of security concern on Covid-19 tracing application. *Open International Journal of Informatics*, 10(2), 155–171.

Sipahi, E. B., & Saayi, Z. (2024). The world's first "smart nation" vision: The case of Singapore. *Smart Cities and Regional Development (SCRD). Journal*, 8(1), 41–58.

Torres-Penalva, A., & Moreno-Izquierdo, L. (2023, October). Innovation and AI: An opportunity for Spanish tourism in the post Covid-19 era. In *International Conference on Tourism and Information and Communication Technologies* (pp. 113-122). Cham: Springer Nature Switzerland.

Van Assche, K., Valentinov, V., & Verschraegen, G. (2022). Adaptive governance: Learning from what organizations do and managing the role they play. *Kybernetes*, 51(5), 1738–1758. DOI: 10.1108/K-11-2020-0759

Wendler, F. (2022). Climate change policy in the EU: From the Paris agreement to the European Green Deal. *Framing Climate Change in the EU and US After the Paris Agreement,* 65-117.

Wonglimpiyarat, J., & Yuberk, N. (2005). In support of innovation management and Roger's Innovation Diffusion theory. *Government Information Quarterly*, 22(3), 411–422. DOI: 10.1016/j.giq.2005.05.005

Chapter 2
Data Quality in the Surveillance Economy:
Challenges of Digital Governance in the Paradox of Data Decontextualization

Younes Karrouk
https://orcid.org/0009-0005-4967-5513
Abdelmalek Essaadi University, Morocco

Felipe Rodolfo Debasa Navalpotro
https://orcid.org/0000-0001-6459-1469
Rey Juan Carlos University, Spain

ABSTRACT

Data is considered the new oil of the current world economy. Therefore, it is necessary to analyze the quality of the data as a preliminary phase in the interaction processes with algorithms and artificial intelligence. This chapter explores the critical importance of data quality within the surveillance economy and its implications for digital governance. It addresses the challenges of ensuring accurate, reliable data in an era of pervasive data collection and usage. The discussion highlights strategies for improving data governance practices to enhance privacy and accountability in AI-driven environments.

DOI: 10.4018/979-8-3693-6945-6.ch002

INTRODUCTION

A paradox exists in contemporary society: while billions of individual data points are generated and recorded through increasingly ubiquitous digital surveillance practices in the surveillance economy, sociotechnical systems have become increasingly "datafied", progressively moving away from the social contexts that give them meaning (West,2017). The initial collection of data for a specific purpose or objective will end up serving purposes far from the initial purpose. The authors of the present chapter describe this situation as the "Paradox of Data Decontextualization". This term highlights the disconnection between the enormous amount of data generated and its disconnection from the social context that gives it meaning (Saura et al., 2024). It reflects how data, rather than faithfully capturing reality, becomes an abstraction that may not accurately represent human experiences, thus creating challenges for governance and public accountability within the surveillance economy (Shandler, 2019). To better understand this paradox, it is essential to explore the historical foundation of data collection and how it has evolved into a tool of control and power. Since the earliest civilizations, humans have collected data to record, control, and organize knowledge. It is a fact through which writing is born, and, therefore, history appears since humans can store and externalize memory (Lyulyov et al., 2024).

In Ancient Egypt and Mesopotamia, data was stored on clay tablets and papyrus, recording fundamental aspects of social, economic and religious life, such as taxes, censuses and commercial transactions. These early archival systems represented a close relationship between data and its cultural context. As civilizations advanced, data collection took on an increasingly formalized role, with the emergence of centralized archives and state libraries in medieval and early modern times, facilitating more efficient administration of territories (Manning, 2013). In public discourse, the relational data practices of the surveillance economy are often considered a "wicked problem," with a tension between data ubiquity, subjective qualities, semiotic meanings, and public accountability (Butler and Brooks, 2023). Crucial elements in this tension and in the conversion to numbers within this digital governance and worldview regime are concerns about data quality (e.g. accuracy, provenance, and representativeness). It remains to be seen whether the data will "speak for itself," as these concerns suggest.

The "Paradox of Data Decontextualization" affects the interpretation of data, has a significant impact on data quality, and raises questions about the ethical and responsible use of users' digital footprint. When data is collected and analyzed without consideration for the context in which it was generated, there is a risk that these data will lose precision, representativeness and relevance (Grindrod, 2016). This phenomenon is amplified in the surveillance economy, where the enormous amount of data generated may contain errors, duplications, or information that is irrelevant for certain analytical purposes. Poor quality data can distort the results of artificial intelligence systems and decision-making algorithms, leading to biased or incorrect interpretations. Thus, the disconnection between data and its context not only poses a problem of interpretation, but also compromises the reliability and usefulness of the data, exacerbating governance and accountability challenges. Furthermore, the user will have doubts about their digital behavior since they will not know what may happen in the future with their own digital footprint.

In this way, a clear example of the problems arising from low data quality in the surveillance economy are decision-making algorithms in the judicial system. When these algorithms are based on decontextualized or biased data, there is a high risk that the resulting decisions will reinforce biases and structural inequalities. Arrest and criminal record data, for example, may reflect biased police practices, but when used without context in predictive algorithms, they perpetuate injustices and produce results that do not accurately reflect social reality. This example shows how data quality is essential for the ethical and responsible operation of surveillance and algorithmic decision systems. In this aspect, criminal law has a great field of work to study equity in the legal models of surveillance capitalism (Zuboff, 2023) especially due to the sensitivity of the data and criminal issues.

Likewise, drawing on the work of 20th-century philosopher, engineer, and public intellectual Vannevar Bush, a historical analysis of data quality concerns in contemporary democracies is undertaken as a memetic realignment within a broader history of surveillance by numbers. and non-human governance. It is argued that this data quality cycle associated with the "surveillance economy", currently at the height of transnational discussion, digital governance legislation and regulation in various jurisdictions around the world (Cuéllar & Huq, 2020), represents the next stage in a historic techno-epistemic policy of data quality within the price-indifference regime of neoliberal governance models that emerged after World War II. Furthermore, it is argued that "data quality" is an ambiguous and contradictory concept, deeply intertwined with social practices, logic, and policies of inequality, privilege, and bias. The paper traces how data quality became politically and socially significant within surveillance economies and what its implications are for addressing questions of responsibility, accountability and legitimacy. The focus is on data quality in its role as a control mechanism, governance technique, and organizing principle distributed within public discourse on data practices in the surveillance economy (Purwanto et al., 2020).

The "Data Decontextualization Paradox" reveals a fundamental contradiction in the surveillance economy: although a massive amount of data is collected with the intention of gaining a deeper understanding of human behaviors and patterns, the process of "datafication" It strips that data of the contexts that give it meaning.

This paradox suggests that, by attempting to capture and quantify human complexity, digital surveillance systems end up producing incomplete or distorted representations of reality. This disconnection can lead to erroneous interpretations and poor decisions, since it is based on data that does not accurately reflect the social, cultural or emotional conditions of individuals. Ultimately, the paradox highlights the limits of a purely quantitative and technocratic view of society, urging the need for governance approaches that recognize and mitigate these limitations. We cannot affirm at the moment that the different artificial intelligence programs and software correct these deviations. We found numerous examples of biases carried out by artificial intelligence programs (Osoba and Welser, 2017).

Finally, the Paradox of the Decontextualization of Data could lead to the proposition, to an extreme degree, that some political systems that do not believe in private property could propose expropriations or nationalizations of archives or data libraries. In surveillance capitalism, this is another asset such as buildings, patents, or industrial machinery.

Understanding the surveillance economy

Much of contemporary life is premised on the generation, collection, and processing of data about individuals, but the kinds of data collected, the technologies used to collect it, and the economic outcomes that follow differ widely across the globe. The chapter situates this variety in data collection within the surveillance economy, a worldwide economic system that concerns surveillance using data. Economic exchanges within the surveillance economy occur through the sale or trade of data about individuals. This data is commonly referred to as "digital exhaust" or "user-generated data" and is often understood by outsiders as a series of clicks, searches, geolocations, and likes. As a result of this ongoing generation and processing, profiles, models, and inferences about individuals are created, usually without their knowledge or consent (Xu et al., 2020). These profiles are sold to companies that, wishing to maximize revenues, use them to offer targeted ads, payment plans, or loans. The surveillance economy is described as a system of heterogeneous economic actors, numerous kinds of data, and diverse technologies and economic strategies, all concerned with the surveillance of individuals using data (Saura and Debasa, 2022).

A typology is presented to frame the surveillance economy's variety and complexity. First, a global overview of contemporary economic exchanges concerning digital data is provided, offering insights into companies, kinds of data, and strategies. Second, grounded in this overview, four dimensions of the surveillance economy are elaborated, differentiating more micro and macro elements. This typology allows refinements of the notion of the surveillance economy by disentangling toolkits, harmonized systems, and systems of living together. Future interventions that could ensure more ethical and equitable practices in the surveillance economy are also suggested while also endeavoring to sketch a horizon of hope (Moore et al., 2021).

The surveillance economy is a term that encompasses a wide range of surveillance practices, including many aspects that are not digital, automated, or capitalist. However, at the center of the surveillance economy situated here, there is a specific history of the use of surveillance technologies for economic exchanges concerning digital data of individuals. Currently, much of everyday life is comprised of the generation, collection, and processing of data about individuals, although there is extreme variation in what kind of data is collected, what technologies are employed to collect it, and what economic outcomes follow. This variation in data collection practices is situated in relation to the surveillance economy, a worldwide economic system concerned with the surveillance of individuals using data (Saura, 2024).

When analyzing the Paradox of Data Decontextualization, a reflection also arises on the role of meaning in data analysis and algorithmic decision making. Disconnecting data from its context of origin not only creates technical and operational problems, but also poses an ethical dilemma: to what extent can algorithmic decisions based on decontextualized data be truly representative or fair? In the surveillance economy, a lack of context can lead to a superficial view of human behaviors, reducing the complexity of individual experiences to numbers and patterns, which dehumanizes the decision-making process (Saura et al., 2022). In doing so, an effort is made to demonstrate how surveillance economies renegotiate, "dataficate," and automate sociotechnical worlds, how this datafication provokes new anxieties and demands for better governance, algorithmic accountability, and auditing practices, and how these audits have their own sociotechnical implications and are offered on the terms of the data owners.

Much of the social activity of the "Today's World" (the latter understood as an academic discipline within Contemporary History) is based on the generation, collection, and processing of data about people (natural or legal), behaviors, elements, or devices. However, the types of data collected, the technologies used to collect it, and the economic outcomes derived from it vary widely around the world. This chapter situates this variety of data collection within the surveillance economy, a global economic system that uses surveillance using data and is based on the mass exploitation of personal information as an economic resource.

Economic exchanges in the surveillance economy occur through the sale or exchange of data. This data is often referred to as "digital waste" or "user-generated data" and is often understood by outsiders as a series of clicks, searches, geolocations, and "likes." However, this simplified view does not capture the complexity of the business models underlying this economy, which include multiple layers of analysis and manipulation of the collected data. As a result of this continuous generation and processing, profiles, models, and inferences are created about individuals, usually without their knowledge or consent (Xu et al., 2020). These profiles are sold to companies that, seeking to maximize their income, use them to offer personalized ads, payment plans or loans. The surveillance economy is described as a system composed of heterogeneous economic actors, diverse types of data, and a variety of technologies and economic strategies, all interested in the surveillance of individuals using data.

The term "surveillance economy" encompasses a wide range of surveillance practices, including many aspects that are not digital, automated, or capitalist. However, at the heart of the surveillance economy presented here is a specific history of the use of surveillance technologies for economic exchanges related to individuals' digital data. Today, much of everyday life is made up of the generation, collection, and processing of data about individuals, although there is extreme variation in what type of data is collected, what technologies are used for its collection, and what the economic results are. that are derived from them. This variation in data collection practices is situated in relation to the surveillance economy, a global economic system concerned with the surveillance of individuals through data.

The intersection of the "Data Decontextualization Paradox" with the surveillance economy also raises important questions about data quality and fairness in its interpretation. When analyzing the Paradox of Data Decontextualization, a reflection also arises on the role of meaning in data analysis and algorithmic decision making. Disconnecting data from its context of origin not only creates technical and operational problems, but also poses an ethical dilemma: to what extent can algorithmic decisions based on decontextualized data be truly representative or fair? In the surveillance economy, a lack of context can lead to a superficial view of human behaviors, reducing the complexity of individual experiences to numbers and patterns, which dehumanizes the decision-making process. In this way, algorithmic systems that operate on poor quality or decontextualized data can perpetuate structural prejudices, disproportionately affecting vulnerable communities. In doing so, an effort is made to demonstrate how surveillance economies renegotiate, "dataficate," and automate sociotechnical worlds, how this datafication provokes new anxieties and demands for better governance, algorithmic accountability, and auditing practices, and how these audits have their own sociotechnical implications and are offered on the terms of the data owners (González-Padilla et al., 2024).

The ethical dimension of the surveillance economy encompasses fundamental questions about individual autonomy. And in relation to law, also equity and its possible criminal implications in the digital age (Nabbosa and Kaar, 2020). Firstly, the massive use of personal data without fully informed, express, and conscious consent raises concerns regarding the right of individuals to exercise control over their information and to determine how it is used. The surveillance economy tends to operate under models of implicit, dubious, or cumbersome, and even coercive consent. In many cases, users are unaware of the scope and implications of their data collection. Furthermore, the potential for algorithmic systems to perpetuate structural inequalities raises questions about justice and non-discrimination, given that the use of biased or decontextualized data can consolidate and amplify social prejudices (Yarger et al., 2019). Furthermore, the opacity and lack of accountability mechanisms in algorithmic decision-making processes challenge the principles of transparency and fairness, as affected individuals mostly lack effective means to challenge or understand such decisions. Ultimately, the surveillance economy requires a strong ethical framework that ensures the protection of individual rights and promotes justice in a context where personal data has become a powerful and ubiquitous commodity.

In the field of criminal law, rigorous intervention in the analysis of coercive data collection behaviors is increasingly necessary, due to the growing exploitation of personal information without the informed consent of individuals. Under models of implicit or forced consent, the surveillance economy has generated practices that pressure users to accept terms that facilitate the massive collection of data, affecting their autonomy and fundamental rights. These practices can lead to significant violations of privacy and, in some cases, constitute abusive conduct that borders on extortion or manipulation of individual will. From criminal law, it is imperative to establish clear limits and sanction those behaviors that, under the appearance of contractual legality, compromise the freedom of decision and the protection of personal data, since the ultimate objective is to guarantee a fair and ethical balance in relationships. between individuals and data collecting entities (Birckan et al.,2018).

The functionality and operability of the overall surveillance economy hinge on a multi-stakeholder system of data agents, a heterogeneous assemblage of humanoid and non-humanoid actors that exercise agency over the production, exchange, and commodification of data. On the one hand, there are the so-called end-users or data subjects, both individual and collective entities, that continue to be surveilled and increasingly automated mentioned above. On the other hand, there are competitive data device assemblages, data service providers and diversity of data brokers offering end-users affordable solutions to offload decision-making tasks to automated systems. The mass adoption and career of the surveillance economy is predicated on this assemblage of actors that enable new forms and standards of interactivity and standardization, as well as a staggering array of new forms of data surveillance and monetization. (Koutsikouri et al.2024)

The proliferation of participatory devices capable of passively producing, processing, and transmitting vast amounts of user-generated data fuels a wide array of economies of good health, automobility, urbanity, sociality, and so forth, which implies a dramatic restructuring of the operations of economic in terms of market and monetary economies. Such devices take the form of ubiquitous sensors embedded in smartphones, smart wearables, smart appliances, and so on, which in turn are connected to robust systems of data server farms and distributed computational infrastructures. Here, data surveillance takes the technological form of software processes that process input data in accordance with pre-defined parameters and outputs. These software processes are designed to facilitate the packing of data, often by means of sampling, filtering, and aggregation, the creation of data metadata describing the data packages, the streaming of data packets to server farms, the storage and processing of data in controlled environments, and the active repacking of data by means of reprocessing, filtering, aggregation, and so on, and the subsequent provision of different data by data brokers to their clients. This multi-actor assemblage continues to be ongoing and increasingly debated by critics and proponents alike in regards to its desirability, effectiveness, trustworthiness, justice, and so on.

Importance of data quality in surveillance

Data quality, being fundamental to the proper functioning of AI systems, poses significant challenges in terms of governance within constitutional regimes. In the surveillance economy, the absence of constitutional safeguards regulating the use of algorithmic systems puts at risk the fundamental rights of individuals, such as privacy, equality and non-discrimination. Since data processed by AI systems can affect decisions that profoundly impact people's lives (for example, in areas such as access to credit, jobs, or even criminal justice), controlling data quality becomes in a matter not only technical, but also constitutional.

The constitutional regimes of many countries protect fundamental rights, but the speed at which AI systems and the surveillance economy evolve has outpaced the ability of existing legal frameworks to adapt to new challenges. This creates a regulatory gap where data quality failures, whether deterministic or non-deterministic, can undermine principles such as the presumption of innocence, due process, or protection against discrimination. In this context, the lack of statistical representativeness or relevance in the data used by AI could lead to biased decisions that disproportionately affect certain groups, violating the principles of equity and justice enshrined in many constitutional texts.

To address these issues, constitutional regimes must evolve to integrate specific safeguards that regulate data quality in AI systems and, more broadly, in the surveillance economy. This could include regulations requiring data quality audits, transparency in information collection and processing processes, and legal liability for actors who use low-quality or decontextualized data. Such measures would not only protect individuals from potentially unfair automated decisions but would also strengthen public confidence in the use of AI and ensure that constitutional principles of justice and protection of fundamental rights are upheld in the digital age. One way to integrate the problem of data quality into the scientific and academic debate on constitutional law is through the exploration of its direct impact on the protection of fundamental rights and possible emerging human rights in the digital age.

The massive use of data in artificial intelligence systems and the surveillance economy poses significant risks to rights such as privacy, non-discrimination, and access to truthful and complete information, which are at the core of human rights. In this sense, the constitutional debate could be expanded to consider data quality as a fundamental prerequisite to protect these rights, emphasizing that decisions made with inaccurate, biased, or decontextualized data can lead to violations of human and fundamental rights. Legal academia and constitutional law could develop a framework that conceptualizes the right to "personal data integrity," requiring that any information processing meets rigorous quality standards to ensure the protection of individuals. This approach would allow data quality to be recognized not only as a technical issue, but as a key dimension to safeguard fundamental rights and prevent abuses in an increasingly digitalized and automated context.

Challenges of data quality in the surveillance economy

Volume, velocity, and scale of data. Generative Artificial Intelligence data.

One of the main assumptions of the surveillance economy lies in the proposition that we have entered a digital era in which economies as complex as the surveillance economy depend on personal data for their operation. This poses a considerable challenge in terms of the volume, speed and scale of data collected, processed and monetized. Limiting the debate on general surveillance to electronic surveillance itself oversimplifies the problem and encourages a reductionist approach that views these issues solely as issues of security and freedom in the digital realm. However, critical reflections on the transformations driven by the surveillance industry and Big Data demonstrate that the scope of this phenomenon is much broader and more complex, encompassing ethical, legal and social dimensions that go far beyond electronic surveillance. (Aho & Duffield, 2020; Zuboff, 2023). With this research we categorically affirm that we are facing a much deeper and more urgent challenge, which implies a reconceptualization of the limits and implications of the surveillance economy society of Current World.

Big Data, characterized by the exponential growth of large data sets, has been accompanied by significant advances in analysis models, driven largely by the increase in computational processing power. It must be said that we are still waiting for the arrival of quantum computing and that we know little about its interaction with generative artificial intelligence. An analysis carried out by Vantune demonstrated that the Greek crisis in the Eurozone was anticipated two years earlier by studying patterns in the succession of a keyword identified from the massive analysis of financial news processed by RavenPack Analytics. This example illustrates how Big Data and artificial intelligence can have a powerful predictive capacity (Saura et al., 2023), although at a considerable cost that limits their application to sectors with high economic resources. The main drawback of applying technologies of this magnitude in areas such as public policy, public health problems and market regulation is that governments, health agencies or regulatory entities often lack the financial capacity to access the necessary private services. This poses a new barrier to access to technologies that could potentially generate great social benefits if they were more accessible.

However, there are numerous sources of institutional and non-institutional data produced by public authorities and available on the Internet, which can be processed at low cost. This democratization of data access can contribute to social development using open government data, a movement that advocates transparency, citizen participation and social innovation. Open government data offers a valuable alternative to commercial Big Data, allowing academic institutions, non-governmental organizations, and other entities to access data sets that can be analyzed without the high costs associated with private providers. This approach may be especially relevant in contexts where equitable access to information and responsible use of data are considered fundamental rights within the framework of constitutional regimes.

The inclusion of generative artificial intelligence in this ecosystem adds an additional dimension of complexity. They analyze pre-existing data and generate new content, exponentially multiplying the volume of digital information. For this reason, new representations, simulations, and predictions appear that can directly influence decision making. The ability to generate text, images and simulations allows profiles and inferences about individuals to be even more sophisticated and detailed, expanding the scope of the surveillance economy and its ethical implications. The possibility of creating realistic content with generative AI also raises questions about the veracity and authenticity of data, as well as the potential manipulation of information, which can lead to tangible harm to individuals. This calls for an urgent review of data quality and authenticity regulations, given that generative AI systems could amplify the biases and errors present in Big Data, compromising both the accuracy of inferences and the fairness of automated decisions.

The surveillance economy, relying on Big Data and generative AI, also raises a set of ethical and legal challenges in relation to fundamental rights, such as the right to privacy, equity, and justice. As the use of big data analysis technologies expands in areas such as health, mobility, or the economy, it is crucial that constitutional regimes and international law consider these developments when defining safeguards to protect human rights in the digital age. This not only implies adopting transparency measures in data collection and processing, but also regulating the quality of the data and guaranteeing that its analysis and use are aligned with the principles of equity and public responsibility.

Thus, the interaction between open data, commercial Big Data and generative AI must be the subject of a deeper debate within constitutional law, exploring how to balance technological innovation with the protection of individual rights. The surveillance economy not only transforms the economic structure, but also the ethical and legal principles that govern our societies, which requires a regulatory and academic response that is up to these complex contemporary challenges. With this research we highlight the need for an interdisciplinary scientific debate. The debate on data quality itself will be followed in the immediate future by that of the data generated by generative artificial intelligence (Canali, 2020).

Variety and veracity of data

Data variety refers to the different forms that data can take: structured, semi-structured and unstructured. Transactional records from banks, satellite images from foresters, and WhatsApp messages from smallholder farmers can provide many valuable insights into an economy. Bank transaction data is typically structured, while income from agriculture and commerce may be somewhat less structured (Bai et al., 2018). National statistical offices, central banks, commercial banks, tax authorities and credit agencies receive data in a structured format. More recently, satellite imagery and information technology data from mobile phone and internet users have enabled more complete and reliable national accounts. The ability to integrate structured, semi-structured and unstructured data facilitates richer and more dynamic analysis, allowing policymakers and businesses to make informed decisions in real time. This variety of data allows us to respond in an agile manner to changes in the market, agricultural conditions and consumer needs, especially in a digital governance context where precision and speed are required.

The veracity of the data refers to the veracity or credibility of the data. Unreliable data can lead to distorted income measures. Consumers move economic transactions from the formal to the informal sector. Farmers report incorrect income to the tax authority, companies underreport labor, and oligopolistic firms collude on prices. Satellite records can present problems with cloud cover, quality of ground readings, and less reliable classification systems (Lobell et al., 2021). Phone records can contain erroneous or incomplete data, especially in the case of prepaid cell phones, and people can be traced through loans of other people's phones. The lack of veracity in data affects economic measurements and raises problems of social justice and equity. When the income of informal sectors, such as small farmers, is underestimated, public policies tend not to benefit them adequately, thus reinforcing pre-existing inequalities. In this context, a credible data system is essential for political and economic decisions to fairly distribute the necessary resources and supports.

Trust between the government, producers, consumers and satellite service providers is necessary for the successful implementation of a SCBD system (System of Comprehensive Business Data). Legal frameworks such as the General Data Protection Regulation (GDPR) in the European Union (Saura et al., 2021) promote data integrity and veracity by imposing strict rules on how data is collected, stored and shared. Likewise, business incentives to improve data quality, such as reducing regulatory risks and improving consumer trust, are essential in sectors where the accuracy of information is essential for the competitiveness and sustainability of companies. The variety and veracity of data also poses ethical challenges in digital governance, as automated decisions based on low-quality data can lead to exclusions or unfair decisions. Therefore, the creation of data quality monitoring systems that respect individual rights and social equity is vital for responsible and transparent digital governance.

Data Privacy and Security Concerns

Our treatment of risks, including privacy and security, is intended as just a partial view to begin identifying and problematizing central challenges in the different dimensions of digital governance. The objective is to identify areas where better institutional mechanisms and laws can offset risks that are judged to be significant, particularly where self-regulatory mechanisms have not been regulating effectively. Our aim is not to offer a normative program but to contribute to informed policy debates intended to enhance rather than diminish the activities that are necessary for digital governance to occur.

There is a basic trade-off that requires an individual's level of comfort with governance: with more data collection and analysis by other actors in society, whether state or business, there is more potential knowledge and better surveillance and management of risk at the potential cost of personal information relating to identity, behavior, and social network being compromised. The issue is not whether people should have individually or collectively enforceable rights; the question is instead, rights to what level of privacy and security and under what circumstances (Saura et al., 2023a). It is important to respect how people use privacy to assimilate themselves with the different groups to which they belong, how they manage stigma, their face work in society. Innumerable digital governance relations are not just about probability, risk, and consequences. They are instead expressions of social order, identities, political relationships, the demonstration of competence or failure, and the definition of what is public and supposed to be private (Quach et al.2022).

Digital governance in the surveillance economy

Amid political awareness of data-driven phenomena, an agile response poses challenges to government actors who grapple with weighing myriad options, as well as gauging their scope and social implications. Initial responses differ as some states expedite attempts to furnish means to monitor and control digital platforms, while others explore factors most conducive to civic, commercial, and political exploitation of data reserves. Such explorative states are either unlikely to be able to respond quickly enough or need to hope such sums remain unexploited. Given the techno-design choices being contested and the significant political stakes involved, the development of cross-national common ground is equally wanting. With states caught between either unventured domains outgunned by moves of other actors or ill-advised responses to innovation, agency remains problematic. In the absence of governance frameworks adequate to the challenge posed by the surveillance economy, societal forces perceive the market and recourse to existing governance infrastructures as the only options (Breaugh et al.2023). The unprecedented accumulation of data through ever-intensifying digitalization of every aspect of life exacerbates disparity in agency. As unprecedented and vast fortunes are amassed, effects on the political landscape remain observable through challenges of mounting inequality. Digital governance of social media platforms by means of contestation of forceful code infrastructure developments constitutes various new political battlegrounds across western democracies. Attempts to fully disentangle data-driven conduct of domains of socio-political life, in turn, intensify a drive for the hegemony of AI infrastructure in response to perceived techno-political threats. Under conditions of historical contingency, the problematic consciousness addressed posits an avenue for grasping premises for the horizon of collective design choices free of existing power constraints.

From a political-economic perspective, regulations are less restrictive sets of sequential moves by states or supragovernmental organizations to regain or maintain control of economic activities. However, this structuration and transmission of governance norms often become taken for granted, as is apparent in the context of the EU's privacy laws. At times, regulatory guidelines are reactivated into efforts at governance design under the pressure of state actors or by codes themselves, as was the case in the introduction of the federal Computer Fraud and Abuse Act in the US or attempts by the Netherlands to urge a 'cyber peace regime' upon the UN. Digital governance can be defined as a move in the direction of expanded competitive advantage through the exploitation of digital technologies via the expectation of collective or individual outcomes in terms of control policy or new designs.

The term “proxy” refers to mediation, thus signifying a curious move back to the general. In a mediation scenario, objects (faster-than-McLuhan feats) are set in motion upon subjects (Warren, 2002). Data proxies do not implicate innocence on the part of what is rendered external, i.e., social ties, interaction forms, and subjectivities. Speculation upon reintegrating consciousness is equally bereft of innocence, carrying with it a sense of guilt in withstanding the imperative to passage through spectacle. The remainder of the narrative chronologizes impossible attempts to assume control of or detach oneself from technological extensions and toxic networks of circulation. Such attempts are doomed spin.

Technological solutions for data quality

Concern about data quality is not new. There is substantial academic provision of research into concepts, problems, and solutions for data quality. The traditional focus has been on information technology (IT) data structures, data standards, and business processes to improve data quality. Many of these technological solutions, together with new data technologies such as data mining, machine learning, and artificial intelligence, are becoming more widespread as data is being transformed into a raw material business in the surveillance economy.

Using ontologies, this earlier research has also pointed towards a taxonomy of remedies. Monitoring, Verification, and Compliance actions are automated descriptions of Venice's Canal Water Quality Monitoring Reaction system for hiring this mitigation actions set (Bettinetti et al.,1996). Attention is paid to how new data technologies within each remedy class influence its implementation with new conditions and more or less awareness. The widening leak of quality issues is analyzed in relation to a snowball trajectory of integrity issues with increasing scale, speed, persistence, and interpretation. It becomes apparent how mirroring narratives built on geolocation tracking feeds can lead to disinformation cascades and mass manipulation.

Lack of quality of data in size, fidelity, and abstraction seriously undermines the ability of self-learning control, optimization, and prediction systems to enhance jobs and generate safe environments. Attention on new conundrums in shaping an increasingly autonomous market in surveillance data in the midst of moving towards a voluntary label for AI systems with risk in content. Both fronts overlap when non-safety justifications of deep learning systems once trained or self-learning solutions are driven by disputable quality data. Continuous learning systems fail to meet safety requirements with non-stationary data streams, quickly leading to data deluge and swamping consequences.

Automated quality finding, monitoring, and scoring is underdeveloped academically, slowing progress in making big data comparable in low-level statistics or signal processing treatment. The recent Smart Water Networks Clean Act activity in the public domain requests a fix to measure ingress of flat loading on the water quality index of raw data feeds. A collective design effort of architectures, earning rules, and signal processing kernels improved on that index's MAPE from above 20% to below 5% by 2025. Processing precedence on the low pass of minimum needed sample size to build a quality index for AGDD curves is needed, though, as those indices apply post-processing. Modeling length of pipe distance in residence and distribution stations in the EST library, with ex-ante MAPE in width of 15%, inspired bounded controls on monitoring nodes with AI success quantiles as baselines. (Luo et al.2022)

Likewise, data quality in the digital economy is a multi-faceted problem. Many different kinds of data sets are involved, users vary widely in their identity, skills, and intention, and some parties wish to increase the use of data while others search to limit it. Multiple actors, including data brokers, carry data from one party to another, with limited accountability for their quality. Academic thinking on quality of data has mostly focused on the description of criteria, without a good understanding of what drives bad quality. It is suggested to start with an analysis of failures, followed by initiatives focused on known causes of bad quality.

Data quality in the digital economy is a concern for all involved parties, either in the role of data provider, merchant, or user. Different actors are involved in this data economy on different levels, for example, internet giants like Apple, Google, Amazon, and Meta at the brokerage level, adding data, blending, cleaning, measuring, and selling it to multiple others. Many actors, especially the smallest, are mainly data consumers, for purposes like marketing, recruitment, and credit scoring. Financial and reputational risk of these data users is huge, with multiple misuses and scandals. Data providers are often unaware of the data economy. (Fernandez et al.2020). Finally, public or private, governmentally or independently controlled, data protection authorities should monitor all market actors on methods for influencing quality, including considerations of privacy, scale, and ethics. Considering the broad scope of the problem, such authorities could be advised to start with dedicated domains, for example, focusing first on specific social sectors like the housing market and fraud detection or specific types and sources of data. Without proactively tackling known causes of bad quality, no success is expected.

Discussion

The analysis of data quality within the framework of the surveillance economy underscores the pivotal role digital governance must assume in shaping its structure. Simultaneously, it reveals a range of ethical challenges inherent to this paradigm. The Paradox of Data Decontextualization is central to these challenges, which highlights the tension between the extensive volume of data collected and the corresponding loss of contextual meaning. As a result, the representativeness and utility of such data are significantly undermined. This paradox constitutes a complex dilemma that extends beyond technical considerations, encompassing social, ethical, and legal dimensions. Effectively addressing these challenges necessitates targeted, context-specific approaches tailored to the nuances of each case and discipline to mitigate their adverse consequences.

A closely related concern centers on how decontextualized and low-quality data can distort decision-making processes, particularly in systems driven by artificial intelligence and algorithmic governance. This issue is especially critical in the context of public decision-making and digital public governance. Evidence from areas such as judicial decision-making demonstrates that reliance on biased or incomplete data perpetuates systemic inequalities and risks eroding public trust in these systems. This concern reflects broader apprehensions regarding the absence of robust accountability and oversight mechanisms within the surveillance economy, where data, stripped of their original context, are transformed into abstract instruments that often exacerbate social inequities rather than resolve them. The resulting dehumanization of decision-making processes through datification poses a profound threat to the ethical integrity of governance systems.

The academic discussion also underscores the ways in which the surveillance economy generates disconnections between individuals and their data, raising critical concerns about autonomy and informed consent. Practices involving implicit or coercive consent often leave individuals unaware of the broader implications of their digital footprints, thereby intensifying the existing power asymmetry between data producers and the entities that monetize their information. Addressing this imbalance requires the development of robust regulatory frameworks that prioritize transparency, accountability, and the ethical use of data. Such frameworks must go beyond ensuring the technical quality of data, incorporating measures that align data collection and usage with principles of fairness and justice. Additionally, they must establish stringent traceability protocols to guarantee that data usage does not result in future repercussions disconnected from their original context.

Future trends and implications

The surveillance economy has crucial implications for the future of social life and democratic governance. This section explores four ways in which the social order could transform in the coming years. First, as trust and data governance become central elements in the economic system, the very notion of the "surveillance economy" will increasingly be seen as a burden on both states and citizens, driving demands to reorganize the data economy in favor of a more transparent model controlled by citizens. Second, the emergence of an invisible economy, which escapes traditional organizational models based on data evidence, will generate serious challenges for social responsibility. This parallel economy makes data accountability and traceability difficult, weakening democratic control over how this data is used in social impact decisions. Third, as the social order becomes increasingly algorithmic and less visible, society's collective abilities to consciously understand how its social metadata is used will be reduced, creating "dark data capitalism". This represents a direct risk to transparency and social empowerment, since crucial decisions could be made opaquely, outside the reach and knowledge of individuals and communities. Finally, the data economy, being capitalist, presents vulnerabilities that could be exploited to restore and further entrench power asymmetries and social inequality, putting the very foundations of society at risk.

Trust and data governance will take on new relevance as they become pillars of the economic system. The organization of data and its custody will begin to be seen as positive aspects of democratic life, while mass surveillance will be perceived as a burden to be avoided. This will drive the development of economic policies and political decisions that encourage the responsible management of data assets, such as trusts or cooperatives. These alternative approaches to data management are likely to prioritize values of equity, inclusion and sustainability, in contrast to the commercial exploitation of personal data. Directly involving citizens in the formulation of data governance policies will be a central objective, and representative administration schemes will emerge to complement collective ownership systems.

The new social order will become less visible, predictable and controllable. Much of the economy will not be understood through dominant models of organizing based on data evidence or through access to public data. Those who fail to adapt to a data-driven growth model will be marginalized or even abandoned. For many, their digital footprints will remain invisible, weakening social responsibility. As the social order becomes algorithmic and less visible, society's collective abilities to understand how its social metadata is used will diminish. With interests at stake that go beyond mere monetary gain, new spheres of data evidence will be persistently sought and deployed, shaping a "dark data capitalism": a managerial social order that renders many of the political and ethical ideals of the Enlightenment, such as individualism, freedom and equality (Sadowski, 2020). This model of data capitalism could lead to a state of permanent surveillance, in which individuals not only lose their privacy, but also their autonomy in decision-making.

The "surveillance economy" can be understood as an ideal construction of a manageable and well-understood social order, useful in current struggles against the most flagrant abuses of social data. However, the data economy has been shaping the social order for more than three decades and is capitalist in nature. As a result, underlying power asymmetries and social inequality will become even more entrenched, and the ability to influence the basic terms of social life will be restricted to a fortunate few. In this context, individual and collective rights are likely to become subordinated to commercial interests, while social and civic technologies that could protect the principles, rights or norms of conduct necessary for a democratic and sustainable social order will be hindered or even intentionally suppressed.

Moreover, the integration of generative artificial intelligence into the surveillance economy amplifies these challenges by exponentially increasing the volume of data and introducing new layers of complexity. While generative AI has the potential to enhance predictive capabilities and create sophisticated simulations, it also raises critical questions regarding authenticity, bias, and the ethical implications of its outputs. These technologies necessitate a reevaluation of existing data governance practices to address the risks associated with misinformation and manipulation, which could further erode public trust in digital systems and provoke social resistance. In this context, these challenges must also be situated within a broader historical and sociopolitical framework, drawing attention to how data quality has emerged as a central issue in the governance of contemporary digital economies. A historical analysis of surveillance practices reveals a trajectory marked by increasing abstraction and commodification of data, culminating in the current landscape of surveillance capitalism. This evolution underscores the urgent need for a paradigm shift that redefines data governance as a fundamental component of digital social governance, extending beyond a purely technical issue.

In order to address this debate must engage diverse stakeholders from multiple fields of knowledge, fostering an open and interdisciplinary discourse. Such an approach is essential to addressing the multifaceted nature of these challenges and ensuring the ethical and equitable governance of digital ecosystems. To approach the Paradox of Data Decontextualization requires a multidisciplinary approach that integrates perspectives from law, economics, contemporary world history, ethics, technology, social sciences, and computer science. Legal frameworks must evolve to recognize data quality as an intrinsic human rights issue, treating digital footprints as an inalienable extension of personal identity. Similarly, constitutional law must ensure that data-driven decision-making respects principles of equity and non-discrimination. Furthermore, criminal law should begin to examine these issues, as the irresponsible use of personal digital footprints could potentially constitute criminal offenses.

At the same time, technological innovations must focus on improving data quality through the implementation of rigorous monitoring and auditing systems capable of mitigating biases and inaccuracies. This approach would not only strengthen the ethical integrity of data-driven systems but also foster public trust in the governance of digital ecosystems.

CONCLUSIONS

In this systematic investigation into the growing prominence of data platforms as intermediaries between personal data collection channels and their use in the economy, the term "surveillance economy" refers to an economy designed to collect and monetize personal data. as a new fundamental commodity. This is qualitatively distinguished from the information economy, which focuses on the use of shared data to innovate business practices, products and services. In contrast, the surveillance economy radically transforms the operational mechanisms of the information economy by commodifying personal data and prioritizing its monetization through programmatic micro-segmentation in an intentionally opaque information space, defined by the surveillance paradigm. The design features of these data platforms are largely informed by intellectual property laws, digital sovereignty, and complementary regulatory interventions at a systemic level. Guided by a modus operandi that acts outside of social control, activities such as the automated trading of personal data flows trigger what is called "epistemic corruption." This epistemic corruption alters the knowledge base on which decisional power is distributed in social systems, which requires urgent and radical regulatory responses.

The socio-technical assembly of data platforms and their activities is analyzed through the case of Meta, considered the largest and most complex data platform in the world. It is thus observed how the original purpose of social networks, focused on facilitating social connectivity, has been completely transformed to turn them into intermediaries whose main purpose is to collect and commercialize the greatest possible amount of personal data. The social consequences of this surveillance economy include the systematic weakening of autonomy at both the social and neural levels, epochal transitions in global political economies, and the "Hobbesian trap" of social systems incentivized to act preemptively in a war of information and geopolitical surveillance, all in a context that is outside social and democratic control.

The conclusions identify the specific factors and challenges of the global advertising surveillance economy, which social actors, organizations and institutions must address. This includes the need for responses to consider epistemic power, disruptions caused by the Internet of Things (IoT), other areas of surveillance (such as politics and security) and coordinated regulatory action at a transnational level. Furthermore, we have detected that it is becoming imperative for criminal law to address the most coercive aspects of the surveillance economy, establishing sanctions for abuses in the collection and use of personal data. Criminalizing invasive practices or practices without explicit consent would help establish clear limits, thus protecting fundamental rights such as privacy, autonomy and individual freedom. These criminal mechanisms would allow additional protection against possible rights violations that cannot be mitigated by civil law or administrative regulation alone.

Work must be done in the immediate future on the need for a comprehensive, transversal and even interdisciplinary regulatory framework of several elements: a holistic understanding of the surveillance economy, jointly managed observational data platforms, and the separation of supply and demand dynamics. surveillance economy data. This framework is presented as an existentially crucial change, aimed at societies evolving organically towards a higher evolutionary order, based on knowledge and understanding, instead of the indiscriminate exploitation of personal data.

Research must be directed towards a comprehensive, transversal and even interdisciplinary regulatory framework of several elements: a holistic understanding of the surveillance economy, jointly managed observational data platforms, and the separation of the data supply and demand dynamics of the surveillance economy. surveillance. This framework is presented as an existentially crucial change, aimed at societies evolving organically towards a higher evolutionary order, based on knowledge and understanding, instead of the indiscriminate exploitation of personal data.

REFERENCES

Aho, B., & Duffield, R. (2020). Beyond surveillance capitalism: Privacy, regulation and big data in Europe and China. *Economy and Society*, 49(2), 187–212. DOI: 10.1080/03085147.2019.1690275

Bai, C., Shi, B., Liu, F., & Sarkis, J. (2018). Banking credit worthiness: Evaluating the complex relationships. In C. Bai, B. Shi, F. Liu, & J. Sarkis [). Elsevier BV.]. *Omega*, 83, 26–38. DOI: 10.1016/j.omega.2018.02.001

Bettinetti, A., Pypaert, P., & Sweerts, J. P. R. A. (1996). Application of an Integrated Management Approach to the Restoration Project of the Lagoon of Venice. In A. Bettinetti, P. Pypaert, & J. P. R. A. Sweerts [). Elsevier BV.]. *Journal of Environmental Management*, 46(3), 207–227. DOI: 10.1006/jema.1996.0017

Birckan, G., Dutra, M. L., de Macedo, D., & Viera, Á. F. G. (2018). Effects of data protection laws on data brokerage businesses. In G. Birckan, M. L. Dutra, D. de Macedo, & Á. F. G. Viera, ICST Transactions on Scalable Information Systems (p. 165673). European Alliance for Innovation.

Breaugh, J., Rackwitz, M., & Hammerschmid, G. (2023). Leadership and institutional design in collaborative government digitalisation: Evidence from Belgium, Denmark, Estonia, Germany, and the UK. *Government Information Quarterly*, 40(2), 101788. DOI: 10.1016/j.giq.2022.101788

Butler, T., & Brooks, R. (2023). On the wicked problem of quantifying and managing non-financial risks and the role of digital technology in providing solutions. *Journal of Risk Management in Financial Institutions*, 17(1), 53–70. DOI: 10.69554/TNPL3644

Canali, S. (2020). Towards a Contextual Approach to Data Quality. In S. Canali [). Multidisciplinary Digital Publishing Institute.]. *Data*, 5(4), 90. DOI: 10.3390/data5040090

Cuéllar, M. F. & Huq, A. Z. (2020). Economies of surveillance.

Fernandez, R. C., Subramaniam, P., & Franklin, M. J. (2020). Data market platforms: Trading data assets to solve data problems. arXiv preprint arXiv:2002.01047.

González-Padilla, P., Navalpotro, F. D., & Saura, J. R. (2024). Managing entrepreneurs' behavior personalities in digital environments: A review. *The International Entrepreneurship and Management Journal*, 20(1), 89–113. DOI: 10.1007/s11365-022-00823-4

Grindrod, P. (2016). Beyond privacy and exposure: Ethical issues within citizen-facing analytics. In P. Grindrod [). Royal Society.]. *Philosophical Transactions. Series A, Mathematical, Physical, and Engineering Sciences*, 374(2083), 20160132. DOI: 10.1098/rsta.2016.0132 PMID: 28336804

Koutsikouri, D., Hylving, L., Raftopoulos, M., Ngwenyama, O., Rowe, F., & Tona, O. (2024). Human Flourishing in the Digital Age: What Responsibilities does/should Researcher (s) Have? Perspectives from the AIS Community. *Communications of the Association for Information Systems*, 55(1), 1.

Lobell, D. B., Tommaso, S. D., Burke, M., & Kilic, T. (2021). Twice Is Nice: The Benefits of Two Ground Measures for Evaluating the Accuracy of Satellite-Based Sustainability Estimates. In D. B.

Luo, H., Lin, L., Chen, K., Antwi-Afari, M. F., & Chen, L. (2022). Digital technology for quality management in construction: A review and future research directions. *Developments in the Built Environment*, 12, 100087. DOI: 10.1016/j.dibe.2022.100087

Lyulyov, O., Pimonenko, T., Saura, J. R., & Barbosa, B. (2024). How do e-governance and e-business drive sustainable development goals? *Technological Forecasting and Social Change*, 199, 123082. DOI: 10.1016/j.techfore.2023.123082

Manning, P. (2013). Big Data in History. In Manning, P. (Ed.), *Palgrave Macmillan UK eBooks*. Palgrave Macmillan. DOI: 10.1057/9781137378972

Moore, E. M., Dau, L. A., & Mingo, S. (2021). The effects of trade integration on formal and informal entrepreneurship: The moderating role of economic development. *Journal of International Business Studies*, 52(4), 746–772. DOI: 10.1057/s41267-020-00386-y

Nabbosa, V. L., & Kaar, C. (2020). *Societal and Ethical Issues of Digitalization*. DOI: 10.1145/3437075.3437093

Osoba, O., & Welser, W. (2017). An Intelligence in Our Image: The Risks of Bias and Errors in Artificial Intelligence. In *O. Osoba & W. Welser*. RAND Corporation. DOI: 10.7249/RR1744

Ptaszek, G. (2020). *From algorithmic surveillance to algorithmic awareness: Media education in the context of new media economics and invisible technologies*. Media.

Purwanto, A., Zuiderwijk, A., & Janssen, M. (2020, June). Citizens' trust in open government data: a quantitative study about the effects of data quality, system quality and service quality. In The 21st annual international conference on digital government research (pp. 310-318).

Quach, S., Thaichon, P., Martin, K. D., Weaven, S., & Palmatier, R. W. (2022). Digital technologies: Tensions in privacy and data. *Journal of the Academy of Marketing Science*, 50(6), 1299–1323. DOI: 10.1007/s11747-022-00845-y PMID: 35281634

Sadowski, J. (2020). Too smart: How digital capitalism is extracting data, controlling our lives, and taking over the world.

Saunders, J. (2023). Surveillance Graphs: Vulgarity and Cloud Orthodoxy in Linked Data Infrastructures.

Saura, J. R. (2024). Algorithms in Digital Marketing: Does Smart Personalization Promote a Privacy Paradox? *FIIB Business Review*, 13(5), 499–502. DOI: 10.1177/23197145241276898

Saura, J. R., & Debasa, F. (Eds.). (2022). *Handbook of research on artificial intelligence in government practices and processes*. IGI Global., DOI: 10.4018/978-1-7998-9609-8

Saura, J. R., Palacios-Marqués, D., & Ribeiro-Soriano, D. (2023a). Privacy concerns in social media UGC communities: Understanding user behavior sentiments in complex networks. *Information Systems and e-Business Management*, •••, 1–21. DOI: 10.1007/s10257-023-00631-5

Saura, J. R., Ribeiro-Navarrete, S., Palacios-Marqués, D., & Mardani, A. (2023). Impact of extreme weather in production economics: Extracting evidence from user-generated content. *International Journal of Production Economics*, 260, 108861. DOI: 10.1016/j.ijpe.2023.108861

Saura, J. R., Ribeiro-Soriano, D., & Palacios-Marqués, D. (2021). Setting B2B digital marketing in artificial intelligence-based CRMs: A review and directions for future research. *Industrial Marketing Management*, 98(October), 161–178. DOI: 10.1016/j.indmarman.2021.08.006

Saura, J. R., Ribeiro-Soriano, D., & Palacios-Marqués, D. (2022). Assessing behavioral data science privacy issues in government artificial intelligence deployment. *Government Information Quarterly*, 39(4), 101679. DOI: 10.1016/j.giq.2022.101679

Saura, J. R., Škare, V., & Dosen, D. O. (2024). Is AI-based digital marketing ethical? Assessing a new data privacy paradox. *Journal of Innovation & Knowledge*, 9(4), 100597. DOI: 10.1016/j.jik.2024.100597

Shandler, R. (2019). The age of surveillance capitalism: The fight for a human future at the new frontier of power. In R. Shandler [). Taylor & Francis.]. *Journal of Cyber Policy*, 4(2), 303–304. DOI: 10.1080/23738871.2019.1637914

Velsberg, O., Westergren, U. H., & Jonsson, K. (2020). Exploring smartness in public sector innovation-creating smart public services with the Internet of Things. *European Journal of Information Systems*, 29(4), 350–368. DOI: 10.1080/0960085X.2020.1761272

Warren, P. L. (2002). A Systems Approach to Mediation: How to Diagram Family and Commercial Disputes. In P. L. Warren, SSRN Electronic Journal. RELX Group (Netherlands). DOI: 10.2139/ssrn.305150

West, S. M. (2017). Data Capitalism: Redefining the Logics of Surveillance and Privacy. In S. M. West []. SAGE Publishing.]. *Business & Society*, 58(1), 20–41. DOI: 10.1177/0007650317718185

Wilson, C., & Mergel, I. (2022). Overcoming barriers to digital government: Mapping the strategies of digital champions. *Government Information Quarterly*, 39(2), 101681. DOI: 10.1016/j.giq.2022.101681

Xu, S., Fu, X., Cao, J., Liu, B., & Wang, Z. (2020). Survey on user location prediction based on geo-social networking data. *World Wide Web (Bussum)*, 23(3), 1621–1664. DOI: 10.1007/s11280-019-00777-8

Yarger, L., Payton, F. C., & Neupane, B. (2019). Algorithmic equity in the hiring of underrepresented IT job candidates. In L. Yarger, F. C. Payton, & B. Neupane []. Emerald Publishing.]. *Online Information Review*, 44(2), 383–395. DOI: 10.1108/OIR-10-2018-0334

Zuboff, S. (2023). The age of surveillance capitalism. Social theory re-wired.

Chapter 3
Re-Assessing Jurisprudential Foundation of Intellectual Property Laws in the Age of Artificial Intelligence

Bhupinder Singh
https://orcid.org/0009-0006-4779-2553
Sharda University, India

Christian Kaunert
https://orcid.org/0000-0002-4493-2235
Dublin City University, Ireland

Kamalesh Ravesangar
https://orcid.org/0009-0004-2154-184X
Tunku Abdul Rahman University of Management and Technology, Malaysia

Hind Hammouch
https://orcid.org/0000-0002-5897-1649
University Sidi Mohamed Ben Abdellah, Fez, Morocco

Anjali Raghav
https://orcid.org/0009-0004-0248-7956
Sharda University, India

DOI: 10.4018/979-8-3693-6945-6.ch003

ABSTRACT

Intellectual property laws, historically conceived along the lines of human innovation and creativity that provide individual or entity have done it granting them rights for their invention. The ascendance of IP from jurisprudential foundations to more abstract principles threatens the traditional underpinnings of many legal doctrines; so too will extend certain AI systems. Rise of AI which leading everything from content to designs and even inventions being spat out by machines raises questions about who gets credit for starting it all. Existing IP systems are unclear in defining and resolving questions such as those relating to the AI-generated works scenario where human authorship is not present a fundamental concept within jurisdictions safeguarding only creative work that has been developed by humans. This chapter focuses on the matter that AI evolves quickly, with greater ability to compromise existing IP rights by creating and adapting protected works more rapidly than ever before.

1. INTRODUCTION AND BACKGROUND

Artificial Intelligence (AI) is increasingly changing the lives from developing new applications to fixing common issues like language identification (Nhemi, 2023). Historically, IP laws have been based on the idea that human creativity and innovation warrant protection by providing incentives to create through proprietary interests for creators. The rise of AI as an unattended creator exposes core assumptions in these pillars, especially the need for human authorship over content, design and inventions, indeed, any creative work (van den Brink et al., 2023). When AI systems start to play a more central role in, and even wholly generate, what was previously the preserve of human creators then it is time we rethink the jurisprudential foundations of IP laws (van Bijsterveld & ten Napel, 2024). This chapter describes increasing challenges attributable to AI on conventional IP architecture (Abbott & Rothman, 2023). At the center of one is debate centered around both authorship and ownership: Who owns a work that was created by AI. What about the authorship of AI should it go to the developer, user or AI system? Questions which fundamentally call into question the assumption of all IP law that at some stage there are humans involved interacting with a system. Secondly, the ability of AI to generate new works based on past creations calls into question established notions of originality and novelty; two foundational principles in copyright and patent law (Abdikhakimov, 2023).

This integration of AI into the creative process also raises larger ethical and legal considerations. But they involve all sorts of normative questions the law ought to answer like, where it should strike a balance between protecting AI-created works and ensuring access for others privileges innovative activity? In addition, the relatively recent move towards grappling with these kinds of issues is a good reminder that it may not take long for such complex questions to require an international level response (since some jurisdictions will likely be more hesitant than others are) (Santoni de Sio et al., 2024). This chapter critically evaluates the jurisprudential basis of intellectual property laws post-the age of AI and reforms that may be concocted to counter these new challenges perhaps, without going too far out on a limb above the sanctimonious notions evolving around IP rights (Abbott et al., 2024).

Figure 1. shows the Dimensions of Introduction Section (Source- Original)

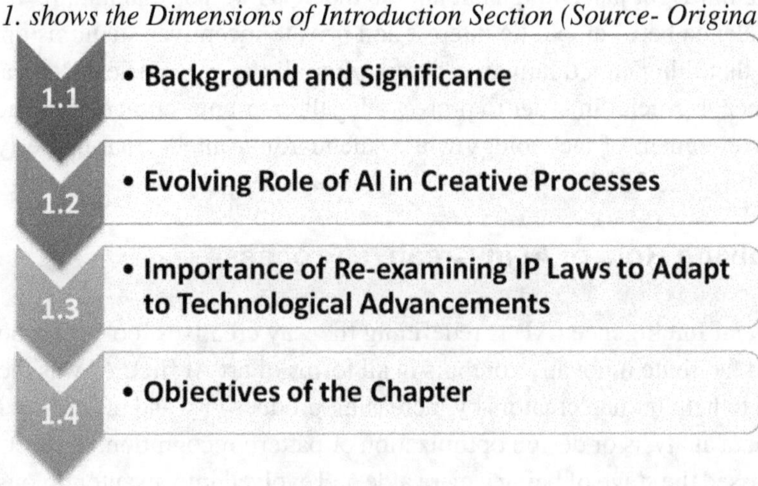

1.1 Background and Significance

The era of Artificial Intelligence (AI) integration into creative and innovative processes brings about a transformation unlike any other, shaking the very foundations on which jurisprudential constructs were laid by developed doctrines at work in intellectual property (IP), laws. IP laws have been developed historically to protect human creativity by means of awarding a monopoly in the form of exclusive rights for innnovators and creators, as incentive for originality amd endeavor. With AI being able to itself produce anything from artistic compositions, all the way through patentable inventions and even far beyond we have a legitimate right to question how these laws can continue functioning in an era where AI is king. Revisiting IP laws in this context is necessitated by the increasing deployment of AI across sectors, which include arts and literature, music as well as technology (Akpuokwe et al., 2024). As AI gets more intelligent, its job as a creator aids in creating the boundary between human and machine contribution to content which opens up many complex issues around "who is an Author?, Who has Ownership?, How do you protect Intellectual Property". The problems he identifies, however, are increasingly underserved by our current IP frameworks based on aspirational human-centric notions of creativity and originality (Lucchi, 2023).

But perhaps a reconsideration of the foundational legal philosophy behind IP laws is in order, not only because it will be required for those laws to continue performing their function efficiently and effectively in this new digital era. More importantly, doing so may assist us all towards fostering innovation without prejudice; protecting some creators' right just enough but not too much; as well as maintaining or restoring the balance between public interest and private incentives stadiums optimally suited to that thing called human progress after all these centuries! Re-evaluating this balance is crucial in order to protect a legally fair environment that encourages the development of technology while safeguarding intellectual property rights (Henderson et al., 2023).

1.2 Evolving Role of AI in Creative Processes

Artificial Intelligence (AI) is redefining the way creatives look to produce, develop and facilitate innovative outputs in all forms of art At first, AI was the helper designed to help human creators by increasing productivity and efficiency in tasks such as data analysis or design optimization or pattern recognition. In recent years, AI has passed the stage of being a mere aide and evolved into an autonomous maker (Jodha & Bera, 2023). Nowadays, AI systems are able to produce original music, visual art and literature, as well as create new technologies without direct human intervention. The creative potential of AI, built on advanced algorithms, machine learning and neural networks is about how well it can analyze mountains of data to detect patterns and create content at least as good or even better than human creativity. From AI-generated works of art fetching tens to even hundreds of thousands at prestigious auctions, to the utilization in film scores and advertising – music by an algorithm. Similarly, AI can also use to innovate in new products and provide the complete design package of an intellectual level where human error may bypass designs which are viable under a dynamic calculation (Igbinenikaro & Adewusi, 2024). This changing role of AI in creativity challenges some traditional ideas around who are an author and what is originality, including both questions about IP rights. Over time, as AI develops further, the future of creativity will increasingly be shaped by it and it may well open up a need for us to rethink how we legally and ethically consider questions around creative ownerships (Kirova et al., 2023).

1.3 Importance of Re-examining IP Laws to Adapt to Technological Advancements

With the growing traction of Artificial Intelligence (AI), by a large margin, how could IP laws keep pace to cater these fast technological advancements and innovations. IP regulations need by nature, were sent to cherish our legacies of expenses and workmanship; in any event they are not moved toward handle the contemporary inquiry that we have wound up with: If AI can without anyone else make new thoughts would it be able utilise them. Without a proper review, the current state of law will not be able to effectively handle issues such as authorship or ownership in an AI-centric reality (Archibong et al., 2024).

This gap could result in legal ambiguities, contests on the ownership of IP rights and problems related to enforcement that can hamper innovation and economic development. While you also have to strike the right balance between protecting AI creations and keeping innovation accessible for everyone. Rethinking IP laws will contribute towards clear policy-making, creating a level playing field for competition and bolstering the further upgradation of technology while respecting legitimate concerns of creators, inventors as well interest society at large.

1.4 Objectives of the Chapter

This chapter has the following objectives to:

- analyze the impact of AI on current IP frameworks
- propose potential reforms to ensure IP laws remain relevant in the AI era

2. THEORETICAL AND JURISPRUDENTIAL FOUNDATIONS OF INTELLECTUAL PROPERTY LAWS

The basic theoretical and jurisprudential underpinning of intellectual property (IP) laws can be traced back to the concept of creativity, invention(s), innovation coupled with balancing between private rights and public interest (Stim, 2024). IP laws have, historically speaking been about protecting the outputs of human intellect which includes inventions; literary and artistic works: symbols names, images used in commerce. Those principles-add the exhaustive reasons for which creators and innovators are able to secure copyright in addition there that may be summed up under these headings-cannot honestly stand on their own as necessary qualities of any law protecting authorial or inventor rights (Tekic & Füller, 2023). The Natural Rights Theory, based on the assertion that humans have a natural right in their "personal creations of ideas," is one of the basic theories behind IP law. It is a theory that has been heavily influenced by the philosophy of John Locke, who believed creators have an inborn right to their creations as if they were flora and fauna. At a higher level, IP rights are perceived as property rights respecting the extensive inputs used by individual authors in creation. This theory enforces the ethical belief that creators should be able to control and profit from what they create (Risse, 2023).

The other subset of the IP law is The Utilitarian Theory, which looks beyond simply protecting private rights and instead makes an evaluation of what benefits society most were created from intellectual property (Vinchon et al., 2023). This view of copyright is grounded in the idea that by assigning monopolies to creators we naturally encourage innovation, as those who are incentivized through profit motive will have a greater reason to commit time and resources. The [general] justification is that IP laws promote the public interest in preventing free riding on new ideas, inventions and creative works by society at large. IP laws seek to redress this, by temporarily limiting access to these creations in order for individual effort required and commercial interest aimed at benefitting the public through increased knowledge distribution/innovation may be rewarded. Besides these theories, Protection of rights were legitimated by the Economic Incentive Theory. This is in essence a utilitarian approach, but one focussed on innovation and the economics of it. Without IP protection, the argument goes that creators and inventors would have no financial incentive to create at all, as their work could be easily copied by others who did not invest in its production. IP laws, therefore, offer a legal framework to assure innovators that they will be able to economically benefit from their efforts and provide them incentive in return for engaging in technological innovation (Kalpokiene & Kalpokas, 2023).

The Personality Theory also helps in creating the jurisprudential groundwork of IP laws especially copyright. In this theory, which is the philosophy of Georg Wilhelm Friedrich Hegel, intellectual creations are another part of the creator_^(s)_own personality (Rayhan & Rayhan, 2023). This view holds that IP rights are important because they prevent the personal expression and identity of a creator from being unjustly usurped when her works fundamentally represent an industrialisation or excretion of one's soul. It has a largely moral bent to it, and talks about the morality of protecting IP while retaining an emotional connection between its creators and their creations (Barrat, 2023).

The level of rationalization for IP law based on Social Planning Theory, is that IP helps to affirm social structures and support cultural development. This paragraph establishes the theory supporting that some of IP laws are to safeguard individual rights, but other part is meant for communitarian purpose; in order social phenomenon and values like increasing cultural diversity, innovation and access to knowledge. These principles imply that the IP laws should be created to mirror and uphold societal standards, which delicately balance private rights vis-à-vis public concerns in order to help innovation as well creativity benefiting society at large (Paraman & Anamalah, 2023). These theories are based on the jurisprudential foundations of IP law that in turn inform and guide how legal frameworks should be developed protecting intellectual property. But new technologies, particularly Artificial Intelligence (AI), are shattering these old foundations (Carobene et al., 2024). Theories of creativity and knowledge developed based on human-centric definitions are incriminated when AI can invent a creative work or legal subject matter without interference from any person. Accordingly, there is a need for a pressing review of the justification to exist areas in this field from theoretical viewpoints that preserve its feasibility under technological change and demands equilibrating between creators/innovators interests versus public interest.

2.1 Jurisprudential Justifications for IP Protection: Theories of IP: Natural Rights, Utilitarian and Economic Incentives

Legitimation of the protection given to intellectual property (IP) rights occupies a prominent place in commercial jurisprudence as well, and what follows summarizes some key justifications for IP which circumscribe individual rights with social benefits. The Natural Rights Theory the jury found: creators have a natural and inherent right to own their creations in reflection of the labour invested by creating them (Miric, & Huang, 2023). The Utilitarian Theory: The idea that Intellectual Property protection encourages innovation by providing those who create with exclusive rights, resulting in there being more knowledge and technology for society (Igbinenikaro & Adewusi, 2024). According to the Economic Incentive Theory, IP rights generate opportunities for profit through a mechanism that rewards innovators with financial returns if they continue investing in creativity and research. The Personality Theory, on the other hand contends that intellectual creations are but an extension of identity of their creator hence to protect personal expression (Gašević et al., 2023). Thus constructed, these theories support strong legal and ethical bases for IP laws so long as such legislation in practice weighs reasonably the recognition of individual creativity against promotion of the public good (Floridi, 2023).

2.2 Traditional Concepts of Authorship and Ownership: Authorship and Ownership in IP Law

Protection and allocation of rights under classical intellectual property (IP) law are grounded in the notions of authorship and ownership (Rehman, 2023). Authorship An author is a person or other entity that writes a novel, book, poem, essay; creator; writer. The concept of authorship stems from this ideal around the possibility to contribute work that was an authentic expression passed through his own intellectual labour, skill and innovative spirit (Pasquinelli, 2023). It is this authorship that can be linked to the work which dictates from whom the economic and moral rights are derived.

Ownership, on the other hand is about who has the legal right to control and economically benefit from a work. If you are found to be the author than normally any intellectual property in your work is owned by you which means that only YOU have the rights over how it may or may not been used, copied and distributed commercially (Adams et al., 2023) This ownership extends to the ability of an author to sell or license these rights for money. Often, particularly in the case of play and works made for hire (i.e. output created by a contractor or an employee as part of duties), ownership will be owned technically by a third party who pays someone to execute creative act from why it stands originally. This flexibility demonstrates the ability of IP law to adjust with different contractual arrangements, so long as it helps inform who should be recognized for their creation and why (Roberts et al., 2023). Yet, the more technology has changed in new ways over time (not least with AI), these simplistic views are also increasingly challenged and a fresh look at how IP law treats them is required.

Figure 2. specifies the Theoretical and Jurisprudential Foundations of Intellectual Property Laws (Source- Original)

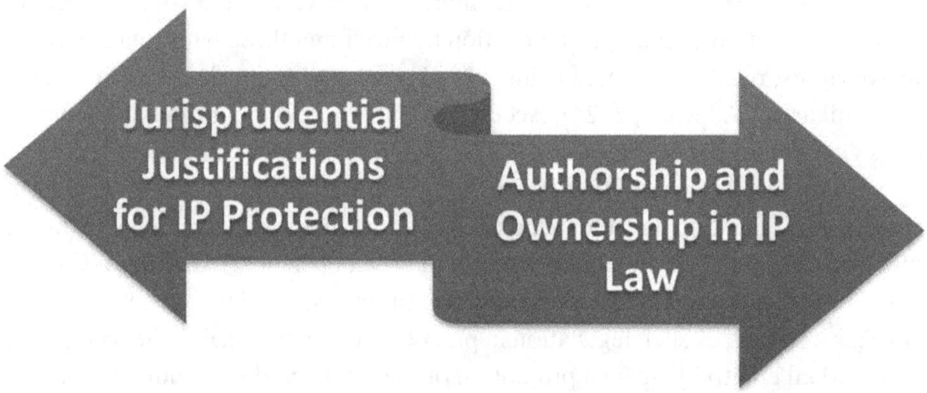

3. IMPACT OF ARTIFICIAL INTELLIGENCE ON INTELLECTUAL PROPERTY

Artificial Intelligence (AI) is changing the face of IP more than we could ever imagine, while offering a slap to the traditional concepts of creativity, authorship and ownership. The effects of IP law from the growing autonomy with which AI systems can generate content, write designs and inventions or other works one day could even extend to how existing legal frameworks have already adapted in response of such technology (Kostenko et al., 2024). Arguably the most significant and immediate impact of AI on IP rests in its attack upon authorship. While traditional IP laws have been invented with the notion of creation and thereby ownership by humans. Nevertheless, modern AI systems create entirely new works with no input from humans. In music, for example: Many people already know that automatic generation or even completion of melodies and lyrics works relatively well at this point. The absence of definitive answers calls into question the foundations of IP law: because human creation is at its heart (Senftleben, 2023).

AI upends not just authorship, but the very idea of ownership in IP. If an invention that qualifies to be patented comes out of the system then who gets ownership on the rights of the patentable execution. Existing legal regimes are not set up to deal with these situations where, instead of a human inventor being responsible for the origin of some product or technology, it was actually created by an autonomous AI like that other massive modernizing force which is currently only just beginning to flatten bushels and harvest plenty (Hirsch-Kreinsen, 2023). Without clear guidance as to how AI-created works should be assigned, legal uncertainty could slow down creative output in a sea of confusion about which rights and obligations rest where.

The sheer scale of data an AI can analyze and outputs being derivative from already existing outputs creates very grey areas concerning copyright infringement as wella s original work. These AI systems are capable of reproducing styles, themes and even entire works with remarkable likeness to real human-made creations a complex replication process that starts crossing boundaries between inspiration and infringement (Hajkowicz et al., 2023). In contrast, if the art is artificially generated to strongly resemble a well-known artist's stylistic work (like AI-generated monet-themed paintings), courts might see this as either an original creation or copyright infringing-derivative (Illia et al., 2023). This gives rise to a confusing state of legal uncertainty over the concept of originality which supports copyright law in its foundations and confounds understanding by making difficult enforcement processes possible on digital platforms. Also, the possible increase in existing IP challenges created by AI is troubling with respect to patent thickets but also over-patenting of minor innovations (La Torre et al., 2023). Due to the powerful ability for AI to produce thousands of potential inventions very quickly, this could inundate patent offices and create a much more complicated and siloed IP environment. And that, in turn, could present genuine innovators with an even bigger obstacle to clear if they want to navigate the patent system and get new products out into the world (Bayer, 2024).

AI offers equally promising prospects for better management and enforcement of IP rights. AI-enabled solutions can improve patent searches, trademark monitoring and detecting copyright infringes which in turn means better IP processes. For example, AI could process and interpret enormous tranches of patent literature to find out prior art work pertaining to new innovations in prevision associated with very expensive a law suit just for inventors along with organisations. Through AI-driven systems, creators and rights holders now also have access to the ability to monitor online platforms for unlicensed use of copyrighted content. The global element of AI development and deployment, on the other hand, only serves to complicate that IP impact further. Such an issue could be a headache for companies working across countries as they would have to deal with different sets of rules on AI-induced works and inventions. Ultimately, international harmonization of IP laws should be a top priority in order to foster the type legal framework that AI innovation can thrive on (Mannuru et al., 2023).

The effects of AI on IP are deep and varied they challenge basic tenets of intellectual property law while simultaneously enabling new paths for creation and anti-piracy efforts (Ruschemeier, 2023). Given the advances made by AI, it is high time for policy-makers and legal professionals in conversation with industry realized that significant aspects of IP laws also merit re-imagination so as to be able to remain adequately effective during this age (Stahl et al., 2023). Addressing these challenges critic raises a need for rethinking about the authorship and ownership, possibly instituting new principles governing AI-generated works and compelling international climate work to deliver an harmonized global intellectual-property framework (Kolides et al., 2023).

3.1 AI and Patent Law: Challenge, Current Legal Position, Patentability

This creates some major issues for traditional patent law, particularly in relation to recognizing AI as an inventor. In patent law, as it has been traditionally thought of for centuries now: inventors are assumed to be people creatures with minds and motivations; individuals or groups can conceive creative ideas. However, the assumption that humans will always be at least partly 'in-the-loop' is compromised as AI systems evolve capable of independently coming up with patentable inventions.

The core of the issue in this debate is whether AI should be eligible to recognition as an inventor (Amariles & Baquero, 2023).

Under current laws, the legal position of AI-produced inventions is mixed internationally. In the US and Europe, patent offices have refused to grant patents on inventions made by AI systems because they were not invented or created in an ordinary sense but rather developed through programming. This position emphasizes one of the main challenges when attempting to integrate AI into a legal culture made on human creativity (Bui & Nguyen, 2023). Therefore, the patentability of AI inventions is a complex subject. AI generated inventions can satisfy the requirements of novelty, non-obviousness and utility but not having a recognized legal entity as an AI inventor creates ambiguity (Biden, 2023). This might limit innovation, because inventors and companies will have some idea in how fair way does they holds the AI generated patents. These challenges must be overcome, and perhaps patent law needs to evolve providing for patenting AIs by setting tangible guideline on the ownership and inventorship of AI-own inventions (Ligthart et al., 2023).

3.2 AI and Copyright Law: Copyrightability of AI-generated Works, Issues of Originality and Creativity and Legal Status

Artificial intelligence (AI) thus intersects copyright law in terms of the extend to which AI-generated works may or not be considered as protectable by Copyright. Copyright law is traditionally based on the idea that any protection and rights should flow to the original work of authorship created by a human. Nevertheless, AI systems increasingly produce music, literature and other creative work prompts questions about the nature of copyrightability essentially whether these works are subject to intellectual property protection at allm or if so who owns it (Tallberg et al., 2023).

All this is what's called originality and creativity which are requisite elements for copyright protection. Courts and copyright offices have traditionally insisted that a work reflect no less than a token amount of creativity on the part of its author. The originality of AI-generated works is sometimes called into question because they often lack the direct manipulation by human artists. The law surrounding these works is an evolving topic that varies depending on the local jurisdiction, but in many places copyright cannot protect content created by AI because it does not fit with human authorship (Garon, 2023). This uncertainty poses serious legal and ethical issues as creators, entrepreneurs, and politicians fight the way to protect AI-generated works while finding ways of making them profitable. The first of these places calls for new legal constructions that allow AI to be recognised as a contributor in creativity, while the second opposes this concept and considers copyright should only be endowed by humans. The law may need to be re-evaluated so that it reflects technological advancements in the evolving AI landscape, and this will inevitably include how we view copyrightable works created by autonomous machines (Hine & Floridi, 2024).

3.3 AI and Trademark Law

The rise of Artificial Intelligence (AI) to have an impact on trademark law is giving way to new considerations regarding the protection and enforcement of brands in today's online economy. One of these points is the implementation AI in production or validation for trademarks. For example, AI can be used to design brand names and logos or develop slogans, thereby raising concerns about the protectability (and inherent distinctiveness) of generated trademarks. In accordance with the old school most trademarks should be highly distinctive and not capable of being mistaken for some other marks that already are existent. But AI adds a level of difficulty to such assessment because the marks generated by an AI might inadvertently infringe upon live trademarks (Khan & Jiliani, 2023).

Artificial intelligence also assists in automated tracking and surveillance of trademark infringement. They sift through a massive amount of databases and online platforms effectively searching for potential trademark infringements (AI tools). But the reliance AI for this work presents concerns over accuracy due to false positives in which non-infringing uses are flagged or it fails to identify potential infringement. Indeed, the capacity of AI to mimic and generate deepfakes or other misleading content generates pitfalls in trademark law around consumer confusion/brand dilution. While AI improves, trademark law will necessarily develop to account for the details of how Al changes brand creation protection and enforcement (Ienca, 2023).

Figure 3. illuminates Impact of Artificial Intelligence on Intellectual Property (Source- Original)

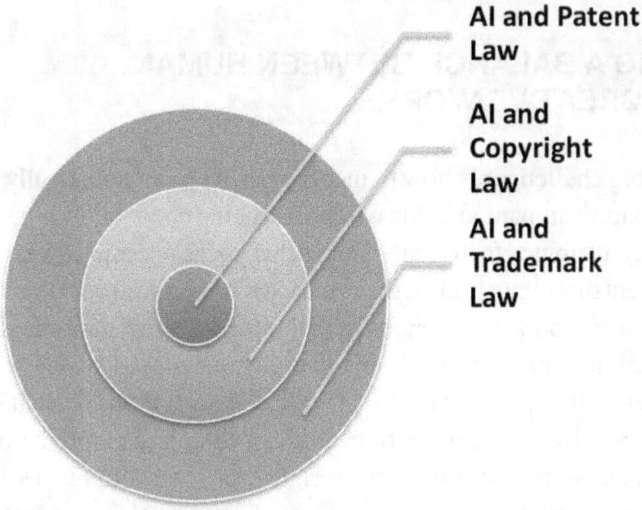

4. REASSESSING JURISPRUDENCE: CHALLENGES AND OPPORTUNITIES

The emergence of Artificial Intelligence (AI) within the realm of creative production and innovation challenges our understanding or imagination, even of traditional notions like authorship as well as ownership in intellectual property (IP). Historically, IP laws have developed under the human assumption that authorship and ownership are attributable to humans. In this new reality, the conventional frames of reference with which we have always looked at every other aspect of our world are not sufficient anymore since AI systems can now produce original content be it artwork or music; inventions or discoveries (Kanbach et al., 2024). Without specifying if AI could (or should) be considered a author or inventor, current IP laws fail to provide for parties involved in extensive use of AI throughout the creation process. There is an increasing recognition of the need to create new definitions and categories in IP law, which take account of a wider variety of AI services. For example, it might mean developing new types of legal subjects for AI-generated works where the author is instead recognized as a tool (not an element) directly within produced work or implementation context; ainsi could there be also some sort hybrid model such that creatorship would belong to not only end-users authors but too partially programmable functions residing at discretion in service with algorithm further responsible under original purpose established originally created fully majority sculpture than submitted system aiding yet allied participants (Zakir & Ali, 2023).

5. STRIKING A BALANCE BETWEEN HUMAN AND AI IN CREATIVE WORKS

The other big challenges is how to incorporate AI more holistically into creative processes, meaning humans and AIs will be bouncing contributions back-and-forth. Unless properly attributed to the real humans that go into creating them, AI can easily pump out content that almost perfectly mimics what people do, and this means thorny issues about attribution will no longer be theoretical. As machines begin replicating and even potentially improving human creativity, a nuanced stance is necessary to avoid depreciating the value of said do:14>>& o.openg…MethodBeatSin Nota This could be achieved by instituting a threshold based approach protecting more and less AI-generated works with protection rights, or even differences in ownership depending on the level of human contribution. For example, a work that is entirely created by AI might be entitled to different IP protections compared to an author who uses some form of the tool. Such a distinction would keep the uniquely human aspects of creativity things like purpose, emotional expression and personal judgment at the heart of who gets to call him/herself an author/owner. At the same time, acknowledging AI as a potential partner could result in new models of co-authorship where human and algorithmic contributions are credited more accurately to reflect the reality behind creativity. So, finding a new definition of authorship and ownership when it comes to AI is one about embracing the evolution in technologies while still recognizing the nature human creative process. This work suggests new definitions of legal principles and frameworks which, in turn represents the adaptation abilities allowed by IP law to bring this intricate relationship between human and machine into a just regards when it comes intellectual property creation (Mariani et al., 2023).

6. PROPOSED LEGAL REFORMS

Many AI technologies are global, as is the exchange of products and services (and data), so it is fundamentally important that countries work together to craft harmonized and effect IP laws capable coping with AI issues. For AI-produced intellectual property, international cooperation is crucial in protecting and managing it at a global level to encourage innovation and economic growth even beyond national boundaries. Rethinking the jurisprudential underpinnings of IP law in the age of AI is not soporific; it must be done as a matter of expediency to keep intellectual property rights afloat. The goal would be to maintain the relevance and effectiveness of law in fostering creativity, innovation, and economic development as AI evolves. This means, the future of IP law would be like treading on thin rope acknowledging that AI is a tool created by humans and should not represent itself as having any rights to invent or benefit from inventions; all while ensuring safeguards are in place for it not to monopolize many areas at global level can ideally protect integrity & sanctity of IP systems (Yas et al., 2024).

Revision in the existing patent laws it cannot be scrapped, need to introduce AI as a part of an invention. There should be legal reforms explicitly regulating the social position of AI in inventorship, with possible acknowledgment by law that an AI system can also act as a co-inventor with human collaborators. This would mean that AI innovation is patented while acknowledging the creative input required by both humans and machines (Roche et al., 2023).

6.1 Amending Copyright Law

However, the time has come for copyright law to evolve in order to encompass AI-generated works. The idea is to allow AI itself to be an author or co-author, so long as its contribution was so significant that without it the study would not have been done. New laws might be written to handle the distribution of creative works produced by AI, in which case copyright may play a role after all. This last approach could include granting copyright to the human developer or operator of AI, with possibly applying co-authorship frameworks that reflect the shared creative activity (Popenici, 2023).

6.2 Reconceptualizing Trademark law

The growing role of AI in the production and administration of trademarks should prompt reform on trademark law to recognize changes. Reforms can clear the distinction of AI-created marks, thereby protecting brand identity within an advanced era of AI technologies. This would include improving AI driven infringement protections and ensuring that trademarks continue to serve as a reliable indication of origin and quality (Gilbert et al., 2023).

6.3 Harmonization on the International Level

International harmonization of legal reforms is essential to address AI and IP challenges. This can, however, provide for tools to facilitate alignment of national laws with emerging international norms which establish consensus in the protection and control over AI-generated works throughout the world. It would also secure consistent, globally harmonised efforts between the reform of AI and IP law to promote cross-border innovation (Sag, 2023).

7. CONCLUSION AND FUTURE SCOPE

The incorporation of Artificial Intelligence (AI) in creative, innovation, and commercial operations has led to disruptive changes for the bedrock principles underpinning classical jurisprudential aspects of Intellectual Property (IP). The kind of redistribution that AI is driving calls for a fundamental reconsideration and overhaul of the legal structures around IP protection, ownership and monetization. IP legal frameworks have been created to protect human creativity and inventiveness, this new realm of AI has rendered them impotent. If AI can produce outputs that are on par with or better than things humans create, then the very notions upon which copyright operates originality and creativity. Laws that cannot identify AI as the creator of author or inventor cause legal grey areas, hamper innovation and breed ownership disputes. The big challenge and one of the reasons I am now working at Wikimedia is that we need to have structures in place where AI can add its own learning to creative works, but still respect human creators getting their just desserts.

This might mean recognizing AI systems as co-inventors at the same level or even forging entirely new patent categories that will account for combined human and AI innovation. Amendments should spell out clear protection for inventions produced by AI, for the security of innovation and transparent inventorship requirements. The second what-if is that copyright law needs to catch up with AI-authored works, and allow for the recognition of an MMI as a co-author when it has made substantial creative contributions. New frameworks could also be created to enable the management of AI-generated content and ensure a more fair and uniform application of copyrighting. If such co-authorship, conjoined with appropriate due diligence or other liability restrictions were put in place by the courts as a starting point for an AI ownership model that ties back to humans developers/operators. Such changes would benefit both AI creators as well as businesses by providing greater transparency and thus more certainty in the commercialization of AI-generated work, while balancing it with interest of human authors. The landscape of trademark laws in terms of AI-created brand development and branding demands to be redefined. The legal reform has to be addressed to the specific issue of trademarks, making certain that AI-generated marks do fulfil both requirements distinctiveness and non-infringement which are at the core of trademark law. This will help to ensure that trademarks retain credibility as indicators of quality and origin, which is essential for consumer confidence.

REFERENCES

Abbott, F. M., Cottier, T., Gurry, F., Abbott, R. B., Burri, M., Ruse-Khan, H. G., & McCann, M. (2024). *International Intellectual Property in an Integrated World Economy* [Connected EBook]. Aspen Publishing.

Abdikhakimov, I. (2023, June). Unraveling the Copyright Conundrum: Exploring AI-Generated Content and its Implications for Intellectual Property Rights. In *International Conference on Legal Sciences* (Vol. 1, No. 5, pp. 18-32).

Adams, C., Pente, P., Lemermeyer, G., & Rockwell, G. (2023). Ethical principles for artificial intelligence in K-12 education. *Computers and Education: Artificial Intelligence*, 4, 100131. DOI: 10.1016/j.caeai.2023.100131

Akpuokwe, C. U., Adeniyi, A. O., & Bakare, S. S. (2024). Legal challenges of artificial intelligence and robotics: A comprehensive review. *Computer Science & IT Research Journal*, 5(3), 544–561. DOI: 10.51594/csitrj.v5i3.860

Alier, M., García-Peñalvo, F., & Camba, J. D. (2024). Generative Artificial Intelligence in Education: From Deceptive to Disruptive.

Amariles, D. R., & Baquero, P. M. (2023). Promises and limits of law for a human-centric artificial intelligence. *Computer Law & Security Report*, 48, 105795. DOI: 10.1016/j.clsr.2023.105795

Archibong, E. E., Ibia, K. U. T., Muniandi, B., Dari, S. S., Dhabliya, D., & Dadheech, P. (2024). The Intersection of AI Technology and Intellectual Property Adjudication in Supply Chain Management. In *AI and Machine Learning Impacts in Intelligent Supply Chain* (pp. 39–56). IGI Global. DOI: 10.4018/979-8-3693-1347-3.ch004

Barrat, J. (2023). *Our final invention: Artificial intelligence and the end of the human era*. Hachette UK.

Bayer, J. (2024). Legal implications of using generative AI in the media. *Information & Communications Technology Law*, 33(3), 1–20. DOI: 10.1080/13600834.2024.2352694

Biden, J. R. (2023). Executive order on the safe, secure, and trustworthy development and use of artificial intelligence.

Bui, T. H., & Nguyen, V. P. (2023). The impact of artificial intelligence and digital economy on Vietnam's legal system. *International Journal for the Semiotics of Law-Revue internationale de Sémiotique juridique, 36*(2), 969-989.

Carobene, A., Padoan, A., Cabitza, F., Banfi, G., & Plebani, M. (2024). Rising adoption of artificial intelligence in scientific publishing: Evaluating the role, risks, and ethical implications in paper drafting and review process. [CCLM]. *Clinical Chemistry and Laboratory Medicine*, 62(5), 835–843. DOI: 10.1515/cclm-2023-1136 PMID: 38019961

Floridi, L. (2023). The ethics of artificial intelligence: Principles, challenges, and opportunities.

Garon, J. (2023). A practical introduction to generative AI, synthetic media, and the messages found in the latest medium. *Synthetic Media, and the Messages Found in the Latest Medium (March 14, 2023).*

Gašević, D., Siemens, G., & Sadiq, S. (2023). Empowering learners for the age of artificial intelligence. *Computers and Education: Artificial Intelligence*, 4, 100130.

Gilbert, S., Anderson, S., Daumer, M., Li, P., Melvin, T., & Williams, R. (2023). Learning from experience and finding the right balance in the governance of artificial intelligence and digital health technologies. *Journal of Medical Internet Research*, 25(1), e43682. DOI: 10.2196/43682 PMID: 37058329

Hajkowicz, S., Sanderson, C., Karimi, S., Bratanova, A., & Naughtin, C. (2023). Artificial intelligence adoption in the physical sciences, natural sciences, life sciences, social sciences and the arts and humanities: A bibliometric analysis of research publications from 1960-2021. *Technology in Society*, 74, 102260. DOI: 10.1016/j.techsoc.2023.102260

Henderson, P., Li, X., Jurafsky, D., Hashimoto, T., Lemley, M. A., & Liang, P. (2023). Foundation models and fair use. *Journal of Machine Learning Research*, 24(400), 1–79.

Hine, E., & Floridi, L. (2024). Artificial intelligence with American values and Chinese characteristics: A comparative analysis of American and Chinese governmental AI policies. *AI & Society*, 39(1), 257–278. DOI: 10.1007/s00146-022-01499-8

Hirsch-Kreinsen, H. (2023). Artificial intelligence: A "promising technology". *AI & Society*, •••, 1–12.

Ienca, M. (2023). On artificial intelligence and manipulation. *Topoi*, 42(3), 833–842. DOI: 10.1007/s11245-023-09940-3

Igbinenikaro, E., & Adewusi, A. O. (2024). Navigating the legal complexities of artificial intelligence in global trade agreements. *International Journal of Applied Research in Social Sciences*, 6(4), 488–505. DOI: 10.51594/ijarss.v6i4.987

Igbinenikaro, E., & Adewusi, O. A. (2024). Policy recommendations for integrating artificial intelligence into global trade agreements. *International Journal of Engineering Research Updates, 6*(01), 001-010.

Illia, L., Colleoni, E., & Zyglidopoulos, S. (2023). Ethical implications of text generation in the age of artificial intelligence. *Business Ethics, the Environment & Responsibility*, 32(1), 201–210. DOI: 10.1111/beer.12479

Jodha, D., & Bera, P. (2023). Copyright issues in the era of Ai-A critical analysis. *Res Militaris*, 13(3), 1737–1748.

Kalpokiene, J., & Kalpokas, I. (2023). Creative encounters of a posthuman kind–anthropocentric law, artificial intelligence, and art. *Technology in Society*, 72, 102197. DOI: 10.1016/j.techsoc.2023.102197

Kanbach, D. K., Heiduk, L., Blueher, G., Schreiter, M., & Lahmann, A. (2024). The GenAI is out of the bottle: Generative artificial intelligence from a business model innovation perspective. *Review of Managerial Science*, 18(4), 1189–1220. DOI: 10.1007/s11846-023-00696-z

Khan, A., & Jiliani, M. A. H. S. (2023). Expanding The Boundaries Of Jurisprudence In The Era Of Technological Advancements. *IIUMLJ*, 31(2), 393–426. DOI: 10.31436/iiumlj.v31i2.856

Kirova, V. D., Ku, C. S., Laracy, J. R., & Marlowe, T. J. (2023). The ethics of artificial intelligence in the era of generative AI. *Journal of Systemics, Cybernetics and Informatics*, 21(4), 42–50. DOI: 10.54808/JSCI.21.04.42

Kolides, A., Nawaz, A., Rathor, A., Beeman, D., Hashmi, M., Fatima, S., Berdik, D., Al-Ayyoub, M., & Jararweh, Y. (2023). Artificial intelligence foundation and pre-trained models: Fundamentals, applications, opportunities, and social impacts. *Simulation Modelling Practice and Theory*, 126, 102754. DOI: 10.1016/j.simpat.2023.102754

Kostenko, O. M., Bieliakov, K. I., Tykhomyrov, O. O., & Aristova, I. V. (2024). "Legal personality" of artificial intelligence: Methodological problems of scientific reasoning by Ukrainian and EU experts. *AI & Society*, 39(4), 1683–1693. DOI: 10.1007/s00146-023-01641-0

La Torre, D., Appio, F. P., Masri, H., Lazzeri, F., & Schiavone, F. (2023). *Impact of artificial intelligence in business and society: Opportunities and Challenges*. Routledge. DOI: 10.4324/9781003304616

Ligthart, S., Ienca, M., Meynen, G., Molnar-Gabor, F., Andorno, R., Bublitz, C., Catley, P., Claydon, L., Douglas, T., Farahany, N., Fins, J. J., Goering, S., Haselager, P., Jotterand, F., Lavazza, A., McCay, A., Wajnerman Paz, A., Rainey, S., Ryberg, J., & Kellmeyer, P. (2023). Minding rights: Mapping ethical and legal foundations of 'neurorights'. *Cambridge Quarterly of Healthcare Ethics*, 32(4), 461–481. DOI: 10.1017/S0963180123000245 PMID: 37183686

Lucchi, N. (2023). ChatGPT: A case study on copyright challenges for generative artificial intelligence systems. *European Journal of Risk Regulation*, •••, 1–23.

Mannuru, N. R., Shahriar, S., Teel, Z. A., Wang, T., Lund, B. D., Tijani, S., Pohboon, C. O., Agbaji, D., Alhassan, J., Galley, J. K. L., Kousari, R., Ogbadu-Oladapo, L., Saurav, S. K., Srivastava, A., Tummuru, S. P., Uppala, S., & Vaidya, P. (2023). Artificial intelligence in developing countries: The impact of generative artificial intelligence (AI) technologies for development. *Information Development*, •••, 02666669231200628. DOI: 10.1177/02666669231200628

Mariani, M. M., Machado, I., Magrelli, V., & Dwivedi, Y. K. (2023). Artificial intelligence in innovation research: A systematic review, conceptual framework, and future research directions. *Technovation*, 122, 102623. DOI: 10.1016/j.technovation.2022.102623

Miric, M., Jia, N., & Huang, K. G. (2023). Using supervised machine learning for large-scale classification in management research: The case for identifying artificial intelligence patents. *Strategic Management Journal*, 44(2), 491–519. DOI: 10.1002/smj.3441

Nhemi, S. (2023). Law Without Lawyers: Examining the Limitations of Consumer-Centric Legal Tech Services. *J. Intell. Prop. & Info. Tech. L.*, 3(1), 15–76. DOI: 10.52907/jipit.v3i1.223

Paraman, P., & Anamalah, S. (2023). Ethical artificial intelligence framework for a good AI society: Principles, opportunities and perils. *AI & Society*, 38(2), 595–611. DOI: 10.1007/s00146-022-01458-3

Pasquinelli, M. (2023). *The eye of the master: A social history of artificial intelligence*. Verso Books.

Popenici, S. (2023). The critique of AI as a foundation for judicious use in higher education. *Journal of Applied Learning and Teaching*, 6(2).

Rayhan, R., & Rayhan, S. (2023). AI and human rights: balancing innovation and privacy in the digital age. *DOI:. 2.2, 35394*.DOI: 10.13140/RG

Rehman, Z. (2023). Beyond Borders: International Law and Global Governance in the Digital Age. *Journal of Accounting & Business Archive Review*, 1(1), 1–12.

Risse, M. (2023). *Political theory of the digital age: Where artificial intelligence might take us*. Cambridge University Press. DOI: 10.1017/9781009255189

Roberts, H., Cowls, J., Hine, E., Morley, J., Wang, V., Taddeo, M., & Floridi, L. (2023). Governing artificial intelligence in China and the European Union: Comparing aims and promoting ethical outcomes. *The Information Society*, 39(2), 79–97. DOI: 10.1080/01972243.2022.2124565

Roche, C., Wall, P. J., & Lewis, D. (2023). Ethics and diversity in artificial intelligence policies, strategies and initiatives. *AI and Ethics*, 3(4), 1095–1115. DOI: 10.1007/s43681-022-00218-9 PMID: 36246014

Ruschemeier, H. (2023, February). AI as a challenge for legal regulation–the scope of application of the artificial intelligence act proposal. In *Era Forum* (Vol. 23, No. 3, pp. 361-376). Berlin/Heidelberg: Springer Berlin Heidelberg. DOI: 10.1007/s12027-022-00725-6

Sag, M. (2023). Copyright safety for generative ai. *Houston Law Review*, 61, 295.

Santoni de Sio, F., Almeida, T., & Van Den Hoven, J. (2024). The future of work: Freedom, justice and capital in the age of artificial intelligence. *Critical Review of International Social and Political Philosophy*, 27(5), 659–683. DOI: 10.1080/13698230.2021.2008204

Senftleben, M. (2023). Generative AI and author remuneration. *IIC; International Review of Industrial Property and Copyright Law*, 54(10), 1535–1560. DOI: 10.1007/s40319-023-01399-4

Stahl, B. C., Brooks, L., Hatzakis, T., Santiago, N., & Wright, D. (2023). Exploring ethics and human rights in artificial intelligence–A Delphi study. *Technological Forecasting and Social Change*, 191, 122502. DOI: 10.1016/j.techfore.2023.122502

Stim, R. (2024). *Patent, copyright & trademark: an intellectual property desk reference*. Nolo.

Tallberg, J., Erman, E., Furendal, M., Geith, J., Klamberg, M., & Lundgren, M. (2023). The global governance of artificial intelligence: Next steps for empirical and normative research. *International Studies Review*, 25(3), viad040. DOI: 10.1093/isr/viad040

Tekic, Z., & Füller, J. (2023). Managing innovation in the era of AI. *Technology in Society*, 73, 102254. DOI: 10.1016/j.techsoc.2023.102254 van Bijsterveld, S., & ten Napel, H. M. (Eds.). (2024). *Culture, Secularization, and Democracy: Lessons from Alexis de Tocqueville*. Taylor & Francis. Abbott, R., & Rothman, E. (2023). Disrupting creativity: Copyright law in the age of generative artificial intelligence. *Fla. L. Rev., 75*, 1141. DOI: 10.4324/9781032641041

van den Brink, M., Dawson, M., & Zglinski, J. (2023). Revisiting the asymmetry thesis: negative and positive integration in the EU. *Journal of European Public Policy*, 1-26.

Vinchon, F., Lubart, T., Bartolotta, S., Gironnay, V., Botella, M., Bourgeois-Bougrine, S., Burkhardt, J.-M., Bonnardel, N., Corazza, G. E., Glăveanu, V., Hanchett Hanson, M., Ivcevic, Z., Karwowski, M., Kaufman, J. C., Okada, T., Reiter-Palmon, R., & Gaggioli, A. (2023). Artificial Intelligence & Creativity: A manifesto for collaboration. *The Journal of Creative Behavior*, 57(4), 472–484. DOI: 10.1002/jocb.597

Yas, N., Elyat, M. N. I., Saeed, M., Shwedeh, F., & Lootah, S. (2024). The Impact of Intellectual Property Rights and the Work Environment on Information Security in the United Arab Emirates. *Kurdish Studies*, 12(1), 3931–3948.

Zakir, M. H., & Ali, S. (2023). CROSS-BORDER TRADEMARK INFRINGEMENT IN THE DIGITAL AGE: JURISDICTIONAL CHALLENGES AND HARMONIZATION EFFORTS. *PAKISTAN ISLAMICUS (An International Journal of Islamic & Social Sciences), 3*(2), 51-69.

Chapter 4
Liberal Democracy, Behavioural Governance, and Communication:
Risks and Opportunities

Sonia Cea Quintana
Rey Juan Carlos University, Spain

ABSTRACT

This article examines the intersection between liberal democracy, behavioural governance, and communication, highlighting their uses, potentialities, and risks. Behavioural economics has introduced innovative approaches in the formulation of public policies, rising new forms of governance and communication with citizens in order to optimise their behaviour. Two decades after the concept appeared, this article takes a current picture of behavioural governance in the world. The research identifies the leading regions and countries, the nature of the units of behaviour and their governmental relationship, as well as their main areas of activity. The findings highlight the prominence of interventions in health, environment and communication, reflecting a global trend towards the use of behavioural knowledge to improve the communication of public policies and overcome cognitive biases enhanced by the media. The authors focus attention on the need for robust regulatory frameworks to ensure ethical deployment and protection of individual rights in this evolving landscape.

DOI: 10.4018/979-8-3693-6945-6.ch004

INTRODUCTION

In 2003, behavioural economists Richard Thaler and Cass Sunstein coined the term "libertarian paternalism". In this foundational article, the authors question the foundations on the pure rationality of the individual and argue that citizens often make suboptimal decisions due to various cognitive limitations or the characteristics of the environment itself. Faced with this reality, libertarian paternalism proposes that states carry out small behavioural interventions in individuals to improve their decisions, without restricting their autonomy and freedom of choice (Sunstein and Thaler, 2003). Subsequently, the same authors would coin the term "nudge" to refer to these behavioural interventions (Thaler and Sunstein, 2008). The success of these publications led to the emergence of the so-called Behavioural Insights (BI) around the world and the birth of behavioural governance (Thaler and Sunstein, 2008; Gofen et al, 2021). Thus, in 2010, Thaler was hired by the British government to develop the Behavioural Insights Team (BIT), the first government unit dedicated to applying the theories of behavioural economics to public policy (Cabinet Office Behavioural Insights Team, 2011).

Meanwhile, Sunstein was appointed director of the Office of Information and Regulatory Affairs (OIRA) by the Obama administration, with the aim of reviewing and improving federal regulations applying these concepts (Sunstein, 2013). His work would later influence the creation of the Behavioural Sciences Team (SBST), forming part of the White House Office of Science and Technology Policy (Social and Behavioural Sciences Team, 2015). The proliferation of these units in various countries around the world and in governments of different political persuasions led libertarian paternalism to be considered a "third way" (Thaler and Sunstein, 2008: 252). In contrast to this support, the 2010s were also marked by strong criticism of nudges, questioning their long-term effectiveness and doubts about a covert manipulation of the citizen by governments (Gigerenzer, 2015; Loewenstein, 2015; Wilkinson, 2013). Similarly, with the arrival of the Trump administration in the US, the SBST ceased to operate and receive funding, as its work was seen to run counter to the deregulation sought by the new administration (Behavioral Scientist, 2017).

The current decade is characterised by a new landscape in behavioural regulation. On the one hand, the application of artificial intelligence to the development of nudges has given rise to more advanced models: hyper nudges (Yeung, 2016; Mills, 2022). These new developments are characterised by improvements in their personalisation and feedback capabilities, significantly increasing their effectiveness and reviving fears of manipulation of individuals (Leonard, 2008; Burr, Cristianini and Ladyman, 2018; Yeung, 2016). On the other hand, there are active efforts by supranational organisations such as the OECD to produce reports and practical guides so that different countries can use these techniques in their policy development (OECD, 2020). Or the European Union's major funding effort to help its member states develop these techniques to solve public health or environmental problems, among others (European Union, 2024). In this way, from the perspective of changing the behaviour of the population, nudging is becoming a powerful ally for countries to implement creative policies aimed at solving the major problems of the time. In this sense, we can highlight how the WHO relied on these techniques during the pandemic to raise awareness and increase vaccination (World Economic Forum, 2021). Or (see BehaviourWorks Australia, 2020) the various attempts by behavioural units to develop strategies to mitigate the effects of communication biases generated by new media environments.

This is an evolving landscape in which the push for artificial intelligence, the technical and financial support of certain supranational organisations, and the attempt by governments to increase the effectiveness of their policies may lead to a resurgence of behavioural governance and its application around the world. For all these reasons, the aim of this article is to carry out a detailed study of the state of behavioural governance. To this end, we will attempt to answer the following research questions (RQ): RQ1) Which are the leading regions and countries in this field?; (RQ2) What is the nature of the behaviour change units in which this knowledge is developed and driven?; (RQ3) What are the main areas of activity in which they operate?

The aim is to provide a comprehensive framework of behavioural governance in its current state. In doing so, we provide an X-ray of its current implementation, while also pointing out potential opportunities and risks that need to be considered due to the lack of proven regulation that protects the interests of the population (Butcher and Beridze, 2019; Taeihagh, 2021).

The originality of this chapter lies in its ability to offer an updated picture of behavioural governance in the world. It highlights the countries where it is most important, the relationship of behavioural units with governments and the main areas of action to which these new communication efforts dedicated to citizen behaviour change are being directed. Twenty years after the concept was first introduced by the authors (Sunstein and Thaler, 2003), and after initial doubts were raised about the long-term effectiveness and durability of these techniques (Gigerenzer, 2015; Loewenstein, 2015; Wilkinson, 2013), this enables us to evaluate their present significance and to identify prospective opportunities and threats in our democratic contexts, particularly in light of the advent of artificial intelligence and its concomitant concerns regarding the safeguarding of individual privacy and autonomy (Leonard, 2008; Burr, Cristianini and Ladyman, 2018; Yeung, 2017).

Similarly, as previously stated, we believe that contextualisation is essential given the growing influence of supranational organisations in the funding and dissemination of nudging tactics, as well as the development of related manuals in different countries.

To carry out this study, three combined methodological approaches have been used in order to provide a comprehensive and rigorous analysis of the situation. First, bibliometric studies are accessed through scientific databases (Yuan and Sun, 2020), searching for the terms 'nudging and governance' and 'nudging and artificial intelligence'. In this way, we try to substantiate this increased interest. Second, a qualitative analysis identifies the major cognitive distortions that shape contemporary public opinion and change the media environment in which governments operate (Saura and Debasa, 2022). The aim is to show how the current media landscape affects the deliberative capacity of citizens and the modulation of our democratic societies. Finally, data from the OECD[1] Observatory are extracted and analysed to provide an empirical basis for our comparisons. These data are compiled into a range of tables that allow us to produce a range of graphs to test and contrast our research questions, providing an up-to-date snapshot of behavioural governance around the world. Taken together, these integrated methodologies provide a holistic and multi-dimensional view of the phenomenon under study.

Following this introduction, the rest of the study will be structured as follows: first, we will provide a theoretical framework in which the concepts necessary to address these issues will be presented and developed. In the same way, these approaches will allow us to observe the impact of behavioural economic theories in our liberal democracies, offering new paradigms regarding the deliberative capacity of citizens. We will then go on to offer a chart of the various cognitive biases that influence citizen formation in new media environments. Third, we will examine current governance in the world, focusing on both its academic interest and its practical implementation in the different countries of the world. Fourth, the discussion and limitations of research, highlighting the potential and risks of these practices and offering new lines of research. Finally, in order to fulfil our purpose of providing a snapshot of behavioural governance in the world, we will offer conclusions that answer the research questions.

Theorical Framework

Behavioural Economics and its Implications for Liberal Democracy: Pure Individual Rationality vs. Bounded Rationality. Traditional Politicians vs. Decision Architects

In 1955, the multidisciplinary scientist Herbert Simon posited a critique of the notion of pure rationality as it applies to the individual, proposing instead the concept of bounded rationality. This theory posits that individuals make rational decisions, yet are constrained by the cognitive and informational limitations of their environment (Simon, 1955). The advent of these theses directly contravened the tenets of traditional democracies, which were predicated on the individual's capacity to engage in reasoned decision-making (Descartes, 1637; Spinoza, 1670; Leibniz, 1714) and the necessity for democracies to rely on this deliberative rational discourse as the foundation of their legitimacy (Habermas, 1987, 1996). Subsequently, the development of neuroscience corroborated Simon's postulates, underscoring the pivotal role of emotions in rational deliberation (Damasio, 1994; Ledoux, 1996; Sommer and Peterson, 2012).

Consistent with these assertions, behavioural economics uses evidence from psychology and other disciplines to create models that reflect the limits of rationality, willpower, and self-interest to explain how individuals make actual decisions (Mullainathan and Thaler, 2001; Camerer, 2014). Among these theories, the theory of bounded rationality (Simon, 1947, 1955), prospect theory (Kahneman and Tversky, 1979; Kahneman, 2011), expected utility theory (von Neumann and Morgenstern, 1944), theory of planned behaviour (Ajzen, 1991, 2012) or cognitive dissonance theory (Festinger, 1957; Harmon-Jones and Mills, 1999) stand out. Combined, these theories move us away from a model of perfect rationality to a model of individuals making decisions that are influenced by cognitive biases, emotional reactions, the environment, and time and form constraints. For behavioural economists, therefore, the architecture of decision-making is key (Thaler, and Sunstein, 2008; Thaler, 2015; Sunstein, 2016). For these authors, public policy makers must be decision architects, creating an environment that leads citizens to make the best decisions to achieve their welfare, always ensuring freedom of choice. Likewise, they stress the need to know the cognitive biases of citizens in order to design these decision environments (Johnson and Goldstein, 2003; Thaler and Sunstein, 2008; Bertrand, Mullainathan, and Shafir, 2006).

In accordance with the recommendations set forth by the authors, our initial objective is to examine the current status of nudges as a technique. Subsequently, we will undertake an analysis of the cognitive biases that exert the greatest influence on citizens in the context of new socio-media environments.

Nudging and Artificial Intelligence: From Nudge to Hypernudge – Personalised Welfare Offers vs. Doubts About Autonomy and Free Choice

The term 'nudge' is used to describe any aspect of the choice architecture that alters people's behaviour in a predictable way without prohibiting any choice or significantly changing their economic incentives. For an intervention to be considered a nudge, it must be simple and inexpensive to avoid (Thaler and Sunstein, 2008). Classifications may be made on the basis of various criteria. In accordance with dual processing theory (see Kahneman, 2011; Sunstein, 2014), two distinct categories of nudges can be identified: The first category of nudges affects behaviour that is maintained by automatic thought processes, without engaging conscious deliberation. The second category of nudges influences attention and deliberative processes through automatic thinking, as evidenced by Hansen and Jespersen (2013). If we consider their objective, we can identify pro-self-nudges, which aim to counteract irrational behaviour in order to maximise the overall benefit for the individual. Conversely, pro-social nudges are identified as non-coercive behavioural measures that encourage individuals to produce public goods and otherwise improve overall social welfare, even when doing so is incompatible with maximising private welfare. Their use for such collective action problems, as present in our societies as climate change, may make this policy tool more prominent in the future (Loewenstein and Chater, 2017; Schmidt and Stenger, 2024).

In light of these developments, the advent of digital devices has given rise to a new field of study, namely digital nudging (DN), which explores the use of nudge-based techniques within digital environments (Sadeghian and Otarkhani, 2023). In this context, the concept of "big nudging" emerges, which refers to the use of big data and artificial intelligence to guide individuals' choices and decisions on a large scale in a more accurate and personalised manner, taking advantage of the vast amount of information available about their behaviours and preferences (Bartmann, 2022). It is also important to consider the role of algorithmic nudges (Saura et al., 2024), which combine AI with nudging techniques to influence an individual's behaviour in a personalised way, based on their specific data and behaviours (Schmauder et al., 2023). The efficacy of these techniques has given rise to the term 'hyper-nudging' (Yeung, 2016; Mills, 2021), reflecting the capacity of these novel nudges to dynamically shape the user's environment of choice in a more subtle and powerful manner. With regard to thematic nudges, early systematic literature reviews indicate that they are predominantly employed in the field of behavioural finance at this nascent stage of development (Aoujil et al., 2023). Notable examples can be found in the field of radiology (see Powell, 2020), the promotion of sustainable use (see Majid, Tussyadiah, and Kim, 2024), the fight against corruption in the public sector (see Villagrasa and Solé, 2022) and even instances of its fraudulent use – a dark nudge – in the food industry (see Brooks et al., 2022).

The enhanced efficacy of these innovations in comparison to conventional ones has given rise to ethical quandaries pertaining to their ramifications for individual autonomy and democratic processes (Bartmann, 2022). Consequently, in recent years, ethical concerns pertaining to privacy violations, manipulation and determinism have been amplified, with the potential to exacerbate existing issues and give rise to new forms of discrimination (De Zárate Alcarazo, 2023). To address this issue, the implementation of value-sensitive design (VSD) and the utilisation of interfaces that facilitate critical reflection are recommended (Schmauder et al., 2023). Similarly, regulatory frameworks are required to guide the development of these technologies, ensuring the rights of citizens, the safety and ethical use of the technologies, and an implementation that ensures the benefit for governments (Yeung, 2016; Floridi, 2015; Leonard, 2008; Weinmann et al., 2016). Consequently, in contrast to conventional nudges, these novel hyper-nudges promise the implementation of personalised government initiatives that are anticipated to enhance individual well-being. Nevertheless, this potential raise concerns surrounding potential misuse.

A Critical Examination of the Main Heuristics and Cognitive Biases Affecting Citizens' Decision-Making in the Information Age

In accordance with the principles espoused by behavioural economists, who accord considerable significance to decision environments, we seek to ascertain which cognitive heuristics and biases have the greatest impact on the rational deliberation of citizens in the context of contemporary socio-media environments.

Heuristics are unconscious mental rules that facilitate the reformulation of complex problems by transforming them into simpler ones. This enables the rapid formation of decisions with the intention of enhancing their efficiency. While not infallible, they are frequently beneficial in the majority of everyday scenarios (Tversky and Kahneman, 1974; Martignon and Gaissmaier, 2011; Kahneman, 2011). Concurrently, cognitive biases represent the patterns of deviation in rational judgement that occur through the utilisation of heuristics. These biases may result in irrational decisions, distorted perceptions of reality, or being manipulated by the insiders of these techniques (Hansen, 2020).

We proceed to identify a list of the principal heuristics and cognitive biases that affect decision-making in the socio-political context, with a particular focus on those that are intensified by citizens' exposure to the new media realities.

The advent of the Digital Revolution has given rise to novel arenas for discourse and deliberation, including the online press, digital platforms on the Internet, and social networks. These spaces engender novel communication environments and facilitate interaction, yet also present considerable challenges for contemporary democracies. These platforms provide a conduit for the dissemination of false information, including hoaxes and cyberbullying, which present a significant and multifaceted challenge to contemporary democracies. These circumstances have significant implications for the formation of our societies, democratic discourse, and citizens' capacity for critical judgement and analysis. This phenomenon has the potential to erode trust in democratic institutions and undermine the electoral process by unduly influencing public opinion, a process known as cognitive warfare (Debasa et al., 2024). The consumption of information through social networks and algorithmic processes has been observed to undermine critical and reasoned judgement, a phenomenon that can be described as filter bubbles (Spohr, 2017), which in turn can contribute to social polarisation.

This phenomenon can be attributed to the tendency of algorithms to present users with content that reinforces their pre-existing ideas or beliefs, thereby fostering what has been termed 'digital bias'. When citizens have only access to online content that corroborates their existing beliefs, the potential for constructive dialogue and engagement, which are vital components of a functioning democracy, is diminished (Daus, 2024). Furthermore, the practice of micro-segmentation and the utilisation of personal data for the purpose of targeted personalised messaging represents a substantial risk. To illustrate, political campaigns may utilise behavioural data amassed by social media platforms to devise highly personalised messages that exploit individuals' psychological vulnerabilities. This not only gives rise to ethical concerns pertaining to privacy, but can also unduly influence public opinion and alter the course of democratic processes in a manner that lacks transparency. The concentration of media power in the hands of a few large technology platforms presents a risk to media diversity and plurality. Companies such as Facebook, Google and X (Diez-Gracia et al., 2023) exert a disproportionate influence over the information consumed globally. The concentration of power in these entities can give rise to indirect censorship (López, 2023), as these platforms possess the ability to moderate and control disseminated content, frequently without sufficient accountability.

Having identified the types of dangers that are characteristic of the present era, we proceed to enumerate the principal heuristics and cognitive biases that influence decision-making within the political and social spheres. We then focus our attention on those biases that are intensified by the citizenry's engagement with the novel media landscapes.

Table 1. Selected cognitive heuristics and biases affecting citizens in new communicative environments.

Denomination	Definition	Social media environment impact
Confirmation bias (Peter Wason, 1960; Nickerson, 1998; Lord and Lepper, 1979; Lerman and Acland, 2018; Sunstein, 2001).	The tendency to seek out, interpret and remember information that confirms pre-existing beliefs and ideologies, and to underestimate information that contradicts them.	- It increases the exposure to low quality sources of information. - This is exacerbated by the use of social media, leading to 'echo chambers'. - Increases polarisation, reinforces ideological divisions and makes it harder to engage with opposing perspectives.
Availability bias (Tversky and Kahneman, 1973; Slovic, 1987, Li and Jager, 2023; Sunstein, 2005; Sunstein, 2002; Weeks and Southwell, 2010).	The assessment of the likelihood of an event is based on the ease with which relevant examples can be recalled. It is observed that recent events and those that are emotionally impactful are more readily remembered.	- Exploitation of recent or shocking events to shape public opinion and promote particular political agendas. - Creates distorted perceptions of the frequency or significance of these events. - Intensifies divisions and emotions in the political debate, as well as differing perceptions of risk and social issues.
Bandwagon Effect (Solomon Asch, 1951; Leibenstein, 1950; Schmitt-Beck, 1996; Kleinnijenhuis et al., 2019; Morton et al., 2015; Khrennikov, 2020)	Adopting beliefs or behaviours because many other people do. Its opposite is the underdog effect (see Vandello and Goldschmied, 2007).	- Voters: Support for a candidate or policy simply on the basis of perceived popularity, rather than reasoned study. - Polls: Demobilisation of minority options. - Media and social media: act as amplifiers of this effect.
Dunning-Kruger Effect (Dunning and Kruger, 1999; Dunning, 2011; Flynn et al., 2017; Mazor and Fleming, 2021).	Those with lesser competence tend to overestimate their abilities and skills.	- Make important political or social decisions based on an overestimation of their own knowledge, which may be detrimental to their well-being (e.g. vaccination). - Increased spread of fake news and misinformation, especially on social networks for rapid information consumption (TikTok). - Society: Contributes to political polarisation and disinformation.
Representativeness bias (Tversky and Kahneman, 1974; Gilovich, Griffin and Kahneman; 2002; Todorov et al., 2005; Iyengar and Kinder, 1987; Vosoughi, Roy and Aral, 2018).	Assessment of the probability of an event on the basis of its similarity to a prototype.	- Formulating opinions based on stereotypes and false generalisations about certain social groups. - Over-representation of extreme and exceptional cases, making them appear representative of certain groups, thus influencing public perception and the political agenda. - Increases polarisation and conflict.

continued on following page

Table 1. Continued

Denomination	Definition	Social media environment impact
The false consensus effect (Ross, Green and House, 1977; Bail et al. 2018; Lelkes, Sood and Iyengar, 2017; Lewandowsky, Ecker, and Cook, 2017; Leviston, Walker and Morwinski, 2012).	Overestimation of the extent to which our beliefs, values and habits are shared by others.	- A distorted view of public opinion, which can influence voting behaviour and perceptions of the legitimacy of election results. - Empowers disinformation and echo chambers: The work of algorithms creates a constant validation of individuals' beliefs. Puede llevar a la polarización y el radicalismo y el desincentivo del pensamiento crítico.
Information overload (Eppler and Mengis, 2004). (Bawden and Robinson, 2020; York, 2013)	Burnout, rejection and sub-optimal decisions can result when people are bombarded with too much information, impairing their ability to process it and make effective decisions. This is considered to be one of the major problems of our time.	- Feelings of being overwhelmed and fed up: Can lead to psychological stress and anxiety, attention and memory problems, social disconnection, reduced cognitive efficiency in vulnerable groups, superficial processing of information and consequently reduced ability to make correct and informed decisions. - It can lead to political demobilisation or the success of anti-systemic ideas.
Cascade of information (Bikhchandani, Hirshleifer, and Welch, 1992; Bikhchandani, Hirshleifer, and Welch, 1992; Vosoughi, Roy, and Aral, 2018; Banerjee, 1992).	It occurs when individuals' decisions are influenced by the actions and decisions of others, rather than based on their own judgement or information.	- Rapid decision-making and opinion-forming, leading to rapid changes in public opinion. - Can encourage the rapid spread of fake news. - Contributes to political polarisation. The viral nature of social media can facilitate this effect by encouraging the bandwagon effect.
Limited attention (Mark, Gudith and Klocke, 2008; Iyengar, Kinder, 1987; Pariser, 2011; Sunstein, 2018).	The human brain is not designed to handle the amount of stimulation and multi-tasking that modern technology requires, which can reduce cognitive efficiency and the ability to concentrate for long periods of time.	- Simplification of the political message and lack of depth in the debate. - Prioritising and viralising sensational or emotional issues that better capture the public's attention, avoiding rational discussion of important issues. -Sharing information without verifying its accuracy, encouraging propaganda and manipulation. Creating echo chambers that contribute to political polarisation.

Source: authors' own work.

As we can see, these cognitive biases, as well as the media environment in which information flows, shape a citizen who subjects his or her decisions to an evaluation in which rational deliberation does not always prevail. In addition, the new political-media environment created by social networks and new media means that information with a strong emotional impact is prevalent among both politicians and the public, leading to more polarised societies and politicians who are more likely to use information with a more emotional charge in order to be effective with their voters. Given this new media landscape, behavioural economics applied to public policy design offers a solution to these and other societal problems, as will be discussed subsequently.

Communication manuals based on behavioural interventions: government communication to overcome cognitive biases in the population

The insights provided by behavioural scientists are having a significant impact on the development of communication strategies. In this sense, behavioural units developed at different levels of administration proffer advice with a view to enhancing the success of different public policies.

Consequently, the United Kingdom's Behavioural Insights Teams (BITs) has developed the so-called 'EAST Framework', a foundational set of recommendations aimed at elucidating and illustrating these interventions. The framework posits that such interventions should adhere to the principles of 'Easy, Attractive, Social, and Timely' (see Behavioural Insights Team, 2014).

In the case of the Canadian government, a Behavioural Insight Playbook has been developed for politicians and communicators. The toolkit provides guidance on the creation of personalised and motivating messages. In a similar manner, they provide tools for the creation of structures with an emphasis on simplicity and memorability (Government of Canada, 2018).

The Australian government, via the Behavioural Economics Team of the Australian Government (BETA), has developed the 'BETA Guide to Applying Behavioural Insights'. This document places particular emphasis on the utilisation of positive reinforcement as a means of fostering the uptake of behaviours that are deemed to be socially beneficial (Behavioural Economics Team of the Australian Government, 2019).

The World Health Organization (WHO) provides guidelines for the design of effective public health communication campaigns. The documents recommend the use of repetitive, clear, and simple messages that appeal to solidarity and include concrete indications (World Health Organization, 2017). In a similar way, the US Department of Health also provides manuals to enhance the dissemination of public health information on social media. These manuals emphasise the significance of developing messages that are readily comprehensible and grounded in evidence from behavioural science (Centers for Disease Control and Prevention, 2011).

In contrast, the OECD has also adopted the creation of communication manuals for the implementation of these policies. These manuals emphasise the personalisation of messages, the use of automatic reminders and the creation of positive and attractive messages (Organisation for Economic Co-operation and Development, 2017).

Furthermore, UNICEF is spearheading the development of these resources with the establishment of Communication for Development (C4D), a communication approach that integrates behavioural techniques. The manual provides strategies for behaviour change in health, education and child protection (UNICEF, 2005).

This illustrates how communication can be utilised as a vital instrument in facilitating the social transitions that these techniques aspire to engender. Similarly, it constitutes a pivotal component in the domain of behavioural governance, particularly in countries and administrations that have adopted it as a means of formulating efficacious responses to the multifarious challenges confronting our societies. It is for these reasons that we propose a study of behavioural governance on a global scale, with the objective of conducting a comprehensive examination of these novel methods of responding to the evolving media, political and social landscape.

Behavioural Governance: Leading Regions, Configuration and Policy Areas of Development

Behavioural governance is the application of behavioural economics to the design of policies and regulations that influence human behaviour in a positive manner. The objective is to establish environments that facilitate decision-making that benefit both individuals and society at large, while ensuring the protection of freedom of choice (Sunstein and Thaler, 2003; Gofen et al., 2021). Behavioural governance is inextricably linked to the concepts of 'soft paternalism' or 'libertarian paternalism' (Sunstein, 2016), which can be defined as a distinctive state-citizen arrangement centred on the implementation of new cultural practices aimed at governing through behavioural change (Pykett, 2016). This approach has resulted in the establishment of behavioural insights (BI) units in various locations worldwide, with the objective of enhancing the efficacy of regulatory measures and optimising the impact of public policy (Barak-Corren and Kariv-Teitelbaum, 2021).

This is a novel and pertinent subject, and as such, it is still in its nascent stages from a practical standpoint. The only X-ray of existing behavioural units in the world was discovered in one of the work areas of the Observatory of Public Service Innovation (OPSI) of the Organisation for Economic Co-operation and Development (OECD). This updated and detailed study of behavioural units permits an analysis and study of the situation of behavioural units in the current period, as well as the establishment of a foundation for future research on their evolution and growth.

Academic Status of Behavioural Governance

In order to conduct a study on the current academic state of governance, we adopted an approach known as bibliometric analysis (Linnenluecke et al., 2020, cited by Lafont et al., 2023), whereby we consulted the Web of Science (WOS) database. As indicated by authors such as Yuan and Sun (2020), this database is widely used to obtain and develop bibliometric sources and studies due to its international prestige in science.

In order to achieve this objective, two searches were conducted. The first of these involved the use of the search terms "TS=(Nudging) AND TS=(Government)", with the aim of gauging the level of interest in the potential application of nudging techniques within the context of political governance. Subsequently, a second search was carried out, utilising the search terms "TS=(Nudging) AND TS=(Artificial Intelligence)", with the intention of observing the extent of interest in the emerging field of research concerned with the application of artificial intelligence in conjunction with nudging techniques.

The results are presented in the following manner: In regard to the initial search, which pertains to the linkage of nudging with governmental entities, the research domain is witnessing a notable expansion, as evidenced by the 452 results yielded. This growth trajectory reached its zenith in 2019, followed by a slight decline in 2020, which could be attributed to the ramifications of the pandemic. The number of publications peaks in 2023 (67), followed by 2022 (54), 2021 (53), 2019 (46) and 2020 (41). A further search combining the terms 'nudging' and 'artificial intelligence' yielded fewer results (108), but also evidenced a growing interest since 2019, with a slight decline in 2023. Therefore, we identify 2022 as the year with the highest number of publications (32), followed by 2023 (26), 2021 (16), 2020 (9), and 2019 (4).

Consequently, there has been a notable surge in research activity within this field since the onset of the pandemic. This has been accompanied by a heightened interest in the application of nudging techniques at the governmental level, as well as in their advancement through the use of artificial intelligence.

Behavioural Insights Units in the World: Regions, Countries, Nature and Areas of Development

As previously stated, the OECD's Observatory of Public Service Innovation was consulted in order to investigate the prevalence of the various behavioural units across the globe. To this end, on 19 June, we accessed the Observatory's website and collated the data in Excel spreadsheets for analysis and comparative study. In accordance with the OECD's information organisation, we proceeded to investigate the presence of these units by region and country, as well as the nature of these units (whether they operate within official bodies or externally), and their areas of study.

Figure 1. BI units by region

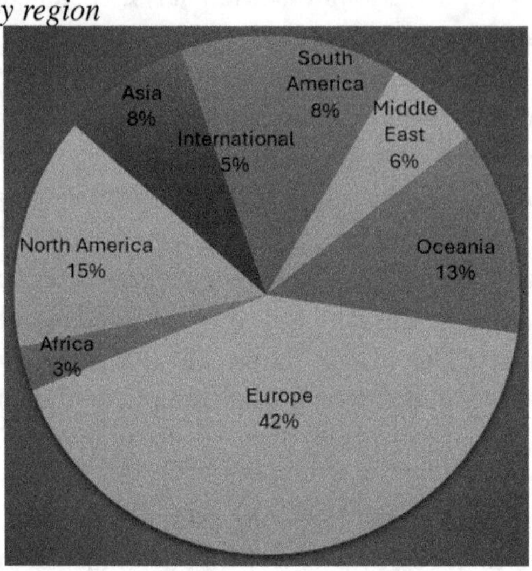

Source: Observatory of Public Service Innovation (OPSI) of the Organisation for Economic Co-operation and Development (OECD).
Produced by: the authors.

The current number of operational units is 329, of which 137 are located in Europe (42% of the total), 48 in North America (15%), 42 in Oceania (13%), 28 in South America (8%), 27 in Asia (8%), 18 are part of international or multinational units (5%), countries in the East (6%), and lastly, 9 are present in Africa (3%). Consequently, Europe is the region with the highest number of BIs in operation (see Figure 1).

Figure 2. BI units in the world. Heat map

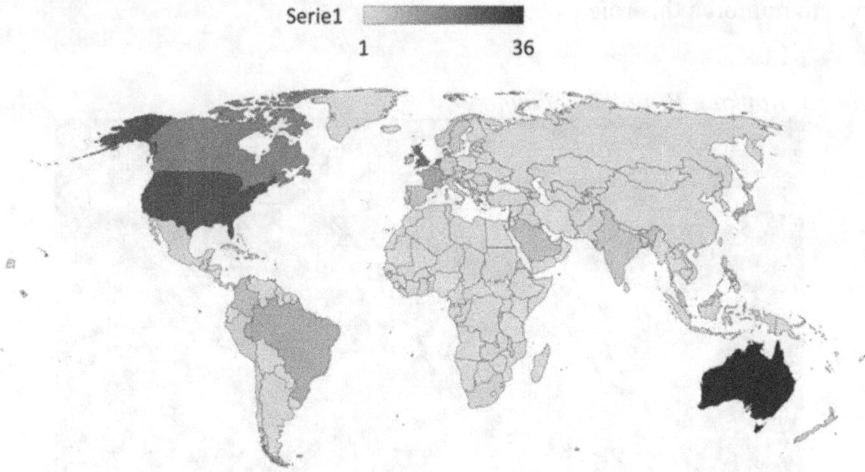

Source: Observatory of Public Service Innovation (OPSI) of the Organisation for Economic Co-operation and Development (OECD)
Produced by: the authors.

As illustrated in the heat map (see Figure 2), the Anglo-Saxon environment is the most prominent in terms of the implementation of behavioural governance. Conversely, this approach is notably absent in China. The implementation of Behavioural Governance is similarly insignificant in Latin America, with notable exceptions such as Cuba and Venezuela. In Europe, the importance of Behavioural Governance appears to be diminished. However, as evidenced by the aforementioned comparison, the presence of units in nearly all member countries makes it the leading subject of study.

A review of the data reveals that, at the country level, there are currently 64 countries with BI units. Australia occupies the top position in the ranking, with 36 units, followed by the United States (28 units), Great Britain (25 units), the Netherlands (24 units), and Canada (18 units). France occupies the sixth position with 11 units, followed by Brazil with 10 units, Switzerland with 8 units, Belgium with 7 units, and Colombia with 7 units (see Figure 2). Therefore, although as previously indicated, the number of units present in Europe is notable (see Figure 1 and Figure 3), the strength of the Anglo-Saxon countries is also evident, with particular focus on Australia, the United States, and Great Britain as sources of development.

In the case of the three main countries, Australia, the USA and the UK, their role is of particular relevance due to the number of units they have providing direct support to central government. This is exemplified by the integration of units within the government structure in the case of Australia and the UK. Furthermore, their extensive implementation in local government, academia and the private sector serves to reinforce this role.

Figure 3. Ranking BI units by country

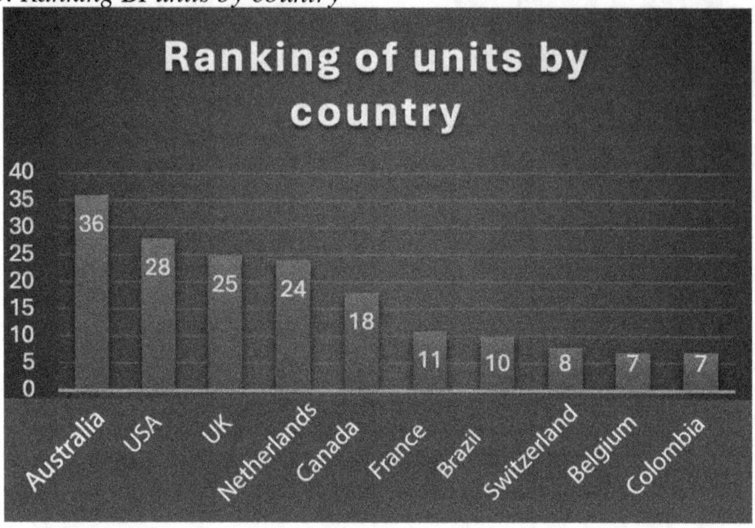

Source: Observatory of Public Service Innovation (OPSI) of the Organisation for Economic Co-operation and Development (OECD)

Prepared by: the authors.

Nature of the Institutions of BI Units in the World

Following the analysis of the countries' developmental progress, we proceeded to examine the financial resources allocated to these initiatives, as well as the institutional frameworks within which they operate. Our objective was to ascertain the primary drivers of development, whether governmental, supranational, academic, or private.

Figure 4. Nature of the Institutions of BI Units in the World.

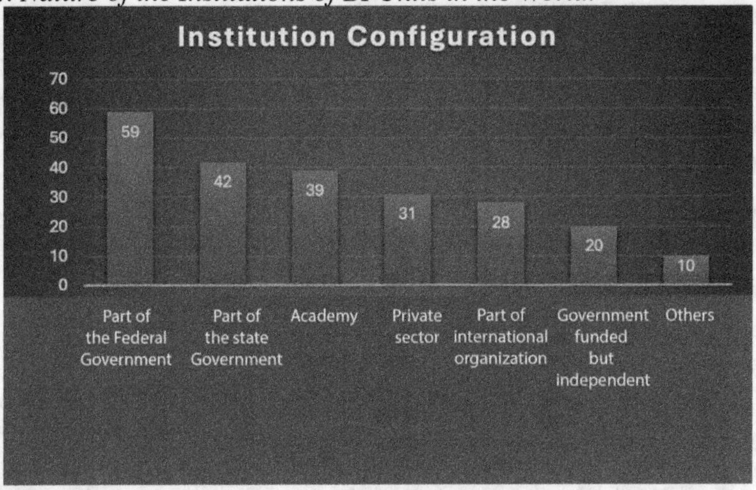

Source: Observatory of Public Service Innovation (OPSI) of the Organisation for Economic Co-operation and Development (OECD)
Prepared by: the authors.

At the time of writing, these units are represented by 229 behavioural institutions around the globe. Of these, 59 are part of the federal government, including the Australian Government's Behavioural Insight Team[2]. Additionally, 42 units are affiliated with state or provincial governments, including the New York City Behavioural Design Team[3]. Thirty-nine units are associated with academic institutions, such as the UBC Decision Insights for Business and Society (UBC-DIBS) in Canada (see https://www.sauder.ubc.ca/thought-leadership/divisions- The remaining 31 units are located in the private sector, including the Behavioural Economics Team at Oxera Consulting in the UK (see https://www.oxera.com/expertise/behavioural-economics/). A further 28 units are part of international organisations, including the Observatory of Public Innovation. The OECD (see https://oecd-opsi.org/) is another notable example. Twenty units are government-funded but operate independently, including the SNCF Transilien Nudge Unit of the Société Nationale des Chemins de Fers in France (see https://www.sncf.com/). Ten units respond to other callings. As the data illustrate, there is a growing interest among governments in having these teams advise national policies directly (see Figure 4).

Practical Application of Behavioural Governance. Main Areas of Development

Behavioural governance is being implemented in a number of areas with the objective of improving effectiveness and optimising public policies. These strategies seek to positively influence citizen behaviour through the implementation of behavioural interventions, with the aim of guiding them towards the desired behaviour. The following section seeks to elucidate the main issues where behavioural governance is trying to promote social behaviour change.

Figure 5. Main areas of activity, BI units worldwide.

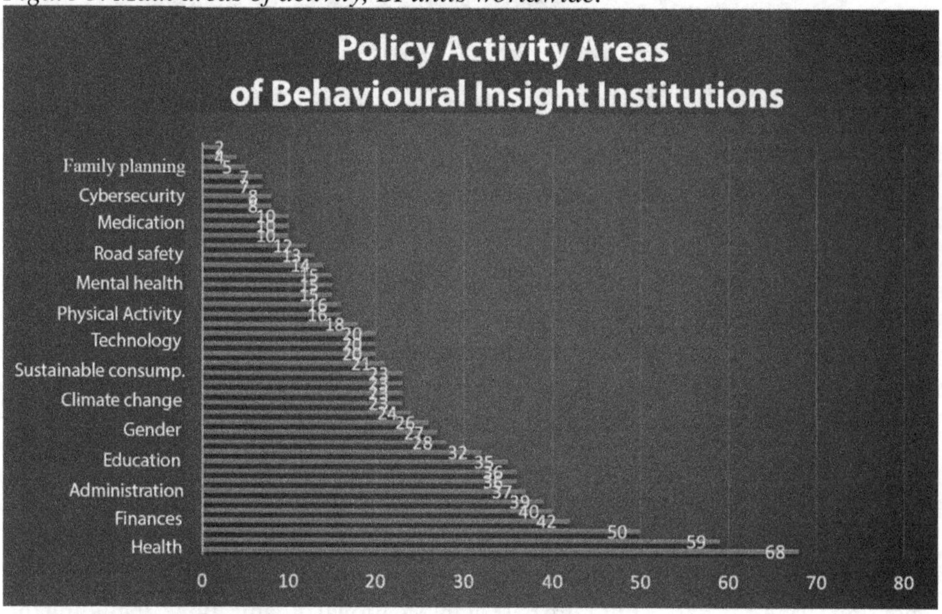

Source: Observatory of Public Service Innovation (OPSI) of the Organisation for Economic Co-operation and Development (OECD)
Produced by: the authors.

The initial observation reveals a preponderance of actions pertaining to health (68 institutions), followed by environment (59), communication (50), finance (42), development (40), and economy (39). In seventh place is the improvement of administration, with 37 institutions dedicated to this pursuit. Following closely behind is work and employment, with 36 institutions similarly engaged in this field. Social welfare and education both occupy tenth place, with 35 institutions each dedicated to the study and creation of policies through behavioural intervention units. For a comprehensive overview of the data, please refer to figure 5. These data demonstrate the significance of developing nudges to foster healthy behaviours in the population, thereby enhancing their well-being (health, ranked 1), followed by the importance of engaging in behavioural changes to improve environmental impact (ranked 2), while relying on communication as a transformative instrument to promote these behavioural changes (ranked 3). In this regard, it is noteworthy to mention initiatives such as those undertaken by the FAO or the International Bank to promote Communication for Development (C4D) (World Congress on Communication for Development, 2007). These initiatives are designed to facilitate communicative actions that seek to engender behavioural change in society, with the ultimate objective of fostering regional development.

Main Areas by Typology of Institution

Subsequently, in consideration of the data provided by the OPSI observatory, we proceed to delineate the following principal domains of activity, classified according to the typology of the institution (for details, please refer to the annex). Consequently, within the institutions comprising the central government, the most significant areas of focus are studies and policies dedicated to environmental interventions (ranked first, 15 institutions), health (ranked second, 14 institutions) and economics (ranked third, 12 institutions). Therefore, it can be concluded that the majority of central governments are concerned with implementing policies that encourage behavioural change with regard to issues that may potentially have an adverse impact on the environment. Amongst these initiatives, the Sustainable Construction team, operating on behalf of the Netherlands Enterprise Agency (see https://english.rvo.nl/), is worthy of particular mention.

A review of the institutions that form part of central or regional governments reveals that education is the primary focus, with eight institutions dedicated to this sector. Health and the environment are also prominent areas of focus, with seven institutions each. Within this branch of government that has more direct contact with citizens, there has been a concern for the development of policies or behavioural studies that lead to improvements in education. Examples of such initiatives include the Public Innovation Laboratory of the Sao Paulo City Council (https://lab11.prefeitura.sp.gov.br/) and its Behavioural Sciences program, whose objective is to increase the efficiency of municipal public services.

In terms of the areas studied by the institutions promoted by academia, the most prominent are health (13 institutions), environment (9 institutions) and social welfare (9 institutions). In this context, it is crucial to acknowledge the significance of academic studies that integrate behavioural sciences with artificial intelligence, with the aim of enhancing preventive diagnoses and fostering attitudinal changes that contribute to an improvement in individual health. In this regard, the Brown University Policy Lab (USA) (see https://thepolicylab.brown.edu/projects/liheap)

is a notable example, with its research on optimising the experience of taking a coronavirus test.

Similarly, the private sector's promoted behavioural units prioritize health-related actions (18 units), followed by environmental actions (second position, 17 units) and communication actions (third position, 16 units). This section will examine the work of the Behavioural Insights Team (BIT) in New York (see https://www.bi.team/) and its initiatives for the development of behavioural interventions in social networks to foster confidence in vaccines in Africa. It will also consider the collaboration of the Danish iNudgeYou institute (see https://inudgeyou.com) with the Danish government to disseminate messages with the objective of increasing the optimism of the population in the context of the coronavirus crisis.

In regard to the promotion of institutions by international organisations, it is observed that the primary objective is the advancement of development amongst populations (10 institutions), followed by health (2nd place, 7 institutions) and communication (3rd place, 7 institutions). In this regard, it is noteworthy to mention UNICEF's Communications for Development (C4D) initiative (see https://www.unicef.org/innocenti/reports/view-all), which provides policy recommendations to inform the formulation of policies and the development of neurotechnology for children. An additional example is the IOM X campaign, which was initiated by the International Organization for Migration with the objective of establishing a participatory communication campaign that would facilitate behavioural change and contribute to the prevention of exploitation and trafficking (see https://iomx.iom.int/about).

In light of the aforementioned, it becomes evident that at the governmental level—that is to say, when considering the various levels of administration collectively—the importance of addressing issues that have their roots in matters pertaining to health or the environment cannot be overstated. Nevertheless, it is businesses and supranational organisations that are prioritising the implementation of these practices in their communication strategies, with the objective of addressing a range of communication and social issues.

Discussion and Agenda for Further Research

As demonstrated throughout this article, we are witnessing a period of reconversion in the social and political landscapes that shape the development of liberal democracies. Subsequently, as the theoretical acceptance of the non-existence of pure individual rationality in decision-making has been established, public administrations are exploring novel methods to influence citizen behaviour in accordance with the promotion of socially desirable behaviours. In this novel context, behavioural governance and the concomitant development of novel communication strategies represent a crucial element.

Two decades after the emergence of the concept of libertarian paternalism (Sunstein and Thaler, 2003), this article aims to present an updated picture of behavioural governance in the world. It identifies leading countries and regions, the configuration of behavioural units and areas of research. Twenty years later, our bibliometric approach has demonstrated that the concept continues to garner academic interest and that artificial intelligence is influencing it, proposing enhancements and raising new ethical considerations. Consequently, if there were any reservations about the long-term impact of nudges (Gigenzer, 2015; Loewenstein et al., 2015), it can be asserted that these units have withstood the test of time.

In terms of leading countries and regions, the study has identified Anglo-Saxon countries and the European continent as the main areas of development. Consequently, following the appointment of Sunstein and Thaler by the British and American governments at their inception, it is evident that their influence has left an indelible mark on these countries, continuing to drive forward development. As the authors observed at the outset, the capacity of libertarian paternalism and its implementation throughout the world led them to conceptualise this technique as a 'third way' (Thaler and Sunstein, 2008: 252). Two decades later, governments of varying political persuasions continue to adopt these techniques, though it is notable that they are predominantly observed in liberal democracies (see Figure 2). With regard to the evolution of these behavioural units, those that receive state funding and are introduced within the government administration itself continue to predominate. However, they have also grown notably towards other lower levels of the administration (see Figure 4). Consequently, after two decades, their evolution has shifted from guiding major policies to policies closer to the citizen, such as local government.

Another objective of this article is to highlight the themes that are explored. In the beginning, as Sunstein (2008) observed, these nudges were created with the intention of enhancing the financial decision-making abilities of individuals. Twenty years later, social issues have also appeared to evolve, and there is now a predominant interest in generating behavioural change on issues related to health, the environment and communication. Furthermore, this illustrates the emergence of novel approaches to the shaping of democratic spaces, which are influenced by nudges and must be considered in their development. As previously discussed in the theoretical framework, the 'prosocial' nudges, which sought to promote collective well-being through individual behavioural change (Hansen and Jespersen, 2013), were the most controversial in terms of their effectiveness. Of particular note are the nudges designed to effect change in environmental behaviour. Consequently, this represents a new challenge for nudges, which must demonstrate their effectiveness in this regard. Similarly, as previously indicated, the profound cognitive biases intensified by the novel media configuration (see Table 1) also present a novel challenge for nudges, which, in view of the paramount importance of communication in their themes, they are prepared to confront (see Figure 5).

In conclusion, the evidence derived from these data suggests that behavioural governance will continue to evolve in the coming years. In light of these developments, it is imperative that the scientific community unite to advocate for the advancement of these technologies in a manner that prioritises the enhancement of citizen well-being and the establishment of robust regulatory frameworks to prevent their misuse and abuse. This perspective has been echoed by numerous scholars, including Leonard (2008), Burr, Cristianini and Ladyman (2018), and Yeung (2016). In light of the aforementioned considerations, and with a view to facilitating the alleviation of the cognitive biases that are intensified by the prevailing media environment, we put forward the following lines of enquiry.

Table 2. Proposed new lines of research: Nudging against cognitive biases amplified by the current media environment.

Cognitive bias	Issues	Lines of research
Confirmation bias, false consensus, Dunning-kruger.	Disinformation, polarisation, reduced deliberative capacity.	-What forms of verification can be devised to prompt individuals to reject false or unverified information? -What strategies might be employed to encourage citizens to engage with information that challenges their existing beliefs? -What communication strategies based on gamification could be developed to encourage the deliberative capacity of the voter?
Information overload	Political demobilisation, successful counter-systemic views	-What forms of behavioural intervention might be employed to assist the citizen in enhancing their capacity to select information? -What kind of AI-promoted care units can be developed to provide individuals with clear and concise summaries of information? -What strategies might these tools adopt in order to ensure that citizens do not abandon their consumption?
Limited attention, cascade of information	Sensationalism, spread of fakenews, volatile opinions, widening of the digital divide.	-What behavioural interventions might be employed to assist citizens in developing greater attention spans? -What actions might be taken to enhance the capacity for retention among specific social groups, such as children, who are increasingly displaying limited attention spans? -What strategies might be employed to enhance access to and comprehension of public information for those who are disadvantaged by the digital divide?

Source: produced by the authors.

Theoretical implications

A comprehensive examination of contemporary governance worldwide enables the observation of a novel configuration of democratic systems and their associated political, social, and communicative decision-making environments.

Firstly, it can be argued that the article not only supports the arguments put forth by behavioural scientists, such as Herbert Simon, who proposed the theory of bounded rationality (Simon, 1955), but also demonstrates the emergence of a new communicative landscape in which cognitive biases are further exacerbated, potentially leading to significant challenges for reflection and deliberation in our democracies. It is therefore our contention that this study presents a novel approach to the exercise of power by governments in the 21st century, while simultaneously offering insights into the evolving role of the citizen, who is increasingly unreflective and susceptible to the influence of information and emotional frameworks.

Secondly, we observe the emergence of these ideas in Western democracies, particularly in those of the Anglo-Saxon tradition. As Sunstein and Thaler have noted, they represent a third way between liberalism and socialism (Thaler y Sunstein, 2008: 252). Indeed, the significance of this phenomenon in these countries and its efficacy in addressing social issues resulting from individual actions (health, environment, communication) illustrate the inclination of liberal democracies to intervene in individuals in a measured manner (see Figure5). However, the absence of transparency and normative and ethical oversight, may result in these actions being perceived as genuine instruments of social control within democratic regimes that, on the surface, may appear to be democratic.

In conclusion, as previously indicated throughout this study, the advent of artificial intelligence has the potential to facilitate more nuanced, beneficial, and efficacious interactions with citizens. However, if not properly regulated, it could result in the concentration of more formidable instruments for influence in the hands of governments, leading to an increase in individuals who are less discerning and more susceptible to technical control (Saura et al., 2022).

Practical implications

This study demonstrates the significance of communication in the context of behavioural governance in the contemporary media environment.

First and foremost, as previously outlined, the capacity to exacerbate certain cognitive biases brought about by the new media landscape is a significant concern. Additionally, the importance governments attach to creating new communication strategies to generate behavioural change and address the challenges threatening the sustainability of our democracies is a crucial consideration. In this way, we posit that the evidence presented in this chapter can be useful in the following respects: Firstly, it is evident that the study effectively highlights the primary cognitive biases that are amplified by social media, which contribute to the polarisation and radicalisation of democratic debate. It is our contention that both the data presented and the in-depth readings of Sunstein and Thaler's thesis (Thaler and Sunstein, 2008; Sunstein, 2013; Sunstein, 2014; Sunstein, 2017) should inform the development of state communication policies that simplify messages, encourage individual deliberation and help individuals identify fake news that may affect their reasoning.

Secondly, it is our contention that the study paves the way for the formulation of novel policies inspired by hypernudges, which could prove more efficacious in addressing issues that demand prompt and decisive government action, such as environmental crises and threats to public health and safety (see Figure 5).

Ultimately, we concur with numerous scholars in our optimism regarding the potential of hypernudges to enhance the well-being of citizens and democratic societies. It is our contention that the advent of new technologies has facilitated the realisation of highly personalised communication through the collation of vast quantities of data (Saura et al., 2023), the monitoring of sentiments (Saura et al., 2022), the enhancement of interaction (Barbosa et al., 2022), and the generation of novel opportunities for both, citizens and governments, to cultivate more advantageous relationships (Lacárcel and Huete, 2023). However, we contend that this vision can only be realised through the establishment of robust regulatory frameworks that safeguard individual autonomy and freedom of choice, ensure informed consent, guarantee the right to withdraw consent at any time, protect the privacy of personal data, and provide comprehensive information and transparency regarding these techniques.

CONCLUSION

This study presents a comprehensive framework for understanding the current state of behavioural governance on a global scale. Two decades after the concept's emergence and following the impact of new methodologies that enhance the effectiveness of these techniques in influencing citizen behaviour, this study presents a comprehensive framework for understanding the current state of behavioural governance globally, elucidating both its opportunities and potential risks. Similarly, we highlight the significance of communication and view these nudging techniques as a novel approach to fostering relationships with citizens with the aim of influencing their behaviour on matters detrimental to their own well-being and social welfare. This highlights the significance attributed to the development of projects pertaining to health, the environment and the advancement of communication policies. The prevalence of these units in Europe, North America and Oceania suggests that a novel approach to the exercise of power is emerging in our democracies.

As we have detailed, we are at an academic moment in research where there is both an interest in applying these tactics to political governance and in building on them to generate more effective communication strategies. The advent of this new context necessitates a fresh examination of the concept of democracy. Individuals are no longer regarded as beings endowed with unquestioning rationality; instead, their decisions are contingent upon a multitude of cognitive factors susceptible to modulation and influence from the surrounding environment. In this regard, the advent of a novel media environment has intensified certain cognitive biases inherent to the individual, giving rise to more polarised societies with diminished capacity to retain information and to facilitate deliberative discourse. In this context, behavioural governance emerges in a new landscape. While it offers governments new communicative tactics to address social issues, it also seeks to generate new communication strategies to overcome biases. It seems inevitable that future developments will be marked by the advance of artificial intelligence and its normative and ethical development. This will lead to new research and application scenarios, which will have to promote a necessary balance between the application of these techniques to improve the welfare of citizens and their necessary regulation to protect their autonomy, deliberation and decision-making capacity.

In conclusion, in response to the research questions posed, the following revelations are offered. With regard to the leading region and countries in the implementation of behavioural units (RQ1), Europe accounts for 42% of the units present in the world (see Figure 1). However, the importance of the Anglo-Saxon area is particularly noteworthy in this respect (see Figure 2). With regard to the ranking of countries with the highest number of units in operation, Australia is in first position with 36 units, followed by the United States with 28 units and Great Britain with 25 units (see Figure 3). With regard to the nature of these institutions (see Figure 4), it can be observed that the majority of them are integrated into the federal government (59 units), followed by those that depend on state, provincial or local government (42 units), with those established within the academic sphere representing the third largest group (39 units). This indicates a preference on the part of governments for these units to engage directly in national policymaking. Finally, with regard to their areas of activity (RQ3), the data indicate a predominance of units studying health (69 institutions, first place), followed by the environment (59 units, second place), with communication in third place (50 units) with a cross-cutting role in promoting behavioural changes in various areas, as well as attempting to address cognitive biases present in the new media landscape (see Figure 5).

REFERENCES

Ajzen, I. (1991). The theory of planned behavior. *Organizational Behavior and Human Decision Processes*, 50(2), 179–211. DOI: 10.1016/0749-5978(91)90020-T

Ajzen, I. (2012). The theory of planned behavior. *Handbook of Theories of Social Psychology*: Volume 1, 438-459. DOI: 10.4135/9781446249215.n22

Aoujil, Z., & Hanine, M. (2023). Artificial Intelligence and Behavioral Economcs: A Bibliographic Analysis of Research Field. *Sustainability*, 15(5), 3949. DOI: 10.3390/su15053949

Asch, S. E. (1951). Effects of group pressure upon the modification and distortion of judgments. In Guetzkow, H. (Ed.), *Groups, leadership and men*. Carnegie Press.

Bail, C. A., Argyle, L. P., Brown, T. W., Bumpus, J. P., Chen, H., Hunzaker, M. F., Lee, J., Mann, M., Merhout, F., & Volfovsky, A. (2018). Exposure to opposing views on social media can increase political polarization. *Proceedings of the National Academy of Sciences of the United States of America*, 115(37), 9216–9221. DOI: 10.1073/pnas.1804840115 PMID: 30154168

Banerjee, A. V. (1992). A simple model of herd behavior. *The Quarterly Journal of Economics*, 107(3), 797–817. DOI: 10.2307/2118364

Barak-Corren, N., & Kariv-Teitelbaum, Y. (2021). Behavioral responsive regulation: Bringing together responsive regulation and behavioral public policy. *Regulation & Governance*, 15(S1). Advance online publication. DOI: 10.1111/rego.12429

Barbosa, B., Saura, J. R., & Bennett, D. (2022). How do entrepreneurs perform digital marketing across the customer journey? a review and discussion of the main uses. *The Journal of Technology Transfer*, 49(1), 69–103. DOI: 10.1007/s10961-022-09978-2

Bartmann, M. (2022). The ethics of ai-powered climate nudging—How much ai should we use to save the planet? *Sustainability (Basel)*, 14(9), 5153. DOI: 10.3390/su14095153

Bawden, D., & Robinson, L. (2020). *Information overload: An overview. Oxford Encyclopedia of Political Decision Making*. Oxford University Press., DOI: 10.1093/acrefore/9780190228637.013.956

Behavioral Scientist. (2017). A Conversation with Bill Congdon, Former Member of the White House Social and Behavioral Sciences Team. Retrieved from Behavioral Scientist Behavioural Economics Team of the Australian Government. (2019). BETA Guide to Applying Behavioural Insights. https://behaviouraleconomics.pmc.gov.au/sites/default/files/resources/beta-guide-applying-behavioural-insights-2019.pdf

Behavioural Insights Team. (2014). EAST: Four Simple Ways to Apply Behavioural Insights. https://www.bi.team/publications/east-four-simple-ways-to-apply-behavioural-insights

BehaviourWorks Australia. (2020). INSPIRE: Behavioural Insights for Better Communication. Retrieved from https://www.behaviourworksaustralia.org/courses/inspire-your-communication

Bertrand, M., Mullainathan, S., & Shafir, E. (2006). Behavioral economics and marketing in aid of decision making among the poor. *Journal of Public Policy & Marketing*, 25(1), 8–23. DOI: 10.1509/jppm.25.1.8

Bikhchandani, S., Hirshleifer, D., & Welch, I. (1992). A theory of fads, fashion, custom, and cultural change as informational cascades. *Journal of Political Economy*, 100(5), 992–1026. DOI: 10.1086/261849

Brooks, R., Nguyen, D. A., Bhatti, A., Allender, S., Johnstone, M., Lim, C. P., & Backholer, K. (2022). Use of artificial intelligence to enable dark nudges by transnational food and beverage companies: Analysis of company documents. *Public Health Nutrition*, 25(5), 1291–1299. DOI: 10.1017/S1368980022000490 PMID: 35232511

Burr, C., Cristianini, N., & Ladyman, J. (2018). An analysis of the interaction between intelligent software systems and human autonomy. *Ethics and Information Technology*, 20(3), 207–221.

Cabinet Office Behavioural Insights Team. (2011). *Annual Update 2010-11*. Retrieved from https://www.bi.team/publications/annual-update-2010-11

Camerer, C. F. (2014). Behavioral economics. *Current Biology*, 24(18), R867–R871. DOI: 10.1016/j.cub.2014.07.040 PMID: 25247364

Centers for Disease Control and Prevention. (2011). The Health Communicator's Social Media Toolkit. https://www.cdc.gov/socialmedia/tools/guidelines/pdf/socialmediatoolkit_bm.pdf

Damasio, A. R. (1994). *Descartes' Error: Emotion, Reason, and the Human Brain*. Putnam Publishing.

Daus, Z. (2024). Socializing the political: Rethinking filter bubbles and social media with Hannah Arendt. *Ethics and Information Technology*, 26(2), 20. DOI: 10.1007/s10676-024-09759-5

de Zárate Alcarazo, L. O. (2023). Sesgos de género en la inteligencia artificial. *Revista de Occidente (Madrid, Spain)*, 502(1).

Debasa, F., & Cuello, Z. (2024). Sociedad actual e identidad digital. In *Historia de la sociedad presente: El mundo Y sus desvelos desde/990* (pp. 143–160). Dykinson. DOI: 10.14679/2545

Descartes, R. (1637). Discourse on the Method of Rightly Conducting One's Reason and of Seeking Truth in the Sciences. (I. Maclean, Trans.). Oxford University Press. (Original work published 1637).

Diez-Gracia, A., Sánchez-García, P., and Martín-Román, J. (2023). Polarisation and emotional discourse in the political agenda on Twitter: disintermediation and engagement in electoral campaigns. *Icono* 14, 21(1).

Dunning, D. (2011). The Dunning-Kruger effect: On being ignorant of one's own ignorance. In Olson, J., & Zanna, M. P. (Eds.), Vol. 44, pp. 247–296). Advances in Experimental Social Psychology. Elsevier Academic Press., DOI: 10.1016/B978-0-12-385522-0.00005-6

Eppler, M. J., & Mengis, J. (2004). The concept of information overload: A review of literature from organization science, accounting, marketing, MIS, and related disciplines. *The Information Society*, 20(5), 325–344. DOI: 10.1080/01972240490507974

European Union. (2024). NUDGE: Nudging consumers towards energy efficiency through behavioural science. *Horizon 2020 Project*. Retrieved from https://www.nudgeproject.eu

Festinger, L. (1957). *A Theory of Cognitive Dissonance*. Stanford University Press. DOI: 10.1515/9781503620766

Floridi, L. (2015). *The Onlife Manifesto: Being Human in a Hyperconnected Era*. Springer., DOI: 10.1007/978-3-319-04093-6

Flynn, D. J., Nyhan, B., & Reifler, J. (2017). The nature and origins of misperceptions: Understanding false and unsupported beliefs about politics. *Political Psychology*, 38(S1), 127–150. DOI: 10.1111/pops.12394

Gigerenzer, G. (2015). On the supposed evidence for libertarian paternalism. *Review of Philosophy and Psychology*, 6(3), 361–383. DOI: 10.1007/s13164-015-0248-1 PMID: 26213590

Gilovich, T., Griffin, D., & Kahneman, D. (2002). Heuristics and biases: The psychology of intuitive judgment. Cambridge University Press. ttps://DOI: 10.1017/CBO9780511808098

Gofen, A., Moseley, A., Thomann, E., & Weaver, R. K. (2021). Behavioural governance in the policy process: Introduction to the special issue. *Journal of European Public Policy*, 28(5), 633–657. DOI: 10.1080/13501763.2021.1912153

Government of Canada. (2018). Behavioural Insights Playbook. https://www.canada.ca/en/innovation-hub/services/reports-resources/behavioural-insights-playbook.html

Habermas, J. (1985). The theory of communicative action: Vol. 1. *Reason and the rationalization of society*. Beacon press.

Habermas, J. (1996). Between Facts and Norms: Contributions to a Discourse Theory of Law and Democracy (W. Rehg, Trans.). MIT Press. (Original work published 1992).

Hansen, K. (2020). Cognitive bias in emergency medicine. *Emergency Medicine*, 37(3), 567–572. DOI: 10.1016/j.emermed.2020.09.001 PMID: 32902161

Hansen, P. G., & Jespersen, A. M. (2013). Nudge and the manipulation of choice. *European Journal of Risk Regulation*, 4(1), 3–28. DOI: 10.1017/S1867299X00002762

Harmon-Jones, E. and Mills, J. (1999). Cognitive dissonance: progress on a pivotal theory in social psychology. DOI: 10.1037/10318-000

Iyengar, S., & Kinder, D. R. (1987). *News that matters: Television and American opinion*. University of Chicago Press., DOI: 10.7208/chicago/9780226388533.001.0001

Johnson, E. J., & Goldstein, D. G. (2003). Do defaults save lives? *Science*, 302(5649), 1338–1339. DOI: 10.1126/science.1091721 PMID: 14631022

Kahneman, D. (2011). *Thinking, Fast and Slow*. Farrar, Straus and Giroux.

Kahneman, D., & Tversky, A. (1979). Prospect Theory: An Analysis of Decision under Risk. *Econometrica*, 47(2), 263–291. DOI: 10.2307/1914185

Khrennikov, A. (2020). Social Laser Model for the Bandwagon Effect: Generation of Coherent Information Waves. *Entropy (Basel, Switzerland)*, 22(5), 559. DOI: 10.3390/e22050559 PMID: 33286331

Kruger, J., & Dunning, D. (1999). Unskilled and unaware of it: How difficulties in recognizing one's own incompetence lead to inflated self-assessments. *Journal of Personality and Social Psychology*, 77(6), 1121–1134. DOI: 10.1037/0022-3514.77.6.1121 PMID: 10626367

Lacárcel, F. J. S., & Huete, R. (2023). Digital communication strategies used by private companies, entrepreneurs, and public entities to attract long-stay tourists: A review. *The International Entrepreneurship and Management Journal*, 19(2), 691–708. DOI: 10.1007/s11365-023-00843-8

Lafont, J., Saura, J. R., & Ribeiro-Soriano, D. (2023). The role of Cooperatives in Sustainable Development Goals: A discussion about the current resource curse. *Resources Policy*, 83, 103670. DOI: 10.1016/j.resourpol.2023.103670

LeDoux, J. E. (1996). *The Emotional Brain: The Mysterious Underpinnings of Emotional Life*. Simon and Schuster.

Leibenstein, H. (1950). Bandwagon, Snob, and Veblen Effects in the Theory of Consumers' Demand. *The Quarterly Journal of Economics*, 64(2), 183–207. DOI: 10.2307/1882692

Leibniz, G. W. (1714). *Monadology* (Rescher, N., Trans.). University of Pittsburgh Press. (Original work published 1714)

Lelkes, Y., Sood, G., & Iyengar, S. (2017). The hostile audience: The effect of access to broadband internet on partisan affect. *American Journal of Political Science*, 61(1), 5–20. DOI: 10.1111/ajps.12237

Leonard, T. C. (2008). Richard H. Thaler, Cass R. Sunstein, Nudge: Improving Decisions About Health, Wealth, and Happiness. *Constitutional Political Economy*, 19(4), 356–360. DOI: 10.1007/s10602-008-9056-2

Lerman, A. E., & Acland, D. (2018). United in States of Dissatisfaction: Confirmation Bias Across the Partisan Divide. *American Politics Research*, 48(2), 246–275. DOI: 10.1177/1532673X18799274

Leviston, Z., Walker, I., & Morwinski, S. (2012). Your opinion on climate change might not be as common as you think. *Nature Climate Change*, 3(4), 334–337. DOI: 10.1038/nclimate1743

Lewandowsky, S., Ecker, U. K. H., & Cook, J. (2017). Beyond misinformation: Understanding and coping with the "post-truth" era. *Journal of Applied Research in Memory and Cognition*, 6(4), 353–369. DOI: 10.1016/j.jarmac.2017.07.008

Li, T., & Jager, W. (2023). How availability heuristic, confirmation bias and fear may drive societal polarisation: An opinion dynamics simulation of the case of covid-19 vaccination. *Journal of Artificial Societies and Social Simulation*, 26(4), 2. Advance online publication. DOI: 10.18564/jasss.5135

Linnenluecke, M. K., Marrone, M., & Singh, A. K. (2020). Conducting systematic literature reviews and bibliometric analyses. *Australian Journal of Management*, 45(2), 175–194. DOI: 10.1177/0312896219877678

Loewenstein, G., Bryce, C. L., Hagmann, D., & Rajpal, S. (2014). Warning: you are about to be nudged. SSRN *Electronic Journal*. DOI: 10.2139/ssrn.2417383

López, A. C. (2023). La globalización de la censura: Nuevas aplicaciones de gobiernos y redes sociales tras el conflicto en Ucrania. *Revista de el Colegio de San Luis*, 13(24), 1–34. DOI: 10.21696/rcsl132420231552

Lord, C. G., Ross, L., & Lepper, M. R. (1979). Biased assimilation and attitude polarization: The effects of prior theories on subsequently considered evidence. *Journal of Personality and Social Psychology*, 37(11), 2098–2109. DOI: 10.1037/0022-3514.37.11.2098

Majid, G. M., Tussyadiah, I., & Kim, Y. R. (2024). Exploring the potential of chatbots in extending tourists' sustainable travel practices. *Journal of Travel Research*, 00472875241247316. Advance online publication. DOI: 10.1177/00472875241247316

Mark, G., Gudith, D., & Klocke, U. (2008). The cost of interrupted work: More speed and stress. *Proceedings of the SIGCHI Conference on Human Factors in Computing Systems*, 107-110. DOI: 10.1145/1357054.1357072

Martignon, L., & Gaissmaier, W. (2011). Heuristic decision making. *Annual Review of Psychology*, 62(1), 451–482. DOI: 10.1146/annurev-psych-120709-145346 PMID: 21126183

Mazor, M., & Fleming, S. M. (2021). The dunning-kruger effect revisited. *Nature Human Behaviour*, 5(6), 677–678. DOI: 10.1038/s41562-021-01101-z PMID: 33833426

Mills, S. (2022). Finding the 'nudge' in hypernudge. *Technology in Society*, 71, 102117. DOI: 10.1016/j.techsoc.2022.102117

Morton, R. B., Muller, S., Page, L., & Torgler, B. (2015). Exit polls, turnout, and bandwagon voting: Evidence from a natural experiment. *European Economic Review*, 77, 65–81. DOI: 10.1016/j.euroecorev.2015.03.012

Mullainathan, S., & Thaler, R. H. (2001). Behavioral Economics. In Smelser, N. J., & Baltes, P. B. (Eds.), *International Encyclopedia of the Social and Behavioral Sciences* (pp. 1094–1100). Elsevier., DOI: 10.1016/B0-08-043076-7/02247-6

Nickerson, R. S. (1998). Confirmation bias: A ubiquitous phenomenon in many guises. *Review of General Psychology*, 2(2), 175–220. DOI: 10.1037/1089-2680.2.2.175

OECD. (2020). *Tools and Ethics for Applied Behavioural Insights: The BASIC Toolkit*. Retrieved from OECD.

Organisation for Economic Co-operation and Development. (2017). Behavioural Insights and Public Policy: Lessons from Around the World. https://www.oecd.org/en/publications/behavioural-insights-and-public-policy_9789264270480-en.html

Pariser, E. (2011). *The filter bubble: How the new personalized web is changing what we read and how we think*. Penguin Press.

Powell, A. C. (2020). Impact of the artificial nudge. *Academic Radiology*, 27(1), 143–146. DOI: 10.1016/j.acra.2019.09.010 PMID: 31818383

Pykett, J. (2016). *Brain Culture: Shaping Policy Through Neuroscience (English Edition)* (1.ª ed.). Policy Press.

Ross, L., Greene, D., & House, P. (1977). The false consensus effect: An egocentric bias in social perception and attribution processes. *Journal of Experimental Social Psychology*, 13(3), 279–301. DOI: 10.1016/0022-1031(77)90049-X

Sadeghian, A. H. and Otarkhani, A. (2023). Data-driven digital nudging: a systematic literature review and future agenda. Behaviour andAmp; *Information Technology*, 1-29. DOI: 10.1080/0144929X.2023.2286535

Saura, J. R. (2024). Algorithms in Digital Marketing: Does Smart Personalization Promote a Privacy Paradox? *FIIB Business Review*, 13(5), 499–502. DOI: 10.1177/23197145241276898

Saura, J. R., & Debasa, F. (Eds.). (2022). *Handbook of research on artificial intelligence in government practices and processes*. IGI Global., DOI: 10.4018/978-1-7998-9609-8

Saura, J. R., Palacios-Marqués, D., & Soriano, D. R. (2021). Digital marketing in smes via data-driven strategies: Reviewing the current state of research. *Journal of Small Business Management*, 61(3), 1278–1313. DOI: 10.1080/00472778.2021.1955127

Saura, J. R., Skare, M., & Riberio-Navarrete, S. (2022). How Does Technology Enable Competitive Advantage? Reviewing State of the Art and Outlining Future Directions. *Journal of Competitiveness*, 14(4), 172–188. DOI: 10.7441/joc.2022.04.10

Saura, J. R., Škare, V., & Dosen, D. O. (2024). Is AI-based digital marketing ethical? Assessing a new data privacy paradox. *Journal of Innovation & Knowledge*, 9(4), 100597. DOI: 10.1016/j.jik.2024.100597

Saura, J. R., Soriano, D. R., & Palacios-Marqués, D. (2022). Assessing behavioral data science privacy issues in government artificial intelligence deployment. *Government Information Quarterly*, 39(4), 101679. DOI: 10.1016/j.giq.2022.101679

Saura, J. R., Soriano, D. R., & Saldaña, P. Z. (2022). Exploring the challenges of remote work on twitter users' sentiments: From digital technology development to a post-pandemic era. *Journal of Business Research*, 142, 242–254. DOI: 10.1016/j.jbusres.2021.12.052

Schmauder, C., Karpus, J., Moll, M., Bahrami, B., & Deroy, O. (2023). Algorithmic nudging: The need for an interdisciplinary oversight. *Topoi*, 42(3), 799–807. DOI: 10.1007/s11245-023-09907-4

Schmidt, R., & Stenger, K. (2021). Behavioral brittleness: The case for strategic behavioral public policy. *Behavioural Public Policy*, 8(2), 212–237. DOI: 10.1017/bpp.2021.16

Schmitt-Beck, R. (1996). Mass media, the electorate, and the bandwagon: A study of communication effects on vote choice in Germany. *International Journal of Public Opinion Research*, 8(3), 266–291. DOI: 10.1093/ijpor/8.3.266

Scientist. (2017). A Conversation with Bill Congdon, Former Member of the White House Social and Behavioral Sciences Team. Retrieved from Behavioral Scientist

Simon, H. A. (1947). *Administrative Behavior: A Study of Decision-Making Processes in Administrative Organizations*. Macmillan.

Simon, H. A. (1955). A Behavioral Model of Rational Choice. *The Quarterly Journal of Economics*, 69(1), 99–118. DOI: 10.2307/1884852

Slovic, P. (1987). Perception of risk. *Science*, 236(4799), 280–285. DOI: 10.1126/science.3563507 PMID: 3563507

Social and Behavioral Sciences Team. (2015). *Social and Behavioral Sciences Team annual report 2015*. The White House. Retrieved from https://sbst.gov/download/2015%20SBST%20Annual%20Report.pdfBehavioral

Somit, A., & Peterson, S. A. (2012). Biopolicy: A Critical Linkage. *Biopolicy: The Life. Science & Public Policy*, 10, 3–11. DOI: 10.1108/S2042-9940(2012)0000010002

Spinoza, B. (1670). *Theological-Political Treatise* (Shirley, S., Trans.). Hackett Publishing. (Original work published 1670)

Sunstein, C. R. (2002). *Risk and reason: Safety, law, and the environment*. Cambridge University Press.

Sunstein, C. R. (2006). The availability heuristic, intuitive cost-benefit analysis, and climate change. *Climatic Change*, 77(1-2), 195–210. DOI: 10.1007/s10584-006-9073-y

Sunstein, C. R. (2013). *Simpler: The future of government.* Simon and Schuster.

Sunstein, C. R. (2014). *Why Nudge?: The Politics of Libertarian Paternalism.* Yale University Press., DOI: 10.12987/yale/9780300197860.001.0001

Sunstein, C. R. (2016). The ethics of influence. DOI: 10.1017/CBO9781316493021

Sunstein, C. R. (2017). *Behavioral insights and public policy: Lessons from around the world.* Cambridge University Press.

Sunstein, C. R., and Thaler, R. H. (2003). Libertarian Paternalism Is Not an Oxymoron.

Sunstein, C. R., & Thaler, R. H. (2003, 3). Libertarian Paternalism Is Not an Oxymoron. *The University of Chicago Law Review. University of Chicago. Law School*, 70(4), 1159–1202. DOI: 10.2307/1600573

Sunstein, C. R. (2001). *Echo chambers: Bush v. Gore, impeachment, and beyond.* Princeton University Press.

Thaler, R. H. (2015). *Misbehaving: The Making of Behavioral Economics.* W. W. Norton and Company.

Thaler, R. H., & Sunstein, C. R. (2008). *Nudge: Improving decisions about health, wealth, and happiness.* Yale University Press.

Todorov, A., Mandisodza, A. N., Goren, A., & Hall, C. C. (2005). Inferences of competence from faces predict election outcomes. *Science*, 308(5728), 1623–1626. DOI: 10.1126/science.1110589 PMID: 15947187

Tversky, A., & Kahneman, D. (1973). Availability: A heuristic for judging frequency and probability. *Cognitive Psychology*, 5(2), 207–232. DOI: 10.1016/0010-0285(73)90033-9

Tversky, A., & Kahneman, D. (1974). Judgment under uncertainty: Heuristics and biases. *Science*, 185(4157), 1124–1131. DOI: 10.1126/science.185.4157.1124 PMID: 17835457

Tversky, A., & Kahneman, D. (1974). Judgment under Uncertainty: Heuristics and Biases. *Science*, 185(4157), 1124–1131. DOI: 10.1126/science.185.4157.1124 PMID: 17835457

UNICEF. (2005). Strategic Communication for Behaviour and Social Change in South Asia. https://www.unicef.org/cbsc/files/Strategic_Communication_for_Behaviour_and_Social_Change.pdf

Vandello, J. A., Goldschmied, N. P., & Richards, D. A. (2007). The appeal of the underdog. *Personality and Social Psychology Bulletin*, 33(12), 1603–1616. DOI: 10.1177/0146167207307488 PMID: 18000097

Villagrasa, Ó. C., & Solé, J. P. (2022). Nudging e inteligencia artificial contra la corrupción en el sector público: Posibilidades y riesgos. *Revista Digital De Derecho Administrativo*, (28), 225–258. DOI: 10.18601/21452946.n28.08

Vosoughi, S., Roy, D., & Aral, S. (2018). The spread of true and false news online. *Science*, 359(6380), 1146–1151. DOI: 10.1126/science.aap9559 PMID: 29590045

Wason, P. C. (1960). On the failure to eliminate hypotheses in a conceptual task. *The Quarterly Journal of Experimental Psychology*, 12(3), 129–140. DOI: 10.1080/17470216008416717

Weinmann, M., Schneider, C., & Brocke, J. (2016). Digital nudging. Business and Amp. *Business & Information Systems Engineering*, 58(6), 433–436. DOI: 10.1007/s12599-016-0453-1

Wilkinson, T. M. (2013). Nudging and Manipulation. *Political Studies*, 61(2), 341–355. DOI: 10.1111/j.1467-9248.2012.00974.x

World Economic Forum. (2021). How nudging can boost COVID-19 vaccinations. Retrieved from https://www.weforum.org/agenda/2021/08/nudging-covid-19-vaccination/

World Health Organization. (2017). Communicating Risk in Public Health Emergencies: A WHO Guideline for Emergency Risk Communication (ERC) Policy and Practice. https://www.who.int/publications/i/item/9789241550208

Yeung, K. (2016). 'hypernudge': Big data as a mode of regulation by design. Information, Communication andAmp. *Information Communication and Society*, 20(1), 118–136. DOI: 10.1080/1369118X.2016.1186713

York, C. (2013). Overloaded by the news: Effects of news exposure and enjoyment on reporting information overload. *Communication Research Reports*, 30(4), 282–292. DOI: 10.1080/08824096.2013.836628

Yuan, B. Z., & Sun, J. (2020). Bibliometric analysis of research on the maize based on top papers during 2009-2019. *COLLNET Journal of Scientometrics and Information Management*, 14(1), 75–92. DOI: 10.1080/09737766.2020.1787110

ENDNOTES

1. https://oecd-opsi.org/about/
2. See reference: https://behaviouraleconomics.pmc.gov.au/, accessed 20th July 2024.
3. See the following reference: https://www.nyc.gov/site/opportunity/portfolio/behavioral-design-team.page, accessed on 20th July 2024

Chapter 5
Leveraging Big Data in SMEs:
Pathways to Effective Application

Aissa Mosbah
https://orcid.org/0000-0003-4092-8789
Dhofar University, Oman

ABSTRACT

Scholars who have studied big data in Small and Medium Enterprises (SMEs) often focus on the technicalities/applicability and factors that encourage or inhibit its use. Therefore, the question of "how could SMEs leverage big data in view of their limited resources as compared to large firms?" remains unanswered. This chapter assesses the realities concerning SMEs adoption of big data and proposes guiding measures to help SMEs overcome the impeding challenges and optimize their use, particularly for better decision making. While SMEs limited adoption of big data is attributed to the limited resources, complexity and/or underestimation of their benefits, the main challenges are often cost, data privacy and security, lack of in-house capabilities, lack of IT skills and analytic expertise, and lack of a supportive culture. We argue that a successful big data system must encompass key budgets, IT infrastructure, data architecture, management/governance, security/privacy, data analytics and skilled workforce. Measures of big data's effective application and implications are discussed.

DOI: 10.4018/979-8-3693-6945-6.ch005

INTRODUCTION

Advances in technologies and processes, such as mobile broadband connections, cloud computing, and digitalization have enabled SMEs to generate enormous volumes of data, known as "Big Data". Big data, one of the key features of Industry 4.0, is changing the way organizations think and strategize their operations and activities (World Economic Forum, 2023). Big data are applicable to nearly all business functions, allowing managers to use data for better decision-making and exploit new business opportunities (Wang & Wang, 2020; Mutasher et al., 2022). Their analysis generates accurate insights that help managers take informed decisions. With reference to investments, the analyzed data improve forecasts, lower equity uncertainty, and decrease firm's cost of capital (Begenau et al., 2018).

SMEs are important economic agents and are expected to play a fundamental role in growing economies by creating jobs and boosting innovation. They represent over 60% of business stock in almost every economy. This rate is much higher in some countries. For example, they represent 99% of all companies in (U (European Commission, 2014; 2020). The OECD (2023) report on financing, data and growth of SMEs acknowledges that between 2015 and 2017 these firms contributed 47% to 69% of all new jobs generated by non-micro SMEs.

Although much has been written on the topic of big data in the business context, the extent to which Small and Medium Enterprises (SMEs) benefit from it and how they use it is not well documented. Indeed, although SMEs are increasingly integrating digital marketing strategies with data sciences (Saura et al., 2023), many researchers warn that the level at which SMEs embrace big data is not satisfactory, and these firms run the risk of being left behind on this matter (Coleman et al., 2016). Willetts et al. (2020) note that SMEs have made a good move towards some data related technologies such as cloud computing and e-commerce SMEs but are slowly adopting analytical technologies required by big data and business Intelligence. The OECD (2022, p: 135) report quotes that *"Yet SMEs are less aware of the potential and need for them to implement better data governance."* Nonetheless, for firms that have not yet turned to big data, this could have often occurred because they lack the necessary resources particularly undercapitalization (Wang and Wang, 2020), the implementation process is time-consuming or expensive (Adadi, 2021) and complex as it requires specialist infrastructure and skillsets (Willets et al., 2020). Sometimes this is because managers underestimate the real benefits of their analytics; they do not know where to start, they are busy with day-to-day operations.

Scholars and researchers who have dealt with the issue of big data in SMEs have focused on: the technicalities/applicability (Rising et al., 2014), benefits, challenges and barriers (see. e.g. Coleman et al., 2016; Iqbal et al., 2018; Wellettis et al., 2020; OECD, 2022), or factors encouraging or inhibiting its use (see. e.g. Wessels and

Jokonya, 2022; Mosbah et al., 2023). Many researchers have assessed these factors based on the TOE model (Technological, Organizational and Environmental factors), focusing on readiness and intention for use or adoption (see. Tien et al., 2020; Wessels and Jokonya, 2022; Baig et al., 2023; Maroufkhani et al., 2023) and raising awareness of the utmost importance of data use readiness in supporting competitiveness and triggering growth for SMEs. Although the TOE model has been particularly valuable for assessing biga data feasibility and planning and offers insights into strategic decision-making in organizational settings, it sometimes lacks specificity for certain industries and fails to quantify some organizational and environmental factors with accuracy. Moreover, numerous studies -discussed along with this study- have highlighted the poor and improper application of big data in the context of SMEs and urged managers to initiate approaches to streamline its use and optimize its impact (see. Eg. Adadi, 2021; OECD, 2022; World Economic Forum, 2023).

The current study emerges to fill these gaps. It poses two main questions: (i) to what extent do SMEs use big data? And (ii) how can they use it effectively? By answering these questions, the study draws a picture on the realities of big data applications within SMEs. This implies assessing the requirement of having a big data system, as well as the challenges hindering its proper use. Considering SMEs' limited resources, the study proposes measures to overcome these challenges for better and optimized use of big data.

Therefore, the significance of this paper will not just be captured in its attempt to showcase the big data within SMEs or on stressing out the factors that impede its proper use, but also through the set of measures it proposes, which are expected to add practical contribution to managers, in the first place, as well as policy makers. These measures draw the pathways to effective application of big data. The remainder of the chapter encompasses sections that compare SMEs to large firms, and discusses the importance of big data for businesses, use and requirements of big data within small firms as well as challenges of big data in SMEs with reference to a case study on the healthcare industry. The last section proposes measures for effective application of big data.

The Resource-Based View (RBV) and SMEs

The Resource-Based View (RBV), a theory developed in the context of strategic management, stresses the role of internal resources in procuring competitive advantage and competitiveness. It suggests that a firm's ability to surpass competitors is contingent upon the possession and protection of resources that must be valuable, rare, inimitable, and non-substitutable (VRIN). Resources are classified into tangible (e.g., employees, equipment, capitals) or intangible (e.g., organizational culture, reputation, learning, and knowledge).

The SMEs category encompasses three main groups; micro enterprises, small enterprises and medium enterprises, and they are often defined based on two main criteria; number of employees and annual turnover. Among the three classifications, however, micro enterprises account for the large majority (Gherhes et al., 2016). They represent small shops and outlets that are seen everywhere across streets, malls and markets. For instance, in the European Union, SMEs are defined as having less than 250 employees and either an annual turnover not above €50 million or a balance sheet total of 43 million or less. Large firms, on the other hand, are firms that exceed the thresholds (European Commission, 2020).

Numerous characteristics distinguish SMEs from large firms, including size, resource capacity, organizational structure, growth propensities, and market impact, and the orientation for innovation. SMEs are known for their overrepresentation in the overall business stock, job provision, remarkable contribution to regional development, lack or shortage of resources, lower competitiveness and sustainability prospects, higher flexibility, localized focus, quicker decision-making and swift adaptation to market changes (Huang, 2009; Spithoven, 2013; Mosbah and Debili, 2014; Rauwerda and Graaf, 2021; Arsawan et al., 2022; Lopez-Torres, 2023; González-Padilla, 2024). On the other hand, large firms tend to have greater financial resources, market access, international expansion, economies of scale, strategic alliances and perhaps some political and institutional influence. They typically navigate mass customization strategies and invest heavily in research and development (R&D) activities.

Within smaller-sized firms, management functions and the decision-making processes lay often in the hands of a few leaders/entrepreneurs. This is supported by simpler organizational structures, which allow for more responsive decision-making procedures but undermine the ability of rapid scaling up. Contrarily, large firms enjoy much better resources with access to capital, technological capacity and human/intellectual resources, which grant them the advantage of operating at a larger scale and often dominate market share (Ghosh, 2004; Gherhes et al., 2016). Furthermore, SMS' adoption of digital platforms, as a source of data, is motivated by their necessity to establish a flexible and fluid network of partners whereas large firms are propelled by strategic benefits and low complexity and adoption costs (Marzi et al., 2023).

Another important difference lies in the orientation and propensities for innovation. SMEs are more responsive and innovative, often targeting niche markets or unique offerings given their relatively smaller scale and lower bureaucratic restraints. It has been noticed that provision of flexitime and flexi-leave in SMEs supports innovation because they provide the mental space and diversity required for creating, sharing and exploiting knowledge (Kotey, 2023). In contrast, large firms notably focus on R&Ds spendings to drive incremental innovation and benefit from economies of scale. Also, SMEs tend to differ from large firms for the purpose of big data usage. For instance, it has been recently advocated that big data analytics help large firms for value adding (decreasing costs and improving efficiency via process innovation) but it benefits SMEs for sales (Saura et al., 2023; Conti et al., 2024).

Thus, while these variations in organizational characteristics, resources, socio-economic impact, and innovation approaches underscore dissimilar strategies and growth abilities between SMEs and large firms, a proper use of big data by SMEs carries promising potential to overcome their limited resources and enhance competitiveness.

Importance of big data for businesses

According to IBM, the global data leader, the concept of big data refers to any type or size of data that is beyond the ability of traditional relational databases to capture, manage, and process. Big data are obtained from different sources and have three main forms: unstructured, semi-structured, and structured data. Data size varies from terabytes to zettabytes. Besides, the "Big data analytics" is the usage of cutting-edge analytic techniques to derive insights from these data. Big data are characterized by five Vs: Volume, Variety, Velocity (often including real-time data that are generated and updated at a fast pace), Veracity (accuracy and trustworthiness of different data sets must be assessed upfront), and Value (firms must realize the value and benefits of big data). Figure 1, proposed by Coleman et al. (2016), proposes seven components of a big data system (infrastructure). Starting with an appropriate infrastructure system is crucial for SMEs to reinforce their competitiveness in the marketplace (Rising et al., 2014).

Figure 1. Infrastructure of a big data system

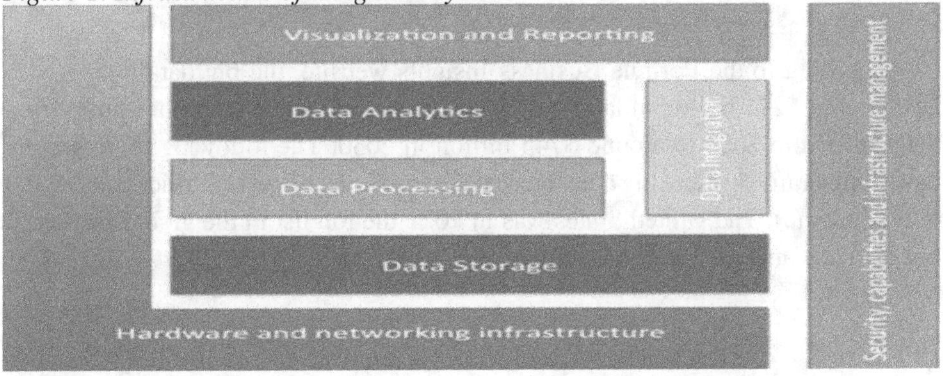

Source: *Coleman et al. (2016)*

The **sources** of big data are no longer limited to traditional data related to employees, customers, suppliers, financial transactions and so on, but are becoming more complex. Social media platforms, mobile devices, Internet of Things (IoT), and artificial intelligence (AI) allow firm to generate extensive and heterogeneous data. One angle through which a the uniqueness big data environments is captured is through their support for unstructured and semi-structured data. Unstructured data contains texts such as survey responses, documents, social media posts, emails, and/or call transcripts, as well as video, audio, image files. Semi-structured data, on the other hand, comprise activity logs from websites, mobile applications, networks, servers along data from industrial devices, and IoT devices. Meanwhile, the infrastructure of big data encompasses many technologies and tools, such as storage repositories, processing engines, NSQL databases, SQL query programs, data lake and warehouse platforms, commercial platforms, and managed services (Stedman, 2022). Managing the big data system require various skills. Figure 2 lists the big data skills that firms must have by selecting the right talents who are capable of managing the big data system effectively.

Figure 2. Big data skills

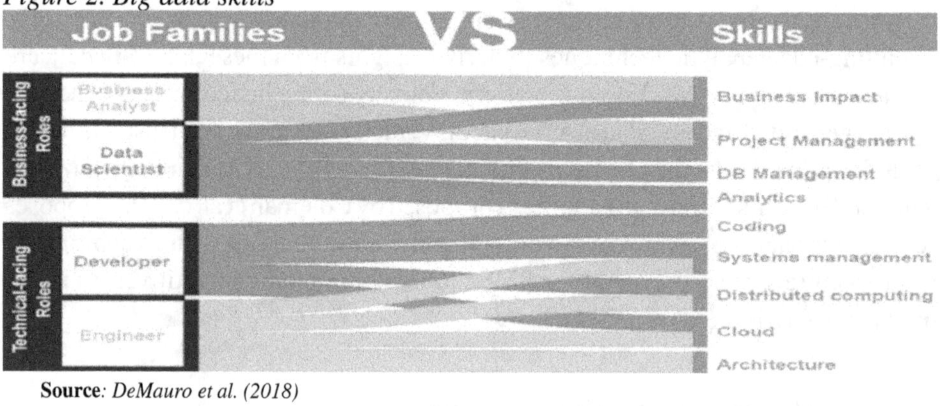

Source: *DeMauro et al. (2018)*

According to the Fortune Business Insights website, the big data market size has reached $271 billion in last year (2022) and is projected to further jump from $307 billion in 2023 to around $745 billion in 2030. The following three sectors have comparatively more big data firms: telecommunications, IT services, and R&D (CBS website). The United States was in 2021 the top list in the global market of big data and analytics with an estimated 51% market share.

Figure 3. Global market share of big data and business analytics in 2021

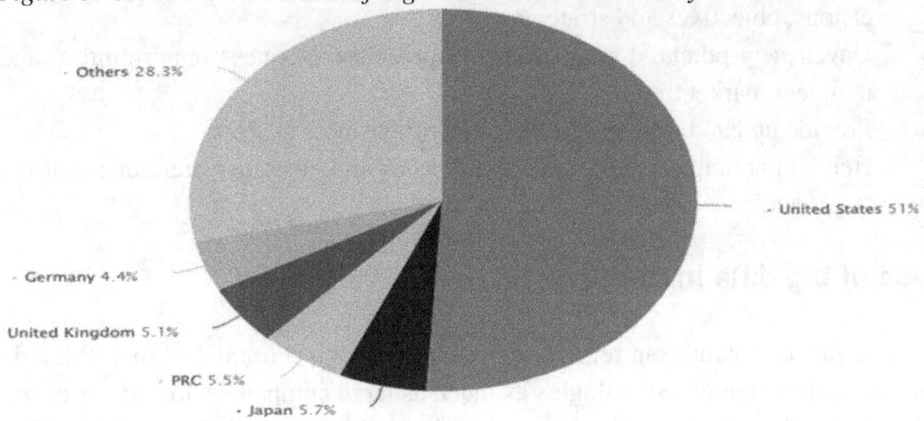

Source: *Statista website*

The Enterprise Strategy Group (ESG), a pioneer IT, research, and strategy corporation, and the division of TechTarget, Inc., conducted a study in 2022 on organizational technology spending based on a survey of 706 senior IT leaders across North America, Western Europe, and Asia Pacific. The study found that the boom in technology spending continues as businesses invest growingly in artificial intelligence, cybersecurity, and clouds. In specific, 62% of firms plan to increase spending next year (2022) relative to 2021, 69% expect to increase spending on cybersecurity, and 65% plan to raise spending on cloud infrastructure (ESG, 2022)

Small businesses can use data analytics to perform several types of analysis such as statistical analysis, text analysis (data mining), predictive analysis, diagnosis analysis, and prescriptive analysis. Big data has many **benefits** for businesses and carries with it a new culture of decision-making (McAfee and Brynjolfsson, 2012). This includes empowering firms with competitive advantages over rivals provided they are processed and analyzed appropriately (Taylor-Sakyi, 2016), and assisting firm managers in the design of new paths to foster innovation by taking decisions that are driven from data (Pappas et al., 2017).

One of the early empirical studies on the relationship between big data and business performance was conducted by a team from Harvard, MIT, and McKinsey based on interviews with 330 executives from North American companies. The study assessed the impact of data-driven decisions on performance and revealed that although not all companies embraced data-driven decision-making, companies which considered themselves data-driven had better performance as measured through financial and operational objectives (McAfee and Brynjolfsson, 2012).

In fact, big data and analytics have the power to yield the following benefits (Stedman, 2022; Iqbal et al., 2018):

- o Generate actionable evidence that allow managers to design data-driven decisions, objectives and strategies.
- o Unveil new potential cost savings approaches, business opportunities, and incipient market trends.
- o Provide updated information on different business aspects.
- o Helps in anticipating the underlying needs and customer preferences of the target audience.

Use of big data in SMEs

One fact that stands out regarding this question points to the fact that SMEs do not take advantage of technologies as much as large companies do and are generally slow in the adoption of business-related technologies, including big data. This could be explained by the ability of large firms to have their own internally built or externally acquired data teams or form strong alliances with data-specialized firms. SMEs seem not able engage in this kind of alliance or do not wish to do so, and therefore, risk being left behind (Coleman et al., 2016) if they cannot convey the current technological changes and trends of big data, e-commerce, and artificial intelligence. In support of this trend, there is an argument that SMEs are still trying to understand the essential conditions needed to enhance their performance using big data (Ghasemaghaei, 2018).

As a matter of fact, available statistics land support to this assumption. Figure 2 indicates that firm size is important for the application of big data in business. For example, it was found in the European context that big data analysis is applied by 33%, 19%, and 10% of large, medium, and small companies, respectively (Binachini and Michalkova, 2019). In the United States however, the overall comparative picture is not much different but looks more promising regarding the extent to which SMEs perceive big data analytics. A survey of Score Association (Service Corps of Retired Executives) found that 45% of small businesses were using some sort of data analytics, while 51% of respondents considered it important (Weston, 2022). Notably, these rates vary across countries and regions, with lower rates expected in developing countries.

Figure 4. Big data analysis by SMEs in the EU

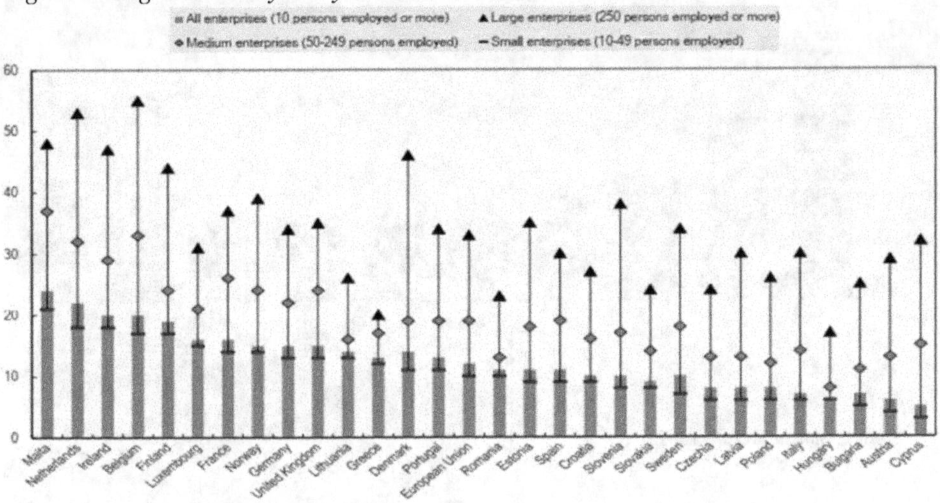

Source: *OECD (Binachini and Michalkova, 2019)*

Data analytics is used for a variety of functions and activities. A CBF study conducted by the Dutch Ministry of Economic Affairs in 2018 for this purpose among SMEs revealed that 26 percent of the participating individuals mentioned that they used big data for marketing/sales tasks, whereas approximately 20 percent of them used it for pre-sales. HR use represented the lowest rate with only six percent. Although these statistics are specific to the Netherlands, they draw a picture that reflect much-similar patterns elsewhere; where it is expected that big data -and particularly its analytics- are expected to dominate in the marketing function. Indeed, the marketing emphasis can be attributed to a few factors. First, owing to the importance of the marketing function in modern business activities. Production, sourcing, distribution and resource allocations all depend on demand estimation which in turn necessitates data from the market. Second, data related to customers and their needs can be collected quickly and cheaply using social media platforms. SMEs do indeed rely heavily on and benefit tremendously from social media platforms (Belás et al., 2021; Rakshit et al., 2021; Kedi et al., 2024). Third, the launching of new products cannot be successful without a thorough understanding of customer taste, which requires the collection and analysis of consumer data prior to production.

Figure 5. Usage of big data among Netherlands SMEs in 2018

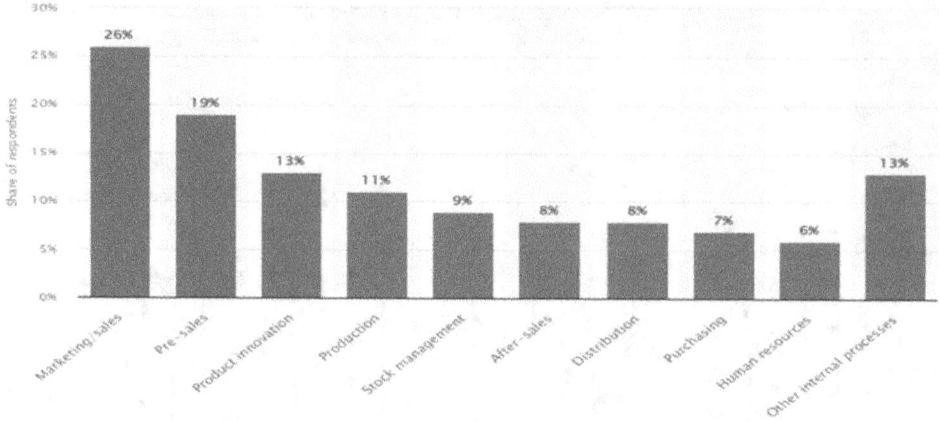

Source: *Statista website (2023)*

Challenges facing the adoption of big data

A review of scholarly publications demonstrates multiple challenges that SMEs face in their endeavor towards the adoption of big data. Table 1 lists the challenges that most appear in the literature with their sources. The primary challenges are: cost, privacy and security, lack of in-house capabilities, lack of IT skills and analytic expertise, and a lack of supportive culture.

Table 1. Challenges of big data use among SMEs

Source	Challenges
Willetts et al. (2020)	Knowledge and skills barriers/ regulatory barriers/ technical barriers/ organizational barriers/ resource barriers.
Karim et al., (2017)	Strategy barriers/ technology barriers/ policy barriers/ organizational barriers/ legal Barriers.
Lee (2017)	Data quality/ data security/ privacy/ investment justification/ data management.
Soroka et al. (2017)	Cost structure/ lack of in-**house capabilities for the selection, installation, configuration and maintenance of complex IT systems.**
Ardagna et al. (2016)	Data quality and diversity/ data security and privacy/ configurability and negotiation/ societal and organizational challenges/ data modeling.
Coleman et al. (2016)	Lack of understanding/ domain specialists' dominance/ cultural impediments and related conservatism/ deficiency of in-house data analytic talents/ talent shortage and costs in the labor market/ dearth of business cases/ shortage and unaffordable external business analytics services/ financial barriers/ non-transparent software market/ poor modeling/ data security and privacy concerns.

continued on following page

Table 1. Continued

Source	Challenges
Zimmerman (2016)	Shortage of IT skills or staff/ data protection and security/ high investment and operating costs/ internet connection speeds.
Sen et al. (2016)	Data storage/ poor processing and analytics potential/ security and privacy issues.
Rising et al. (2014)	(1) Technology-related challenges, (2) Organization-related challenges, (3) Strategy-related challenges.

5. CHALLENGES: THE HEALTHCARE INDUSTRY CASE

The extent of the risk posed by these challenges varies among firms, depending on their size but also varies based on sectors. The challenges faced in the healthcare industry for instance can be summarized into three broad categories: data itself, accessibility, and translation (Adibuzzaman et al., 2017). First, healthcare data may seem very large until they are analyzed for the purpose of answering specific clinical questions. Thus, it is not uncommon that after considering the selection criteria, large data will only produce small or very small sets of clinical cases (small cohort), which makes it nearly impossible to attain answers with strong statistical confidence. This provides poor insights for managers and cannot help in making the informing decisions. Figure 6 depicts this issue.

Figure 6. Example of big data producing small cohorts when considering clinical selection criteria.

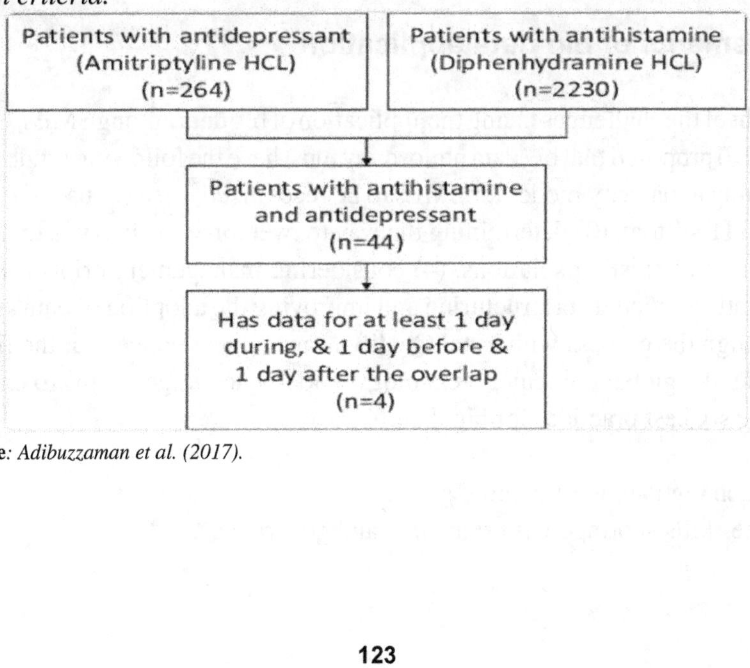

Source*: Adibuzzaman et al. (2017).*

Furthermore, clinical data tend to be poorly integrated within clinics as they are often captured in various systems; each with a somewhat dissimilar intent. This can be seen in the different diagnoses that a patient receives from a different doctor for the same symptoms. In addition, manual reports encompassing doctors' follow-up of the patient may not be stored together with those resulting from the laboratory and X-ray room. Another issue with data in the medical context relates to sparse and insufficient data on drug administration and infusion. This also makes it extremely difficult to reconstruct therapeutic processes for outcome studies.

Second, the accessibility and sharing of patient data for scientific work, validation, and reproducibility pose another critical challenge that can be briefed in three concerns: privacy, sharing ability, and proprietary rights. Privacy means that data are protected by laws, and, because of fear of litigation, providers are discouraged from sharing it even after it is de-identified (via the removal of all direct identifiers). As such, sharing it with other business partners (such as labs, partner hospitals, and government bodies) remains complicated. Adibuzzaman et al (2017) give example, of a large system called "Informatics for Integrating Biology and the Bedside (i2b2)" which is an initiative undertaken by multiple Healthcare partners. The system was designed to gather data for scientific research. Each hospital is required to transform their data into SQL after de-identification. This process not only requires great effort to implement and adjust to the system but also helps to fulfill all the steps to make data available in it. Finally, translating the research findings driven by big data into clinical practices constitutes another serious problem due to the poor understanding of the benefits and risks of data-driven decision support systems. For example. Although machine-learning algorithms perform with good accuracy, they do not provide good interpretations or consider the clinical context of the outcomes.

Requirements of big data application

In light of the challenges facing the application of big data among SMEs, Coleman et al. (2016) proposed that big data philosophy must have the following fundamentals: (1) deciding a maturity model for SMEs to be recognized, then (2) use of the latest/advanced IT system, (3) determining the way to overcome the barriers that impede the adoption of existing solutions, (4) considering management priorities and the role of maturity models in structuring and improving the adoption of data analytics, and (5) align the process with Total Quality Management concept of the firm.

Oracle, the global computer technology leader, encourages firms to ensure the following six best practices for big data:

- Match big data with specific goals.
- Ease skills shortage with standards and governance.

- Create a center of excellence to optimize knowledge transfer.
- Align unstructured data with structured data and correlate different types and sources.
- Plan the discovery lab for performance.
- Align with the operating model of the cloud.

Given the fact that the analytical processes and models of big data can be both human- and machine-based, leading SMEs and startups, including those in emerging markets, are in a permanent quest for data specialists. Currently, data science is one of the top well-paying professions. Yet, within this race for talents, firms from developed countries benefit the well-trained graduates of their universities and from government schemes that attract overseas expatriates with IT and Data science skills. In many developing countries firms re increasingly relying on returning students but more increasingly -like in the case of China- on returning migrants who are known as "returnees" (Liu, 2023; Mosbah and Daghrir, 2017; Mosbah et al., 2018).

Proposed measures: a pathway to effective application of big data among SMEs

Embracing big data by SMEs is a multifaceted process that necessitates addressing a combination of organizational, technological, and environmental encounters. Good leadership, tailored solutions and external support are strategic to unlocking the promise of big data in SMEs. Further benefits can be derived from collaborative initiatives with technology providers, tech-related service firms and training programs, allowing them to bridge the gaps with large firms. In this regard, the World Economic Forum (2023) argues that data holds immense potential to revolutionize SMEs and advocates that its effective use requires reliable IT infrastructure, active leadership, data-centric culture, and proactive strategic conception.

Analyzing and making sense of big data eventually brings new prospects for IT firms but also offers massive opportunities for data producers and users. Managing big data is not an easy task. The European Commission (2014) resembles big data as an ocean made of tiny information which is difficult to manage even for large companies. The same commission adds that modern technological advancements procure SMES with a bundle of chances to fish for the same opportunities as large corporations. However, the question that may be posed at this point is "how can SMEs exploit big data to boost their operations?". Considering the realities discussed above alongside insights available in the literature we recommend the following measures to be implemented by SMEs to overcome the barriers that impeded the use of big data and maximize its impact on their firms:

- Formulate a clear strategy concerning the use of and aims behind the big data.
- Seek sponsorship and efficient collaborative solutions with technology providers
- Use open-source tools and platforms such as Hadoop and Apache Spark
- Leverage on free/cheaper cloud-based solutions
- Establish smaller infrastructure systems and scale up
- Focus on predictive analysis to help in decision making
- Recruit talented fresh graduates and part time university students
- Encourage a culture of learning from Massive Open Online Courses (MOOCs),
- Cooperate with research institutes, universities and large companies for data analytics purpose
- Outsource analytics to small/unknown service providers that are available in freelance platforms such as Upwork, assess their performance and costs regularly by comparing with other providers
- Ensure effective inter-departmental cooperation for data management and analytic purpose
- Once grown to a certain level, make informed decisions regarding the degree of centralization on the analytics (single unit vs departmental)

CONCLUSION

This study questioned the realities of big data usage by SMEs. The main question posed here was: what shapes the realities of SMEs use of big data and what can be done to apply it effectively? to answer these questions, this study has to first gather relevant statistics and insights from various reports and scientific research articles to draw a picture of the realities of big data applications within SMEs, the requirement of having a big data system, and the challenges hindering the proper use of big data. The study has then proposed a framework encompassing a set of measures to overcome the various challenges faced by SMEs in their use of big data and optimize its use considering their limited resources.

The extant literature indicates that scholars and researchers who have dealt with the topic of big data among SMEs focus on the technicalities/applicability, benefits and challenges, or factors that encourage or inhibit their use. Although SMEs are making good use of some technological aspects like e-commerce, they are noticeably late, relative to large firms, in the use of big data and business-related technologies, and, therefore, risk being left behind if they cannot convey the technological changes that underpin today's business environment. For firms which have not yet turned to big data, this could have occurred because of process complexity, limited resources and/or because their managers underestimate the real benefits of big data analytics, they do not know from where to start, they are busy with day-to-day operations, and/or they lack the necessary resources. Furthermore, SMEs face multiple challenges that impede the smooth use of big data, including cost, data privacy and security, lack of in-house capabilities, lack of IT skills and analytic expertise, and lack of a supportive culture.

Among the measures proposed in this chapter regarding the effective and efficient use of big data is the "must" to start off somewhere on the right system then scale it up, taping on free solutions and wisely tradeoff cost with efficiency to adopt additional solutions and components, and adopting cloud computing. In terms of skills, SMEs can rely on Massive Open Online Courses (MOOCs) and seek to enhance business knowledge of current IT staff. Externally, SMEs must seek networking and cooperation with governments, universities, and specialized research institutes. Overall, these measures reflect three broad avenues of opportunities: organizational, technological and external/cooperational.

This study is among a few attempts to discuss big data from the SMEs resource constraints perspective and, accordingly, proposes some measures to guide these firms in their implementation and management. Propose adoption of big data and their analytics is crucial for decision making, operations, strategic planning and the overall performance. By doing so, we somehow add to the application of the RBV into further theoretical boundaries, address a pressing challenge that faces SMEs with actionable solutions, and set a foundation for more- probably interdisciplinary- research.

Theoretical and practical implications

The observations made in this chapter not just demonstrate how intangible assets like big data capabilities and their analytics can be taped by resource-constrained firms like SMEs but the measure proposed here can also showcase how scarcity in resources can be moderated through wise resource management (particularly financial and human) and market opportunities and alliances.

At the firm level, the chapter is likely to clarifies, through the measures, how SMEs can practically tap on various solutions in the use of big data to support operational efficiency and improve their competitive edge. It also encourages them to leverage external resources, such as collaboration with universities, consultation firms, technology suppliers to overcome internal resource weaknesses.

Furthermore, the insights of this chapter can create awareness among external stakeholders such as government agents whose support is very helpful in streamlining and facilitating the process of big data adoption. While improved data governance creates viable opportunities for SMEs to develop, more attention must be paid to engaging various institutions in data policy making. Policy makers are therefore expected not only to facilitate and encourage this process but play a key role in it (OECD, 2022). The insights of this chapter might help them develop support initiatives, subsidies, and training initiatives tailored just to SME.

Limitations and recommendations

As seen in this chapter, the level of understanding concerning the application of big data in SMEs is unsatisfactory. The current work has attempted to contribute to this topic, but it is not without limitations. Here we highlight two limitations of this approach and propose how they could be improved/overcome through future research to improve the output and our understanding of this issue. First, in this chapter we explored this topic using information and statistics available in reports and academic papers. Therefore, we recommend future researchers conduct empirical studies using qualitative methods to collect data from data managers and experts affiliated with different institutional bodies in charge of data and IT infrastructure. The collection and analysis of in-depth data allows gathering firsthand insights on the topic. Issues to be focused include aims and purposes of data usage, their departmental sources and focus, how data budgets are allocated and the nature and impact of institutional support on this matter if any. Researchers could also seek to understand what role is played by external collaboration with third party businesses, such as suppliers, service providers, distributors and financial institutions, in SMEs big data management (collection, storage, analysis and sharing) and how does this add to or limit the overall performance of firms supply chains. This is so important due to the role of supply chains in nowadays business environment. Finally, we believe that focusing on SMEs from developing countries and their innovative (cheap and/or open source) solutions on the matter of big data adoption are of utmost importance.

REFERENCES

Adadi, A. (2021). A survey on data-efficient algorithms in big data era. *Journal of Big Data*, 8(1), 1–54. DOI: 10.1186/s40537-021-00419-9 PMID: 33425651

Adibuzzaman, M., DeLaurentis, P., Hill, J., & Benneyworth, B. D. (2017). Big data in healthcare–the promises, challenges and opportunities from a research perspective: A case study with a model database. [). American Medical Informatics Association.]. *AMIA ... Annual Symposium Proceedings - AMIA Symposium. AMIA Symposium*, 2017, 384. PMID: 29854102

Ardagna, C. A., Ceravolo, P., & Damiani, E. (2016, December). *Big data analytics as-a-service: Issues and challenges. In 2016 IEEE international conference on big data (big data)*. IEEE.

Arsawan, I. W. E., De Hariyanti, N. K., Atmaja, I. M. A. D. S., Suhartanto, D., & Koval, V. (2022). Developing organizational agility in SMEs: An investigation of innovation's roles and strategic flexibility. *Journal of Open Innovation*, 8(3), 149. DOI: 10.3390/joitmc8030149

Azeem, M. M., & Kotey, B. (2023). Innovation in SMEs: The role of flexible work arrangements and market competition. *International Journal of Human Resource Management*, 34(1), 92–127. DOI: 10.1080/09585192.2021.1961162

Baig, M. I., Yadegaridehkordi, E., & Nizam Bin Md Nasir, M. H. (2023). Influence of big data adoption on sustainable marketing and operation of SMEs: A hybrid approach of SEM-ANN. *Management Decision*, 61(7), 2231–2253. DOI: 10.1108/MD-06-2022-0778

Begenau, J., Farboodi, M., & Veldkamp, L. (2018). Big data in finance and the growth of large firms. *Journal of Monetary Economics*, 97, 71–87. DOI: 10.1016/j.jmoneco.2018.05.013

Belás, J., Amoah, J., Dvorský, J., & Šuleř, P. (2021). The importance of social media for management of SMEs. *Economics & Sociology (Ternopil)*, 14(4), 118–132. DOI: 10.14254/2071-789X.2021/14-4/7

Bianchini, M., & Michalkova, V. (2019). Data Analytics in SMEs: Trends and Policies. OECD SME and Entrepreneurship Papers No. 15. Available at: https://www.oecd.org/industry/smes/SME-Outlook-2021-Country-profiles.pdf

Casey, T., Krishnamurthy, K., & Abezgauz, B. (2013). *Who Should Own Big Data? strategy+business*. Available at: http://www.strategybusiness.com/article/00211?gko=44b8e

CBS website. Are SMEs ready for big data? Available at: https://www.cbs.nl/en-gb/about-us/innovation/project/are-smes-ready-for-big-data-

Coleman, S., Göb, R., Manco, G., Pievatolo, A., Tort-Martorell, X., & Reis, M. S. (2016). How can SMEs benefit from big data? Challenges and a path forward. *Quality and Reliability Engineering International*, 32(6), 2151–2164. DOI: 10.1002/qre.2008

Conti, R., de Matos, M. G., & Valentini, G. (2024). Big data analytics, firm size, and performance. *Strategy Science*, 9(2), 135–151. DOI: 10.1287/stsc.2022.0007

Conti, R., de Matos, M. G., & Valentini, G. (2024). Big data analytics, firm size, and performance. *Strategy Science*, 9(2), 135–151. DOI: 10.1287/stsc.2022.0007

DeMauro, A., Greco, M., Grimaldi, M., & Ritala, P. (2018). Human resources for Big Data professions: A systematic classification of job roles and required skill sets. *Information Processing & Management*, 54(5), 807–817. DOI: 10.1016/j.ipm.2017.05.004

Enterprise Strategy Group - ESG. (2022). 2022 Technology Spending Intentions Survey. Available at: https://www.esg-global.com/2022-technology-spending

European Commission. (2014). Helping SMEs fish the big data ocean. Available at: https://digital-strategy.ec.europa.eu/en/news/helping-smes-fish-big-data-ocean

European Commission. (2020). *What is an SME?* Retrieved from https://single-market-economy.ec.europa.eu/smes/sme-fundamentals/sme-definition_en

Ghasemaghaei, M. (2018). Improving organizational performance through the use of big data. *Journal of Computer Information Systems*, 60(5), 395–408. DOI: 10.1080/08874417.2018.1496805

Gherhes, C., Williams, N., Vorley, T., & Vasconcelos, A. C. (2016). Distinguishing micro-businesses from SMEs: A systematic review of growth constraints. *Journal of Small Business and Enterprise Development*, 23(4), 939–963. DOI: 10.1108/JSBED-05-2016-0075

Ghosh, A. (2004). Increasing market share as a rationale for corporate acquisitions. *Journal of Business Finance & Accounting*, 31(1-2), 209–247. DOI: 10.1111/j.0306-686X.2004.0006.x

González-Padilla, P., Navalpotro, F. D., & Saura, J. R. (2024). Managing entrepreneurs' behavior personalities in digital environments: A review. *The International Entrepreneurship and Management Journal*, 20(1), 89–113. DOI: 10.1007/s11365-022-00823-4

Huang, X. (2009). Strategic decision making in Chinese SMEs. *Chinese Management Studies*, 3(2), 87–101. DOI: 10.1108/17506140910963602

Iqbal, M., Kazmi, S. H. A., Manzoor, A., Soomrani, A. R., Butt, S. H., & Shaikh, K. A. (2018). A study of big data for business growth in SMEs: Opportunities & challenges. In *2018 International conference on computing, mathematics and engineering technologies (iCoMET)* (pp. 1-7). IEEE. DOI: 10.1109/ICOMET.2018.8346368

Kedi, W. E., Ejimuda, C., Idemudia, C., & Ijomah, T. I. (2024). Machine learning software for optimizing SME social media marketing campaigns. *Computer Science & IT Research Journal*, 5(7), 1634–1647. DOI: 10.51594/csitrj.v5i7.1349

Liu, L. (2023). Analysis of the Challenges of Overseas Students Returning to China for Employment in the Labor Market—Based on the Re-discussion of the Value of Western Higher Education.

Lopez-Torres, G. C. (2023). The impact of SMEs' sustainability on competitiveness. *Measuring Business Excellence*, 27(1), 107–120. DOI: 10.1108/MBE-12-2021-0144

Maroufkhani, P., Iranmanesh, M., & Ghobakhloo, M. (2023). Determinants of big data analytics adoption in small and medium-sized enterprises (SMEs). *Industrial Management & Data Systems*, 123(1), 278–301. DOI: 10.1108/IMDS-11-2021-0695

Marzi, G., Marrucci, A., Vianelli, D., & Ciappei, C. (2023). B2B digital platform adoption by SMEs and large firms: Pathways and pitfalls. *Industrial Marketing Management*, 114, 80–93. DOI: 10.1016/j.indmarman.2023.08.002

McAfee, A., & Brynjolfsson, E. (2012). Big Data: The Management Revolution. Available at: https://hbr.org/2012/10/big-data-the-management-revolution

Mosbah, A., Ali, M. A., Aljubari, I. H., & Sherief, S. R. (2018). Migrants in the High-Tech and engineering sectors: an emerging research area. In *2018 IEEE Conference on Systems, Process and Control (ICSPC)* (pp. 234-237). IEEE. DOI: 10.1109/SPC.2018.8704139

Mosbah, A., Alrawi, M. A., & Noorita, M. T. (2023). Empowering small and medium enterprises with data analytics for enhanced competitiveness. 2023 IEEE 13th International Conference on Control System, Computing and Engineering (ICCSCE), 25–26 Aug 2023, Penang, Malaysia.

Mosbah, A., & Daghrir, F. (2017). High-tech immigrant entrepreneurship: A concise review. *International Journal of Technical Research & Science*, 2(2), 96–100.

Mosbah, A., & Debili, R. (2014). Development of Algerian SMEs in the age of mosglobalization. *Journal of business and social development, 2*(1), 37-48.

Mutasher WG, Aljuboori AF. (2022). New and Existing Approaches Reviewing of Big Data Analysis with Hadoop Tools. *Baghdad Science Journal*. 1;19(4):0887-.

OECD. (2022). Financing growth and turning data into business: Helping SMEs scale up. https://shorturl.at/HbGKn

Pappas, I., Jaccheri, L., Mikalef, P., & Giannakos, M. (2017). Social innovation and social entrepreneurship through big data: developing a research agenda.

Rakshit, S., Mondal, S., Islam, N., Jasimuddin, S., & Zhang, Z. (2021). Social media and the new product development during COVID-19: An integrated model for SMEs. *Technological Forecasting and Social Change*, 170, 120869. DOI: 10.1016/j.techfore.2021.120869

Rauwerda, K., & De Graaf, F. J. (2021). Heuristics in financial decision-making: The selection of SME financing by advisers in an increasingly diverse market. *Management Decision*, 59(7), 1728–1749. DOI: 10.1108/MD-09-2019-1269

Rising, C. J., Kristensen, M., & Tjerrild-Hansen, S. 2014. Big data too big for SMEs? Available at: http://web.stanford.edu/class/msande238/projects/2014/GainIT.pdf

Saura, J. R., Palacios-Marqués, D., & Ribeiro-Soriano, D. (2023). Digital marketing in SMEs via data-driven strategies: Reviewing the current state of research. *Journal of Small Business Management*, 61(3), 1278–1313. DOI: 10.1080/00472778.2021.1955127

Sen, D., Ozturk, M., & Vayvay, O. (2016). An overview of big data for growth in SMEs. *Procedia: Social and Behavioral Sciences*, 235, 159–167. DOI: 10.1016/j.sbspro.2016.11.011

Soroka, A., Liu, Y., Han, L., & Haleem, M. S. (2017). Big data driven customer insights for SMEs in redistributed manufacturing. *Procedia CIRP*, 63, 692–697. DOI: 10.1016/j.procir.2017.03.319

Spithoven, A., Vanhaverbeke, W., & Roijakkers, N. (2013). Open innovation practices in SMEs and large enterprises. *Small Business Economics*, 41(3), 537–562. DOI: 10.1007/s11187-012-9453-9

Statista (2023). Usage of big data among SMEs in the Netherlands in 2018, by business unit. Available at: https://www.statista.com/statistics/915577/usage-of-big-data-among-smes-in-the-netherlands-by-business-unit/

Stedman, C. (2022). The ultimate guide to big data for businesses. Available at: https://www.techtarget.com/searchdatamanagement/The-ultimate-guide-to-big-data-for-businesses

Taylor-Sakyi, K. (2016). Big data: Understanding big data. *arXiv preprint arXiv:1601.04602*.

Tien, E. L., Ali, N. M., Miskon, S., Ahmad, N., & Abdullah, N. S. (2020). Big data analytics adoption model for Malaysian SMEs. In *Emerging Trends in Intelligent Computing and Informatics: Data Science, Intelligent Information Systems and Smart Computing 4* (pp. 45-53). Springer International Publishing. DOI: 10.1007/978-3-030-33582-3_5

Van de Vrande, V., de Jong, J. P. J., Vanhaverbeke, W., & de Rochemont, M. (2009). Open innovation in SMES: Trends, motives and management challenges. *Technovation*, 29(6-7), 423–437. DOI: 10.1016/j.technovation.2008.10.001

Wang S, Wang H. (2020). Big data for small and medium-sized enterprises (SME): a knowledge management model. *Journal of Knowledge Management*, 29;24(4):881-97.

Wessels, T., & Jokonya, O. (2022). Factors affecting the Adoption of Big Data as a Service in SMEs. *Procedia Computer Science*, 196, 332–339. DOI: 10.1016/j.procs.2021.12.021

Wessels, T., & Jokonya, O. (2022). Factors affecting the adoption of big data as a service in SMEs. *Procedia Computer Science*, 196, 332–339. DOI: 10.1016/j.procs.2021.12.021

Weston, B. (2022). Infographic: Are You Taking Advantage of Marketing Data? Available at: https://www.score.org/resource/blog-post/infographic-are-you-taking-advantage-marketing-data

Willetts, M., Atkins, A. S., & Stanier, C. (2020). Barriers to SMEs adoption of big data analytics for competitive advantage. In *2020 Fourth International Conference On Intelligent Computing in Data Sciences (ICDS)* (pp. 1-8). IEEE. DOI: 10.1109/ICDS50568.2020.9268687

World Economic Forum. (2023). Data Unleashed: Empowering Small and Medium Enterprises (SMEs) for Innovation and Success. Available online at: https://www3.weforum.org/docs/WEF_Data_Unleashed_Empowering_Small_and_Medium_Enterprises_(SMEs)_for_Innovation_and_Success_2023.pdf

Zimmermann, V. (2016). SMEs and digitalization: The current position, recent developments and challenges. *KfW research*. No. 138.

Chapter 6
Unethical Design in TikTok and Its Connection to Surveillance Capitalism and Collective Intelligence

Eva Abajo Pérez
Rey Juan Carlos University, Spain

ABSTRACT

In an increasingly digitalized world, social media has transformed communication and information consumption, but it has also raised ethical concerns regarding privacy and mental health, particularly among young people. The study of TikTok, one of the most popular platforms, offers an opportunity to examine how addictive design captures users' attention, while surveillance capitalism commodifies their data. This analysis highlights the need for ethical design, promoting practices that prioritize transparency and user well-being.

INTRODUCTION

In an increasingly digitalized world, social media has become an integral part of our lives, transforming how we communicate, interact, and consume information. Checking notifications has become a reflexive, almost automatic act, performed

DOI: 10.4018/979-8-3693-6945-6.ch006

without thought or questioning. According to the "Digital 2024: Global Overview Report" by DataReportal, the average internet user currently spends 6 hours and 40 minutes online daily, with 2 hours and 23 minutes devoted to social media. The most widely used platforms include Facebook, WhatsApp, Instagram, and TikTok. The exponential growth of the social media has created new opportunities for communication, information access, and entertainment (Saura et al., 2024). However, these opportunities are tempered by ethical concerns surrounding data handling, privacy, and the mental and physical health effects on users, particularly the youth, who are one of the most vulnerable demographics and more prone to addiction-related issues.

In a context where data is often referred to as the "new gold" and the economy is increasingly based on capturing users' attention, some tech companies are leveraging the design and functionalities of their systems to exploit user vulnerabilities, thereby increasing the time spent on digital platforms. The goal is to maximize the amount of data collected. In this scenario, the phenomenon of "surveillance capitalism" takes center stage. This term, popularized by sociologist Shoshana Zuboff, refers to the commodification of personal data, wherein personal information is transformed into a product bought and sold for profit. Tech companies collect and analyze this data to predict our behavior and sell these predictive products to commercial clients for financial gain. The vast amount of information generated by online social interactions, also known as collective intelligence, is a valuable resource for companies, who use it as a tool to direct advertising, influence user behavior, and secure economic benefits.

Given the growing concerns over social media design, it is essential to examine whether platforms are intentionally engineered to be addictive and capture users' attention. Unethical platforms often use persuasive visual elements that benefit advertisers, manipulating users to increase ad visibility and prioritize commercial goals over privacy and transparency. Ethical design, on the other hand, focuses on transparency, helping users understand how their actions and data are used.

TikTok, one of the most downloaded mobile apps globally, has rapidly grown in popularity, with over a billion active users. Powered by AI, TikTok's algorithm personalizes content recommendations, making the platform highly engaging. However, its addictive design has raised concerns about privacy, content manipulation, and user well-being. This research aims to analyze TikTok's design principles and how they relate to broader issues such as surveillance capitalism and collective intelligence. TikTok's success, especially among younger users, and its unique algorithm, highlight important implications for ethical design and privacy.

As social media's impact on daily life grows, so do concerns about addiction, user safety, and privacy. The European Union is pushing for regulation to address these issues, advocating for ethical platform designs that protect mental health. Recent reports suggest a "right to not be digitally disturbed" proposing measures like disabling notifications by default, limiting screen time, and promoting healthier app usage through changes such as grayscale displays and usage summaries.

This study aims to inform on unethical design practices, using TikTok as a case study, and encourage reflection on how social media shapes society. By understanding these platforms' influence on behavior, we can work toward ethical technology use, ensuring social media serves as a positive tool for communication rather than exploitation.

The general objective of this research is to analyze TikTok's design and its relationship with surveillance capitalism and collective intelligence, evaluating the platform's ethical implications for its users. The general objective will be achieved through the following specific objectives: Identify and describe unethical design practices on TikTok, assessing their ethical implications on user behavior and perception. Relate the concept of surveillance capitalism to TikTok's unethical design. Connect the concept of collective intelligence with TikTok. Identify the negative consequences of unethical design in social media.

Theoretical Framework

Social Media Industry and Digital Addiction

In recent years, social media has gained considerable momentum and has become an essential part of daily life for thousands of people (Ochoa & Barragán, 2022). What began as simple communication tools has evolved into a cultural phenomenon that shapes how we communicate, interact, and build digital communities. The social media phenomenon has left an indelible mark on contemporary society, especially among young people, who have adopted it as a fundamental resource for socialization (Tejada et al., 2023). Since the Covid-19 pandemic in 2020, the social media industry has experienced exponential growth. According to the "Digital 2024" report by DataReportal, the number of social media users increased by 5.2%, surpassing 5 billion globally, representing a growth of 266 million in 2023. This rise is also reflected in the average time users spend on social media, which has reached 2 hours and 23 minutes per day. This exponential increase in users has facilitated the creation and expansion of innovative platforms, with the most popular being Facebook, WhatsApp, Instagram, and TikTok—the latter gaining significant popularity among young people.

This growing use of social media as a daily activity has raised ethical concerns regarding the management of user-shared data, privacy, and decision-making within this digital ecosystem (Baier, 2018). Additionally, the increased time spent on these platforms has led to rising concerns about potential addiction. Various studies and research help us understand the reasons behind this phenomenon. Experts such as

David Greenfield, psychologist and founder of the Center for Internet and Technology Addiction in West Hartford (Connecticut), argue that the magnetic appeal of social media stems from how our impulses and neurological connections respond to its content. Social media has become a dynamic social environment that facilitates constant interaction, information sharing, and coordination of actions among users (Orihuela, 2008). This constant communication is closely tied to dopamine, a neurotransmitter that regulates emotions and affectivity (Trujillo et al., 2000), suggesting that social media can trigger emotional and affective responses due to the various interactions and social rewards they offer. Social media addiction is classified as a behavioral disorder, similar to gambling addiction, where the compulsion is focused on a specific activity (Griffiths, 2000).

Neuroimaging studies like FMRI and SPECT show similarities in brain activation between social media addiction and substance addiction, particularly in areas related to reward and memory (Lin et al., 2014). Interactions and notifications on social media release dopamine, a neurotransmitter associated with reward and pleasure, creating a reinforcement cycle that drives constant use (Koob & Volkow, 2010). Robert Sapolsky introduced the concept of the "Magic Maybe," which explains the dopamine cycle associated with the use of electronic devices and social media. The dopamine surge when receiving a notification reinforces the need to continually seek that gratification, generating a cycle of constant reward-seeking. This dynamic has been pointed out by former Facebook employees (Sean Parker, Chamath Palihapitiya), who describe the platform as a "social validation feedback loop" designed to exploit human psychological vulnerabilities. Psychological factors such as the "Fear Of Missing Out" (FOMO) also contribute, creating anxiety about being disconnected from the gratifying experiences others share on social media, thus driving the need for constant connection and checking (Przybylski et al., 2013).

Surveillance Capitalism

Numerous studies support the theory that social media addiction is not coincidental (Balakrishnan & Griffiths, 2017). Authors like Zuboff and Maxmin have highlighted how the design of digital platforms can manipulate users to make decisions based on economic and business factors rather than social ones. Social media platforms are designed to be highly attractive and addictive, with companies using techniques such as intermittent reinforcement and constant notifications to capture user attention and encourage repeated interaction (Fogg, 2018). This combination of elements significantly contributes to their addictive potential. This addiction phenomenon fuels an emerging economic model known as surveillance capitalism (Saura and Debasa, 2022).

The term "surveillance capitalism" was coined by Shoshana Zuboff in her book *The Age of Surveillance Capitalism* to describe an economic system where companies generate enormous profits by collecting and analyzing personal user data. In this system, companies use digital technologies to monitor, track, and analyze online behavior to predict and influence decisions. These companies are typically digital platforms and social media networks that offer "free" services in exchange for collecting user data, which is then used to target specific, personalized advertising. The main providers of this data and information are companies working with ICT infrastructure. Surveillance capitalism raises concerns about autonomy, privacy, and the power of large tech corporations in modern society. This concept is closely related to collective intelligence, which involves gathering information about society to predict behaviors and influence global decision-making.

According to Shoshana Zuboff (2023), personal information has become the foundation for a new global economic order that threatens democracy. Companies like Google, Facebook, and others have capitalized on this model, using user data as raw material for analysis and monetization. Surveillance capitalism also argues that social media networks are built on reward-use models, where users need to obtain recurring rewards to increase their engagement and usage time (Zuboff, 2019). In this context, tech companies are developing psychology-based strategies aimed at increasing technology usage by people, with the ultimate goal of boosting corporate profits (Boddy & Dominelli, 2017). Overall, the primary goal of a social media platform is to increase user activity to generate more data (Carlson et al., 2018).

Unethical Vs. Ethical Design in Social Media

In some cases, digital architectures are intentionally designed to provoke specific behavior, and this is where the concept of ethical design becomes relevant (Sunstein & Thaler, 2003). Ethical design refers to ways of creating products and services that pursue positive moral goals over profits (Kilgour et al., 2020). Ethical design in social media involves structuring information architecture in such a way that users are fully aware of their actions and behaviors. This means users must have complete control over their information and understand how it is used (Lyulyov et al., 2024).

In contrast, unethical design in social media involves organizing visual elements in such a way that they encourage behaviors that economically benefit advertisers. This may include persuasive techniques to attract users or manipulate their actions to increase ad visibility (Kampf, 2014) and (Greene et al., 2019). In this design, companies seek to modify user behavior through the analysis of user data interactions and participation on social networks (Zuboff, 2019). To achieve unethical design in social media, advertisers pursue three main objectives (Saura et al., 2021):

- Engagement Goal: to provoke actions that increase the average time users spend interacting with the social network. This can be achieved by implementing new functionalities or features that encourage interaction, such as story polls, comments, sharing content, etc. The goal is to keep users engaged and active on the platform for as long as possible.
- Growth Goal: to increase the average time users spend on the social network over time, regardless of how it is achieved. This may involve strategies such as increasing the number of notifications to keep users hooked, establishing partnerships with other social networks to expand the user base, or providing highly personalized content that maintains long-term user interest. The focus is on ensuring that the social network grows consistently and retains users effectively.
- Advertising Goal: to ensure users interact uninterruptedly with the network's advertising. To achieve this, strategies can be implemented to make advertisements more intrusive and harder to ignore, such as placing ads between feed posts, incorporating auto-play video ads, or using advanced targeting techniques to deliver highly relevant ads to users. The goal is to maximize advertising revenue by ensuring users are constantly exposed to ads while using the platform.

The authors identified 10 performance measures and 4 ethical design measures used by social media companies to increase user engagement and achieve online behavior modification, sometimes without users being aware of this effect, aimed at increasing the profitability of their business models.

Performance Measures

The performance measures include: image or video view duration, which helps predict total session time and duration on the platform; time per visit, which determines the total daily and weekly time a user is connected; and the number of pages viewed in one visit, indicating the amount of images or videos consumed. Additionally, interactions are measured to evaluate content quality and relevance to the user, and user sentiments are assessed to predict emotional states and personalize the displayed content. Recent and top searches reveal the type of content users want to see, helping personalize the feed, while personality type, determined by user habits, allows relevant content to appear in the first posts of the feed. Click-through rates are also considered to measure user interaction capability, crucial for advertising monetization. Finally, the number of times the app is visited without interactions is tracked to assign a specific value to each user, reflecting their engagement with the platform.

Ethical Design Measures

Choice Architecture: The way the app is structured to channel user attention and shape action. In this way, users are constructed as passive actors who perform the actions the social network creates for them. The issue arises when users believe they are making their own decisions, even though the social network's architecture is already designed with that objective in mind. The structure of social networks is designed for users to make decisions from an economic, rather than a social, perspective.

Session Value: This is the value of a session per user, where the number of actions is classified as engagement. This value is one of the most relevant factors because it determines the types of advertisers who will display their ads and the percentage of profitability they will achieve. Consequently, social networks will attempt to treat users with higher session values more delic

Notification Design: element that establishes a link with users even after they have disconnected from social media platforms. The content in notifications is incomplete, merely informing users that there is information or content that requires their attention. In this way, notifications prompt users to access the social media platform to view the full content, and once inside, the platform provides relevant information based on profile data to prolong the session. Social media platforms thus use notifications to increase data collection and profitability.

Engagement Level: This metric measures the amount of time a user spends performing actions such as commenting, liking, sharing, and other interactions. This measure is crucial for assessing user quality, as it reflects the profitability of social media platforms in terms of advertising returns.

Methodology

For this chapter, a structured methodology ensured a rigorous analysis of the topic. It included a detailed literature review and critical analysis of existing research, facilitating the collection and evaluation of relevant information from various sources for a deeper understanding.

An extensive search was conducted using academic databases like Google Scholar, RefSeek, BASE, Web of Sciences, Sage Journals, and Dialnet, as well as non-academic sources such as news articles. The focus was on books, scientific articles, studies, news, and testimonies related to ethical design in social media, surveillance capitalism, and collective intelligence. Keywords included "unethical design in social media," "surveillance capitalism," "collective intelligence," and "TikTok." Search filters prioritized recent and high-quality publications.

The literature analysis involved several stages. Information sources were categorized to identify trends and patterns in unethical social media design and its connection to surveillance capitalism and collective intelligence. This structured the information coherently and facilitated result synthesis. A deductive analysis identified TikTok's unethical design practices, focusing on how user data is collected and used, and how these align with surveillance capitalism. Additionally, TikTok's role in facilitating content creation and sharing was linked to collective intelligence. A critical analysis followed, evaluating the ethical implications of TikTok's design practices, including platform addiction, behavioral manipulation, and mental health issues.

The next step established theoretical connections between unethical design and TikTok's features, linking them to surveillance capitalism. This analysis drew on key works, such as *The Age of Surveillance Capitalism* (2019) by Shoshana Zuboff, which examined how tech companies monetize data collection. Zuboff's insights were crucial for understanding TikTok's strategies.

The article *Ethical Design in Social Media: Assessing the Main Performance Measurements of User Online Behavior Modification* (2021) by Saura, Palacios-Marqués, and Iturricha-Fernández provided a solid framework for evaluating TikTok's ethical implications and design strategies within the context of social media ethics.

Finally, *How Social Media Uses UX Design to Keep Users Engaged: Case Study: TikTok* (2024) by M. Syrjälä offered a detailed study of TikTok's UX design, highlighting its role in capturing user attention. This case study shed light on specific mechanisms TikTok employs to sustain engagement, offering practical insights into unethical design tactics and their impact on user behavior.

Analysis of Results

Origin and Characteristics Of Tiktok

In an increasingly intrusive digital world, TikTok has emerged as a social media giant, captivating millions of users with its dynamic short-video format. However, behind its attractive design and overwhelming success lies a set of unethical strategies closely tied to surveillance capitalism. This analysis aims to uncover the questionable practices that underpin TikTok's empire.

TikTok is a social media platform of Chinese origin characterized by its short, dynamic video format. The app allows users to create and share videos with music, animations, and visual effects, lasting between 15 seconds and 10 minutes. It offers a wide variety of content, from dances, entertainment, and humor to viral challenges and creative trends. Its intuitive and appealing design, combined with its personalized algorithm (Saura, 2024), makes it a highly addictive platform that has captivated millions of users worldwide. It was created by the tech company ByteDance in 2016 under the name Douyin and founded by entrepreneur Zhang Yiming. In 2017, the company acquired Musical.ly, another popular short-video platform based in the United States, and later merged it with Douyin in 2018, resulting in what we now know as TikTok. This strategic merger was key to TikTok's success, allowing it to capitalize on Musical.ly's strong user base in the West while leveraging Douyin's technology and experience in the Chinese market. Since then, TikTok has become one of the most downloaded apps globally, with an exponentially growing user base.

The COVID-19 pandemic in 2020 accelerated TikTok's growth, contributing to its worldwide adoption and transforming it into a phenomenon that continues to reshape the global social media landscape. In early 2021, TikTok partnered with Shopify, boosting the platform's advertising strategies and promoting the development of businesses and brands. According to the latest data from the "Digital 2024" report, compiled by Data Reportal, We Are Social, and Meltwater, TikTok has reached 1.562 billion monthly active users, making it the fifth most used social network globally, with a 7.4% share of total usage. Its primary audience consists of users aged 16 to 24, who have turned it into a space for self-expression, creativity, and building digital communities. TikTok's influence on contemporary digital culture is undeniable, particularly among Gen Z and millennials.

User Interface (Ui) Design

TikTok's success can be attributed to its distinctive features and functionalities, its innovative design, and the core principles upon which it is built. The platform's UI design, with a focus on simplicity and usability, seeks to offer a smooth, engaging, and addictive user experience. The interface is minimalist, relying on intuitive gestures like swipes and taps for navigation. Focused on short video viewing, it captures users' attention from the very first moment. One of the standout features of its design is that it places audiovisual content at the center of the experience, with short, dynamic videos automatically playing as soon as the app is opened. Unlike other platforms, TikTok doesn't have a homepage or start button; instead, videos begin playing immediately, immersing users in a continuous flow of content. This "content-first" strategy grabs users' attention from the start and encourages them to dive into an ongoing stream of videos. This approach has resulted in users spending more time on the app compared to competitors.

TikTok's interface features a bottom navigation bar that provides quick access to key sections: Home, Friends, Create, Inbox, and Profile. The Home section is split into "For You," where the algorithm curates personalized content, and "Following," which shows videos from users' followed creators. The "Create" icon opens the camera and editing tools, allowing users to make and customize their own videos with various effects and filters. The "Friends" section enables users to interact with content from their followers and followed accounts, while the "Inbox" allows private messaging for personal interactions.

Algorithm

The key to TikTok's success lies in its "For You" feed algorithm, which functions as the platform's brain. This artificial intelligence system is designed to select and display highly relevant and engaging content for each user. TikTok defines its algorithm as a carefully curated stream of videos based on each user's interests. This recommendation system allows users to easily discover content and creators they enjoy, creating a unique and personalized experience. Unlike other recommendation systems, TikTok's algorithm is not static. It is constantly evolving, learning from users' interactions and preferences. Over time, the algorithm refines its ability to select content that genuinely attracts users, adapting to their tastes and behaviors on the platform. As a result, most users spend the majority of their time on the "For You" feed, drawn by its addictive and dynamic nature. In this way, TikTok's algorithm uses natural language processing and computer vision to rank content, considering several factors to determine recommendations. These factors include:

- User interactions: The algorithm records data on the videos users have watched, liked, shared, or added to favorites, the videos they watch to the end, as well as the accounts they follow, comments they post, and videos they create. It also considers instances where users have marked videos as "Not Interested" or reported inappropriate content.
- Video information: The algorithm collects data on the videos users search for or interact with, such as captions, sounds, hashtags, and effects. Based on this information, the algorithm determines what type of content may interest the user and recommends it on their "For You" feed.
- Device and account settings: The algorithm takes into account certain device and account settings, such as language preference, country settings, and mobile device type. Although these settings affect system performance, they have less weight compared to user interactions and video information.

The algorithm also avoids recommending duplicate content, previously viewed videos, spam, or disturbing material. Importantly, it does not prioritize follower count, giving all users an equal opportunity to succeed on the platform.

Community

Beyond its attractive design and intelligent algorithm, another reason for TikTok's popularity is its strong sense of community, as it is a platform based on social interactions where, particularly, young people form their own virtual communities. The platform has become a space where people freely express themselves, share their passions, create trends, and connect with others. TikTok offers a wide range of editing tools, filters, and effects that allow users to personalize their creations and unleash their creativity.

Users use the app to escape reality, to interact socially, to express themselves, and to connect with others. Personal motivations play a significant role in how people interact with the platform (González-Padilla et al., 2024). A feature that fosters this strong sense of community is its interactive nature, which goes beyond the number of followers creators accumulate and includes "likes," comments, and reposts. This active community participation is essential to understanding how TikTok functions, as it encourages the creation and replication of viral videos, the formation of duets between creators, and constant interaction between users. TikTok trends, such as dance challenges, humor, or recipes, also contribute to the sense of community.

With all these features, TikTok has managed to dominate the digital landscape, captivating millions of users. Its innovative design, focus on community, and personalized algorithm have propelled its rise, making it an essential platform for creative expression, social connection, and entertainment. Its popularity has even drawn the interest of competitors. Companies like Meta, owner of Facebook and Instagram, which face challenges in attracting and retaining users under 25, have incorporated similar features into their platforms, such as Instagram's "Reels".

However, TikTok's rapid growth has sparked debates about its impact on society, design ethics, and user privacy. Concerns have been raised by parents, educational institutions, and political leaders about issues related to addiction and data collection for economic purposes. In recent years, TikTok has been continuously threatened with foreign bans. In 2020, India permanently banned TikTok due to security concerns over user data collection. The U.S. government has threatened to ban TikTok entirely unless an ownership change agreement is reached with its parent company, ByteDance. Additionally, the European Commission is also investigating TikTok's practices regarding privacy and data protection.

Unethical Design in Tiktok

Beneath the simple and functional features of TikTok, designed to provide an engaging user experience, lie design principles and psychological foundations that, from an ethical perspective, are questionable. These elements contribute to the app's addictive nature, leading users to spend hours scrolling through content without realizing how much time has passed, often unable to recall the videos they watched after closing the app. These features serve a financial goal closely tied to surveillance capitalism: the longer users spend on social media, the more data they generate, allowing companies to learn more about them, thus making it easier to influence them to buy certain products or behave in specific ways.

This analysis explores how TikTok pursues unethical social media design goals through the various mechanisms and features embedded in its platform. These include the *engagement goal*, aimed at prolonging user interaction with the app; the *growth goal*, focused on increasing active users and frequency of use; and the *advertising goal*, aimed at maximizing engagement with sponsored content and advertisements. These mechanisms are designed to attract and retain users but come with the risk of fostering addictive behaviors.

Tiktok'S Engagement Goal

A key element of TikTok's unethical design is its "*engagement goal*", which aims to keep users hooked on the platform for as long as possible, at any cost. While effective at driving participation and time spent, this approach raises serious ethical concerns due to the strategies employed to achieve it. TikTok uses a combination of appealing design and advanced algorithms to provide a constant stream of highly personalized content, creating an environment where users feel compelled to interact and continue consuming videos without significant pauses. This structure is intentionally addictive, leveraging reward mechanisms that trigger dopamine responses and encourage compulsive use. Through features such as infinite scrolling and the promotion of viral trends, TikTok strives to maximize user engagement, potentially leading to problematic behaviors and the erosion of conscious control over time and actions.

Interface Design

TikTok's user interface is minimalist and easy to use, focusing on highlighting content without unnecessary distractions. This simplicity allows users to navigate the app intuitively, encouraging greater interaction with content and enhancing the user experience. The "For You" page, where users spend most of their time on the platform, is based on Hick's Law, a psychological principle commonly used in user experience (UX) design. Formulated by William Edmund Hick in 1952, the law posits that the more options people are presented with, the more time they need to make a decision. Consequently, the "For You" page minimizes the user's options for what content to view, limiting them to just a few simple actions: scrolling up or down, visiting a creator's profile, or interacting with the video. By reducing the number of choices and the cognitive effort required to decide, TikTok keeps users more engaged and browsing for longer. Moreover, users don't need to click anything to start enjoying content, as entertainment is ready to be consumed without interruptions as soon as the app is opened.

Exploiting The Dopamine Effect

TikTok's design is crafted to exploit human psychology, specifically the brain's reward system, which is activated by the release of dopamine. Dopamine is a neurotransmitter associated with feelings of pleasure and reward, and TikTok's interface is designed to trigger this system repeatedly and consistently. Every time a user encounters an interesting or entertaining video on TikTok, they experience a small release of dopamine. These tactics trigger the brain's reward system, similar to the effects of drug use or addictive behaviors like gambling or excessive shopping. Dopamine releases generate instant pleasure, prompting users to consume content on the platform repeatedly. The primary techniques TikTok developers use to enhance dopamine production include:

Short-Form Content for Quick Consumption

TikTok's ultra-short content, typically ranging from 15 seconds to 10 minutes, caters to modern users who often have limited attention spans. This format allows users to consume large amounts of content in a short time, which can be highly addictive. The brevity of the videos also makes content creation and consumption easier, as users don't need to invest much time in producing or watching videos. This approach allows TikTok to present a wide variety of content, keeping the user experience fresh. However, this format poses ethical concerns. Rapid content consumption may contribute to a diminished attention span and promote compulsive behaviors. By offering short videos, TikTok encourages users to scroll quickly through content, constantly seeking new and exciting stimuli, a potentially harmful experience for younger users who are more susceptible to addictive patterns of use.

Infinite Scrolling

The brevity of the videos is complemented by the app's infinite content feed, also known as "infinite scroll," which allows users to browse through an endless stream of content without needing to click on individual pages. Infinite scroll exploits the human tendency to want to complete a unit of something to achieve satisfaction. Since TikTok's content is endless, users continue scrolling in the hope of reaching an endpoint, which they know they will never reach. This infinite scrolling also fosters addiction, as the brain experiences a dopamine hit while rapidly changing content in the "For You" feed. This neurological high pushes users to keep exploring, creating an addictive cycle. The app's intuitive design and lack of friction keep users engaged without them realizing it. Users scroll from one video to another automatically, unaware of the minutes passing by.

Social Rewards

TikTok's design also promotes constant social validation through mechanisms that trigger dopamine release. Each time a user encounters an interesting or entertaining video, they experience a small dopamine release. This process reinforces scrolling behavior, incentivizing users to continue interacting with the platform in search of more enjoyable stimuli. Gamification elements like "likes," comments, and sharing options contribute to this effect, creating an environment where social rewards become a powerful driver of continuous participation.

The constant social validation offered by these features may be appealing to users, but it also presents significant risks, especially for younger users. Users may develop a dependency on these social rewards as a source of validation and self-esteem. The pressure to achieve certain interaction levels, such as a high number of "likes" or comments, can lead to problematic behaviors and competition among users.

Personalization Algorithm and Attention Manipulation

The most crucial and distinctive element of TikTok is its recommendation algorithm. Based on advanced artificial intelligence (AI) and machine learning techniques, the algorithm collects and analyzes a wide range of user behavior data to deliver personalized and engaging content. It is designed to offer tailored content to each user, increasing the likelihood of satisfaction with the interaction. This strategy creates a reward cycle that reinforces scrolling behavior and prolonged engagement.

Personalization begins with data collection. TikTok records various data points for each user, including interactions with the app, such as liked, commented on, or shared videos, followed accounts, and rewatched videos. This information allows the algorithm to build a detailed profile of user preferences, identifying behavioral patterns and personal trends. The viewing history is another critical component. The algorithm monitors the duration of time spent on each video, measuring "dwell time" to determine which content attracts the user most. Similarly, it tracks whether the user scrolls quickly or lingers on certain videos. This data enables the algorithm to understand which visual or thematic elements are most appealing to each person.

Once the information is collected, AI processes and analyzes the data. Machine learning models identify correlations and patterns, continuously adjusting recommendations based on the most recent data. TikTok's algorithm is highly dynamic, meaning it can adapt quickly to changes in user interests. The AI not only focuses on individual preferences but also considers broader trends across the platform. It can detect which videos are gaining popularity and being shared more frequently, integrating this information into personalized recommendations. This creates a balance between content relevant to the user and emerging trends within the TikTok community.

The final result is a constant stream of content tailored to each user's tastes. By presenting videos aligned with their preferences, TikTok enhances the user experience and increases the likelihood of spending more time on the app. This also contributes to a sense of personalization, making users feel as though the content is designed specifically for them. As the algorithm becomes more accurate, it can predict with greater precision which videos will capture the user's attention (Sarua et al., 2023). This level of relevance makes the app experience more immersive and addictive, as each scroll promises something interesting and entertaining. Users may spend hours exploring content without realizing the time passed, further feeding into the feedback loop created by the algorithm.

The recommendation algorithm raises ethical concerns. By offering highly relevant and engaging content, the app encourages compulsive use, which may harm users' emotional and mental well-being. The algorithm's ability to quickly adapt and capture user attention can lead to addictive behaviors and excessive dependence on the platform. Additionally, the data collection necessary to operate the algorithm raises privacy concerns (Saura et al., 2022). Users are not always aware of the amount of information being gathered or how it is used to influence their behavior. This level of data collection and processing aligns with the surveillance capitalism model, where companies use personal data for financial gain at the expense of user privacy. The algorithm is central to creating an addictive experience on the app, where users are continually drawn to watch more content.

Growth Goal

TikTok's "*growth goal*," is designed to drive continuous use and increase its user base at any cost. This strategy can take various forms, but all share the aim of increasing the amount of time users spend on the platform and the frequency with which they return. A key tactic is the intensive use of notifications, which are sent frequently to grab users' attention and draw them back into the app, creating a sense of urgency and constant relevance. Another strategy involves creating partnerships with other social networks and platforms, extending TikTok's reach and encouraging content sharing, which in turn prompts users to explore and engage more. Additionally, TikTok personalizes content for each user in a way that feels unique and tailored to their interests, leading to a more engaging and immersive experience. The platform's continuous growth is essential for its business model, but the use of these strategies may result in addictive behaviors and erosion of users' free time, raising significant ethical concerns.

Tiktok Notification Design

The design of notifications in social media plays a key role in creating addictive behaviors by keeping users connected even when they attempt to disconnect. These notifications often provide incomplete information, suggesting there is something new to discover, which encourages users to open the app for full details. Once inside, social networks show personalized content, prolonging user engagement and increasing data collection, which boosts profitability.

In TikTok, notifications are crucial to the platform's success but pose risks to users' well-being. By tapping into the need for social validation, notifications can lead to addictive behaviors and social pressure, particularly affecting younger users' mental and emotional health. TikTok uses diferrent notification strategies to maintain user interest, such as alerts for new followers, "likes," comments, direct messages, and mentions. The frequency of these notifications encourages regular app use. Personalization is key, as TikTok tailors notifications based on user activities and preferences, highlighting relevant content and trends, increasing the chances of engagement.

Notifications trigger emotional responses, especially when related to social validation like new "likes" or comments, which can be likened to a small release of dopamine, motivating users to engage more frequently. Additionally, TikTok promotes popular trends and challenges through notifications, fostering a sense of community. However, this can also generate pressure to conform, which may be harmful to users seeking social validation.

New Features

New features are another element that keeps users hooked and counters the disinterest that prolonged use of the app can generate. By introducing new functionalities, TikTok renews the interest of existing users and attracts new ones, thus driving the platform's growth. These new features add variety and freshness to the user experience, preventing monotony and the feeling of having seen everything. This motivates users to keep exploring the platform, discover new ways to interact and consume content, and, ultimately, spend more time on it. Constant updates with new features are an effective strategy for attracting new users and retaining existing ones. Users seeking novel experiences are drawn to the plataform´s new possibilities, while current users find an incentive to return to it and rediscover it.

Some of the most notable features TikTok has introduced in recent years include TikTok Stories a feature similar to Instagram Stories, offering ephemeral content that disappears after 24 hours, creating a sense of urgency and exclusivity; TikTok Nowa feature that allows users to share photos and videos in real-time, fostering spontaneity and social interaction; and the "Repost" feature, which enables users to share content from other users, extending creators' reach and promoting virality.

Advertising Goal

The "*advertising goal*" in TikTok is a critical component of the platform's unethical design, as it seeks to maximize revenue by continuously exposing users to ads. To achieve this, TikTok implements strategies that make advertising more intrusive and harder to ignore, creating an environment where the user experience is constantly interrupted by sponsored content. Among these tactics are ads placed between feed posts, ensuring that users encounter advertisements even when they are simply browsing content. Auto-playing video ads capture users' attention instantly without their prior consent. Another technique is advanced targeting, which allows TikTok to deliver highly personalized and relevant ads to each user, increasing the likelihood of interaction and thus, ad revenue. While this intrusive approach can be highly profitable for the platform and its advertisers, it is often bothersome to users and contributes to growing concerns about social media overuse and its effects on mental health.

TikTok offers a variety of advertising formats that cater to different marketing objectives and strategies. Among the most prominent are: in-feed ads within the user's "For You" feed, which appear as organic videos, allowing for a seamless and natural experience; Top View ads, which appear as the first video upon opening the app, immediately capturing users' attention; Hashtag Challenge ads, where brands create challenges with specific hashtags, encouraging users to generate creative content related to the campaign's theme; Branded Effects, which allow brands to create custom augmented reality filters and lenses for users to apply in their own videos, fostering interaction and brand recognition; Live Ads, or live broadcasts within the app, giving brands the opportunity to present their products or services interactively and in real-time, generating higher audience engagement; and finally, content creators, strategic collaborations between brands and influencers who recommend products and brands.

Surveillance Capitalism

The unethical design of TikTok is not accidental but rather a deliberate strategy closely related to the concept of surveillance capitalism, an economic model in which users' personal data becomes a source of commercial value, and user attention becomes a valuable commodity sold to advertisers. This model relies on the collection, analysis, and exploitation of large volumes of data to predict and modify human behavior for commercial purposes. In this context, TikTok's design drives this business model by not only facilitating data collection but also propelling the cycle of surveillance and monetization characteristic of surveillance capitalism.

TikTok employs deliberate strategies to keep users hooked, maximizing the time they spend on the platform and, consequently, the amount of data they generate. Its intuitive and appealing interface, infinite scrolling, personalized content, speed, and dopamine-triggering effects create an immersive experience, keeping users active for extended periods and generating a constant flow of data. Every interaction, video view, and action on the platform generates data that is collected and analyzed to create detailed user profiles. Data becomes the platform's primary commercial asset and is used for various purposes such as:

Extremely targeted advertising, increasing ad effectiveness and thus advertising revenue. By knowing users' preferences and behaviors, TikTok can serve ads that are more likely to generate interaction, leading to higher advertising income. Ad formats such as In-Feed, Top View, and Hashtag Challenges benefit from this personalization, ensuring that users see sponsored content aligned with their interests. Additionally, user data is sold to advertisers, allowing them to target their campaigns at people most likely to be interested in their products or services.

Consumer behavior control and product development. By analyzing user data, TikTok can predict preferences, tailor advertising to those most likely to engage, and even influence consumer behavior. The platform's recommendation algorithm plays a key role in this process. It uses artificial intelligence and machine learning techniques to analyze the collected data and deliver personalized content that keeps users engaged. This not only enhances the user experience but also maximizes the amount of data generated by extending users' time on the app. The data collected by the algorithm allows TikTok to continuously adjust and improve its recommendations, making the selection of content more accurate and ensuring longer user engagement, which increases the chances of ad clicks.

Creation of detailed user profiles. TikTok collects vast amounts of information, including location, viewing history, social interactions, and content preferences. This data allows for the creation of detailed user profiles, used not only for content and ad personalization but also for predicting future behaviors. This level of detail is valuable to advertisers and other actors in the surveillance ecosystem, who can use this information to influence user decisions and behaviors, identify trends, and develop new features that enhance the user experience and increase engagement on the platform.

Collective Intelligence

User-generated data on TikTok becomes even more significant within its business model when it is shared collectively. TikTok exploits collective intelligence by encouraging the mass creation and dissemination of content across its platform. With its large user base and ability to collect data at scale, TikTok has sparked debate about its potential to contribute to collective intelligence or, conversely, to be used for prediction and behavioral manipulation purposes. Design mechanisms such as the recommendation algorithm and social rewards leverage the knowledge and creativity of users to keep them engaged. This approach not only increases usage time and engagement but also turns users into active participants in data generation, further fueling the cycle of surveillance capitalism.

The large-scale collection of data has raised concerns about its potential use for predicting and manipulating behavior. While collective intelligence may generate benefits for the platform and its users, it can also be used as a tool for manipulation by companies operating under the surveillance capitalism model. Data from collective intelligence can be used to:

Influence users' opinions and behaviors. Through personalized content and targeted advertising, TikTok can influence users' decisions, opinions, and behaviors, shaping their perception of reality and consumption habits. Additionally, the ease of spreading content on TikTok can be used to disseminate false information, misinformation, and propaganda, manipulating public opinion and causing social divisions. TikTok can also use its control over collective intelligence data to limit access to information and control the discourse on the platform.

CONCLUSION

In a context where social media has deeply integrated into people's daily lives and concerns about addiction, especially among young people, are on the rise, this study aimed to analyze and assess TikTok's unethical design and its relationship with surveillance capitalism and collective intelligence. It seeks to shed light on the ethical implications of social media platforms, using TikTok as an example, and encourages deeper reflection on the role these platforms play in people's lives. To achieve this objective, a comprehensive literature review on ethical social media design, surveillance capitalism, and collective intelligence was conducted, along with a critical analysis of TikTok's design practices. Several key conclusions have been drawn, addressing the specific objectives outlined in this study.

The main findings reveal that TikTok employs various unethical design practices that encourage compulsive use of the application, aimed at holding users' attention for as long as possible to maximize data generation and, ultimately, financial gain.

Firstly, TikTok employs an "engagement goal," designed to keep users hooked on the platform for extended periods through techniques such as a simple interface focused on content without distractions, and other methods that exploit human psychology and the brain's reward system by generating instant gratification through dopamine release. Features like infinite scrolling, short video format, social rewards, and the use of advanced algorithms based on artificial intelligence and machine learning are utilized to personalize each user's experience on their "For You" page. These strategies increase the likelihood that users will experience satisfaction when interacting with the platform, creating a reward cycle that reinforces scrolling behavior and prolonged engagement, maximizing interaction time and user commitment. However, all these features create an addictive environment that can lead to compulsive platform use. This addictive design can negatively affect mental health, promoting dependency and compulsive behavior among users.

Secondly, TikTok pursues a "growth goal," aimed at increasing the number of active users and usage frequency. This goal is achieved through personalized notifications, the constant introduction of new features, and the encouragement of viral content creation. These strategies are designed to attract and retain users, increasing their time on the platform. Intensive use of notifications draws users' attention back to the app, establishing a constant connection even when offline, often with incomplete content designed to compel them to return. The personalization of notifications also plays a critical role in sustaining continuous interest and engagement. On the other hand, to keep users hooked, TikTok continuously introduces new features that add variety to the user experience. These updates not only attract new users but also encourage existing ones to explore the platform and discover new ways to interact with and consume content. Notable features like TikTok Stories, TikTok Now, and the Repost function have been implemented to create a sense of urgency, promote social interaction, and expand content creators' reach. However, these strategies can lead to addictive behaviors and increased social pressure, especially among younger users, raising serious ethical concerns about their impact on mental and emotional well-being.

The "advertising goal" aims to maximize revenue through the continuous exposure of users to intrusive and personalized advertisements. TikTok's advertising formats include in-feed ads, auto-playing Top View ads, Challenge Hashtag, Branded Effect, Live Ads, and collaborations with content creators. The platform employs advanced targeting techniques to deliver highly relevant ads to each user, increasing the likelihood of interaction and, consequently, advertising revenue. However, this strategy results in a user experience constantly interrupted by sponsored content, which can be bothersome and detrimental to users. Moreover, the personalization of ads relies on massive data collection, raising significant concerns about privacy and data exploitation (Saura et al, 2023a). All these design strategies that aim to keep users hooked reflect TikTok's prioritization of profit over user ethics and privacy.

Also, after analyzing the platform's characteristics, it has become clear that TikTok's unethical design practices, driven by goals of engagement, growth, and advertising, are not coincidental but rather a deliberate strategy that directly contributes to the cycle of surveillance capitalism. This economic model turns users' personal data into a source of commercial value and commodifies their attention, which is sold to advertisers.

TikTok's design serves as the core engine of this business model, using deliberate strategies to keep users engaged and maximize the time they spend on the platform, thereby increasing the amount of data they generate. Elements such as its intuitive interface, infinite scrolling, personalized content, and dopamine-triggering effects contribute to an immersive experience that retains users for extended periods, ensuring a steady flow of data. Every interaction, video view, and action on the platform generates data that is meticulously collected and analyzed to create detailed user profiles.

These data become the primary commercial asset, used for multiple purposes, including highly targeted advertising, consumer behavior control, and the development of new products and services. By thoroughly understanding users' preferences and behaviors, TikTok can present highly personalized ads that are more likely to generate interaction, resulting in higher advertising revenues. Additionally, user data is sold to advertisers, allowing them to direct their advertising campaigns toward those most likely to be interested in their products or services. The recommendation algorithm is a crucial component of surveillance capitalism, analyzing collected data to offer personalized content that keeps users engaged. This not only enhances user experience but also maximizes the amount of data generated by prolonging app usage. The data collected enables TikTok to continuously adjust and improve its recommendations, making the algorithm increasingly accurate in selecting content that will retain users' attention and increase the likelihood of clicks on advertisements.

TikTok collects a wealth of information, including users' viewing history, location, social interactions, and content preferences. This information allows for the creation of detailed profiles, which are used not only for content and ad personalization but also for predicting future behaviors. This level of detail is extremely valuable to advertisers and other actors in the surveillance ecosystem, who can use this information to influence users' decisions and behaviors, identify trends, and develop new features that enhance user experience and increase platform participation.

TikTok exploits the collective intelligence of its users to generate and disseminate content on a massive scale. While this can foster creativity and interaction, it can also be used to manipulate opinions and behaviors. The platform's ability to influence users' perceptions and decisions through personalized content and targeted advertising is a powerful but potentially dangerous tool. This manipulation power raises the need for more rigorous scrutiny and measures to protect users from abuse. TikTok capitalizes on collective intelligence by incentivizing the mass creation and distribution of content, turning users into active participants in data generation. This approach not only increases usage time and engagement but also fuels the cycle of surveillance capitalism. However, large-scale data collection can also be used for behavioral prediction and manipulation, raising ethical concerns about its influence on users' behaviors and opinions, limiting access to information, and spreading misinformation.

In this way, unethical design in social media leads to several negative consequences that affect both users and society. After analyzing TikTok's unethical platform design, some direct negative consequences for users were identified. One of the most significant consequences of unethical design is addiction. Features designed to maximize interaction and usage time, such as infinite scrolling, personalization, and dopamine rewards, foster compulsive platform use. Users, especially younger ones, may spend hours scrolling through content without realizing how much time they are investing, leading to a loss of control over their time. The rapid and constant consumption of brief content can deteriorate users' attention spans. Platforms that promote fast scrolling and short content cycles can make users accustomed to quick rewards, making it harder for them to focus on more extended, complex tasks. Moreover, excessive social media use can be linked to various mental health issues, including anxiety, depression, and stress. The constant search for social validation through likes, comments, and followers can lead to emotional dependency and impact self-esteem. Exposure to idealized content can also lead to feelings of inadequacy and low self-worth.

Another consequence is the concern over privacy and data security. The business model based on surveillance capitalism involves massive data collection, often without users' full knowledge or informed consent. This data collection raises serious concerns about privacy and security, as personal information can be used to influence user behavior, direct highly specific advertisements, and potentially be sold to third parties. Additionally, algorithmic designs that personalize content can lead to behavioral manipulation and influence public opinion. Platforms can influence purchasing decisions, political beliefs, and other behaviors by presenting carefully curated content that reinforces certain ideas or products. This can lead to the creation of filter bubbles, where users are only exposed to information that reinforces their pre-existing beliefs, reducing opinion diversity and increasing social polarization.

Finally, the ease with which content can be disseminated on platforms like TikTok also facilitates the spread of misinformation and propaganda. Algorithms that prioritize highly interactive content can amplify false or misleading information, affecting users' perception of reality and contributing to widespread misinformation.

In conclusion, while TikTok's design is ingenious and highly effective in achieving its commercial objectives, it raises serious ethical and social concerns. The application of design principles that promote addictive use and the exploitation of personal data for financial gain must be questioned and regulated.

Theoretical Implications

This study presents several significant theoretical contributions to the fields of social media studies, ethical design, and surveillance capitalism. It expands the concept of unethical design, particularly in the context of TikTok, by providing a detailed analysis of the psychological and design tactics used to capture and retain user attention. This expansion is important for the fields of behavioral psychology and user interface engineering, as it deepens understanding of the specific techniques employed by TikTok. Future research can use these findings as a basis to compare other platforms and explore new dimensions of unethical design. Additionally, this work contributes to the theory of surveillance capitalism by showing how TikTok, through its unethical design, operates within this economic model. It illustrates how the platform collects and exploits personal data to generate revenue, providing a concrete example of surveillance capitalism in practice. This analysis could be used to critique other business models based on personal data exploitation and help develop more complex theories about the relationship between digital platforms and surveillance capitalism.

Another key contribution is the new perspective on digital ethics. By discussing the ethical implications of TikTok's design choices, the study provides a foundation for future discussions on how design decisions impact user well-being. This contributes to the literature on technology ethics and social media. Other researchers can use this analysis to evaluate the ethics of various digital platforms and propose ethical design principles and guidelines.

Practical Implications

In addition to theoretical insights, this study offers several practical implications that could influence social media platform design, technology regulation, and digital education strategies. The conclusions could serve as a guide for social media designers aiming to implement ethical design practices. By identifying the specific tactics that promote addiction and compulsive use, designers can avoid these practices and adopt approaches that prioritize user well-being. This includes creating interfaces that encourage mindful use and incorporate features that allow users to better manage their time. Implementing ethical design could enhance platform perception and increase user satisfaction and loyalty.

The study also has implications for policy-making and digital regulation. Its findings could be used to inform the development of laws that protect users from unethical design practices and personal data exploitation. This might involve regulating personalization algorithms, ensuring transparency in data collection, and safeguarding user privacy. Such regulations could contribute to a safer and more ethical digital environment.

Additionally, the results could be used in educational programs to raise awareness of the risks associated with social media use. Educational institutions and non-profit organizations can develop materials and campaigns to inform users, especially younger audiences, about how social media platforms influence behavior through design techniques. Digital education can empower users to make informed decisions and develop healthier usage habits, helping mitigate the negative effects of unethical design.

The study also emphasizes the importance of considering the mental health impact of social media platforms. Mental health professionals could use these findings to develop strategies and therapeutic approaches to help individuals manage their social media use and reduce the risk of addiction. Furthermore, social media platforms could collaborate with mental health experts to implement features that promote emotional and mental well-being. Integrating mental health considerations into platform design could lead to a healthier and more sustainable digital experience.

Limitations and Future Research

The main limitation of this research was the lack of access to specific data on TikTok's internal design and data collection practices, which may affect the depth and accuracy of the findings. To address this limitation, future research could explore additional data collection approaches, such as interviews with industry experts or analysis of internal company documents. Moreover, the time constraints of the investigation limited the ability to conduct a more exhaustive and detailed analysis of certain key aspects.

The scope of the study, covering broad topics such as unethical design, surveillance capitalism, and collective intelligence, inevitably imposed limits on the depth of analysis in certain areas. The breadth of these topics requires a more detailed and specific treatment, which was not possible within the confines of this study. Additionally, the dynamic nature of technology and social media platforms calls for continuous research and adaptation. Since platforms like TikTok are constantly evolving, the findings of this study may quickly become outdated. Therefore, future research must maintain an updated focus and respond to technological changes and user behavior shifts.

Lastly, it would be valuable to explore further the impact of surveillance capitalism on various aspects of society and how users can better protect themselves from unethical practices. This could include research on topics like promoting more conscious use of social media and technology in general, as well as studies examining the long-term effects of social media use on users' mental health and well-being.

To address these limitations and continue advancing knowledge on ethical social media design, several key areas for future research are identified. First, it is necessary to explore more deeply the long-term psychological effects of using social media with addictive design, providing a more comprehensive understanding of the implications of these practices. It is also suggested to study how different regulations affect the design practices of platforms like TikTok, which could offer valuable insights for effective public policy-making. Finally, research should investigate which interventions and design changes are most effective in promoting user well-being without compromising the commercial viability of platforms. This approach would help develop practical solutions that balance commercial interests with ethical responsibility, contributing to a more ethical and user-centered digital world.

REFERENCES

Balakrishnan, J., & Griffiths, M. D. (2017). Social media addiction: What is the role of content in YouTube? *Journal of Behavioral Addictions*, 6(3), 364–377. DOI: 10.1556/2006.6.2017.058 PMID: 28914072

Bhandari, A., & Bimo, S. (2022). Why's Everyone on TikTok Now? The Algorithmized Self and the Future of Self-Making on Social Media. *Social Media + Society*, 8(1), 20563051221086241. DOI: 10.1177/20563051221086241

Boddy, J., & Dominelli, L. (2017). Social media and social work: The challenges of a new ethical space. *Australian Social Work*, 70(2), 172–184. DOI: 10.1080/0312407X.2016.1224907

Carlson, J., Rahman, M., Voola, R., & De Vries, N. (2018). Customer engagement behaviours in social media: Capturing innovation opportunities. *Journal of Services Marketing*, 32(1), 83–94. DOI: 10.1108/JSM-02-2017-0059

Cía, A. (2014). Las adicciones no relacionadas a sustancias (DSM-5, APA, 2013): un primer paso hacia la inclusión de las Adicciones Conductuales en las clasificaciones categoriales vigentes. Neuro-Psiquiatría, 216. Retrieved from: https://revistas.upch.edu.pe/index.php/RNP/article/view/1169

DataReportal. (2024). Digital 2024: Global Overview Report. https://datareportal.com/reports/digital-2024-global-overview-report

Dulenko, V. (2020). How TikTok design hooks you up. *UX Planet*. https://uxplanet.org/how-TikTok-design-hooks-you-up-6c889522c7ed

Dzioba, B. (2021). Addictive by design: How TikTok keeps you hooked. *UX Collective*. https://digitaltattoo.ubc.ca/2021/11/19/addictive-by-design-how-TikTok-keeps-you-hooked/

Europeo, P. (2023). Reglas europeas para combatir la adicción digital. https://www.europarl.europa.eu/news/es/press-room/20231208IPR15767/reglas-europeas-para-combatir-la-adiccion-digital

Fogg, B. J. (2018). *Tiny habits: The small changes that change everything*. Houghton Mifflin Harcourt.

González-Padilla, P., Navalpotro, F. D., & Saura, J. R. (2024). Managing entrepreneurs' behavior personalities in digital environments: A review. *The International Entrepreneurship and Management Journal*, 20(1), 89–113. DOI: 10.1007/s11365-022-00823-4

Greene, D., Hoffmann, A., & Stark, L. (2019). Better, nicer, clearer, fairer: A critical assessment of the movement for ethical artificial intelligence and machine learning. Gupta, S. (2017). Ethical issues in designing internet-based research: Recommendations for good practice. *Canada Journal of Research Practice Journal of Research Practice*, 13(2).

Griffiths, M. D. (2000). Internet addiction: Does it really exist? *Addiction (Abingdon, England)*, 95(8), 1091–1093.

Hao, X. (2022). Estrategias de funcionamiento de TikTok en el proceso de difusión internacional. Universitat Politècnica de València. http://hdl.handle.net/10251/188817

Harwood, J., & Sundar, S. S. (2019). The dark side of social media: A systematic review of negative effects of social media use. *Social Science & Medicine*, 232, 112294.

Holgado, R. (2022,). El peligro del scroll infinito de las redes sociales: estas son las medidas que existen para combatir su adicción. https://www.20minutos.es/tecnologia/aplicaciones/el-peligro-del-scroll-infinito-de-las-redes-sociales-estas-son-las-medidas-que-existen-para-combatir-su-adiccion-5013669/

Howell, C. (2024). Interfaz de usuario de TikTok: Explicando las elecciones de diseño de TikTok.

Iqbal, M. (2024). TikTok Revenue and Usage Statistics. https://www.businessofapps.com/data/tik-tok-statistics/

Kampf, C. (2014). The cultural production of new forms of practice: Social media, CSR and lifelong learning for consumers. In *2014 IEEE International Professional Communication Conference (IPCC)*. DOI: 10.1109/IPCC.2014.7020382

Kharpal, A. (2023, March 16). TikTok confirms the U.S. has threatened ban if Chinese parent ByteDance doesn't sell stake. CNBC. https://www.cnbc.com/2023/03/16/TikTok-us-threatens-ban-if-chineseparent-bytedance-doesnt-sell-stake.html

Kilgour, L., Sutherland, T., & Wood, S. (2020). Introduction to the Minitrack on critical and ethical studies of digital and social media. In *Proceedings of the 53rd Hawaii International Conference on System Sciences*. DOI: 10.24251/HICSS.2020.289

Koob, G. F., & Volkow, N. D. (2010). Neurocircuitry of addiction. *Neuropsychopharmacology*, 35(1), 217–238. DOI: 10.1038/npp.2009.110 PMID: 19710631

Levin, Y. (2022, August 5). Opinion | It Was a Mistake to Let Kids Onto Social Media Sites. Here's What to Do Now. The New York Times. https://www.nytimes.com/2022/08/05/opinion/social-media-parentschildren.html

Lin, H., Potenza, M. N., Wu, H., & Yücel, M. (2014). Aberrant striatal response to reward anticipation in Internet gaming disorder. *Addiction Biology*, 19(3), 423–432. PMID: 24725195

Lopez, J. (2023). Analyzing TikTok UX/UI: Unveiling the Magic Behind User Behavior and the Infinite Scroll.

Lyulyov, O., Pimonenko, T., Saura, J. R., & Barbosa, B. (2024). How do e-governance and e-business drive sustainable development goals? *Technological Forecasting and Social Change*, 199, 123082. DOI: 10.1016/j.techfore.2023.123082

Macit, H. B., Macit, G., & Güngör, O. (2018). A RESEARCH ON SOCIAL MEDIA ADDICTION AND DOPAMINE DRIVEN FEEDBACK. *Mehmet Akif Ersoy Üniversitesi İktisadi Ve İdari Bilimler Fakültesi Dergisi*, 5(3), 882–897. DOI: 10.30798/makuiibf.435845

Montag, C., Lachmann, B., Herrlich, M., & Zweig, K. (2019, July 23). Addictive Features of Social Media/Messenger Platforms and Freemium Games against the Background of Psychological and Economic Theories. *International Journal of Environmental Research and Public Health*, 16(14), 2612. DOI: 10.3390/ijerph16142612 PMID: 31340426

Morrison, S. (2023). TikTok is confusing by design: TikTok isn't the way I want the internet to work, but it's where the internet is going. https://www.vox.com/technology/23780112/TikTok-internet-design-algorithm-for-you-page-ux-ui

Ochoa, F., & Barragán, M. (2022). El uso en exceso de las redes sociales en medio de la pandemia. ACADEMO *Revista de Investigación en Ciencias Sociales y Humanidades*, 9(1). 85-92. https://doi.org/jzjh

Orihuela-Colliva, J. L. (José Luis). "Internet: la hora de las redes sociales". En., 2008-10-14T10:48:23Z, https://hdl.handle.net/10171/2962

Perez, S. (2022, July 13). Kids and teens spend more time on TikTok than YouTube. TechCrunch. https://techcrunch.com/2022/07/13/kids-andteens-watch-more-TikTok-than-youtube-TikTok-91-minutes-in-2021- youtube-56/

Przybylski, A. K., Murayama, K., DeHaan, C. R., & Gladwell, V. (2013). Motivational, emotional, and behavioral correlates of fear of missing out. *Computers in Human Behavior*, 29(4), 1841–1848. DOI: 10.1016/j.chb.2013.02.014

Quintero-Cacique, J. C., & Lesmes-Silva, A. K. (2021). ¿Por qué el ser humano es adicto a las redes sociales? *Revista CONVICCIONES*, 8(15), 6–9.

Sapolsky, R. (2003). Taming stress. *Scientific American*, 289(3), 86–95. PMID: 12951832

Saura, J. R. (2024). Algorithms in Digital Marketing: Does Smart Personalization Promote a Privacy Paradox? *FIIB Business Review*, 13(5), 499–502. DOI: 10.1177/23197145241276898

Saura, J. R., & Debasa, F. (Eds.). (2022). *Handbook of research on artificial intelligence in government practices and processes*. IGI Global., DOI: 10.4018/978-1-7998-9609-8

Saura, J. R., Palacios-Marqués, D., & Iturricha-Fernández, A. (2021). Ethical design in social media: Assessing the main performance measurements of user online behavior modification. *Journal of Business Research*, 129, 271–281. DOI: 10.1016/j.jbusres.2021.03.001

Saura, J. R., Palacios-Marqués, D., & Ribeiro-Soriano, D. (2023a). Privacy concerns in social media UGC communities: Understanding user behavior sentiments in complex networks. *Information Systems and e-Business Management*, •••, 1–21. DOI: 10.1007/s10257-023-00631-5

Saura, J. R., Ribeiro-Navarrete, S., Palacios-Marqués, D., & Mardani, A. (2023). Impact of extreme weather in production economics: Extracting evidence from user-generated content. *International Journal of Production Economics*, 260, 108861. DOI: 10.1016/j.ijpe.2023.108861

Saura, J. R., Ribeiro-Soriano, D., & Palacios-Marqués, D. (2022). Assessing behavioral data science privacy issues in government artificial intelligence deployment. *Government Information Quarterly*, 39(4), 101679. DOI: 10.1016/j.giq.2022.101679

Saura, J. R., Škare, V., & Dosen, D. O. (2024). Is AI-based digital marketing ethical? Assessing a new data privacy paradox. *Journal of Innovation & Knowledge*, 9(4), 100597. DOI: 10.1016/j.jik.2024.100597

Sunstein, C. R., & Thaler, R. H. (2003). Libertarian paternalism is not an oxymoron. SSRN Electronic Journal. DOI: 10.2139/ssrn.405940

Syrjälä, M. (2024). How social media uses UX design to keep user engaged: case study: TikTok (Bachelor's thesis).

Topino, E., Gori, A., Jimeno, M. V., Ortega, B., & Cacioppo, M. (2023). The relationship between social media addiction, fear of missing out and family functioning: A structural equation mediation model. *BMC Psychology*, 11(1), 383. DOI: 10.1186/s40359-023-01409-7 PMID: 37941011

Trujillo, R., Flores, G., & Arias Montaño, J. (2000). Dopamina: Síntesis, liberación y receptores en el Sistema. *BIÓMEDICA*, 1, •••. https://www.revistabiomedica.mx/index.php/revbiomed/article/ view/218

Yang, Z. (2023). How China takes extreme measures to keep teens off TikTok. MIT Technology Review. https://www.technologyreview.com/2023/03/08/1069527/china-TikTokdouyin-teens-privacy/

Zeng, J., & Kaye, D. B. (2022). From content moderation to visibility moderation: A case study of platform governance on TikTok. *Policy and Internet*, 14(1), 79–95. Advance online publication. DOI: 10.1002/poi3.287

Zhao, H., & Wagner, C. (2022). How TikTok leads users to flow experience: Investigating the effects of technology affordances with user experience level and vídeo length as moderators. Internet Research, ahead-ofprint(ahead-of-print). DOI: 10.1108/INTR-08-2021-0595

Zhao, Z. (2021). *Analysis on the "Douyin (TikTok) Mania"*. Phenomenon Based on Recommendation Algorithms., DOI: 10.1051/e3sconf/202123503029

Zuboff, S. (2015). Big other: Surveillance capitalism and the prospects of an information civilization. *Journal of Information Technology*, 30(1), 75–89. DOI: 10.1057/jit.2015.5

Zuboff, S. (2023). The age of surveillance capitalism. In *Social theory re-wired* (pp. 203–213). Routledge. DOI: 10.4324/9781003320609-27

Zuboff, S., & Maxmin, J. (2004). *The support economy: why corporations are failing individuals, and the next episode of capitalism*. Penguin.

Chapter 7
Role of Data Analytics to Sustainability in Apparel Supply Chain Management

Kamalendu Pal
https://orcid.org/0000-0001-7158-6481
University of London, UK

ABSTRACT

Textile companies have gradually realized that data is essential for improving sales and revenue margins because clothing brands and retailers must develop manufacturing and sale styles that resonate with customers. In recent decades, with advancements in various categories of data analytics and artificial intelligence techniques (e.g., machine learning), the value of data-driven applications has been well acknowledged by textile clothing retailers as they use these predictive software outputs for regular operational decision-making. This chapter reviews retail businesses and their products' manufacturing data analytics and presents a scalable business intelligence framework using a graph data model and its management system. The chapter also highlighted that big data technologies and related supporting resources (e.g., Internet of Things enable capturing, storing, processing, and sharing data) in real-time help to make business operational decisions faster and effective way.

DOI: 10.4018/979-8-3693-6945-6.ch007

INTRODUCTION

Textiles and clothing are a significant part of the world's economy (Pal & Yasar, 2020). In 2000, the world's consumers spent around one trillion United States currency on clothing – split roughly one-third in Western Europe, one-third in North America, and one-quarter in Asia. Seventy percent of total world exports are in clothing and textiles. Significant parts of the sector are dominated by developing countries, particularly in Asia (Pal, 2023). Moreover, in recent years, the textile and clothing business world has been disrupted by the coronavirus pandemic (COVID-19) and a move to remote working, digital customer experience revolutions, ongoing clothing retail business turmoil, and an economic slowdown. Textile manufacturers are coming across unprecedented changes in cost reduction and performance improvement.

Many textiles and clothing companies have relied on and continue to rely on timely decision-making with the help of business operational data, interpretation, and decision-making by using artificial intelligence (AI) techniques, which guide them to navigate uncertain times. However, while having data and the right technology in place is essential, the ability to turn data into insights and insights into action is where businesses see value begin to materialize. Additionally, textile and clothing companies harnessing AI's power to augment data-driven decision-making further enhance their capabilities, drive more value, and maximize business impact.

Graph data models play crucial roles in today's data-driven decision-making. Graphs are supported by mathematical graph theory-based representations and computations that enable flexible and powerful evaluations of domain objects and their relationships. Thus, graph analytics and graph mining have become popular among academics and practitioners of different business domains, such as analyzing customer engagement in the retail clothing industry. Also, business data can be abstracted as a graph where vertices represent heterogenous domain objects like products, sales orders, or telephone calls, and edges represent relationships between those objects. One of the main objectives of this chapter is to present an example of graph data-based business intelligence applications for the clothing industry. However, the textile and clothing industry's real-world operations are complex and challenging.

Figure 1. Textile industry and its dependencies with related industrial business processes

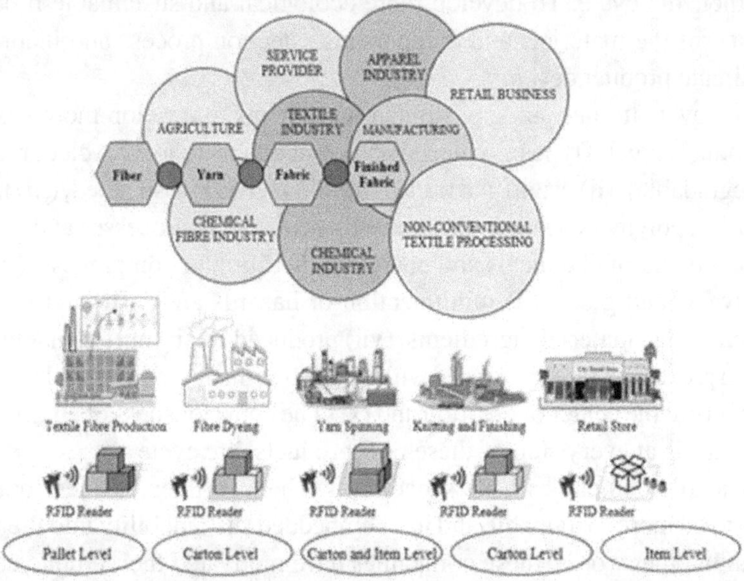

Textile and garment manufacturing are complex and consist of very long chains of operational activities, from raw materials to the fabrication of finished products. The textile and clothing production process comprises different industries and their integrated efforts. For example, agriculture, chemical, and textile industries work in a coordinated way to produce natural and synthetic fibers, the main ingredients of fashion and commercial textile products for industrial use. It presents a significant challenge to textile manufacturers. Researchers (Pal, 2017) described an industrial world with challenges to maintaining sustainability for controlling environmental pollution inequality in global environmental policies and organizational approaches. Academics and practitioners are introducing new business models emphasizing resource waste prevention and focusing on work practice efficiency. A simplistic textile and clothing business model consists of procurement of textile fiber, fiber colouring, yarn preparation, knitting and finishing the products and sending them to sales outlets, as shown in Figure 1.

The growing population and increased consumption of textile products are causing higher environmental burdens on air, water, and soil associated with producing raw materials, manufacturing ingredients, and ultimate items of interest. Besides, the disposal of textile products at the end of use requires more consideration. For example, textile products are usually made from various materials and ingredients chosen by considering the design, purpose of the item, and performance needed for use. The adequate selection of materials, components, and constituent ingredients provides an immense opportunity for the overall sustainability of textile products through their life cycle. To develop more ecological and sustainable products, in what concerns the materials and components selection process and incorporation in the ultimate product design.

In this way, materials, and constituent ingredients to develop more sustainable textile products are: (i) type of material and components (e.g., recycled, recyclable, and biodegradable), (ii) origin and transportation methods associated, (iii) materials (e.g., textiles, polymers, leather) produced by ecofriendly processes and the use the minimum amount of chemicals and energy in their production process, (iv) water-based solvents and glues, (v) minimization of hazards and restricted substances, (vi) the renewable material ingredients, (vii) produced by simplified manufacturing production processes, (viii) produced with innovative manufacturing technology with sustainability at the center of creation and (xi) The consciousness of environmental-related issues is at every step of these new products' life cycle.

Many textile companies have successfully changed their business operational activities to be more sustainable and have embedded sustainability into their regular functions. In other words, these companies have motivated their employees with a sense of sustainable corporate steward that helps them to engage in more sustainable-supporting corporate activities. When employees integrate environmental and societal sustainable-related issues in corporate decisions, sustainability progress manifests in individual business goals, decisions, and actions. Business process-generated data drives these decisions and actions. This way, using available data for analytics design has also started to get immense value for handling business operations. However, estimates of the data value are required to accurately understand how data can contribute value to the textile's regular business operations and how to manage the collection and use of various data types.

This chapter's main objective is to highlight a systemic approach for the textile industry, the value of data, and data analytics in day-to-day operations. It includes product and service personalization to win the game of customer experience. In order to understand the broad sources of data in the textile industry, the chapter uses Professor Michael Porter's value chain model to identify the data sources in the textile industry. Data collection and processing power provide the information system architecture for any industry, and this chapter provides a new technology-based approach to provide a solid foundation. Next, the chapter provides an example of the textile industry's sales data processing using a graph data model. In the last section, the chapter concludes with future research directions and concluding remarks.

BACKGROUND OF CUSTOMER EXPERIENCE

Textile and clothing retail enterprises with data-driven cultures understand and appreciate how to use data and analytics throughout business operations (Pal, 2023). These enterprises use data in decision-making, performance monitoring, and product development. They constantly look for new ways to measure the enterprise and its operational environment. Sophisticated analytics and intelligent computing techniques are at the center of how businesses with data-driven cultures compete. These enterprises also recognize the limits of data and analytics. They acknowledge failures, learn from them, and conduct frequent experiments with business operational data (Pal, 2023).

Examples of organizations with data-driven cultures include Capital One, Procter & Gamble, Google, and Amazon are the few examples (Pal, 2023). Academics and practitioners highlight that developing a data-driven culture is difficult, but organizational performance lags behind its business. Industry-specific research also shows that businesses are not improving or are even getting worse. It is discouraging since business organizations without a data-driven culture make inferior decisions, engage in less innovation, and have less talent than competitors.

One of the valuable retail business lessons is to focus on customer engagement and provide a superior customer experience. The five digital forces of mobility, big data, cloud service, social media, and analytics have empowered retailers to reimagine the shopper's journey. In this era of the physical-to-digital world, easy connectivity, radically changing consumer behaviour, listening to customers, and contextually engaging customers with deep personalization are the best bets for long-term profitability and customer loyalty. It implies a transformational change in the underlying business model, processes, and tools.

Across different industries, many organizations have created successful business models by institutionalizing interactions, which enables seamless and continuous conversations with customers across every contact point. However, it consistently questions the practitioners and operation managers on the usefulness of continuous interactions. The other important issue is sufficiently consistent interactions. Inconsistent interactions can often lead to consumer mistrust, potentially making such efforts more damaging than enriching.

Customers are social entities, and understanding their buying behaviour is challenging. Often, practitioners compare their retail buying behavioural signatures with those of a football player within the penalty box and maneuvering to put the ball to the goal. At the same time, customers and retailers are increasingly adopting digital channels, which has resulted in the availability of and access to product data, reviews and comparisons, price, promotions, and stock levels. This ubiquitous availability of rich data has pushed digital customer interactions towards transactions. While customers are demanding more from retailers – lower prices, better value, extensive range, quicker fulfillment – information democratization is the overarching theme. Customers consistently seek better deals, which has commoditized retail, forcing retailers to differentiate themselves through value-added interactions. A transaction becomes critical and value-added when it involves a personalized interaction – it creates a serendipitous experience by enriching product discovery.

In order to foster long-term relationships, retailers must offer meaningful personalization. With various digital forces at play and, more significantly, use cases connecting two or more digital channels, a one-to-one relationship with customers may no longer be a distant dream – it is an approaching opportunity that needs to be seized. The operations, marketing, technology, and corporate teams will have to come together to define the constructs of designing and delivering these personalized interactions, which means that the rules of the retail game need to be redefined.

Advantage of Retail Product Personalization

Textile products are essential commodities for human society. The textile industry's operational practices have been changing rapidly in recent decades, and its business activities are considered responsible for their day-to-day work that affects society directly or indirectly. The increase in human population has demanded approaches that are more adaptable to the sustainability and ecology of the textile industry. In addition, trends in textile product development are influenced by the globalization of manufacturing networks, digitization of business operations, and multifaceted consumer expectations related to operational sustainability. Consequently, industry experts seek detailed information regarding the environmental impact of textile products' constituent elements, products, and production processes.

Figure 2. Diagrammatic representation of textile product sales activities

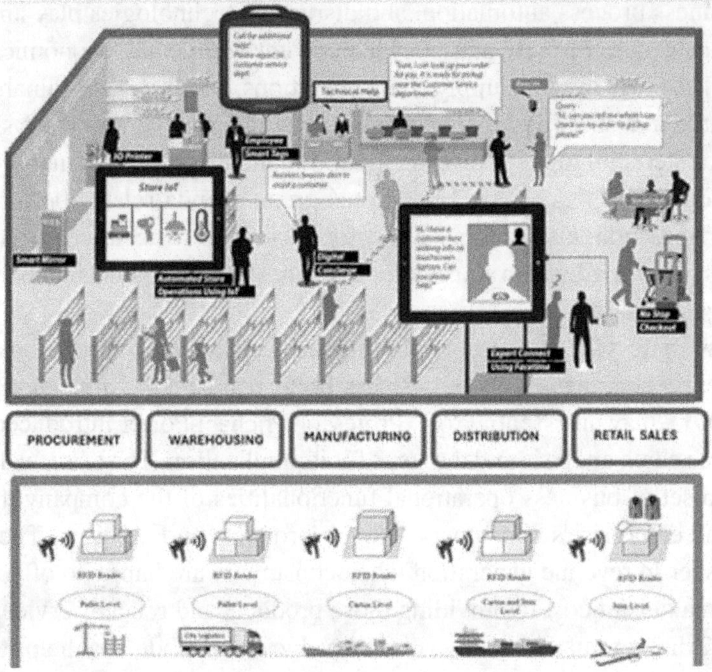

Besides, textile product manufacturing has often fragmented, and a globally dispersed production network acts as a significant stimulus in industry-specific supply chain network deployment and value creation for the entire business operations. Historically, the concept of supply chain operations (or *value chain network* for business prosperity) and management practice is getting much more complex due to business processes outsourcing and their product traceability monitoring for regulatory purposes and quality assurance management. Supply chain operation managers appreciate the importance of enforcing assessment through achievement by using data-driven decision metrics. The crucial ingredients of traceability management are business process-related data gathering, data processing, data-driven decision-making, and secure information-sharing system architecture (Pal, 2023). In this way, it creates an essential ingredient for an attractive industrial operation management using technologies. Business process-generated data drives these decisions and actions. This way, using available data for analytics design has also started to get immense value for handling business operations. However, estimates of the data value are required to accurately understand how data can contribute value to the textile's regular business operations and how to manage the collection and use of various data types.

Textile manufacturing and retailing activities have changed in recent decades due to business process automation, and disruptive technologies play an essential role. The influences of these activities include environmental, economic, societal, and as well as those of their supply chain operations. Moreover, sustainability is all around textile industries and manufacturing activities and has become a significant challenge and crucial topic of investigation. The inclusion of sustainability-related business activities enhances the operational green agenda-related performance of the enterprises, and it also presents a way for businesses to accumulate a new set of advantages that provide them attain competitiveness by using sustainability agendas around regular operations.

In order to assess the organizational competitive advantage of operations, strategic management techniques, such as business performance and *value chain analysis* (Porter, 2001), play an essential role. Professor Michael Porter introduced the concept of value chain analysis and the steps for its application. The term "value chain" describes a set of business operational functionalities of the company that brings value to the enterprise's consumers through products and services. The business benefits usher in revenue generation when consumers are happy to offer the costs over the break-event cost in providing those products and related services.

Figure 2 diagrammatically describes the value chain model that helps to identify and assess those value-creating activities comprising an industrial business operation (e.g., textile manufacturing and sales). The value chain analysis model consists of business activities that a textile company can use to analyze and deliver a product or a service. This analysis considers a series of business activities related to raw materials procurement and the sale of finished products. The series of activities consists of (i) coming materials and putting them in temporary storage and warehouses around manufacturing plants for material management purposes, (ii) logistical production management that involves in the transformation of raw materials into semi-finished or finished materials, and calculating the expenditure for the final outputs (e.g., goods and services), (iii) next, it consider the business storage and transportation costs from manufacturing plants to the sales shops for ultimate consumers, (iv) product market-based identity or banding and sales related communication, and finally (v) sales of the products to consumers and after-sales service plan.

The value chain analysis also considers four operational support functionalities: (i) the administration and management part of the planning activities that includes the procurement of materials and services, (ii) the deployment of technological infrastructures for processing raw materials to finished products, (iii) required staffs recruitment and training related strategic actions, and (iv) manufacturing business infrastructures that look after the financial, legal, and public service-related issues.

In this way, Porter describes breaking down a business operational activity that represents the primary constituent building blocks of competitive advantage. Operational supervisors can then assess how individual business operations enhance the value of the final product or service. It is also evident from the research that industrial business process operations can be rewarded and create added value to the revenue streams by using big data analytics. The critical idea behind this added value is generating insightful data analysis and using the data analysis's ultimate results with industrial partners so that operation managers can act collaboratively.

The recent types of data analytics require sophisticated and robust information and communication technology provision, modern data structures utilization, and management ability to enhance day-to-day activities' operational efficiency quickly and promptly. Moreover, researchers urged industrial manufacturing companies to deploy new data-acquiring methods (e.g., Radio Frequency Identification (RFID) tags, nanotechnology-based techniques, and Sensors) and data storage repositories supported by the new generation of package software systems (e.g., enterprise resource planning (ERP), supplier relationship management (SRM)) to improve industrial operations scheduling (Pal, 2021).

Textile and clothing businesses face a regular operating environment where disruptive technologies drive continuous changes in business-delivery models and skill sets at every level. It has been widely recognized that big data technologies and IoT enable capturing, storing, processing, and sharing data in real time, further driving transparency and visibility in the daily operations of the clothing business to make faster and more effective decisions (Keikhosrokiani, 2022a, 2022b). Academics and practitioners (Pal, 2020a; Pal, 2020b; Pal, 2021) highlight the consequential views of disruptive technology implementation as a strategic decision to improve business competitive advantages.

Figure 3. Value chain analysis model

Sustainability-related issues are the other important factors essential to new industrial value chain operational activities. Sustainability practices provide the safest route to governmental regulations and customer satisfaction (Pal, 2023). Industrial data analytics provide a way to address social issues and create value-added economic revenue (Pal, 2023) while optimizing the operating environment and the effects of the green environment (Pal, 2021).

Moreover, the ramifications of massive-collected data analyses on Lean, Agile, Resilient, Green, and Economical (LARGE) issues outcome are providing some guidelines for different categories of supply chain operations (Chun Wu, 2003) (Dora et al., 2016) (Baramichai et al., 2007) (Srivastava, 2007) in present years. Some researchers put forward the panacea of the LARGE ideas of industrial operations as a value-added manifestation. The following section briefly presents a selection of LARGE concepts based on recent research.

RECENT SUPPLY CHAIN DATA ANALYTICS RESEARCH

Industrial manufacturing businesses require to place sustainable work practices to comply with international institution guided regulations. Big data analytics are helping businesses to achieve social dimensions and improve economic values while optimizing the green effects related to corporate sustainability.

In addition, the research articles reviews of the researcher-works realised that some western countries (e.g., United Kingdom, United States of America, and Germany) are using vast business operation related data collection and analyses for supply chain management. Developing countries (e.g., India, China) are also under the microscope of industrial manufacturing sustainability related research works. Figure 4 presents a diagrammatic visualization of sustainability related research for few countries.

Figure 4. Recent research on manufacturing industry and supply chain

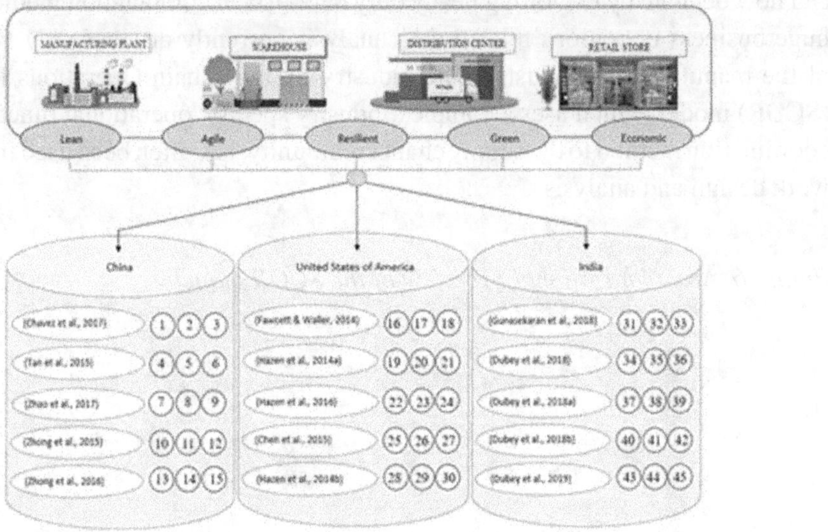

Figure 5. Legend

1. Delivery Flexibility
2. Cost and Quality
3. Customer Satisfactions
4. Manager Competence Skills
5. Case of Optimal Decision
6. Analytic Infrastructure Model
7. Green Supply Chain
8. Inherent Risk
9. Total Cost Management
10. Manufacturing with Sensor Networks
11. Business Case Study
12. RFID Technology
13. Big Data Processing Technologies
14. Decision Make Model
15. Big Data Interpretation
16. Supply Chain Agility
17. Capacity Analysis
18. Operational Dynamics
19. Correlational Decision Analysis
20. Prediction Through Profiling
21. Collaborative Supply Chain
22. Manufacturing Organizations
23. Senior-Level Supply Chain Managers
24. Big Data Based Decisions
25. Factor Analysis
26. Senior Executive Managers
27. Technological Capabilities
28. Big Data Framework for Supply Chain
29. Structural Equation Modelling
30. Operational Dynamics Analysis
31. Big Data Processing Technologies
32. Supply Chain Performance
33. Top Management Commitment
34. Big Data Processing Technologies
35. Decision Make Model
36. Organizational Flexibility
37. Resource Complementarity
38. Organizational Compatibility
39. Temporal Orientation
40. Big Data Based Business Operations
41. Decision Make Model
42. Collaborative Performance
43. Senior-Level Supply Chain Managers
44. Supply Chain Resilience
45. Big Data Analytics

This research works described various application areas in various manufacturing industries and the utilization of big data processing-related issues. The main agenda is to show that business operational practices that in the past were carried out on speculative or time-consuming complex mathematical modelling of reality can now be done by exploiting heavy duty data-driven computation methods. Such huge business operations related data analysis currently drives nearly all aspects of the manufacturing industry. The industry Supply Chain Operations Reference (SCOR) model, which uses a complex industry specific operational functionalities coordination method to the supply chain community, has often been used in research work design and analysis.

Figure 6. An organizational overview of the SCOR model

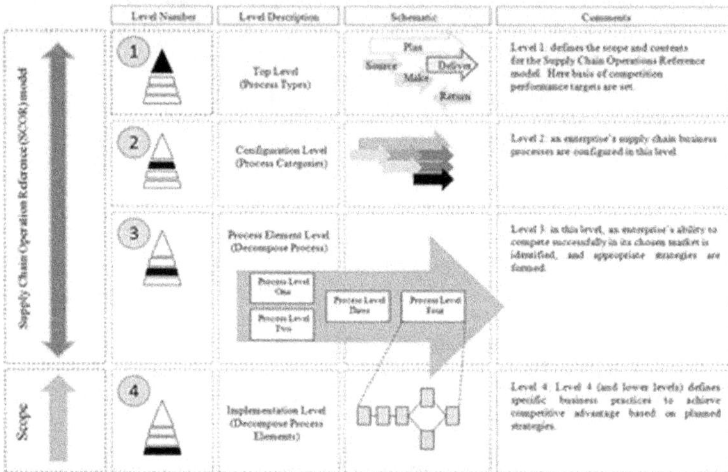

The SCOR model considers customer engagement information, regular business transactions, and market economic indicators related issues. In this analysis, the SCOR model uses a standardized multi-level business operation with Key Performance Indicators (KPIs) over various levels of activities. The SCOR method uses five-elements based operational strategy: Plan (P), Source (S), Make (M), Deliver (D), and Return (R) – from the suppliers' supplier to customers' customers, and all aligned with leading enterprise's operational strategy, material, work, and information flow. Figure 6 presents the SCOR model's operations.

In this way, every process metric uses aspects of a performance characteristic for operational, tactical, and strategic performance measurements across the whole business operations.

Significant technological advancements have been achieved in textile product production, transportation, and sales-related activities, in recent years. Often this achievement relates to a new generation of industrial businesses processes data capture, storage, and processing methods. Textile industry-specific data is uploaded daily in massive quantity to different storage platforms in the form of text, image, audio and video, through various media such as blogs, emails, social networks, photo and advertising hosting services. Besides, textile industries business operational data are stored on individual corporation data storages. Many companies (e.g., Google, Microsoft, Facebook, and Twitter) are also collecting a large amount of data about the web users, their related interaction activities with the social media, and this data is commonly termed as Big Data (Pal, 2018).

BIG DATA SIGINAFACE AND DATA ANALYTICS

Big Data is a common technical phrase that describes a significant volume of structured and unstructured data produced by various industrial business processes. For ordinary people's understanding, it is often presented with different numbers of Vs. (e.g., 4V – that is, Volume, Velocity, Variety, Veracity, and 5Vs or 6Vs), moreover, it describes the challenge the business world needs to address.

Figure 7 presents a brief overview of big data for industrial use and some relevant socio-technical issues for business application development. For example, consumer behavioural characteristics to design and develop recommendation systems.

Figure 7. A conceptual view of big data for industrial use

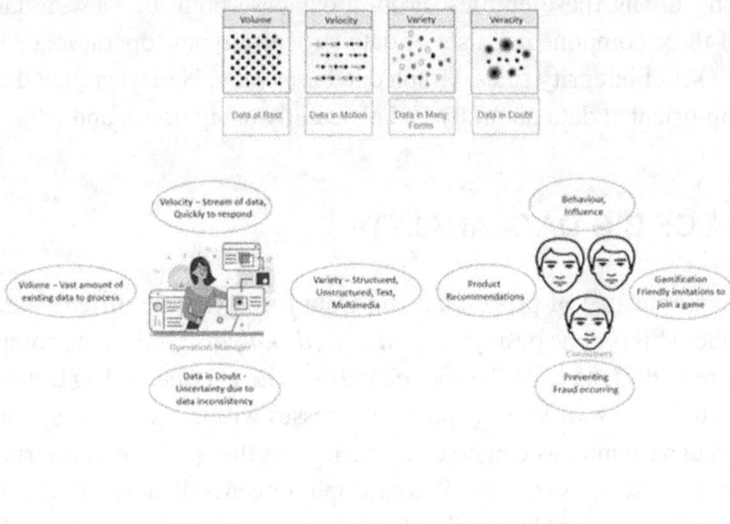

Academics and practitioners are assessing bottlenecks in various industrial applications. These bottlenecks have been tackled by various categories of data management models and algorithms. The following section discusses various databases developed to store significant data for analysis.

DATA PROCESSING AND INDUSTRIAL APPLICATIONS

Data processing systems have historically been inseparable technological means for regular manufacturing and distribution operations. In the 1970s, manufacturing business operations were coordinated with the help of third-generation programming (i.e., COBOL) applications (e.g., material management, raw material procurement, human resource management, and transportation). The early 1980s gifted relational data management systems for industrial application development.

However, with the increased volume of semi- or unstructured and interconnected data, storing data in relational databases has become tedious and inefficient since these information processing systems have constrained data models and deal poorly with relationships. The drawbacks of traditional database systems, particularly the relational data model, to mitigate the needs of industrial applications have led to the development of new-generation database technologies. Among them, Graph Databases are calling the attention of the database community because, in trendy projects where a database is needed, the extraction of worthy information relies on processing the graph-like structure of the data. Activity around graph databases flourished in today's industrial applications.

One of the most essential elements conforming to a database is its '*database model*' or simply '*data model*.' In the most general sense, a data model needs a collection of conceptual tools to model representations of real-world *entities* and the relations among these entities. From a database point of view, a data model consists of three components: a set of data structure types, operators or inference rules, and a set of integrity rules. Graph databases (e.g., Neo4j) are good at storing relationship-oriented data naturally and efficiently using nodes and edges.

THE ERA OF BIG DATA ANALYTICS

The main objective of processing Big Data is to generate differentiated, trustworthy value. This is done by applying *advanced analytics* against the complete data collection, regardless of scale. To understand the critical issues of Big Data, one must understand the *data sources* of business processes within industrial applications.

Graph database models can be characterized as those where data structures for the schema and instances are modelled as graphs or generalizations of them and data manipulation is expressed by graph-oriented operations and type constructors. The advantages of using a graph data model are that it introduces a level of abstraction that allows more natural modelling of graph data, query languages, operations, and algorithms for storing and querying graphs. A few essential preliminaries of graph databases are described below.

Graph Database Preliminaries:

Graph databases store data in the form of *nodes*, *edges*, and *relationships* that provide index-free adjacency. Figure 7. Represents a simple product-order database. A graph is a pair G = (V, E) of sets such that E ⊆ (V x V). The elements of V are vertices or nodes of the graph G, and the element of E are its *edges* or *relationships*. Because academic literature on graph theory typically talks about vertices and edges, which available graph database and its APIs operate on nodes and relationships respectively, these terms are used interchangeably in this chapter.

Order – The order of a graph G, denoted by |G|, is the number of vertices of G. Its number of edges is denoted by ||G||.

Incident Vertex – A vertex v is incident with an edge e if $v \in$ e; then e is an edge at v. An edge $\{x, y\}$ can be written as xy.

Vertex Degree – The set of all edges in E at a vertex v is denoted E(v). The degree of a vertex v, denoted as d(v), is the number |E(v)| of edges at v.

Figure 8. Characteristics of relational and graph database

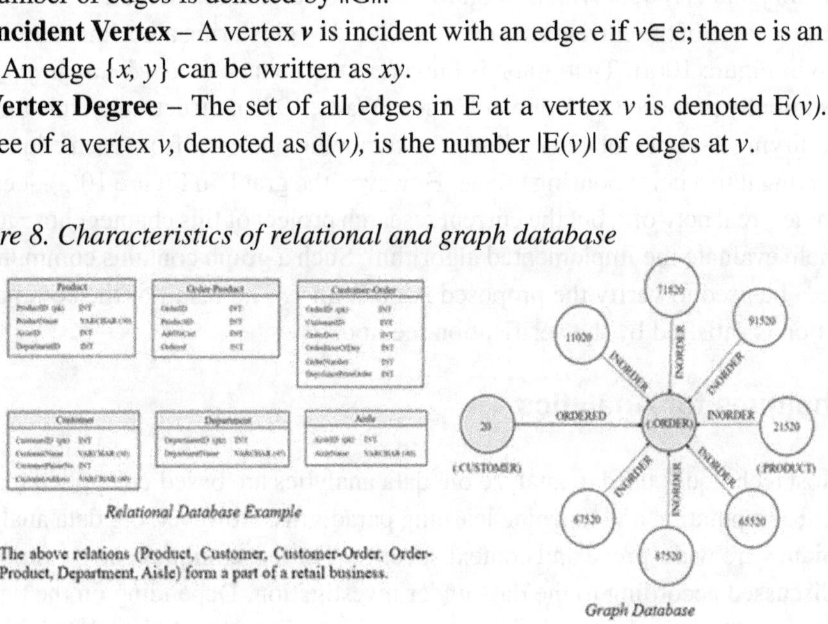

Subgraph – Given two graphs G = (V, E) and G' = (V', E'), G' is a subgraph of G, written as G' ⊆ G and G' contains all the edges $xy \in$ E with x, y ∈ V', then G' is an induced subgraph of G.

Path – A path is a non-empty graph P = (V, E) of the form V = $\{x_0, x_1, \dots x_k\}$, E = $\{x_0x_1, x_1x_2, \dots x_{k-1}x_k\}$. The number of edges in a path is its length.

BIG DATA ANALYTICS

A simple definition is that "BI is a wider group of software applications, technologies, infrastructure, and processes for gathering, storing, accessing, and analyzing data to help business users make operational decisions" (Watson, 2009). The methodology used in this chapter's research is based on the cross-industry standard process for the data mining model conceived initially by IBM research in the mid-1990s. The model consists of six phases for conducting a data mining project. The six phases are (i) understanding business, (ii) data understanding which deals with the initial data collection and analysis, (iii) data preparation, (iv) modelling, (v) evaluation, and (vi) deployment. Figure 10 (b) represents the model.

The research of the current chapter is evaluated by clustering algorithm on a graph shown in Figure 10(a). That graph is known as the connected *caveman graph*, and it was initially proposed by Duncan J Watts (Watts, 1999). Structurally, it is formed by modifying a set of isolated k-cliques by removing one edge from each clique and connecting it to a neighbouring clique. However, the graph in Figure 10(a) does not resemble a real network, but the current research project of this chapter chose it as it will help evaluate the implemented algorithm. Such a graph contains communities that can be used to verify the proposed Algorithm 1. The result of the community detection is satisfied by the verification method.

Techniques for Analytics

Most techniques used to analyze big data analytics are based on applied mathematical computation and machine learning paradigms. However, big data analytics techniques are widespread and context specific. These techniques can be classified and discussed according to the data under investigation. Depending on the type of data, four central big data analytics can be defined: (i) text analytics: this technique is used to find out relevant information from textual data, (ii) audio analytics: techniques deployed to extract information from unstructured audio data. Customer service telephone conversations with customers are the primary source of audio analytics. Some of the main techniques used for audio analytics include large vocabulary, continuous speech recognition and phonetics-based systems, (iii) video analytics: methods used to monitor and analyze video streams. Video analytics has been mainly used as a replacement for labor-intensive observation. In addition, many business applications of video analytics are being used in manufacturing to collect data on customer demographics and preferences, and (iv) social media analytics: techniques used to analyze structured and non-structured data from social media channels (e.g., Twitter, Facebook). Some exciting techniques used to analyze social media data are community detection, social influence analysis and link prediction.

Many successful enterprises have invested large sums of money in business intelligence and data warehousing tools and technologies. These enterprises believe that up-to-date, accurate and integrated information about their supply chain, products and customers is critical for their survival.

In order to solve a problem, the Big Data-based application uses intelligent reasoning in automated software that helps users apply analytical and scientific methods to business decision-making. The software applications that focus on the industrial decision support systems, providing Big Data-based tools to support a user's global supply chain reasoning process to develop a solution to the problem.

Figure 9. Typical types of Big Data application systems

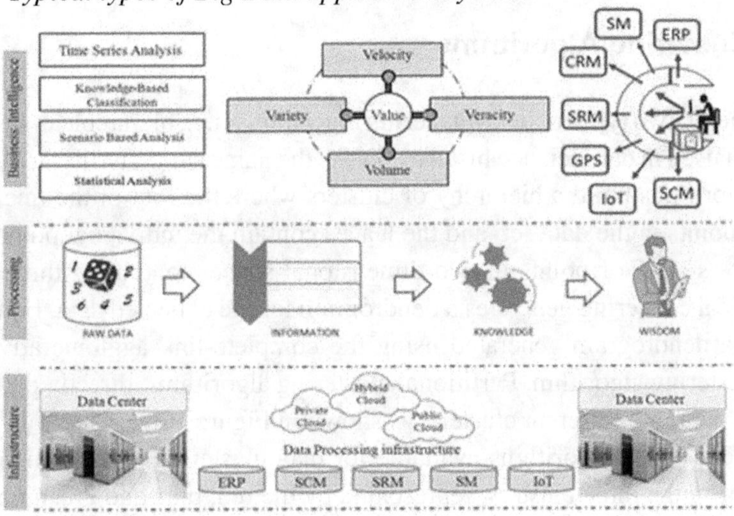

Once the industrial business process data is collected, it needs to be stored for processing purposes. In the data processing phase, the collected data is analyzed for business operational decision making. Data analysis is broadly classified into two different categories: (i) exploratory, and (ii) confirmatory. The main objective of exploratory analysis is to discover patterns and model the data. Exploratory data analysis is usually followed by a phase of confirmatory data analysis which aims at model validation. Many mathematical techniques have been proposed to perform data analysis. Statistical pattern recognition and machine learning is often used with predicative analysis that consists of finding relationships among objects in consideration and predicting future events, based on the knowledge obtained. Pattern recognition comprises of three phases: data representation, learning and inference.

Data Representation

In order to analyze the collected data, the analysis process needs an appropriate representation scheme to represent the data. Again, this representation involves picking a set of properties to identify the objects of interest in the data set. A d-dimensional vector $x = (x_1, x_2, \ldots x_d)^T$ represents each object, where x_p, $p \in [d]$ denotes a feature. The features may be *numerical*, *categorical* or *ordinal*. For example, a written textual artifact may be represented using the words in the artifact; in which case each x_p denotes a word in the artifact. An image may be presented by the pixel intensity values. In this case, x_p is the numerical intensity value at the pth pixel.

Data Clustering Algorithms

In general, two types of data clustering algorithms (i.e., hierarchical, partitional) have been used in data science historically. As the name suggests, hierarchical clustering algorithms build a hierarchy of clusters where the root of the tree contains all the n points in the data set, and the leaves contain the individual points. Figure 10(a) shows a set of points in two-dimensional space, containing three clusters. Hierarchical clustering generates a dendrogram for the collected data. Figure 10(b) presents a dendrogram generated using the complete-link agglomerative hierarchical clustering algorithm. Partitional clustering algorithms, directly partition the collected data into different clusters, as shown in Figure 10(c). There are different types of clustering algorithms available for data clustering. For example, Figure 10(c) depicts the three clusters, represented by the red, blue and green points, and obtained using the *k*-means algorithm.

Figure 10. Various categories of data clustering

(a) (b) (c)

The methodology used in this chapter's research is inspired by the cross-industry standard process for the data mining model conceived initially by IBM research in the mid-1990s. The model consists of six phases for conducting a data mining project.

The six phases are (i) understanding business, (ii) data understanding which deals with the initial data collection and analysis, (iii) data preparation, (iv) modelling, (v) evaluation, and (vi) deployment. Figure 11 (b) represents the model.

Figure 11. Connected caveman graph of six cliques.

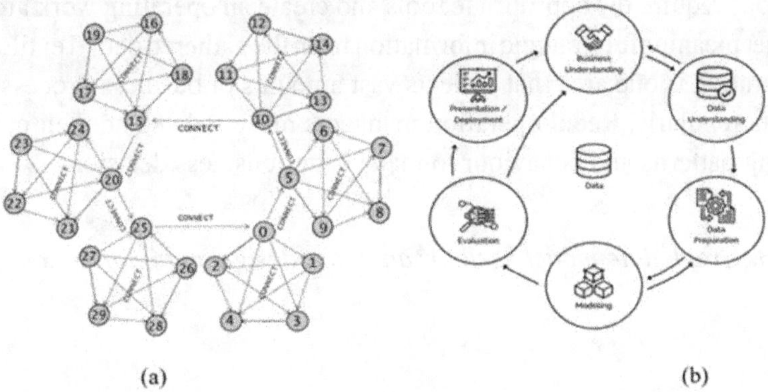

(a) (b)

The research of the current chapter is evaluated by clustering algorithm on a graph shown in Figure 10(a). That graph is known as the connected *caveman graph*, and it was initially proposed by Duncan J Watts (Watts, 1999). However, the graph in Figure 10(a) does not resemble a real network, but the current research project of this chapter chose it as it will help evaluate the implemented algorithm. Such a graph contains communities that can be used to verify the algorithm in Figure 12. The result of the community detection is satisfied by the verification method.

Figure 12. Louvain community detection algorithm

```
G be the initial network;
while Put each node of G in its own community do
    while some nodes are moved do
        foreach Node in the network do
            place n in its neighboring community including its own which maximizes
            the modularity gain;
        end
    end
    if the new modularity is higher than the previous modularity then
        G = the network between communities of G;
    else
        Terminate;
    end
end
```

RETAIL SALES DATA ANLYTIC EXAMPLE

Big data analytics are playing an essential role in today's textile business. It is geared towards storing, processing, and visualizing many real-time business process-related data. In order to do these data-related activities, industrial analytics applications require the appropriate tools and create an operating work area, which helps to get meaningful strategic information from the gathered data. Textile business retail operation is one area that collects vast amounts of business-processes operational data regularly. Retail operation managers must understand their consumer's purchasing patterns and behaviour to make better business decisions.

Figure 13. Graph data model used for database design and information generated

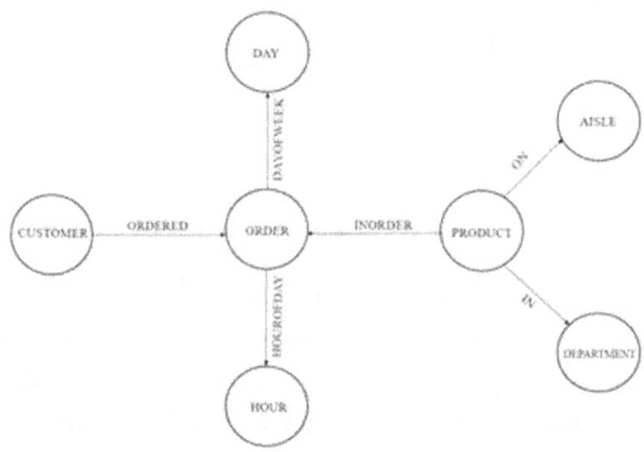

Big data analytics are playing an essential role in today's textile business. It is geared towards storing, processing, and visualizing many real-time business process-related data. In order to do these data-related activities, industrial analytics applications require the appropriate tools and create an operating environment. Retail operation managers must understand their consumer's purchasing patterns (as shown in Figure 14) and behaviour to make better business decisions.

Figure 14. Number of orders placed at various hours of a particular day

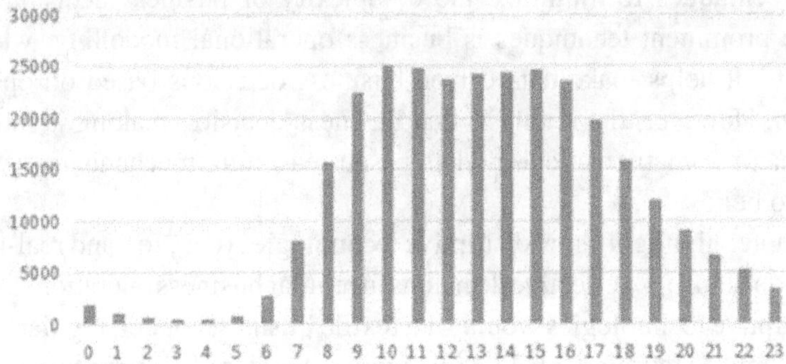

FUTURE RESEARCH DIRECTIONS

As big data-based textile sales analytics are getting prominence, their implementations use different techniques for regular operation management. Researchers are using artificial intelligence-based network technologies to solve different types of operational issues, and one of the prominent issues is algorithmic recommendation systems. This chapter presented the Louvain clustering algorithm to produce non-overlapping clusters of products and evaluate the influence of an overlapping community clustering algorithm. In the future, the current research will consider more detailed information regarding textile retailing data (e.g., order timestamp, customer demographics, and other relevant geographic details) to enhance the recommendation system. Another important characteristic of future projects is applying the service-oriented processing capability of analytics. Besides, the current project wants to include seasonal variations of products from customers' requirements, and it needs to include the organizational capability to deploy new information and communication technologies (e.g., augmented reality (AR), virtual reality (VR) (Keikhosrokiani, 2023) and inclusion of new technologies to capture real-time data streams (i.e., IoT, RFID technology).

CONCLUSION

This chapter presents the essential need for data-driven business decisions for operational efficiency. Even when facing a straightforward decision, the number of problem characteristics that need to be considered can exceed business operation managers' ability of imagination. However, business managers have used different tools and techniques to minimize the complexity of business decision-making. One of the prominent techniques is business operational modelling, which uses spreadsheets. It helps make data-driven business decisions based on operational information. However, the reality is that business decision-making is much more complex than the mathematical models-based reasoning mechanisms would lead managers to believe.

This chapter highlights how disruptive technologies (e.g., IoT and real-time data analytics) can help make effective decisions in regular business operations. Although not all disruptive technologies would fit a textile business model, regular operation managers should stay alert by looking around to identify disruptive exogenous forces and looking in to assess resources and capabilities. This chapter presented that disruptive technologies and big data are entwined in two ways. Firstly, big data tools and techniques are fueling disruptive technologies. Secondly, disruptive technologies are generating bid data. However, practitioners must implement strategies and operational plans to leverage these disruptive technologies.

In order to exemplify new innovative ideas, this chapter presents a graph-based framework for data analytics for textile product sales management. Textile manufacturing and sales business processes collect vast amounts of retail data regularly. These data are interlinked as a network of activities, and traditional methods are not promising for identifying existing relationships between products. The central objective of this chapter is to present a way that can be used to get insights into the data quickly. Besides, it is realized that graph databases are easy to deploy for high-dimensional data in real-world applications. The chapter uses the 'Louvain Algorithm' to find network communities in retail transactional data and produces a customer recommendation system using the Neo4j graph database.

REFERENCES

Akter, S., Wamba, S. F., Gunasekaran, A., Dubey, R., & Childe, S. J. (2016). How to improve firm performance using big data analytics capability and business strategy alignment? *International Journal of Production Economics*, 182, 113–131. DOI: 10.1016/j.ijpe.2016.08.018

Arunachalam, D., Kumar, N., & Kawalek, J. P. (2018). Understanding big data analytics capabilities in supply chain management: Unravelling the issues, challenges and implications for practice. *Transportation Research Part E, Logistics and Transportation Review*, 114, 416–436. DOI: 10.1016/j.tre.2017.04.001

Baesens, A. (2014). *Analytics in a big data world: The essential guide to data science and its applications, John Wiley & Sons, Hoboken, New Jersey, USA. DOI:*DOI: 10.1002/9781119204183

Baramichai, M., Zimmers, E. W.Jr, & Marangos, C. A. (2007). Agile supply chain transformation matrix: An integrated tool for creating an agile enterprise. *Supply Chain Management*, 12(5), 334–348. DOI: 10.1108/13598540710776917

Davenport, T. H. (2006). *Competing on analytics, Harvard Business Review*. Harvard Business Press., DOI: 10.5860/CHOICE.44-6322

Davenport, T. H., & Harris, J. G. (2007). *Competing on analytics – the new science of winning*. Harvard Business School Publishing Corporation., DOI: 10.5465/amr.2005.17293788

Dora, M., Kumar, M., & Gellynck, X. (2016). Determinants and barriers to lean implementation in food-processing SMEs—A multiple case analysis. *Production Planning and Control*, 27(1), 1–23. DOI: 10.1080/09537287.2015.1050477

Dubey, R., Gunasekaran, A., & Childe, S. J. (2018a). Big data analytics capability in supply chain agility: The moderating effect of organizational flexibility. *Management Decision*. Advance online publication. DOI: 10.1108/MD-01-2018-0119

Dubey, R., Gunasekaran, A., Childe, S. J., Fosso Wamba, S., Roubaud, D., & Foropon, C. (2021). Empirical investigation of data analytics capability and organizational flexibility as complements to supply chain resilience. *International Journal of Production Research*, 59(1), 1–19. DOI: 10.1080/00207543.2019.1582820

Dubey, R., Gunasekaran, A., Childe, S. J., Luo, Z., Wamba, S. F., Roubaud, D., & Foropon, C. (2018b). Examining the role of big data and predictive analytics on collaborative performance in context to sustainable consumption and production behaviour. *Journal of Cleaner Production*, 196, 1508–1521. DOI: 10.1016/j.jclepro.2018.06.097

Dubey, R., Gunasekaran, A., Childe, S. J., Roubaud, D., Wamba, S. F., Giannakis, M., & Foropon, C. (2019b). Big data analytics and organizational culture as complements to swift trust and collaborative performance in the humanitarian supply chain. *International Journal of Production Economics*, 210, 120–136. DOI: 10.1016/j.ijpe.2019.01.023

Dubey, R., Gunasekaran, A., Childe, S. J., Wamba, S. F., & Papadopoulos, T. (2016). The impact of big data on world-class sustainable manufacturing. *International Journal of Advanced Manufacturing Technology*, 84(1–4), 631–645. DOI: 10.1007/s00170-015-7674-1

Fawcett, S. E., & Waller, M. A. (2014). Supply chain game changers—mega, nano, and virtual trends—and forces that impede supply chain design (ie, building a winning team). *Journal of Business Logistics*, 35(3), 157–164. DOI: 10.1111/jbl.12058

Fosso Wamba, S., Gunasekaran, A., Papadopoulos, T., & Ngai, E. (2018). Big data analytics in logistics and supply chain management. *International Journal of Logistics Management*, 29(2), 478–484. DOI: 10.1108/IJLM-02-2018-0026

Giannakis, M., & Louis, M. (2016). A multi-agent based system with big data processing for enhanced supply chain agility. *Journal of Enterprise Information Management*, 29(5), 706–727. DOI: 10.1108/JEIM-06-2015-0050

Govindan, K., Cheng, T. C. E., Mishra, N., & Shukla, N. (2018). Big data analytics and application for logistics and supply chain management. *Transportation Research Part E, Logistics and Transportation Review*, 114, 343–349. DOI: 10.1016/j.tre.2018.03.011

Gunasekaran, A., Papadopoulos, T., Dubey, R., Wamba, S. F., Childe, S. J., Hazen, B., & Akter, S. (2017). Big data and predictive analytics for supply chain and organizational performance. *Journal of Business Research*, 70, 308–317. DOI: 10.1016/j.jbusres.2016.08.004

Hazen, B. T., Boone, C. A., Ezell, J. D., & Jones-Farmer, L. A. (2014). Data quality for data science, predictive analytics, and big data in supply chain management: An introduction to the problem and suggestions for research and applications. *International Journal of Production Economics*, 154, 72–80. DOI: 10.1016/j.ijpe.2014.04.018

Hazen, B. T., Skipper, J. B., Ezell, J. D., & Boone, C. A. (2016). Big Data and predictive analytics for supply chain sustainability: A theory-driven research agenda. *Computers & Industrial Engineering*, 101, 592–598. DOI: 10.1016/j.cie.2016.06.030

Keikhosrokiani, P. (2022a). Big Data Analytics for Healthcare: Datasets, Techniques, Life Cycles, Management, and Applications. In Big Data Analytics for Healthcare: Datasets, Techniques, Life Cycles, Management, and Applications. DOI: 10.1016/C2021-0-00369-2

Keikhosrokiani, P. (2022b). Handbook of research on consumer behavior change and data analytics in the socio-digital era. In Handbook of Research on Consumer Behavior Change and Data Analytics in the Socio-Digital Era. DOI: 10.4018/978-1-6684-4168-8

Keikhosrokiani, P. (2023). *Handbook of Research on Consumer Behavioral Analytics in Metaverse and the Adoption of a Virtual World*. IGI Global., DOI: 10.4018/978-1-6684-7029-9

*Pal,K.(2016). Supply Chain Coordination Based on Web Service, Supply Chain Management in the Big Data Era, Hing Kai Chan, Nachiappan Subramanian, and Muhammad Dan-Asabe Abdulrahman (edited Book Chapter), IGI Publication, Chapter 9, 137-170.*https://doi.org/DOI: 10.4018/978-1-5225-0956-1.ch009

Pal,K.(2017). Supply Chain Coordination Based on Web Services, in Chan H K, Subramanian, N. and Abdulrahman, M D (Edited), Supply Chain Management in the Big Data Era Chapter 9, 137-171, IGI Global Publishing, Hershey PA, USA. https://doi.org/DOI: 10.4018/978-1-5225-0956-1.ch009

Pal,K.(2020b). Information sharing for manufacturing supply chain management based on blockchain technology, in cross-Industry Use of Blockchain Technology and Opportunities for the Future, I. Williams (Edited), 1-17, IGI Global Publication, 701 E Chocolate Avenue, Hershey, PA, USA 17033. https://doi.org/DOI: 10.4018/978-1-7998-3632-2.ch001

*Pal,K.(2021). Applications of Secured Blockchain Technology in Manufacturing Industry, in Blockchain and AI Technology in the Industrial Internet of Things, Subhendu Kumar Pani, Biju Patnaik, Sian Lun, & Xingcheng Liu (Edited), Chapter 10, January 2021, IGI Global Publication, 701 E Chocolate Avenue, Hershey, PA, USA 17033.*https://doi.org/DOI: 10.4018/978-1-7998-6694-7.ch010

*Pal,K.(2023). Drivers of Sustainable Supply Chain Management Using Internet of Things-Based Blockchain Technology, in Government Impact on Sustainable and Responsible Supply Chan, Atour Taghipour (Edited), Chapter 10, 171-201, IGI Global Publication, 701 E Chocolate Avenue, Hershey, PA, USA 17033.*https://doi.org/DOI: 10.4018/978-1-6684-9062-4.ch010

Pal, K., & Yasar, A. (2020a). Internet of Things and blockchain technology in textile manufacturing supply chain data management. *Procedia Computer Science*, 170, 450–457. DOI: 10.1016/j.procs.2020.03.088

Porter, M. (2001). The value chain and competitive advantage. In *Understanding Business: Processes; Barnes, D. (Edited)* (pp. 50–66). Routledge., DOI: 10.1201/9781420025569.ch8

Srivastava, S. K. (2007). Green Supply-Chain Management: A State-of-the-Art Literature Review. *International Journal of Management Reviews*, 9(1), 53–80. DOI: 10.1111/j.1468-2370.2007.00202.x

Supply Chain Council. (2010). http://supply-chain.org/f/down-load/726710733/SCOR10.pdf

Trkman, P., McCormack, K., de Oliveira, M. P. V., & Ladeira, M. B. (2010). The Impact of Business Analytics on Supply Chain Performance. *Decision Support Systems*, 49(3), 318–327. DOI: 10.1016/j.dss.2010.03.007

Watts, D. J. (1999). *Small Worlds. The Dynamics of Networks between Order and Randomness*. Princeton University Press., DOI: 10.1515/9780691188331

Wu, C. (2003). Lean manufacturing: A perspective of lean suppliers. *International Journal of Operations & Production Management*, 23(11), 1349–1376. DOI: 10.1108/01443570310501880

Zhao, R., Liu, Y., Zhang, N., & Huang, T. (2017). An optimization model for green supply chain management by using a big data analytic approach. *Journal of Cleaner Production*, 142, 1085–1097. DOI: 10.1016/j.jclepro.2016.03.006

Zhong, R. Y., Huang, G. Q., Lan, S., Dai, Q. Y., Chen, X., & Zhang, T. (2015). A big data approach for logistics trajectory discovery from RFID-enabled production data. *International Journal of Production Economics*, 165, 260–272. DOI: 10.1016/j.ijpe.2015.02.014

Zhong, R. Y., Lan, S., Xu, C., Dai, Q., & Huang, G. Q. (2016). Visualization of RFID-enabled shopfloor logistics Big Data in Cloud Manufacturing. *International Journal of Advanced Manufacturing Technology*, 84(1–4), 5–16. DOI: 10.1007/s00170-015-7702-1

Chapter 8
Exploring a Smart City and the Epicenter of Megatrends in Innovation With Artificial Intelligence: The Case of Dubai

Maria Amparo Diaz-Llairo
University of Barcelona, Spain

ABSTRACT

This article explores the transformative role of Artificial Intelligence (AI) in urban development, focusing on Dubai as a pioneering smart city at the epicenter of global technological trends. Through a comprehensive case study, this research investigates Dubai's integration of AI within its socio-economic and infrastructural frameworks, illustrating its evolution from a regional hub to a global leader in smart city innovations. The study highlights the multifaceted applications of AI in Dubai's public services, transportation, healthcare, and environmental management, demonstrating how these initiatives enhance urban functionality and set new standards for global urban development. The findings offer insights into the strategic implementation of AI, showcasing Dubai's approach as a model for future smart cities and providing a framework that blends technological advancements with sustainable urban planning.

DOI: 10.4018/979-8-3693-6945-6.ch008

AI-DRIVEN INNOVATION IN SMART CITIES: EXPLORING DUBAI AS AN EPICENTER OF MEGATRENDS

The integration of AI in urban development is transforming how cities worldwide are designed, managed, and experienced, enabling new models of governance and public service delivery. Among global examples of AI-driven urbanism, Dubai stands out as a particularly unique case, demonstrating AI's potential to reshape the urban landscape in the Middle East. As a city-state that has rapidly emerged as a global hub for technology and innovation, Dubai's strategic approach to smart city initiatives illustrates how AI can be harnessed to address urban challenges while enhancing socio-economic and environmental outcomes. Dubai's commitment to becoming a smart city is driven not only by ambitions for technological advancement but also by broader geopolitical, cultural, and economic imperatives. Positioned at the crossroads of East and West, Dubai's AI initiatives aim to present a Middle Eastern model of urban innovation, placing the city as a leading force in the global smart city movement (Faccia et al., 2023; Marri et al., 2019).

Dubai's unique blend of characteristics—including its rapid economic development, strategic position as a trade hub, and top-down governance model—creates an ideal environment for examining the broader implications of AI integration in urban settings. Unlike many Western cities, Dubai operates within a centralized governance structure that allows for swift, large-scale deployment of new technologies, facilitating rapid transformation across its urban infrastructure (Yiğitcanlar et al., 2020a). Furthermore, Dubai's socio-economic landscape, shaped by high urbanization rates, a diverse expatriate population, and a strategic focus on sustainability, positions the city as a testing ground for AI applications in non-Western, rapidly developing contexts (Barbosa et al., 2024). This unique setting provides a valuable case for examining how AI can be tailored to meet the specific needs and challenges of cities in emerging economies, adding diversity to the predominantly Western-focused literature on AI and urban innovation (Rjab and Mellouli, 2019; Saura et al, 2022).

While a substantial body of research exists on AI applications in smart cities, a noticeable gap remains in studies focused on Middle Eastern urban contexts, where unique socio-political and cultural dynamics shape the adoption and impact of technology. Most existing literature concentrates on Western examples, primarily addressing the technical aspects of AI without fully exploring the social, economic, and environmental dimensions of its implementation in diverse global settings (Lim et al., 2021; Shareef and Altan, 2021). Additionally, current research on AI in urban development often emphasizes functional applications, such as traffic management, energy systems, and public services. However, these studies frequently lack a holistic analysis of how AI shapes the socio-economic landscape, governance structures, and cultural frameworks in cities outside the West (Kuberkar and Singhal, 2024). This study addresses this gap by providing an in-depth, multi-dimensional analysis of Dubai's AI-driven transformation, illustrating how AI influences not only infrastructure and service efficiency but also urban policy, public–private partnerships, and the socio-economic fabric of the city.

Dubai's approach to AI integration offers a new lens for understanding AI's potential in urban governance, particularly within emerging economies. As a city that has successfully positioned itself as a global leader in innovation, Dubai's smart city model holds interest not only for regional policymakers but also for urban planners and scholars worldwide seeking to understand how AI can support sustainable development. Unlike traditional city development models, Dubai's vision for a smart city incorporates ambient intelligence and interconnected urban environments supported by AI-enhanced public services. This research explores Dubai's holistic approach to AI, analyzing how the city's strategic deployment of AI impacts sectors such as healthcare, transportation, public services, and environmental management, establishing Dubai as an example of how AI can drive comprehensive urban transformation in diverse global contexts (Bibri et al., 2023; Yiğitcanlar et al., 2020a).

The objectives of this study are threefold: (a) to investigate the extent of AI integration across various sectors of urban life in Dubai, including public services, healthcare, transportation, and environmental management; (b) to assess the implications of these AI applications for sustainable urban development, with a focus on economic, social, and environmental impacts; and (c) to position Dubai as a model for other cities seeking to leverage AI in creating smarter, more resilient urban environments. By systematically analyzing Dubai's deployment of AI, this research contributes original insights into the operational, economic, and ecological benefits of AI for urban governance while offering a practical framework for cities aiming to adapt AI-driven models to their unique socio-economic and cultural contexts (Kuberkar and Singhal, 2024; Manzoor et al., 2021).

The originality of this study lies in its combination of theoretical analysis and empirical case study, bridging a critical gap in the literature on AI-driven smart cities in the Middle East. This research not only contributes to academic knowledge by expanding the scope of AI and smart city studies to include a Middle Eastern perspective but also offers practical applications for policymakers, urban planners, and technology developers. By highlighting the challenges and successes of Dubai's AI-driven approach to urban governance, this study provides actionable insights for other cities worldwide seeking to implement similar technologies. The findings are expected to inform future smart city strategies, promoting sustainable development and enhancing urban quality of life through intelligent systems and data-driven decision-making processes (Bibri et al., 2023).

In conclusion, Dubai's strategic approach to AI highlights the transformative potential of technology not only as a tool for urban optimization but also as a catalyst for redefining urban governance and societal structures. This study positions Dubai as a global blueprint for AI-driven urban development, contributing to a broader discourse on the role of technology in sustainable urban futures. By examining Dubai's journey, this research provides valuable insights into the ongoing conversation on AI and urban evolution, underscoring the importance of strategic, ethical, and inclusive approaches to technology in the modern cityscape (Herath and Mittal, 2022; Kinder et al., 2023).

Overall, Dubai's transformation into a smart city and its embrace of AI have positioned it as a global epicenter of innovation and a trailblazer in using advanced technologies to address the challenges of urbanization, creating a sustainable, efficient, and livable city for its residents and visitors. Dubai's smart city project aims to improve the quality of life and governance, making it the most dynamic city in terms of seamlessness, safety, and impact. In summary, Dubai's focus is on becoming a smart city (Virtudes et al., 2017).

This study meticulously examines Dubai as a smart city and the epicenter of megatrends in innovation with AI, highlighting how its integration of AI has positioned it as a global leader in innovation.

Dubai 2040 Vision: Pioneering Global Smart City Innovation and Citizen Happiness

Dubai's 2040 Vision is a comprehensive strategy led by His Highness Sheikh Mohammed bin Rashid Al Maktoum, designed to position Dubai as a global leader in urban innovation and sustainability. Central to this vision is the concept of achieving

"المركز الأول"

(al-markaz al-awwal), meaning "first place" or "number one," in smart city advancements and citizen happiness.

In his book My Vision, Sheikh Mohammed bin Rashid Al Maktoum emphasizes his firm rejection of the word "impossible," asserting that it is a label created by those unwilling to leave their comfort zones. According to Sheikh Mohammed bin Rashid Al Maktoum, "impossible" is a term used by individuals who are either lazy or lack resilience, reflecting a fear of challenges and resistance to progress. He argues that self-confidence and a willingness to face challenges are essential for achieving success and excellence. This perspective aligns with his vision for Dubai as a global leader, with an unwavering commitment to becoming the best in all endeavors (Al Maktoum, 2012).

This roadmap envisions a city where infrastructure, technology, and environmental stewardship are harmonized to enhance residents' quality of life and establish global benchmarks in sustainable urban planning (United Arab Emirates [UAE] Government, n.d.d; Dubai Electricity and Water Authority [DEWA], n.d.).

The 2040 Vision integrates advanced technologies across public sectors to enhance operational efficiency and citizen well-being. For example, Dubai's AI-driven traffic management system is projected to reduce congestion by 30%, improving daily commute times and contributing to overall resident satisfaction (Dubai Future Foundation, n.d.). Additionally, initiatives led by DEWA have achieved notable improvements in air quality and water conservation, reflecting the city's commitment to sustainable urban development. Dubai aims to source 75% of its energy from renewables by 2050 (DEWA, n.d.).

Sustainable mobility solutions, such as autonomous public transportation and smart parking systems, are also prioritized. These initiatives are expected to lower emissions by 20% and reduce parking search times by 40%, directly supporting Dubai's Happiness Index, a metric central to Sheikh Mohammed bin Rashid Al Maktoum 's vision of a livable, resident-focused city. Cultural heritage initiatives like the Safeguarding Civilization project leverage AI to preserve Dubai's cultural assets, fostering a strong sense of identity and pride among residents (Dubai Government, n.d.).

Aligned with Dubai's Vision 2040, the UAE has invested extensively in science, technology, and sustainable development. Strategic government initiatives foster innovation, collaboration, and technological advancement across key sectors. For example, the Open Labs Platform, launched in 2018, provides a comprehensive database of advanced scientific equipment and laboratories. It connects prominent research institutions like the Mohammed bin Rashid Space Centre and Khalifa University, enhancing research capabilities and reducing costs by 30%. This platform reinforces Dubai's smart city infrastructure by facilitating innovation in critical sectors (UAE Government, 2024).

The Mohammed bin Rashid Innovation Fund further supports this vision by allocating AED 2 billion to promote sustainable, market-driven innovation in priority sectors. The Mohammed bin Rashid Innovation Fund's Guarantee Scheme and Innovation Accelerator offer financial and non-financial support to UAE-based innovators, particularly in advanced sectors such as ICT, space science, and nuclear technology, which are integral to Dubai's smart city goals (Ministry of Finance, 2024). These programs attract global talent, support local innovators, and encourage economic diversification, aligning with Dubai's strategic objectives for sustainable growth.

The UAE's focus on specific science and technology sectors reflects its commitment to becoming a smart, interconnected city. Space science initiatives, including the Mohammed bin Rashid Global Space Challenge and the Mars 2117 project, underscore Dubai's ambitious vision for space exploration. ICT is fundamental to Dubai's digital governance and data analytics capabilities, enabling AI integration across various sectors (Dubai Future Foundation, 2024).

Dubai is also a leader in 3D printing applications for construction, healthcare, and manufacturing. Investments in nuclear technology further support clean, efficient energy goals, enhancing the city's resilience as a smart city (Emirates Scientists Council, 2024; UAE Government, 2024).

By fostering a knowledge-based society through initiatives like the Mostaqbal Portal and Popular Science Arabia magazine, the UAE encourages scientific engagement and literacy, inspiring Arab youth to pursue careers in science and technology. The Mohammed bin Rashid Centre for Accelerated Research facilitates collaborative research on critical scientific challenges, funding projects such as the Global Space Challenge. These efforts accelerate advancements in space science and other cutting-edge fields, demonstrating Dubai's holistic approach to smart city development. This approach integrates sustainable growth, technological advancement, and global collaboration (Dubai Future Foundation, 2024).

The Dubai 2040 Vision exemplifies an ambitious yet pragmatic approach to transforming Dubai into a global leader in smart city innovation. Through strategic investments, technological advancements, and a commitment to sustainability, Dubai is setting a benchmark for future urban development worldwide.

Economic Vision and Development: Dubai D33 Economic Agenda

Launched by His Highness Sheikh Mohammed bin Rashid Al Maktoum, the Dubai D33 Economic Agenda is an ambitious initiative designed to double the size of Dubai's economy by 2033. The agenda aims to establish Dubai as a global hub for trade, finance, and innovation, with a strong focus on sustainability, digital transformation, and economic self-sufficiency. Sheikh Mohammed bin Rashid Al Maktoum's vision underscores the resilience and competitiveness necessary to position Dubai as a leading example of sustainable urban economic growth.

Central to the D33 Agenda is the expansion of Dubai's foreign trade. The plan envisions increasing its value from AED 14.2 trillion to AED 25.6 trillion while adding 400 new cities to its trade network. This strategy also targets a significant boost in Foreign Direct Investment (FDI), with annual contributions expected to rise from AED 32 billion to AED 60 billion, culminating in a total inflow of AED 650 billion by 2033. These ambitious targets highlight Dubai's status as a premier global investment destination (UAE Government, n.d.a).

The D33 Agenda places significant emphasis on digital transformation, aiming to generate AED 100 billion annually from digital advancements. This goal is supported by substantial investments in AI, automation, and smart city technologies. These initiatives align with Dubai's broader vision of fostering innovation as a central driver of economic and societal progress.

The agenda also prioritizes sustainable development and self-sufficiency, particularly in energy production. By 2050, Dubai aims to source 75% of its energy from renewable sources, reinforcing the city's commitment to environmental sustainability. This strategy complements Dubai's efforts to balance economic growth with ecological responsibility, further solidifying its position as a global leader in sustainable urban development.

The Dubai D33 Economic Agenda exemplifies a forward-thinking approach to economic growth, blending innovation, sustainability, and strategic investments. By enhancing trade networks, accelerating digital transformation, and advancing renewable energy initiatives, Dubai continues to set a benchmark for modern, resilient urban economies.

Theoretical Framework

This research is anchored in urban innovation theories and Everett Rogers's diffusion of innovations theory, providing a dual theoretical foundation for examining the role of AI in Dubai's urban development. Urban innovation theories offer insights into the dynamic changes in urban governance and infrastructure, emphasizing how cities adopt and integrate new technologies to enhance public services and economic efficiency. These theories contextualize Dubai's efforts to become a leading smart city and help explain how AI can catalyze shifts in urban management and public interaction (Shareef and Altan, 2021).

The diffusion of innovations theory, developed by Rogers (1962), offers an additional lens through which to understand the adoption patterns of AI technologies within Dubai's urban fabric. According to this theory, innovations are adopted through a process that includes awareness, interest, evaluation, trial, and adoption stages. By applying this framework, the study examines how Dubai's government, public institutions, and residents interact with AI technologies, focusing on factors influencing adoption rates, perceived benefits, and societal acceptance. This perspective is particularly relevant for understanding Dubai's unique governance structure, which enables streamlined, large-scale implementation of technological advancements.

By combining these two theoretical perspectives, the study provides a holistic view of AI's role in shaping urban governance, societal norms, and infrastructural efficiency. The theoretical framework supports a detailed exploration of how AI integration influences sustainable urban development, aligns with Dubai's strategic goals, and contributes to global urban innovation trends (Yiğitcanlar et al., 2020b).

Methodology

Research Design

This study employs a case study approach to analyze Dubai's integration of AI within its urban infrastructure. A case study design is particularly suited to this research because it emphasizes exploring a single, unique instance—Dubai's comprehensive AI-driven smart city model—in depth and within its real-life context (Yin, 2015). The case study approach facilitates a thorough understanding of how AI functions across various sectors in Dubai, including transportation, healthcare, public services, and environmental management, providing insights into the city's strategies, challenges, and successes. This research design enables a qualitative interpretation of how AI influences urban governance, infrastructure efficiency, and public engagement.

Data Collection

Data for this study were collected from primary and secondary sources to ensure comprehensive coverage of Dubai's AI initiatives. Secondary data were gathered from government reports, academic articles, white papers, policy documents, and press releases from Dubai's government agencies, including Smart Dubai and the Dubai Future Foundation. These documents provided valuable insights into the strategic goals, technological implementations, and policy frameworks guiding AI integration in Dubai.

In addition to document analysis, primary data were obtained through interviews with key stakeholders involved in Dubai's AI projects, including city planners, policy advisors, and technology experts. A total of 15 semi-structured interviews were conducted over six months, from January to June 2023. Interview participants were selected based on their involvement in AI policy-making, implementation, or management within Dubai's public sector. The semi-structured format allowed for open-ended discussions, enabling participants to share their experiences and perspectives on AI's role in urban development, including its benefits, challenges, and impact on the local population.

Data Analysis

Data analysis was conducted using a thematic approach, which is well-suited for identifying patterns, themes, and insights in qualitative data (Braun and Clarke, 2006). For secondary data, thematic coding was applied to documents and reports to identify recurring themes related to AI applications, governance, sustainability, and socio-economic impact. Thematic analysis allowed the study to categorize findings into key areas, such as AI's role in public service efficiency, economic development, and environmental sustainability.

Limitations of the Methodology

While this methodology allows for a deep, context-specific analysis of AI in Dubai's urban infrastructure, it is not without limitations. The single-case study design limits the generalizability of the findings, as they may not apply to cities with different socio-political or economic contexts. Additionally, reliance on secondary data restricts the study to existing documentation, which may not capture all perspectives. Future research could address these limitations by conducting comparative studies or longitudinal analyses to observe the long-term impact of AI in urban environments (Silverman, 2020).

Analysis of Results

Smart Dubai Strategy

His Highness Sheikh Mohammed bin Rashid Al Maktoum, Vice President and Prime Minister of the UAE and Ruler of Dubai, has played a pivotal role in advancing Dubai's position as a global leader in AI and smart city initiatives. His vision emphasizes transforming Dubai into a "smart city" through substantial investments in AI and digital technologies, establishing the city as a global innovation model. Under his leadership, Dubai has launched key initiatives such as Smart Dubai and the Dubai Future Foundation, both of which leverage AI, the Internet of Things, and other advanced technologies to enhance urban governance, transportation, healthcare, and environmental management (Faccia et al., 2023; Yiğitcanlar et al., 2020a).

A major milestone in His Highness Sheikh Mohammed bin Rashid Al Maktoum's efforts to institutionalize AI occurred in 2017 with the creation of the UAE Ministry of AI. This ministry, the first of its kind globally, reflects the sheikh's commitment to positioning Dubai and the UAE at the forefront of technological and innovative progress. The Ministry of AI serves as a strategic overseer, setting national AI objectives that align with Dubai's vision of a smart city. In collaboration with entities such as the Digital Dubai Authority and Smart Dubai, the ministry facilitates cross-sector partnerships, upholds regulatory standards, and promotes ethical AI practices. Through these efforts, the Ministry of AI strengthens Dubai's capacity to integrate AI across diverse sectors, from public safety to healthcare, advancing His Highness Sheikh Mohammed bin Rashid Al Maktoum's vision of Dubai as a pioneering smart city (Government of Dubai, 2022).

His Highness Sheikh Mohammed bin Rashid Al Maktoum's leadership has also propelled the Dubai Blockchain Strategy, making Dubai the first city globally to fully integrate blockchain technology into public services. This initiative has significantly enhanced operational efficiency and service quality across all levels of government (Marri et al., 2019; Virtudes et al., 2017).

Introduced in 2017, the Smart Dubai 2021 strategy aimed to position Dubai as the world's smartest and happiest city, focusing on six strategic dimensions: living, governance, environment, economy, mobility, and people. This comprehensive, cross-sectoral initiative sought to create seamless urban experiences, enable paperless governance, and leverage AI-driven data insights to support informed decision-making (Smart Dubai, 2021). Key applications under this strategy include DubaiNow, which consolidates over 130 services, and UAE PASS, a secure digital identity platform—both of which have substantially streamlined government services, enhancing accessibility and efficiency for residents (Digital Dubai Authority, 2023a).

The integration of advanced digital tools has led to substantial improvements in service delivery metrics. For instance, AI-powered platforms such as DubaiNow and UAE PASS have achieved a 98% user satisfaction rate, reduced service processing times by 80%, and attained a 90% adoption rate among residents. Additionally, AI-driven chatbots have played a key role in supporting citizen engagement, offering timely assistance, and enhancing the overall service experience. These results highlight the impact of Dubai's digital transformation in public services, demonstrating advancements in administrative efficiency and service accessibility enabled by AI and digital solutions.

As shown in Table 1, Dubai's application of AI across sectors such as healthcare, transportation, and public safety has significantly improved operational efficiency and citizen satisfaction. These accomplishments support Dubai's broader goals of innovation-driven urban governance and improving residents' quality of life.

Table 1 highlights the diverse integration of AI across key sectors within Dubai's smart city framework, showcasing its transformative impact on public services, infrastructure, and citizen experiences. Each sector is examined through the lens of specific AI technologies and quantifiable metrics, emphasizing Dubai's accomplishments relative to global benchmarks. These applications not only enhance operational efficiency but also align with theoretical models that support citizen acceptance and adaptive learning in smart cities. Case studies are included to demonstrate Dubai's pioneering role and the practical outcomes of its AI deployment.

Table 1. AI Integration and Impact Across Key Sectors in Dubai's Smart City Framework

Sector	Specific AI Technologies	Quantifiable Impact	Global Benchmark	Theoretical Framework / Academic Insight	Dubai Case Examples
Transportation	Predictive traffic management, smart parking, autonomous vehicles	30% reduction in congestion; 20% improvement in commute times	10% reduction above global city averages in congestion (e.g., Singapore, Tokyo)	Diffusion of Innovations Theory (Rogers): Explains adoption patterns, benefits, and citizen adaptation rates	RTA's Autonomous Vehicles Initiative for public transit; Smart Parking Dubai with real-time space tracking
Public Safety	Predictive policing, facial recognition, smart surveillance	40% faster emergency response; 25% decline in crime incidents	First MENA city to implement predictive AI in policing	TAM: Assesses citizen trust and perceived value of AI in public safety	Dubai Police AI Surveillance Network; DEWA's biometric access with facial recognition
Healthcare	Predictive diagnostics, AI-based telemedicine, medical imaging	20% improvement in early diagnosis; 25% reduction in wait times	Above-average AI health application in MENA; comparable with global leaders (e.g., U.S.)	Health Belief Model: Investigates public acceptance and ethical implications of AI in healthcare	AI Telemedicine via Dubai Health Authority; Rashid Hospital's AI Diagnostics for disease prediction
Utilities	Smart grid technology, predictive energy load management	35% increase in energy efficiency; 40% fewer power outages	15% higher efficiency than global averages (e.g., Amsterdam, Seoul)	Environmental Determinism Theory: Emphasizes tech adaptation to optimize local environmental resources	DEWA's Smart Grid for real-time energy and water management; AI in Water Conservation by Dubai Municipality

continued on following page

Table 1. Continued

Sector	Specific AI Technologies	Quantifiable Impact	Global Benchmark	Theoretical Framework / Academic Insight	Dubai Case Examples
Education	AI-driven personalized learning, virtual tutors, adaptive assessment	25% increase in learning outcomes; higher engagement rates	Higher AI education integration than global peers (e.g., New York, London)	Constructivist Learning Theory: Links AI in personalized tutoring to improved student engagement	AI Learning Labs in Dubai Schools; Smart Dubai's AI Tutor and Virtual Classroom Program
Retail and Commerce	Customer behavior analytics, demand forecasting, logistics AI	30% increase in sales forecast accuracy; 20% cut in supply chain costs	Comparable with retail innovation hubs (e.g., Singapore, Tokyo)	Consumer Behavior Theory: Analyzes how AI-driven personalization affects consumer satisfaction	AI-Powered Shopping Insights at Dubai Mall; AI for Logistics at Emirates Post

Note. RTA = Roads and Transport Authority; MENA = Middle East and North Africa; TAM = Technology acceptance model. Source: Own elaboration based on sources from UAE Government (n.d.b), Dubai Health Authority (2021), and DEWA (2018b).

Dubai's Leadership in AI-Driven Urban Transformation

The results of this case study methodology offer a detailed examination of Dubai's pioneering role in the AI sector. This study synthesizes findings from multiple authoritative sources to validate Dubai's leadership in AI-driven innovation through careful data collection and structured presentation, including comparative tables. The analysis benchmarks Dubai's progress against global standards, revealing its unique approach to integrating AI across various urban sectors and its impact on advancing technology-driven urban governance.

Dubai has positioned itself as a global benchmark for AI-integrated urban infrastructure, shaping the future of smart cities worldwide. This comprehensive analysis emphasizes the extensive application of AI in public services, healthcare, environmental management, and other critical sectors, highlighting the strategic initiatives and outcomes that define Dubai's visionary approach.

Smart Dubai Strategy

Key tools like DubaiNow, which consolidates over 130 government services, and UAE PASS, a secure digital identity platform, have significantly streamlined public service delivery, improving accessibility and efficiency for Dubai's residents (Digital Dubai Authority, 2023b).

With a 98% user satisfaction rate, an 80% reduction in service processing times, and a 90% adoption rate for digital services among residents, these AI-driven applications highlight Dubai's substantial progress in enhancing public service efficiency. AI-powered chatbots also play a pivotal role in citizen support, providing timely responses and improving overall service quality. These outcomes underscore Dubai's success in digital transformation, particularly in public administration, where AI has streamlined processes and improved service accessibility, aligning with the city's broader goals of innovation-driven governance and enhanced quality of life.

AI-Powered Public Safety and Tourism Enhancements

Since the 2020 Expo, Dubai has introduced a series of AI-driven innovations to enhance public safety, most notably by establishing Smart Police Stations. These self-service stations operate 24/7 and offer over 60 police services—ranging from crime reporting and traffic assistance to community services—without human intervention. By providing multi-lingual support and enabling contactless service, the smart police station initiative contributes to Dubai's strategic goal of automating public services, enhancing accessibility, increasing efficiency, and improving user satisfaction while significantly reducing response times (Government of Dubai Media Office, 2021).

Furthering its commitment to a technology-driven approach, Dubai Police has integrated AI and predictive policing technologies to enhance crime prevention. Through the analysis of historical crime data, these AI systems anticipate potential security threats, enabling law enforcement to allocate resources more strategically. The success of this approach is evident in the reported 50% reduction in response times and a 20% decrease in crime rates, underscoring Dubai's effective use of AI in optimizing resource management and bolstering urban safety (Dubai Police, 2022).

Additionally, Dubai has deployed smart patrol vehicles equipped with license plate recognition systems and real-time data connectivity. These advanced patrol units enable real-time data sharing, improving law enforcement response and ensuring coordinated action across units. The integration of AI-based crime analysis and facial recognition in surveillance systems further reflects Dubai's commitment to using technology to enhance public safety and build public trust. These tools not only strengthen preventative security measures but also highlight the transparency and reliability embedded within Dubai's law enforcement operations.

Dubai's deployment of predictive policing, automated crime analysis, and AI-powered surveillance reflects a proactive, technology-focused approach to public safety. By integrating these AI solutions, Dubai fosters an environment of security and public trust, reinforcing its position as a global leader in smart city development. This approach highlights the transformative potential of AI in enhancing law enforcement effectiveness and improving public safety outcomes (González-Padilla et al., 2024).

In the tourism sector, AI is pivotal in enhancing the visitor experience (Lacarcel and Huete, 2023), positioning Dubai as a technologically advanced destination. AI-guided tours, virtual reality experiences, and multi-lingual translation applications provide tourists with a seamless, personalized experience. Data show a 20% increase in tourist satisfaction, a 30% improvement in crowd management, and a 40% reduction in wait times at popular attractions, illustrating AI's significant impact on tourism infrastructure. These innovations align with Dubai's broader strategic goal of becoming a high-tech tourism hub, further reinforcing its global reputation as an innovative and accessible city for visitors.

Dubai's Leadership in AI-Driven Urban Transformation

The case study results in this article provide an in-depth analysis of Dubai's ascent as a leader in AI innovation. The study organizes findings through meticulous data collection and clear tabular structures, enhancing readability and facilitating comparison. By synthesizing information from diverse sources and referencing key works in the field, the study supports its conclusions on Dubai's pivotal role as a forerunner of innovation in the AI sector. Through rigorous comparison and benchmarking against global standards, the analysis offers valuable insights into Dubai's unique approach to AI integration and its implications for broader technological advancement.

Dubai has emerged as a global leader in integrating AI into urban infrastructure, setting benchmarks for cities worldwide. This in-depth analysis explores the extensive applications of AI in public services, healthcare, and environmental management, underscoring the city's pioneering strategies and outcomes.

Revolutionizing Healthcare Through AI Integration in Dubai

Dubai's healthcare sector is undergoing a transformative shift with the integration of AI, solidifying the city's position as a global leader in medical technology innovation (Li et al., 2023). This section explores the strategic initiatives driving these advancements, focusing on how AI is reshaping healthcare delivery and contributing to improved health outcomes, increased life expectancy, and enhanced healthcare accessibility. By leveraging scientific, technological, and natural resources, AI applications in Dubai are redefining mental and physical healthcare practices, benefiting individuals and communities on a global scale.

As part of a global shift in healthcare (Alhussain et al., 2022), Dubai has harnessed AI to advance its medical infrastructure. This analysis explores the emirate's strategies that place it at the forefront of medical technology innovation. AI applications have redefined healthcare paradigms by enhancing diagnosis accuracy, treatment precision, and preventive care, addressing the population's physical and mental health needs (AlSuwaidi and Moonesar, 2021). Moreover, Dubai's approach underscores its dedication to democratizing healthcare access, blending scientific and technological advancements to improve outcomes for all residents.

The Global Burden of Disease Study (Institute for Health Metrics and Evaluation [IHME], 2019) indicates that bacterial strains contribute to over ten percent of global mortality, including a significant proportion of sepsis-related deaths. Dubai has integrated AI-driven data analytics and personalized interventions into its healthcare system, markedly improving disease prevention and treatment strategies (Liu et al., 2024). The prevalence of these bacterial strains highlights the urgent need for advanced prevention measures, innovative antibiotics, and the development of new vaccines. The interaction of various microorganisms within the human body deepens our understanding of disease mechanisms, an area where AI's analytical capabilities prove particularly valuable (Panthee et al., 2022).

The human microbiome has garnered significant attention in this ecosystem due to its critical role in health. Imbalances in the microbiome can lead to autoimmune diseases, chronic inflammation, and metabolic disorders. The gut microbiome is central to overall health, influencing physiological, cognitive, and mental functions (De Vos et al., 2022). AI is pivotal in profiling gut bacteria, identifying biomarkers, and proposing novel therapeutic approaches. This use of AI enables Dubai's healthcare system to advance personalized nutrition, antibiotic development, and targeted antibacterial treatments.

A notable AI application in Dubai's healthcare system is the Salama Electronic Medical Record initiative, launched by the Dubai Health Authority. This centralized system consolidates patient records across hospitals, improving access to medical histories, enhancing diagnostic accuracy, and reducing redundancy in testing. These features contribute to an efficient, patient-centered healthcare model, aligning with Dubai's strategic vision for advanced healthcare (Dubai Health Authority, 2023). Additionally, Dubai's collaborations with the Dubai Future Foundation and leading technology firms emphasize predictive diagnostics. By leveraging AI algorithms to detect early indicators of chronic diseases such as diabetes and cardiovascular conditions, these partnerships enable timely interventions that align with Dubai's goals of extending life expectancy and improving quality of life (Dubai Future Foundation, 2023a).

Key metrics highlight the impact of these AI applications, including a 50% reduction in diagnosis times, a 60% improvement in early detection accuracy, and a 40% decrease in emergency wait times. The Salama Electronic Medical Record system and AI-powered medical imaging enhance patient care and optimize resource allocation, reflecting Dubai's broader commitment to efficiency and technological advancement in healthcare.

These AI-driven initiatives underscore Dubai's leadership in personalized and preventive healthcare. AI applications are transforming conventional practices into data-driven, sustainable healthcare models that address modern public health challenges. By advancing AI for diagnosis, personalized treatment, and remote monitoring, Dubai demonstrates how smart technology can be leveraged to improve health outcomes, patient satisfaction, and system efficiency.

AI's role in Dubai's healthcare extends to supporting personalized medicine by enabling customized treatment plans based on individual patient data, resulting in a 25% improvement in health outcomes (National Institutes of Health, 2024). When benchmarked against global standards, Dubai's achievements surpass those of advanced cities such as Boston and London, particularly in patient data analytics and personalized healthcare protocols.

AI-Driven Environmental Sustainability Initiatives in Dubai

This section examines the strategic use of AI in supporting Dubai's ambitious environmental sustainability and restoration efforts. As Dubai rapidly transforms into a modern metropolis, the environmental impacts of urbanization have become increasingly evident. In response, the city has integrated AI-driven innovations to balance urban growth with ecological preservation, advancing its goals in sustainable urban planning and environmental conservation (Bibri et al., 2023).

Dubai has leveraged AI to develop resilient environmental management practices, using the technology to optimize natural resource management, mitigate ecological risks, and enhance the environment's capacity for restoration (Jamali, Ahmad, et al., 2024). Central to the city's environmental vision, known as the "Mother City" concept, is the integration of biomimetic principles drawn from biological sciences and advanced AI. This approach enables Dubai to design self-regenerating urban landscapes that reduce maintenance costs while promoting sustainable living environments (AL-Dabbagh, 2022). For instance, biomimetic solutions like shark skin–inspired surface designs and V-formation-inspired structures for energy efficiency demonstrate Dubai's commitment to nature-inspired urban design. However, integrating biomimicry into urban planning poses challenges that require careful management to avoid unintended environmental consequences (AlAli et al., 2023).

Dubai is also at the forefront of using virtual biodomes powered by AI simulations to evaluate and implement eco-centric policies. These digital biodomes allow for cost-effective testing and forecasting of conservation outcomes, aligning urban development with environmental priorities. As models for sustainable urban planning, these virtual environments support investment frameworks that prioritize natural preservation, fostering a global sustainability perspective among Dubai's residents and stakeholders (Cüce et al., 2017).

Furthermore, Dubai utilizes AI-enabled carbon-based nanomaterials for advanced water purification, demonstrating remarkable efficiency in pollutant removal and offering solutions for localized and large-scale applications. This innovative approach is particularly valuable in water-scarce regions, reinforcing Dubai's leadership in addressing critical sustainability challenges. However, the use of these nanomaterials requires careful evaluation of their long-term environmental and health impacts (Jangid and Inbaraj, 2021; Sharma, 2021).

In energy management, AI is advancing sustainable practices across Dubai. AI-driven smart grid technologies and demand forecasting systems have improved energy distribution efficiency by 20%, reduced power outages by 30%, and decreased operational costs by 25%. Moreover, AI has contributed to a 15% reduction in Dubai's environmental footprint, showcasing the technology's role in optimizing energy resources and ensuring reliable, cost-effective distribution. These AI-powered initiatives highlight Dubai's commitment to climate resilience and efficient energy use (Dubai Municipality, 2023).

Furthering its sustainability objectives, Dubai has launched the Green Spine project, a 40-mile eco-corridor featuring solar-powered trams, pedestrian pathways, cycling tracks, and over one million trees. This initiative exemplifies Dubai's commitment to sustainable urban infrastructure, enhancing green transportation options and air quality (Dubai Municipality, 2023). Additionally, AI-enabled water management systems have been instrumental in boosting water recycling rates and cutting freshwater consumption by 35%, underscoring Dubai's proactive approach to resource conservation.

Dubai's commitment to environmental sustainability extends to public safety through the Oyoon (Eyes) project, an AI-powered smart surveillance system. By utilizing facial recognition, this system monitors public spaces such as malls, airports, and metro stations in real time, enhancing situational awareness and balancing rapid urban growth with environmental stability. By reducing congestion by 20%, improving public transport efficiency by 15%, lowering accident rates by 25%, and cutting emissions by 15%, these AI applications highlight Dubai's dedication to fostering a sustainable, safe, and efficient urban environment (Dubai Police, 2022).

Dubai has effectively harnessed AI to drive environmental improvements. The city has improved its air quality index by 40% through AI-driven traffic flow optimization and industrial emissions management. Additionally, AI-enabled water conservation and energy management systems, led by the DEWA, have increased water recycling, reduced freshwater consumption by 35%, and enhanced public building energy efficiency by 25%. These metrics underscore Dubai's successful use of AI in environmental conservation, positioning it as a global model for sustainable urban management (Bibri et al., 2023).

Supporting these efforts, the UAE Air Quality Index—accessible via the Ministry of Climate Change and Environment's app—uses AI to deliver real-time air quality data from satellite imagery. This platform facilitates data-driven decision-making and pollution reduction strategies, underscoring Dubai's commitment to environmental stewardship. Through these comprehensive initiatives, Dubai stands out among global cities, such as San Francisco, as a leader in sustainable AI integration for environmental management.

Dubai's multi-faceted AI strategy for environmental sustainability integrates urban planning inspired by natural processes, virtual policy simulations, and practical water and energy management applications. These initiatives embody Dubai's vision for a sustainable, technologically advanced future, establishing it as a global leader in AI-driven environmental management. As Dubai continues to expand its AI capabilities, it offers a model of how technology and nature can coexist synergistically to promote planetary well-being.

Empowering Communities: AI's Role in Dubai's Social and Cultural Framework

This analysis explores the transformative role of AI in fostering societal empowerment and cohesion within Dubai (Sırmaçek et al., 2023). Dubai's approach to AI-driven social empowerment includes initiatives that strengthen community engagement, promote cultural preservation, and tackle some of humanity's most complex challenges. Through the strategic implementation of AI solutions, Dubai aims to optimize systems that safeguard against crises, building a resilient and adaptable society.

A significant component of Dubai's empowerment strategy is the redefinition of educational paradigms through initiatives such as the "School for Wisdom" program (Aliabadi et al., 2023). This initiative emphasizes culturally grounded critical thinking and equips students with skills to navigate the complexities of emerging technologies. By doing so, Dubai enriches educational experiences across generational lines, fostering a society prepared to engage with technological advancements. AI's contribution to this program is particularly notable, with reported increases in student engagement by 40%, 100% remote access to educational resources, and an extended educational reach by 30%. AI-based learning platforms, adaptive tools, and virtual classrooms illustrate Dubai's AI-enhanced education model, personalizing and expanding learning, making quality education accessible to a wider demographic.

Cultural heritage, recognized as a cornerstone of societal identity, represents a critical focus within Dubai's AI strategy. The "Safeguarding Civilization" initiative exemplifies Dubai's commitment to cultural preservation, integrating cultural awareness into public policy frameworks to protect tangible and intangible heritage (Jamali, Moonesar, and Al Suwaidi, 2024). This initiative promotes cross-cultural understanding and dialogue, reinforcing Dubai's dedication to preserving its heritage amid rapid modernization.

In the economic realm, Dubai addresses inclusivity through the network divide concept, a strategy designed to foster collaborative economic networks. This initiative seeks to dismantle barriers to economic participation, encouraging innovation through synergy across diverse social sectors. Another pioneering concept, public AI, proposes utilizing aspects of AI as a public good to tackle global issues, such as climate change and public health. This initiative advocates for a framework that ensures AI's sustainability and consistent performance, aligning technological advancement with the public's long-term welfare.

Dubai's strategic use of AI within its social and cultural policies exemplifies its commitment to societal resilience, cultural integrity, and inclusive economic growth. In Dubai, AI is not merely a technological tool; it catalyzes community cohesion, an agent for safeguarding cultural heritage, and a foundation for building inclusive and innovative economic frameworks (Marri et al., 2019).

Pioneering Knowledge Access: The Mohammed bin Rashid Library and AI Integration

The Mohammed bin Rashid Library, inaugurated as one of Dubai's premier knowledge institutions, exemplifies the pioneering use of AI in promoting access to information and fostering a culture of lifelong learning. As a state-of-the-art facility, the library leverages AI-driven systems to enhance user experiences through personalized recommendations, automated cataloging, and efficient resource management. Key features include AI-powered virtual assistants that guide visitors through the library's extensive digital and physical collections, offering real-time support and improving information accessibility (Mohammed bin Rashid Library Foundation, 2023). Furthermore, the library integrates AI technologies for language processing, enabling multi-lingual support and instant translations to cater to Dubai's diverse population. This technological integration reflects Dubai's commitment to creating inclusive, innovative spaces that transcend traditional library functions, establishing the Mohammed bin Rashid Library as a model for how AI can revolutionize public knowledge institutions globally. Through this initiative, Dubai promotes educational advancement and reinforces its strategic vision of becoming a global leader in AI-driven knowledge dissemination and cultural preservation.

AI and the Pursuit of Happiness in Dubai's Smart City Agenda

Central to Dubai's smart city strategy is the objective of enhancing resident happiness. This goal is embodied in initiatives such as the Happiness Meter, a real-time feedback tool that measures resident satisfaction with government services. Similarly, the Dubai Now application includes a "Happiness Services" category, which provides residents with access to essential community resources such as emergency contacts, charitable services, and mental health support, directly contributing to their well-being (Smart Dubai, 2021).

Further supporting this focus on happiness, Dubai has introduced Customer Happiness Centers and the Happiness Agenda—initiatives designed to enhance the public service experience. Staff in these centers undergo specialized training focused on delivering satisfaction-oriented services, reflecting Dubai's commitment to integrating happiness into its governance framework. Through these efforts, Dubai demonstrates how AI and smart city technologies can foster a well-being-centric approach to urban governance, reinforcing the city's dedication to improving quality of life as a foundational element of its smart city vision.

Building Resilient Urban Systems: Dubai's AI-Powered Infrastructure

The strategic integration of AI in optimizing Dubai's urban and administrative systems has significantly enhanced the efficiency and resilience of governance and public services. The emirate of Dubai has actively leveraged AI to improve its infrastructure, positioning technology as a key driver of societal advancement. This analysis explores how AI optimization has bolstered efficiency and resilience in service delivery across various levels of governance and society, demonstrating Dubai's commitment to incorporating AI as a cornerstone of its infrastructure development (Virtudes et al., 2017).

This article introduces the concept of the responsible robot and explores how sustainable development has become integral to robotics strategies, particularly in advancing sectors such as agriculture, construction, disaster relief, and healthcare. Dubai Municipality has implemented robots to enhance the construction process, further solidifying Dubai's reputation as a leader in urban development and technological innovation. These robots, designed to evaluate and test construction materials, can conduct rapid, in-depth chemical analyses and X-ray examinations of materials like cement. Builders now receive precise results in just eight minutes, a significant improvement over the previous four-day wait. This advancement not only streamlines operations but also improves safety, reduces labor intensity, and supports the long-term sustainability of new construction. The introduction of construction robotics exemplifies Dubai Municipality's ongoing efforts to set global standards for innovation in urban development, livability, and sustainability.

AI-driven robotics are transforming industries and recalibrating Dubai's alignment with global sustainable development goals. This analysis further explores the concept of balanced books, which addresses the obsolescence of traditional monetary policy mechanisms in light of AI (Kinder et al., 2023) and how AI enhances financial stability, fostering sustainable growth. It examines the potential of AI to refine monetary policy adjustments through real-time macroeconomic trend analysis and predictive adjustments. Dubai's strategic initiatives leverage AI to empower societies, optimize systems, protect against vulnerabilities, and promote collective growth.

Much of the discussion is dedicated to zero-margin, where mobile edge computing redefines data processing and storage paradigms. The role of AI in surpassing traditional data centers, thus enhancing the speed and reliability of data transmission, is critically assessed in the context of Dubai's smart city initiatives. This includes analyzing the impact of AI-driven mobile edge computing on data processing and storage, highlighting the potential for improved speed and reliability in data transmission (Manjula et al., 2022). The landscape (De'Shazer, 2024) suggests that these advancements could enhance global justice systems and reduce legal uncertainties in a rapidly globalizing society.

The synthesis highlights AI's profound impact on Dubai's infrastructure, driving a transformation that extends across public service sectors and redefines the urban experience. The city's trajectory points toward a future where AI's integration into the societal fabric optimizes systems, fostering a resilient and forward-thinking metropolis.

Exploring Emerging AI and Connectivity Technologies in Dubai

This study investigates two pivotal technological advancements poised to redefine computational capacity and global connectivity: quantum computing and the evolution of satellite-based internet infrastructure. Grounded in empirical data and industry projections, this analysis explores the potential impacts, opportunities, and challenges surrounding the adoption of quantum computing and the integration of satellite internet connectivity (Rozenman et al., 2023). By examining technological trends, market forecasts, and societal implications, this research highlights the transformative potential of these technologies, emphasizing opportunities for cross-sectoral innovation and collaboration. Dubai's smart city initiatives are at the forefront of leveraging AI in data processing and storage paradigms, positioning the emirate as a leader in technological advancement (Marri et al., 2019).

The convergence of quantum computing (Ammar, 2023) and advanced internet connectivity marks a pivotal moment in technological progress, with far-reaching implications for scientific advancement, economic growth, and societal transformation. This section explores the synergies between these emerging trends, assesses their potential impact across various domains, and identifies key challenges in their implementation.

Quantum computing has emerged as a revolutionary force in computational science, offering exponential advancements in processing power compared to traditional computers. Recent progress in quantum hardware has propelled the field forward, achieving critical milestones in qubit scalability and error correction. Quantum computing promises applications across diverse fields, including accelerated scientific research, optimization in supply chain management, and complex logistics. However, realizing its full potential requires overcoming significant obstacles such as error correction, interoperability, and data security. Collaborative initiatives, such as the Open Quantum Institute (Shammah et al., 2023) and the development of open-source frameworks like Qibo, are crucial in creating accessible and inclusive quantum computing solutions.

Dubai's strategic investments in quantum technology further solidify its position as a leader in next-generation computing. Initiatives such as the Dubai Quantum Computing Center support research in quantum algorithms, cryptography, and simulations, which are set to transform sectors such as logistics, finance, and urban development (Dubai Future Foundation, 2023b). Through partnerships with global technology leaders like International Business Machines Corporation, Dubai empowers regional researchers by providing access to quantum resources, accelerating innovation within the UAE.

To enhance cybersecurity, the Dubai Electronic Security Center is investigating applications of quantum cryptography. By leveraging quantum encryption, Dubai aims to safeguard critical sectors, recognizing that advancements in quantum technology could potentially compromise traditional encryption protocols. Through investments in quantum-resistant cryptographic methods, Dubai seeks to future-proof its digital infrastructure across key domains such as finance, healthcare, and national security (Dubai Electronic Security Center, 2023).

The advancement of global internet connectivity, driven by satellite and communications technologies, is set to usher in a new era of accessibility and collaboration. Satellite internet solutions, such as SpaceX's Starlink, provide high-speed, low-latency connectivity to remote and underserved regions, helping to bridge the digital divide and democratize global access to information. Integrating 5G and future 6G networks

(Salh et al., 2021) with satellite internet connectivity could revolutionize communication networks, enabling emerging technologies like the Internet of Things, edge computing, and quantum computing. However, challenges related to the widespread adoption of satellite internet—such as cost, space debris management, and equitable access—demand careful regulatory and economic planning.

In conclusion, the convergence of quantum computing and global satellite internet connectivity represents a paradigm shift in computational and communication capabilities, offering vast opportunities for innovation, economic growth, and societal advancement. To fully harness the potential of these technologies, concerted efforts from government bodies, industry stakeholders, and the scientific community are essential to overcoming technical challenges, ensuring equitable access, and fostering a collaborative ecosystem that supports sustained innovation. As the implications of quantum computing and global connectivity continue to unfold, stakeholders must remain vigilant and approach these advancements with a commitment to responsibly leveraging them for the collective benefit.

Strategic AI Integration: Shaping Dubai's Future Urban Landscape

Dubai's strategic deployment of AI within its public services framework has significantly enhanced operational efficiency and service delivery. Notably, smart traffic management systems powered by real-time data analytics have played a crucial role in reducing traffic congestion by an impressive 20% (Kuberkar and Singhal, 2024). These systems employ dynamic traffic flow optimization, reducing travel times and lowering carbon emissions, directly contributing to Dubai's environmental sustainability objectives.

Moreover, predictive maintenance technologies integrated into Dubai's public transportation network have improved operational efficiency by 15%. These AI-driven systems facilitate maintenance scheduling based on predictive data insights, reducing system downtime and extending the functional lifespan of essential infrastructure. In addition, AI has transformed emergency response services in Dubai, cutting response times from 15 to 7 minutes—an improvement that significantly enhances survival rates and crisis outcomes.

Dubai's ability to rapidly scale and implement these advanced technologies, compared to other global cities like Singapore (Smart Nation Singapore, 2023) and Helsinki, can be attributed to its centralized governance model. This model enables expedited decision-making and policy implementation, supported by robust public–private partnerships that streamline the introduction of new technologies (Digital Dubai Authority, 2022).

Table 2 offers a detailed comparison of emerging technologies being actively implemented within Dubai's smart city framework. It examines the diverse applications of AI, blockchain, 6G connectivity, and quantum computing, reviewing each technology based on its specific use cases, measurable impacts, future applications, global context, and illustrative case studies. These examples underscore Dubai's dedication to pioneering advancements, improving operational efficiency, and fostering a technology-driven urban ecosystem that serves as a global benchmark. This comparative analysis aligns with the UAE's strategy to position Dubai as a hub for innovation and digital transformation.

Table 2. Comparative Analysis of Emerging Technologies in Dubai's Smart City Development

Technology	Use Cases in Dubai	Quantifiable Impact	Future Applications	Global Comparison	Case Examples
AI	Predictive healthcare diagnostics, real-time traffic management, smart policing through facial recognition	20% reduction in healthcare wait times; 30% drop in traffic congestion	AI-driven climate analytics	Leading in MENA; comparable to advanced cities	DubaiNow app for integrated e-government services; DEWA's Smart Grid for energy management; Smart Dubai's Happiness Index for public satisfaction; AI-driven surveillance by Dubai Police
Blockchain	Secure public service transactions, digital identity verification, land registry management	30% faster processing of government services; enhanced data security	Blockchain in digital passports	First city to implement at scale in public sector	UAE PASS for digital identity; Dubai Land Department's Blockchain-Based Property Registry; DubaiPay platform for secure payments; Blockchain-secured healthcare records for data integrity
6G Connectivity	Infrastructure for ultra-fast internet, autonomous vehicle support, industrial IoT applications	Projected 10x data transfer speed	Autonomous 6G-enabled vehicles	Testing phases in select global cities	Dubai 6G Readiness Initiative; Dubai Roads and Transport Authority's autonomous vehicle trials; IoT logistics and real-time data monitoring supported by 6G in smart city projects
Quantum Computing	Energy load balancing, advanced cryptographic security, desalination process optimization	Enhanced energy distribution efficiency; cybersecurity in early stages	Environmental modeling, AI processing boost	Early development globally with few implementations	Technology Innovation Institute's Quantum Research Center; DEWA's quantum initiatives for energy solutions; Dubai Quantum Lab's RandD in quantum algorithms; Exploration of quantum-safe encryption in financial sectors

Note. RandD = Research and Development. Source: Own elaboration based on sources from UAE Government (n.d.c), DEWA (2018a), Technology Innovation Institute (2021).

Dubai leads the way among global smart cities with remarkable performance metrics, particularly in public safety, healthcare, and environmental management. The city's AI-driven strategies have resulted in impressive outcomes: a 50% reduction in emergency response times, a 50% decrease in diagnostic times, and a high 90% citizen satisfaction rate with Smart Police Stations. These achievements set Dubai apart, demonstrating how effectively the city leverages AI to enhance public safety and healthcare services.

In environmental management, Dubai excels by significantly reducing freshwater consumption by 35% and decreasing its carbon footprint by 30%, surpassing the performance of other cities like Singapore and Helsinki. These accomplishments underscore Dubai's commitment to sustainable urban development and efficient resource management.

While Singapore (Smart Nation Singapore, 2023) showcases strong AI applications in traffic management, achieving a 25% reduction in road congestion and a 20% decrease in traffic incidents, New York demonstrates leadership in digital governance, with 80% citizen adoption of digital government services and a 75% reduction in online service processing times (New York City Open Data, 2023).

Helsinki provides a commendable example in environmental management, achieving a 35% improvement in waste recycling rates and a 25% reduction in energy consumption in public buildings. These advancements reflect the city's efforts to integrate AI to promote sustainability.

In sum, Dubai stands out as a benchmark in multiple sectors, establishing itself as a global model for AI-driven smart city initiatives. The city's comprehensive approach to AI integration serves as a blueprint for enhancing urban resilience, sustainability, and innovation, setting a high standard for future smart city development worldwide.

The Road Ahead: Dubai's Blueprint for Global AI Leadership

Dubai stands as a leader among global smart cities, particularly in public safety, healthcare, and environmental management, showcasing how AI can be harnessed to elevate urban resilience, sustainability, and innovation. The city's AI-driven initiatives yield remarkable outcomes across these sectors, positioning Dubai as a benchmark for comprehensive, technology-driven urban development.

Dubai has made substantial advancements in public safety, achieving a 50% reduction in emergency response times, a 20% reduction in crime rates, and a 90% citizen satisfaction rate with its Smart Police Stations. These metrics reflect Dubai's effective use of AI in fostering a safer urban environment, highlighting best practices that other cities can emulate.

In healthcare, Dubai's AI applications have contributed to a 50% reduction in diagnostic times and a 60% increase in early detection accuracy, significantly improving patient outcomes and operational efficiency. The city's integration of AI in healthcare demonstrates how predictive analytics and real-time health monitoring can transform urban healthcare systems, aligning with global standards of patient-centered care (Digital Dubai Authority, 2022).

In environmental management, Dubai's smart grid technology, operated by the DEWA, has facilitated a 35% reduction in freshwater consumption, a 40% improvement in air quality, and a 30% reduction in its carbon footprint. These achievements position Dubai as a model for sustainable resource management and environmental conservation, reinforcing its commitment to green urban development (Digital Dubai Authority, 2022).

Singapore has also achieved notable successes in traffic management, realizing a 25% reduction in road congestion and a 20% decrease in traffic incidents by deploying smart traffic systems. These outcomes highlight Singapore's effective use of AI to enhance urban mobility, contributing to a more efficient and sustainable transportation network (Singapore Ministry of Health, 2021).

New York stands out for its robust digital governance infrastructure, with 80% of citizens adopting digital government services and a 75% reduction in processing times for online services. This widespread digital transformation underscores the city's commitment to providing accessible, user-friendly government services (New York City Mayor's Office of Technology, 2023).

Helsinki has made significant contributions to environmental management, with AI-driven initiatives achieving a 35% improvement in waste recycling rates and a 25% reduction in energy consumption in public buildings. These results reflect Helsinki's dedication to sustainability and efficient resource utilization, offering a model for cities aiming to incorporate AI into their environmental policies (Helsinki Smart City Project, 2021).

Dubai's achievements across multiple sectors, particularly in public safety, healthcare, and environmental management, establish it as a global exemplar in AI-driven smart city initiatives. The city's holistic approach to AI integration offers valuable insights and strategies for other urban centers aiming to enhance operational efficiency, sustainability, and quality of life through innovative technologies. Dubai's success further solidifies its position as a global leader in urban AI integration, setting a benchmark for future smart city developments worldwide.

Dubai's substantial investments in AI research and development have cemented the city's role as a pioneer in urban AI applications, placing it at the forefront of global smart city initiatives. As part of its strategy to become a leading hub for technology and innovation, Dubai has developed proprietary AI algorithms that have been adopted by other prominent cities, contributing to advancements in urban management and planning on a global scale (Saura et al., 2024). Ranking among the top five cities globally for AI innovation in urban development, alongside New York, Tokyo, and Amsterdam, Dubai's achievements reflect its unique state-driven innovation model. Through strategic partnerships with multi-national technology companies, Dubai has accelerated the adoption and implementation of cutting-edge AI solutions throughout its urban framework (Digital Dubai Authority, 2022).

Dubai's AI-driven governance model and adaptive urban planning strategies underscore its commitment to enhancing urban living through advanced technology, establishing a replicable model for other cities seeking to harness AI for sustainable urban development. By systematically applying AI across various sectors, Dubai demonstrates how a well-coordinated smart city framework can transform urban experiences and set new global standards.

In particular, Dubai's successful integration of AI into public services, healthcare, and environmental management has redefined the urban landscape, cementing the city's reputation as a benchmark for global smart city initiatives. The city's achievements provide valuable insights into how AI can improve urban living, offering critical lessons in strategic planning, stakeholder collaboration, and sustainable development practices (Kinder et al., 2023). Dubai's comprehensive AI-driven strategies not only contribute to global discussions on urban innovation but also offer a practical roadmap for other cities aiming to integrate AI into their urban ecosystems.

In conclusion, Dubai's strategic integration of AI and advancements in quantum technology and smart infrastructure have reshaped the urban experience, positioning the city as a global leader in smart city development. From healthcare and public safety to environmental sustainability and community engagement, Dubai exemplifies the transformative potential of technology in enhancing quality of life, security, and urban efficiency. These initiatives set a high global standard and provide a replicable model for cities worldwide seeking to leverage technology to create smart, secure, and sustainable urban environments. Dubai's innovative approach to AI integration serves as a blueprint for the future of urban development, showcasing the profound impact of technology-driven governance on the modern cityscape (Digital Dubai Authority, 2022).

DISCUSSION

The findings of this study underscore the transformative role of AI in urban development, using Dubai as a case study to illustrate the multi-dimensional impacts of AI integration on economic, environmental, and social frameworks. Consistent with previous research, this study affirms that AI can significantly improve the operational efficiency of urban services, optimize resource allocation, and enhance residents' quality of life (Manzoor et al., 2021; Yiğitcanlar et al., 2020a). However, in contrast to earlier studies that have predominantly focused on Western smart cities, this research contributes to the limited body of literature on AI-driven urbanization in Middle Eastern cities, highlighting the unique challenges and opportunities in the context of Dubai.

Building on the work of Saura et al. (2022), who explored data privacy in AI applications, this study also addresses the ethical and governance dimensions of AI integration, which are crucial for ensuring sustainable urban development. By placing Dubai's AI initiatives within this framework, the study adds depth to the discourse on how ethical considerations in AI can influence urban policies, aligning smart city projects with global sustainability goals (Bibri et al., 2023). Dubai's governance model, which promotes public–private partnerships and centralized decision-making, is a valuable example of how cities can effectively manage AI projects to foster transparency, collaboration, and accountability.

This study also extends the literature on AI's environmental impacts by examining Dubai's implementation of smart energy and water management systems, as highlighted in recent works by Kuberkar and Singhal (2024). AI-powered infrastructure in Dubai has led to significant reductions in energy consumption and carbon emissions, underscoring the broader applicability of such systems in global environmental sustainability initiatives. By addressing environmental and operational benefits, the research emphasizes AI's role as a holistic solution for cities seeking to balance technological innovation with sustainable practices.

Furthermore, this research provides unique insights into the socio-economic impact of AI on urban life, an area that has been less explored in Middle Eastern smart city studies. Dubai's integration of AI in healthcare, transportation, and public services demonstrates a comprehensive approach to enhancing urban functionality, echoing the calls from scholars like Lim et al. (2021) for a multi-sectoral approach to AI-driven urbanization. By contextualizing Dubai's advancements within the broader smart city literature, this study identifies AI as a catalyst for socio-economic transformation, positioning the city as a replicable model for other regions aspiring to develop sustainable, high-tech urban centers.

CONCLUSION

This study contributes to the growing body of knowledge on AI in urban development by offering a comprehensive, case-based analysis of Dubai's AI integration across multiple sectors, including healthcare, public services, transportation, and environmental management (Kuberkar and Singhal, 2024; Lim et al., 2021). Unlike prior research, which often focuses on Western smart cities, this study highlights a distinctive Middle Eastern model, thus enriching the existing literature by exploring Dubai's unique approach to smart city transformation (Yiğitcanlar et al., 2020b). By examining Dubai's journey, this research demonstrates the potential of AI not only as a technological tool but also as a strategic framework for achieving urban sustainability, operational efficiency, and socio-economic resilience within a dynamic and rapidly evolving city (Bibri et al., 2023).

The study underscores Dubai's success in leveraging AI across multiple domains. In healthcare, AI-driven predictive analytics and personalized treatment models have enabled Dubai to enhance patient care, reduce diagnostic times, and improve operational efficiency, positioning the city as a global leader in medical innovation (Alhussain et al., 2022; Liu et al., 2024). The city's deployment of AI in transportation has optimized traffic flows, minimized congestion, and lowered carbon emissions, serving as a replicable model for other global cities (Kuberkar and Singhal, 2024). Additionally, Dubai's use of AI in environmental management, from water conservation to air quality monitoring, highlights the potential of technology to address pressing environmental challenges (Bibri et al., 2023). These achievements emphasize how AI can serve as a holistic solution for cities aiming to balance technological innovation with sustainable practices (Doorn, 2021; Saura et al., 2022).

From a governance perspective, Dubai's centralized model and public–private partnerships have facilitated the rapid integration of AI technologies across sectors, showcasing a blueprint for agile governance that other cities can emulate (Digital Dubai Authority, 2022). This model has enabled Dubai to advance its smart city objectives while maintaining strong oversight, transparency, and public engagement, which are crucial for fostering trust in AI-driven initiatives (Marri et al., 2019). The study suggests that policymakers globally can learn from Dubai's approach, particularly in creating frameworks that promote collaboration, innovation, and ethical AI usage (Kinder et al., 2023).

While this study highlights significant achievements, it is important to acknowledge its limitations. As a single-case study, the findings may not be universally applicable to cities with different socio-political or economic contexts, limiting the generalizability of the results). Additionally, the rapid evolution of AI technology may challenge the long-term relevance of these findings. Future research could build upon this study by exploring similar AI applications in diverse urban settings, conducting comparative analyses, or using longitudinal research designs to assess the long-term impact of AI on urban development (Rjab and Mellouli, 2019; Yiğitcanlar et al., 2020b).

This study also highlights the need for ongoing ethical and governance considerations as AI continues to influence urban policy (Saura et al., 2023). As previous research has indicated, the ethical deployment of AI is critical for maintaining public trust and ensuring that the benefits of AI are equitably distributed across all societal segments (Saura et al., 2022). As cities move towards AI-driven models, addressing data privacy, algorithmic bias, and inclusivity will be essential for creating socially responsible smart cities (Sharma, 2021; Sırmaçek et al., 2023).

In conclusion, Dubai's approach illustrates the transformative potential of AI in reshaping urban landscapes and setting new standards for smart city development worldwide. By examining Dubai's AI initiatives, this study provides valuable insights for cities worldwide seeking to harness AI to address the challenges of rapid urbanization, environmental sustainability, and socio-economic inequality (Shareef and Altan, 2021). The city's strategic use of AI redefines its urban and economic frameworks and offers a replicable model for global smart city initiatives. With Dubai serving as a case study, this research underscores the importance of strategic planning, stakeholder collaboration, and a solid ethical foundation for cities aiming to build smarter, more resilient, and more inclusive urban environments. Future research should continue to explore AI's role in urban governance, its implications for sustainability, and its potential to transform the socio-economic fabric of cities worldwide (Lim et al., 2021; Rozenman et al., 2023).

Practical Implications

The findings underscore the importance of AI in enhancing urban resilience, operational efficiency, and sustainability. Dubai's implementation of AI-driven energy management, traffic optimization, and personalized healthcare illustrates how AI can optimize resources, reduce environmental impact, and improve the quality of life for residents (Manzoor et al., 2021; Saura, 2024). Cities facing similar urbanization challenges can adopt AI strategies prioritizing collaboration across sectors to promote transparency, accountability, and scalability in urban governance. Additionally, the study emphasizes ethical AI deployment, suggesting that clear regulatory guidelines are essential for ensuring data privacy and ethical standards in urban applications of AI (Saura et al., 2022).

This research underscores the importance of strategically integrating AI within urban infrastructures to enhance efficiency and adaptability. For city planners and municipal authorities, Dubai's AI deployment strategies offer a replicable model for urban innovation. These strategies have streamlined city operations and significantly improved public transportation, healthcare, and environmental management service delivery, creating a more livable and sustainable urban environment (Kuberkar and Singhal, 2024). The study provides practical guidelines for implementing AI tools that optimize real-time traffic management, energy consumption, and emergency services.

Additionally, the study illustrates the benefits of AI for the corporate sector, driving business efficiency and innovation. By leveraging AI for data analytics, predictive maintenance, and customer engagement, businesses can enhance operational efficiencies and offer personalized customer experiences (Faccia et al., 2023). The article highlights best practices for integrating AI into business processes and includes case studies showing how AI has led to substantial cost savings and increased revenue. It also discusses the need to invest in AI training and development to cultivate a technologically skilled workforce capable of managing and advancing AI systems.

From a policy perspective, the study's findings provide governmental entities with evidence-based recommendations to promote a supportive environment for AI integration. The research advocates for policies that foster AI research and development, encourage public–private partnerships, and uphold ethical standards in AI deployment. It also recommends establishing governance frameworks to address data privacy, security, and accountability, ensuring that AI advancements benefit all social segments without exacerbating inequalities (Shareef and Altan, 2021).

For public sector officials, the study's practical implications highlight ways to enhance service delivery through AI. Examples from Dubai's experience show how AI can optimize resource allocation, improve public health monitoring, and enhance educational outcomes (Saura et al., 2022). Recommendations are provided for adopting similar models in cities worldwide, tailoring AI solutions to meet local needs and capabilities.

Finally, the study addresses the long-term sustainability and alignment of AI projects with global sustainability goals. It emphasizes the importance of ongoing evaluation and adaptation of AI systems to ensure they remain effective and beneficial as urban environments evolve. The study proposes frameworks for continuous learning and improvement, incorporating feedback mechanisms to help AI systems adapt to changing urban dynamics and technological advancements (Bibri et al., 2023).

Theoretical Implications

This study's examination of Dubai's AI-driven transformation in urban landscapes not only reinforces existing theories but also introduces new avenues for theoretical exploration in smart city development. The integration of AI in urban governance and public services in Dubai provides a practical foundation for theorizing the relationship between technology and urban development strategies (Rjab and Mellouli, 2019; Saura et al, 2023). It enhances our understanding of how AI can drive innovation and efficiency in urban contexts, challenging traditional theories of urban planning and management (Bibri et al., 2023).

The research findings reveal significant gaps in existing theoretical frameworks regarding the adaptability and scalability of AI technologies in diverse urban settings. Dubai's success in implementing AI initiatives suggests a need to revise urban development theories to include the dynamic influences of AI and its impact on sustainable urban planning. This study contributes to academic discourse by recommending that future theoretical models account for the rapid integration of technological innovations and consider the regulatory and ethical implications accompanying them (Yiğitcanlar et al., 2020b).

Based on insights from Dubai's experience, this section provides a roadmap for future research on AI integration in urban environments. It emphasizes the need for empirical studies that examine the long-term outcomes of AI adoption in urban management, the socio-economic effects on urban residents, and the environmental implications of widespread AI use. Integrating AI in Dubai's infrastructure calls for a synthesis of theories from urban planning, information technology, and social sciences (Lim et al., 2021). Such a cross-disciplinary approach could yield innovative theoretical frameworks that more accurately reflect the complexities of modern urban ecosystems, enabling researchers to better analyze and predict the impacts of AI on urban futures, leading to more robust and inclusive development strategies (Manzoor et al., 2021).

Limitations and Future Research

Acknowledging the limitations of this study is crucial for transparency and sets the foundation for future research. As a case study focused on Dubai, the findings may not universally apply to cities with different socio-economic or political contexts. Additionally, data limitations and the rapidly evolving nature of AI technology may affect the long-term relevance of the study's conclusions (Yiğitcanlar et al., 2020b). Future research could address these limitations by conducting comparative studies across multiple cities or using longitudinal studies to assess the sustained impact of AI on urban governance and development.

Future research should also explore AI's integration in diverse urban contexts, examining how cultural, economic, and regulatory factors shape the success of AI-driven smart city initiatives. Comparative research between Middle Eastern and Western cities could help identify universal versus region-specific challenges in AI implementation. Additionally, further research is needed to evaluate the socio-economic impact of AI on urban populations, particularly in areas such as job markets, social equity, and quality of life. Studying AI's role in addressing emerging challenges, including climate resilience and public health crises, could offer valuable insights for policymakers and urban planners worldwide.

In summary, this study positions Dubai as a model for AI-driven urban transformation and underscores the importance of strategic, ethical, and sustainable AI deployment in smart city planning. By offering a framework that integrates practical applications and theoretical perspectives, this research contributes to advancing global discourse on AI's role in shaping urban futures and supports the creation of smarter, more livable cities for future generations.

Added Value and Broader Impact

This research contributes to academic and practical understandings of AI in smart cities. Academically, it bridges a notable gap by presenting a holistic model for AI integration in urban settings, covering social, environmental, and economic dimensions (Shareef and Altan, 2021). Practically, the study highlights specific strategies and technologies used in Dubai, offering a blueprint for other cities seeking to implement AI sustainably. Drawing on Dubai's public–private partnerships and centralized governance model, the research suggests adaptable frameworks that policymakers and urban planners can consider when integrating AI into city infrastructures (Saura et al., 2022).

This study adds original value by providing a comprehensive, case-based examination of AI's integration in a Middle Eastern smart city. Unlike prior research focusing primarily on technological advancements, it integrates theoretical perspectives with empirical data, offering a model of AI-driven urbanization that is both locally relevant and globally applicable (Shareef and Altan, 2021). Furthermore, the research contributes to the advancement of urban governance models, offering insights into policy implications that can inform the development of regulatory frameworks for AI in diverse urban contexts.

In conclusion, the findings extend beyond Dubai, offering valuable insights into the scalability of AI technologies in cities worldwide. By providing a strategic and ethical framework for AI deployment, this research supports urban planners, policymakers, and researchers in leveraging AI for sustainable urban development. The study contributes a model that addresses the economic, social, and environmental dimensions of AI integration, advancing the discourse on its potential to reshape urban landscapes across varied socio-political settings.

COMPETING INTERESTS

The authors of this publication declare there are no competing interests.

FUNDING

This research received no specific grant from any funding agency in the public, commercial, or not-for-profit sectors. Funding for this research was covered by the author of the article.

REFERENCES

AL-Dabbagh, R. (2022). Dubai, the sustainable, smart city. *Renewable Energy and Environmental Sustainability*, *7*, 3. Advance online publication. DOI: 10.1051/rees/2021049

Al Maktoum, M. B. R. (2012). *My Vision: Challenges in the Race for Excellence*. Motivate Publishing.

AlAli, M., Mattar, Y., Alzaim, M. A., & Beheiry, S. (2023). Applications of biomimicry in architecture, construction and civil engineering. *Biomimetics*, *8*(2), 202. Advance online publication. DOI: 10.3390/biomimetics8020202 PMID: 37218788

Alhussain, G., Kelly, A., O'Flaherty, E. I., Quinn, D. P., & Flaherty, G. (2022). Emerging role of artificial intelligence in global health care. *Health Policy and Technology*, *11*(3), 100661. Advance online publication. DOI: 10.1016/j.hlpt.2022.100661 PMID: 35991006

Aliabadi, R., Singh, A., & Wilson, E. (2023). Transdisciplinary AI education: The confluence of curricular and community needs in the instruction of artificial intelligence. In Schlippe, T., Cheng, E. C. K., & Wang, T. (Eds.), *Artificial Intelligence in Education Technologies: New Development and Innovative Practices* (pp. 137–151)., DOI: 10.1007/978-981-99-7947-9_11

AlSuwaidi, S., & Moonesar, I. A. (2021). UAE resident users' perceptions of healthcare applications from Dubai Health Authority: Preliminary insights. *Dubai Medical Journal*, *4*(1), 10–17. DOI: 10.1159/000513489

Ammar, J. (2023). Analyze business context data in developing economies using quantum computing. https://doi.org//arXiv.2311.08048DOI: 10.48550

Barbosa, B., Saura, J. R., & Bennett, D. (2024). How do entrepreneurs perform digital marketing across the customer journey? A review and discussion of the main uses. *The Journal of Technology Transfer*, *49*(1), 69–103. DOI: 10.1007/s10961-022-09978-2

Bibri, S. E., Alahi, A., Sharifi, A., & Krogstie, J. (2023). Environmentally sustainable smart cities and their converging AI, IoT, and big data technologies and solutions: An integrated approach to an extensive literature review. *Energy Informatics*, *6*(1), 9. Advance online publication. DOI: 10.1186/s42162-023-00259-2 PMID: 37032812

Braun, V., & Clarke, V. (2006). Using thematic analysis in psychology. *Qualitative Research in Psychology*, *3*(2), 77–101. DOI: 10.1191/1478088706qp063oa

Cüce, E., Nachan, Z., Cuce, P. M., Sher, F., & Neighbour, G. B. (2017). Strategies for ideal indoor environments towards low/zero carbon buildings through a biomimetic approach. *International Journal of Ambient Energy*, *40*(1), 86–95. DOI: 10.1080/01430750.2017.1372807

De Vos, W. M., Tilg, H., Van Hul, M., & Cani, P. D. (2022). Gut microbiome and health: Mechanistic insights. *Gut*, *71*(5), 1020–1032. https://www.ncbi.nlm.nih.gov/pmc/articles/PMC8995832/. DOI: 10.1136/gutjnl-2021-326789 PMID: 35105664

De'Shazer, M. (2024). Advancing legal reasoning: The integration of AI to navigate complexities and biases in global jurisprudence with semi-automated arbitration processes (SAAPs). https://doi.org//arxiv.2402.04140DOI: 10.48550

Digital Dubai Authority. (2022). *Dubai blockchain strategy*. https://www.digitaldubai.ae/initiatives/blockchain

Digital Dubai Authority. (2023a). Smart city initiatives and digital transformation projects. https://www.digitaldubai.ae

Digital Dubai Authority. (2023b). *UAE PASS and digital transformation*. https://www.digitaldubai.ae

Digital Government Singapore. (2022). *AI in Singapore's smart city development*. https://www.smartnation.gov.sg/nais/

Doorn, N. (2021). Artificial intelligence in the water domain: Opportunities for responsible use. *The Science of the Total Environment*, *755*, 142561. Advance online publication. DOI: 10.1016/j.scitotenv.2020.142561 PMID: 33039891

Dubai Electricity and Water Authority. (2018a). *DEWA is first utility in the world to work with Microsoft to utilize quantum computing*. https://www.dewa.gov.ae/en/about-us/media-publications/latest-news/2018/07/dewa-is-first-utility-in-the-world-to-work-with-microsoft-to-utilise-quantum-computing

Dubai Electricity and Water Authority. (2018b). *Smart initiatives for enhanced energy efficiency*. https://www.dewa.gov.ae

Dubai Electricity and Water Authority. (2023). *DEWA becomes the world's first utility organization to integrate ChatGPT.* Government of Dubai. https://www.dewa.gov.ae/en/about-dewa/news-and-media/news/2023/01/dewa-first-to-integrate-chatgpt

Dubai Electricity and Water Authority. (2023). *DEWA Smart Grid and energy efficiency initiatives*. https://www.dewa.gov.ae/en/about-us/media-publications/latest-news/2023/07/dewas-smart-grid-an-effective

Dubai Electricity and Water Authority. (n.d.). Smart Grid Strategy. https://www.dewa.gov.ae/en/about-dewa/smart-initiatives/smart-grid-strategy

Dubai Electronic Security Center. (2023). Dubai Cyber Security Strategy 2023. https://www.desc.gov.ae/wp-content/uploads/2023/pdfs/dcss_EN_2023.pdf

Dubai Future Foundation. (2023a). Dubai Centre for Artificial Intelligence. https://www.dubaifuture.ae/dubai-centre-for-artificial-intelligence

Dubai Future Foundation. (2023b). AI Program government services. https://www.dubaifuture.ae/ai-program-government-services

Dubai Future Foundation. (2024). Mostaqbal Portal: Advancing Science and Technology in Arabic. https://www.dubaifuture.gov.ae

Dubai Future Foundation. (n.d.). About Us. https://www.dubaifuture.ae/about-us/

Dubai Government. (n.d.). Dubai 3D Printing Strategy. https://u.ae/en/about-the-uae/strategies-initiatives-and-awards/strategies-plans-and-visions/innovation-and-future-shaping/dubai-3d-printing-strategy

Dubai Health Authority. (2023). Salama: The Integrated Electronic Medical Record Initiative. https://www.dha.gov.ae/en/media/news/762

Dubai Municipality. (2023). *Sustainability and environmental management in Dubai*. https://www.dm.gov.ae/municipality-business/environment-sustainability-technical-guidelines/

Dubai Police. (2022). Smart policing and innovation in public safety. https://www.dubaipolice.gov.ae/wps/portal/home/aboutus/overview

Emirates Scientists Council. (2024). UAE Advanced Science Agenda 2031: Supporting Research and Innovation. https://www.esc.ae

Faccia, A., Le Roux, C. L., and Pandey, V. (2023). Innovation and e-commerce models, the technology catalysts for sustainable development: The Emirate of Dubai case study. *Sustainability, 15*(4), Article 3419. [REMOVED HYPERLINK40 FIELD] DOI: 10.3390/su15043419

González-Padilla, P., Navalpotro, F. D., & Saura, J. R. (2024). Managing entrepreneurs' behavior personalities in digital environments: A review. *The International Entrepreneurship and Management Journal, 20*(1), 89–113. DOI: 10.1007/s11365-022-00823-4

Government of Dubai. (2022). *UAE-National Strategy for Artificial Intelligence 2031*. https://ai.gov.ae/wp-content/uploads/2021/07/UAE-National-Strategy-for-Artificial-Intelligence-2031.pdf

Government of Dubai Media Office. (2021). Four new smart police stations inaugurated in Dubai. *Dubai Media Office*. https://www.mediaoffice.ae/en/news/2021/September/27-09/Four-Smart-Police

Helsinki Smart City Project. (2021). *Autonomous vehicles and environmental management strategies*. https://www.hel.fi/static/kanslia/Julkaisut/2021/helsinki-city-strategy-2021-2025.pdf

Herath, H. M. K. K. M. B., & Mittal, M. (2022). Adoption of artificial intelligence in smart cities: A comprehensive review. *Journal of Cleaner Production*, *330*, 140105. Advance online publication. https://www.smartnation.gov.sg/initiatives/urban-planning/. DOI: 10.1016/j.jclepro.2023.140105

Institute for Health Metrics and Evaluation (IHME). (2019). *Global Burden of Disease Study 2019 (GBD 2019) results*. Seattle, WA: IHME, University of Washington. Retrieved from https://ghdx.healthdata.org/gbd-2019

Jamali, D., Ahmad, I., Aboelmaged, M. G., & Usman, M. (2024). Corporate social responsibility in the United Arab Emirates and globally: A cross-national comparison. *Journal of Cleaner Production*, *434*, 140105. Advance online publication. DOI: 10.1016/j.jclepro.2023.140105

Jamali, D., Moonesar, I., & Al Suwaidi, H. (2024). AI and sustainable urban planning in Dubai. *Journal of Smart Cities and Urban Innovation*, *12*(1), 85–102.

Jangid, P., & Inbaraj, M. P. (2021). Applications of nanomaterials in wastewater treatment. *Materials Today: Proceedings*, *43*(5), 2877–2881. https://www.sciencedirect.com/science/article/pii/S2214785321001693. DOI: 10.1016/j.matpr.2021.01.126

Kinder, T., Stenvall, J., Koskimies, E., Webb, H. L., & Janenova, S. (2023). Local public services and the ethical deployment of artificial intelligence. *Government Information Quarterly*, *40*(4), 101865. Advance online publication. DOI: 10.1016/j.giq.2023.101865

Kuberkar, S., & Singhal, T. K. (2024). Adoption of AI-enabled smart city services from citizens' perspective. *Journal of Urban Technology and Innovation*, *12*(1), 56–72.

Lacarcel, F. J., & Huete, R. (2023). Digital communication strategies used by private companies, entrepreneurs, and public entities to attract long-stay tourists: A review. *The International Entrepreneurship and Management Journal*, *19*(2), 691–708. DOI: 10.1007/s11365-023-00843-8

Li, P., Bastone, A., Mohamad, T. A., & Schiavone, F. (2023). How does artificial intelligence impact human resources performance: Evidence from a healthcare institution in the United Arab Emirates. *Journal of Innovation and Knowledge*, *8*(2), 100340. Advance online publication. DOI: 10.1016/j.jik.2023.100340

Lim, T., Rajabifard, A., Khoo, V., Sabri, S., & Chen, Y. (2021). The smart city in Singapore: How environmental and geospatial innovation lead to urban livability and sustainability. In H. M. Kim, S. Sabri, and A. Kent (Eds.), *Smart cities for technological and social innovation: Case studies, current trends, and future steps* (pp. 13–27). Elsevier. DOI: 10.1016/B978-0-12-818886-6.00003-4

Liu, S., Wang, L., & Gao, R. X. (2024). Cognitive neuroscience and robotics: Advancements and future research directions. *Robotics and Computer-integrated Manufacturing*, *85*, 102610. Advance online publication. DOI: 10.1016/j.rcim.2023.102610

Manjula, S., & Raj, A. (2022). Assessment of waste management through mobile edge computing and deep learning. *International Journal of Advanced Research in Science. Tongxin Jishu*, •••, 297–315. DOI: 10.48175/IJARSCT-3186

Manzoor, B., Othman, I., Durdyev, S., Ismail, S., & Wahab, M. H. (2021). Influence of artificial intelligence in civil engineering toward sustainable development: A systematic literature review. *Applied System Innovation*, *4*(3), 52. DOI: 10.3390/asi4030052

Marri, A. A., Albloosh, F., Moussa, S., & Elmessiry, H. (2019). Study on the impact of artificial intelligence on government e-service in Dubai. In *Proceedings of the 2019 International Conference on Digitization* (pp. 153–159). IEEE. DOI: 10.1109/ICD47981.2019.9105866

Ministry of Finance. (2024). Mohammed bin Rashid Innovation Fund (MBRIF). https://www.mof.gov.ae

Mohammed bin Rashid Library Foundation. (2023). *Revolutionizing knowledge access with AI at the Mohammed bin Rashid Library*. https://www.mbrl.ae/smart-services

National Institutes of Health. (2024, April 18). *Using AI to shape the future of treatment personalization*. National Center for Advancing Translational Sciences. https://ncats.nih.gov/news-events/news/using-ai-to-shape-the-future-of-treatment-personalization

New York City Mayor's Office of Technology. (2023). *New York City AI initiatives in public services*. https://www.nyc.gov/content/oti/pages/artificial-intelligence

New York City Open Data. (2023). *Digital services and AI applications in healthcare*. https://www.nyc.gov/opendata

Panthee, B., Gyawali, S., Panthee, P., & Techato, K. (2022). Environmental and human microbiome for health. *Life (Chicago, Ill.)*, *12*(3), 456–456. DOI: 10.3390/life12030456 PMID: 35330207

Rjab, A. B., & Mellouli, S. (2019). Artificial intelligence in smart cities: Systematic literature network analysis. In *Proceedings of the 12th International Conference on Theory and Practice of Electronic Governance* (pp. 259–269). Association for Computing Machinery. DOI: 10.1145/3326365.3326400

Rogers, E. M. (1962). *Diffusion of innovations* (1st ed.). Free Press.

Rozenman, G. G., Kundu, N. K., Liu, R., Zhang, L., Maslennikov, A., Reches, Y., & Youm, H. Y. (2023). The quantum internet: A synergy of quantum information technologies and 6G networks. *IET Quantum Communication*, *4*(4), 147–166. DOI: 10.1049/qtc2.12069

Salh, A., Audah, L., Abdullah, Q., Noorsaliza, A., Shah, N. S. M., Mukred, J. A. A., & Hamzah, S. A. (2021). Development of a fully data-driven artificial intelligence and deep learning for URLLC application in 6G wireless systems: A survey. https://doi.org//arxiv.2108.10076DOI: 10.48550

Saura, J. R. (2024). Algorithms in Digital Marketing: Does Smart Personalization Promote a Privacy Paradox? *FIIB Business Review*, *13*(5), 499–502. DOI: 10.1177/23197145241276898

Saura, J. R., Palacios-Marqués, D., & Ribeiro-Soriano, D. (2023). Digital marketing in SMEs via data-driven strategies: Reviewing the current state of research. *Journal of Small Business Management*, *61*(3), 1278–1313. DOI: 10.1080/00472778.2021.1955127

Saura, J. R., Ribeiro-Navarrete, S., Palacios-Marqués, D., & Mardani, A. (2023). Impact of extreme weather in production economics: Extracting evidence from user-generated content. *International Journal of Production Economics*, *260*, 108861. DOI: 10.1016/j.ijpe.2023.108861

Saura, J. R., Ribeiro-Soriano, D., & Iturricha-Fernández, A. (2022). Exploring the challenges of remote work on Twitter users' sentiments: From digital technology development to a post-pandemic era. *Journal of Business Research*, *142*, 242–254. DOI: 10.1016/j.jbusres.2021.12.052

Saura, J. R., Ribeiro-Soriano, D., & Palacios-Marqués, D. (2022). Assessing behavioral data science privacy issues in government artificial intelligence deployment. *Government Information Quarterly*, *39*(4), 101679. Advance online publication. DOI: 10.1016/j.giq.2022.101679

Saura, J. R., Skare, M., & Riberio-Navarrete, S. (2022). How does technology enable competitive advantage? Reviewing state of the art and outlining future directions. *Journal of Competitiveness*, *14*(4), 172–188. DOI: 10.7441/joc.2022.04.10

Saura, J. R., Škare, V., & Dosen, D. O. (2024). Is AI-based digital marketing ethical? Assessing a new data privacy paradox. *Journal of Innovation & Knowledge*, *9*(4), 100597. DOI: 10.1016/j.jik.2024.100597

Shammah, N., Roy, A. S., Almudéver, C. G., Bourdeauducq, S., Butko, A., Cancelo, G., Clark, S. M., Heinsoo, J., Henriet, L., Huang, G., Jurczak, C., Kotilahti, J., Landra, A., LaRose, R., Mari, A., Nowrouzi, K., Ockeloen-Korppi, C., Prawiroatmodjo, G., Siddiqi, I., & Zeng, W. J. (2023). Open hardware in quantum technology. https://doi.org//arxiv.2309.17233DOI: 10.48550

Shareef, S., & Altan, H. (2021). Sustainability at an urban level: A case study of a neighborhood in Dubai, UAE. *Sustainability (Basel)*, *13*(8), 4355. Advance online publication. DOI: 10.3390/su13084355

Sharma, R. (2021). Nanotechnology: An approach for water purification [Review]. *IOP Conference Series. Materials Science and Engineering*, *1116*(1), 012007. Advance online publication. DOI: 10.1088/1757-899X/1116/1/012007

Silverman, D. (2020). *Qualitative research* (5th ed.). SAGE Publications.

Singapore Ministry of Health. (2021). *AI innovation in Singapore healthcare*. https://www.moh.gov.sg/newsroom/transforming-healthcare-through-technology

Sırmaçek, B., Gupta, S., Mallor, F., Azizpour, H., Ban, Y., Eivazi, H., Fang, H., Golzar, F., Leite, I., Melsión, G. I., Smith, K., Nerini, F. F., & Vinuesa, R. (2023). The potential of artificial intelligence for achieving healthy and sustainable societies. In Mazzi, F., & Floridi, L. (Eds.), *The ethics of artificial intelligence for the sustainable development goals* (pp. 65–96). Springer., DOI: 10.1007/978-3-031-21147-8_5

Smart Dubai. (2021). *Smart Dubai 2021 strategy*. https://u.ae/en/about-the-uae/strategies-initiatives-and-awards/strategies-plans-and-visions/strategies-plans-and-visions-untill-2021/smart-dubai-2021-strategy

Smart Dubai. (2022). *Smart Dubai happiness index*. https://smartdubai.ae/happiness-index

Smart Nation Singapore. (2023). *Using Data for Urban Planning*.

Technology Innovation Institute. (2021). *TII's Quantum Research Center starts building UAE's first quantum computer*. https://www.tii.ae/news/tiis-quantum-research-center-starts-building-uaes-first-quantum-computer

UAE Ministry of Foreign Affairs. (2024, October 28). *Cabinet approves UAE's stance on AI policy to reinforce its global leadership in technology.* https://www.mofa.gov.ae/en/mediahub/news/2024/10/28/28-10-2024-uae-technology

United Arab Emirates Government. (2024). Open Labs platform. https://www.uae.gov.ae

United Arab Emirates Government. (n.d.a). D33 Economic Agenda details. UAE Government Publications. https://uae.gov.ae

United Arab Emirates Government. (n.d.b). Dubai AI and Smart City Initiatives. https://u.ae/en/about-the-uae/strategies-initiatives-and-awards

United Arab Emirates Government. (n.d.c). UAE PASS for digital identity verification. https://u.ae/en/about-the-uae/strategies-initiatives-and-awards/uae-pass

United Arab Emirates Government. (n.d.d). UAE Strategy for Artificial Intelligence. https://u.ae/en/about-the-uae/strategies-initiatives-and-awards/strategies-plans-and-visions/government-services-and-digital-transformation/uae-strategy-for-artificial-intelligence

Virtudes, A., Abbara, A., & Sá, J. H. M. (2017). Dubai: A pioneer smart city in the Arabian territory. *IOP Conference Series. Materials Science and Engineering*, *234*, 052071. Advance online publication. DOI: 10.1088/1757-899X/245/5/052071

Yiğitcanlar, T., Desouza, K. C., Butler, L., & Roozkhosh, F. (2020a). AI in urban governance: Dubai's AI-driven transformation in urban planning. *Journal of Urban Technology*, *27*(2), 131–150.

Yiğitcanlar, T., Desouza, K. C., Butler, L., & Roozkhosh, F. (2020b). Contributions and risks of artificial intelligence (AI) in building smarter cities: Insights from a systematic review of the literature. *Energies*, *13*(6), 1473. Advance online publication. DOI: 10.3390/en13061473

Yin, C., Zhang, X., Chen, H., Wang, J., Cooper, D., & David, B. (2015). A literature survey on smart cities. *Science China. Information Sciences*, *58*(10), 1–18. DOI: 10.1007/s11432-015-5397-4

ADDITIONAL READING

Bibri, S. E., Alahi, A., Sharifi, A., & Krogstie, J. (2023). Environmentally sustainable smart cities and their converging AI, IoT, and big data technologies: An integrated approach to urban planning. *Energy Informatics*, *6*(9). Advance online publication. DOI: 10.1186/s42162-023-00259-2 PMID: 37032812

Dubai Future Foundation. (2023). The role of AI in healthcare and public services. https://www.dubaifuture.ae/dubai-centre-for-artificial-intelligence

Kuberkar, S., Singh, S., & Singhal, T. K. (2024). Adoption intention of artificial intelligence enabled smart city services from citizens' perspective. *International Journal of Human Capital in Urban Management*, *9*(1), 29–46. DOI: 10.22034/IJHCUM.2024.01.03

Lim, T. K., Rajabifard, A., Khoo, V., Sabri, S., & Chen, Y. (2021). The smart city in Singapore: How environmental and geospatial innovation lead to urban livability and environmental sustainability. In H. M. Kim, S. Sabri, and A. Kent (Eds.), *Smart cities for technological and social innovation* (pp. 29–49). Academic Press. https://doi.org/DOI: 10.1016/B978-0-12-818886-6.00003-4

Yigitcanlar, T., Desouza, K. C., Butler, L., & Roozkhosh, F. (2020). Contributions and risks of artificial intelligence (AI) in building smarter cities: Insights from a systematic review of the literature. *Energies*, *13*(6), 1473. Advance online publication. DOI: 10.3390/en13061473

KEY TERMS AND DEFINITIONS

6G Connectivity: The next generation of wireless technology promises ultra-fast data transfer speeds, low latency, and support for advanced applications like autonomous vehicles and industrial IoT.

Artificial Intelligence (AI): A field of computer science focused on creating systems capable of performing tasks that typically require human intelligence, including visual perception, speech recognition, and decision-making.

Blockchain: A decentralized, distributed ledger technology that records transactions across multiple computers, ensuring security and transparency. In smart cities, it supports applications in digital identity, land registry, and secure public transactions.

Public Safety AI: AI technologies specifically designed for law enforcement and emergency response, including predictive policing and real-time surveillance to improve response times and public safety outcomes.

Quantum Computing: An emerging field that leverages quantum-mechanical phenomena to perform complex calculations at unprecedented speeds, with potential applications in energy management, cryptography, and AI enhancement.

Smart City: An urban area that uses digital technologies, such as the Internet of Things (IoT) and artificial intelligence (AI), to enhance the quality of urban services, improve efficiency, and promote sustainable development.

Sustainable Urban Development: A planning and development strategy that balances technological advancements with environmental preservation, aiming to create resilient, energy-efficient, and ecologically balanced urban spaces.

APPENDIX

Questions and Answers

1. What is the overall problem presented in this case?

The case examines Dubai's integration of AI into its urban infrastructure to drive sustainable development, public safety, and efficiency. It serves as a benchmark for global cities aiming to leverage AI for urban transformation.

2. What are the factors affecting the challenges in this case?

Key factors include Dubai's unique socio-economic context, centralized governance, rapid technological adoption, public-private partnerships, and its vision to establish itself as a global AI hub.

3. Discuss the managerial, organizational, and technological issues related to this case.
   - **Managerial issues:** Scaling AI initiatives across sectors, maintaining data privacy, and ensuring ethical AI deployment.
   - **Organizational challenges:** Aligning stakeholder interests and adapting governance models to support rapid innovation.
   - **Technological demands:** Building infrastructure to support large-scale AI, such as smart grids and predictive analytics.
4. What role do different players (decision-makers) play in implementing and managing AI applications?

Decision-makers, including government bodies like the Ministry of AI, Digital Dubai Authority, and Smart Dubai, work closely with technology firms and research institutions. These entities drive AI initiatives, establish regulatory frameworks, and ensure equitable benefits for all. The Ministry of AI provides strategic oversight and facilitates partnerships, aligning projects with national goals.

5. What are the possible alternatives and pros and cons for addressing the challenges of AI integration in urban management?
   - **Expand public-private partnerships:** Enhances resources and expertise but may require complex coordination.
   - **Adopt a decentralized approach:** Improves transparency and public engagement but could slow decision-making and innovation.

6. What emerging technologies could be considered to enhance AI's role in addressing urban challenges?

Emerging technologies such as quantum computing, blockchain for secure data management, and 6G connectivity could improve AI's effectiveness by enhancing data processing speeds, security, and urban connectivity.

7. What is the recommended solution for management in this case, and why?

A balanced approach combining centralized governance with public engagement is recommended. This strategy enables rapid AI deployment while addressing ethical and societal concerns, fostering an inclusive model of technological advancement.

Epilogue and Lessons Learned

Epilogue

Dubai's AI-driven smart city model positions it as a global leader in urban development. Its success highlights AI's transformative potential to enhance urban efficiency, sustainability, and quality of life. This case serves as a blueprint for cities worldwide to harness AI for addressing urban challenges.

Lessons Learned

- **Centralized governance enables rapid innovation:** A centralized model facilitates swift decision-making critical for large-scale AI deployment.
- **Public-private partnerships enhance resources and expertise:** Collaborations between government and private sectors drives technological advancement.
- **Data privacy and ethics are fundamental:** Prioritizing data privacy and ethical considerations is essential for public trust.
- **Adaptable infrastructure is key:** Investments in flexible infrastructure, like smart grids and digital platforms, ensure scalable and sustainable AI applications.
- **AI drive comprehensive urban transformation:** The integration of AI across multiple sectors exemplifies its potential to create sustainable, smart cities.

Chapter 9
Artificial Intelligence in Data Visualization: Enhancing Research Through Generative Graphs

Oscar Aguado Tevar
https://orcid.org/0009-0001-9245-3167
Nebrija University, Spain

Luis Díaz-Marcos
https://orcid.org/0009-0007-6580-0382
Nebrija University, Spain

Daniel Angel Corral de la Mata
Rey Juan Carlos University, Spain

María García de Blanes Sebastián
https://orcid.org/0000-0002-9169-3337
Rey Juan Carlos University, Spain

ABSTRACT

This research examines how generative artificial intelligence, specifically ChatGPT, can transform the analysis and visualization of educational data in the Community of Madrid. Using university enrollment data processed and normalized in SPSS v27, a methodology was designed to integrate traditional statistical tools with advanced AI capabilities. The data were structured to reveal key trends in enrollment across public and private universities and various fields of knowledge. Iterative prompts created visualizations highlighting sustained growth in private institutions and a preference for Social Sciences and Health Sciences. The methodology addressed challenges of time and complexity in data visualization, though some inconsistencies

DOI: 10.4018/979-8-3693-6945-6.ch009

in generated graphs were observed. Findings demonstrate AI's potential to enhance the understanding of complex data and support evidence-based decision-making in educational management. This hybrid approach highlights how AI tools can complement traditional methods, opening new possibilities for academic planning and educational research.

INTRODUCTION

In recent years, data visualization has emerged as a key tool in higher education, providing an effective way to interpret and analyze complex information. Graphs, in particular, have been widely used to visually represent trends and patterns, facilitating informed decision-making across various fields, including education. Student enrollment data, especially in undergraduate programs (Grado), is essential to identify areas of high demand, optimize institutional resources, and adapt the educational offering. In this context, visualizing this data through graphs is crucial to understanding enrollment trends and student behavior in diverse institutions.

This study focuses specifically on the Community of Madrid, a region with a high concentration of public and private universities, offering a rich source of data on student enrollment. The central question of this research is: How can data visualization tools, especially graphs generated by artificial intelligence (AI), improve the analysis of student enrollment by area of knowledge in universities of the Community of Madrid, and what role can ChatGPT play in creating these graphs to achieve more precise and effective analysis? The main objective of this study is to evaluate ChatGPT's potential to generate suitable graphs that facilitate the analysis of enrollment data. This analysis will include public and private universities, covering various areas of knowledge, and examining student enrollment trends over recent years.

The specific objectives are as follows:

1. To test various types of graphs, such as column, line, bar, area, scatter, and bubble charts, among others, to effectively visualize enrollment data. The suitability of each type of graph to represent the information clearly and meaningfully will be evaluated.
2. To analyze how each type of graph can help visualize enrollment trends over time, differences between public and private universities, and the most demanded areas of knowledge. This will aid in identifying significant patterns in the data that may not be evident without proper visualization.

3. To explore how the AI model ChatGPT can assist in creating complex graphs, reducing the time required to produce accurate visual representations, and facilitating the interpretation of enrollment data.

This study will contribute to understanding educational trends in the Community of Madrid and improving data analysis methods in the academic field. The results will demonstrate how artificial intelligence, particularly in graph generation, can make interpreting large volumes of data more accessible, enhancing strategic decision-making in universities. Through this analysis, recommendations will be offered on best practices for using visualization tools and AI for educational management and the development of more effective academic policies.

Theoretical Framework

Generative Artificial Intelligence: Definition and Characteristics

The concept of generative AI is defined as a specific branch of artificial intelligence focused on creating new data from learned patterns. According to Corchado et al. (2023), its innovative nature lies in its ability to integrate discriminative and generative models, which work together to analyze, model, and produce results in the form of original content. In this regard, Bannister et al. (2023) highlight that generative AI transforms how we process and generate text while redefining learning and knowledge production environments, facilitating adaptive and personalized processes.

This advanced subfield of artificial intelligence focuses on the capacity of systems to create new data based on learned patterns, reproducing fundamental characteristics of pre-existing datasets. This contrasts with traditional AI, which primarily classifies or predicts data based on prior inputs. According to Shang and Huang (2024), generative AI processes existing information and constructs original content, becoming a key tool for generating knowledge in fields such as science, education, and biotechnology.

It also refers to a set of techniques and deep learning models designed to generate data, content, or simulations that mimic real or plausible patterns. These techniques enable the creation of text, images, music, videos, and even three-dimensional models. According to Fanini and Gosti (2024), generative AI can capture and simulate interaction patterns in immersive applications such as 3D environments, using advanced data analysis and processing technologies.

Generative AI utilizes advanced mathematical models, such as deep neural networks, to learn the underlying distributions of the data. These models include architectures like Generative Adversarial Networks (GANs), transformers like GPT, and Graph Neural Networks (GNNs). Dinu et al. (2024) explain that the ability of these architectures to model complex and dynamic relationships has revolutionized their application across various disciplines.

One of the distinctive characteristics of generative AI is its focus on creating synthetic data that can enrich limited datasets, address bias issues, or generate entirely new content. Hassan et al. (2023) emphasize that this capability is particularly useful in situations where original data is insufficient, such as in biomedical analyses or molecular graph modeling.

Origin and Conceptual Evolution

The development of generative AI dates back to early research on deep learning, where the goal was not only to classify data but also to generate new patterns. Generative Adversarial Networks (GANs), introduced by Goodfellow et al. in 2014, marked a milestone by establishing a competitive approach between a generator and a discriminator to create realistic data. This model evolved into more sophisticated applications, such as the creation of hyper-realistic images and the synthesis of complex data (Wang et al., 2023).

The advent of transformers, such as the GPT model, represented another significant advancement. According to Chen et al. (2023), transformers use attention mechanisms to process large volumes of sequential data, enabling them to generate coherent and contextualized text. This capability has expanded the reach of generative AI into domains such as text content creation, machine translation, and sentiment analysis.

Foundational Models and Applications

Generative models like GPT-4 and BERT are advanced deep learning systems designed to process and generate text with high semantic and grammatical coherence. GPT-4, for instance, can answer complex questions, write essays, perform translations, generate summaries, and even assist in coding while maintaining a high level of adaptability and accuracy (Zahid et al., 2024). In contrast, BERT excels in tasks requiring contextual understanding, such as semantic search and sentiment analysis, making it a powerful tool for educational and business applications (Fui-Hoon Nah et al., 2023).

Dhamani (2024) notes that the true potential of these models lies in their ability for continuous learning and flexibility to adapt to different domains. This means that, with appropriate adjustments and training, a model like GPT-4 can be used in both literary analysis and drafting specialized medical reports. This level of adaptability is crucial for expanding the scope of generative AI across various industries.

Bragazzi and Garbarino (2024) highlight the revolutionary promise of generative AI in the healthcare sector, where it is used to generate detailed clinical reports and personalize medical treatments. Its ability to analyze large volumes of data and translate them into comprehensible text makes it indispensable for decision-making in complex clinical environments.

In the academic field, Dashkevych and Portnov (2024) experimented with generative AI to analyze definitions and characteristics of smart cities. Their study demonstrated that AI can synthesize information from multiple sources, providing a coherent and holistic view of multidimensional concepts. This capacity for integration and synthesis is particularly useful in interdisciplinary research, where combining data from different fields is required to draw meaningful conclusions.

Types of Generative AI

Generative AI in Text

Generative artificial intelligence focused on text has significantly transformed the way written content is produced, analyzed, and consumed. Based primarily on models such as Generative Pre-trained Transformers (GPT) and Bidirectional Encoder Representations from Transformers (BERT), this technology uses deep learning to process and generate human-like language coherently and contextually. Generative text AI models, such as GPT-4 and its variants, are trained on vast amounts of textual data to learn patterns, syntax, and semantics, enabling them to generate textual content that mimics human language with great precision (Zahid et al., 2024; Chen et al., 2023).

Main Characteristics

1. Generative text models use attention mechanisms to analyze the context of a conversation or a dataset. This allows them to generate relevant and context-adapted responses, a capability that is fundamental for applications like chatbots and virtual assistants (Dhamani, 2024; Zahid et al., 2024).
2. Generative text models can perform diverse tasks such as content generation, automatic translation, sentiment analysis, text summarization, and scientific writing. This versatility makes them essential tools for researchers, educators, and businesses (Corchado et al., 2023).
3. Through fine-tuning, generative text models can adapt to specific domains like medicine, law, or education. This is achieved by training the model with specialized data, which increases its accuracy in tasks related to those fields (Bragazzi & Garbarino, 2024).

Applications

- Generative models like GPT-4 assist in drafting scientific articles, providing coherent and structured drafts that can later be refined by human authors. This is particularly useful for non-native English researchers aiming to publish in international journals (Lopes et al., 2024).
- In advertising and marketing, generative AI is used to develop slogans, scripts, and campaigns that resonate with specific audiences. Generative models are also being employed in the creation of novels and movie scripts (Panda & Kaur, 2024).
- In education, generative text models help create personalized materials for students, adapting to their specific needs. This includes simplified explanations of complex concepts and generating tailored exercises (Bannister et al., 2023).
- Tools like DeepL and Google Translate have been significantly improved using generative AI, enabling more precise and contextually relevant translations (Hassan et al., 2023).

Generative AI in Video

Generative AI applied to video is an emerging field that combines advanced techniques in image processing, deep learning, and generative neural networks to create audiovisual content. This type of AI has the potential to revolutionize industries such as entertainment, advertising, education, and medicine, offering an innovative way to produce and analyze dynamic visual content.

Main Characteristics

1. Unlike static image generation, generative video models must capture the temporal dynamics between frames, ensuring smooth and logical transitions. This is achieved using architectures such as recurrent networks and 3D convolutional networks (Fan et al., 2023; Hassan et al., 2023).
2. Advances in generative AI have enabled the creation of hyper-realistic videos that are virtually indistinguishable from those produced by humans. This includes the generation of faces, body movements, and highly detailed environmental effects (Tang et al., 2023).
3. Generative video tools allow users to define specific parameters, such as visual style, theme, and duration, offering granular control over the generated content. This is especially useful in cinematic and advertising production (Gangwal et al., 2024).

Applications

- Generative AI facilitates the creation of visual effects, animations, and complete video sequences without extensive recordings. This not only reduces costs but also allows for greater creative experimentation (Qi et al., 2023).
- In education, generative videos are used to create audiovisual materials that explain complex concepts in an accessible way. This includes scientific simulations, interactive tutorials, and visual representations of abstract processes (Apablaza-Campos et al., 2024).
- Generative AI in video has medical applications such as simulating surgical procedures and generating dynamic medical images for diagnostic studies and medical training (Gangwal et al., 2024).
- In areas like security and forensic investigation, generative video models are used to recreate scenarios based on limited data, such as security camera footage or textual descriptions (Fan et al., 2023).

Understanding ChatGPT's Functionality in Graph Creation

Graph creation by ChatGPT is an emerging capability in generative language models, combining natural language processing (NLP) and graph-based reasoning. This theoretical framework details how language models like ChatGPT use instructions and structured data to generate graphs or visual representations, leveraging various theoretical and practical sources of recent research.

Language models such as ChatGPT, trained on vast textual datasets, have demonstrated capabilities to interpret and produce graphical representations by transforming tabular or structured data into visual formats like bar charts, line graphs, and network diagrams. According to Zhang (2023), the model relies on predefined structures and templates, combined with adaptive reasoning, to produce graphs consistent with the provided instructions.

The Generation Process

1. When a graph is requested, ChatGPT analyzes the provided instruction, which generally includes details about the type of graph, axes, and variables. For example, in works like Graph-ToolFormer (Zhang, 2023), it is demonstrated how the model identifies patterns in tabular data and translates them into visual graphs through specific prompts.

2. ChatGPT can extract relevant information from textual or numerical datasets, using reasoning heuristics based on prior learning. Shi et al. (2023) explain how models can interpret relationships between variables and visualize them in explanatory graphs, such as knowledge diagrams or temporal graphs.
3. Graph production uses preconfigured templates. Studies like those of Mountantonakis and Tzitzikas (2023) highlight the use of RDF graphs and prior knowledge structures to enrich the visual representations generated by the model.

Despite its capabilities, ChatGPT has limitations. According to Hollenbeck (2024), the model depends on well-structured and well-defined data to produce accurate graphs. Additionally, it may lack the ability to validate the accuracy of generated graphs, which can lead to errors if the original data is ambiguous or incomplete.

Graph-Based Reasoning

Graph reasoning is a key extension in language models, enabling them to understand and manipulate relationships between data in the form of graphs or diagrams. Zhang (2023) introduced the concept of Graph-ToolFormer, which integrates graph reasoning capabilities through specific prompts that guide the model to generate visual relationships between data nodes.

In practical applications, this capability is crucial for tasks such as knowledge visualization, where nodes represent entities and edges their relationships. For instance, knowledge graphs enriched with RDF data described by Mountantonakis and Tzitzikas (2023) demonstrate how these tools can be integrated into models like ChatGPT to enhance their visual responses.

The Importance of Prompts in Graph Generation

Prompts are the key element that determines the quality of the generated graphs. According to Zhang (2023), a well-formulated prompt should include clear descriptions of the data, specifications about the required graph type, and relevant contextual details.

- It should include a detailed explanation of the dataset, such as the variables involved and their relationships.
- Specify the desired format (e.g., bar chart, scatter plot, line graph, etc.).
- Indicate how the graph will be used and what aspects should be highlighted.

Example: "Generate a scatter plot to visualize the relationship between study hours and exam scores. Use one axis for study hours and another for scores, differentiating by gender."

This ensures that ChatGPT understands the purpose of the graph and generates useful results. According to Mountantonakis and Tzitzikas (2023), prompts can be adjusted for more specific tasks, such as generating interactive graphs. This includes requesting functionalities like dynamic filters or dual-axis graphs.

A fundamental component for improving the accuracy of generated graphs is data quality. Hollenbeck (2024) emphasizes that data must be preprocessed to avoid interpretation errors.

Types of Charts

According to IBM (2024), charts are essential tools for visually and comprehensibly representing data. They enable users to intuitively analyze complex information, facilitating the identification of patterns, trends, and relationships that might be challenging to uncover in data tables. On platforms like IBM® Cognos® Analytics, charts offer a wide variety of options that allow data to be visualized from different perspectives, each suitable for highlighting specific aspects of the information.

When selecting a chart type, it is important to consider the analysis objective and the nature of the data. Each chart type has a unique purpose and is designed to highlight different data characteristics, such as comparisons, trends, or proportions. Below is a description of the main types of charts available in IBM® Cognos® Analytics and their most common applications.

Column charts are ideal for comparing discrete data or showing how variables change over time. This type of chart clearly visualizes differences between categories and is useful for observing variations over a given period. Bar charts, similar to column charts, use horizontal bars and are useful for showing comparisons between different data series, especially when categories have long labels.

When aiming to represent proportions, pie charts are the most suitable option. These charts effectively show how each category contributes to the total. Additionally, area charts highlight the magnitude of changes over time. Stacked area charts are particularly useful for showing the relationship between parts and the whole, visualizing both the change and the distribution of categories.

Line charts are perfect for showing trends over time, allowing the comparison of multiple data series simultaneously. This type of chart is essential for tracking variables over prolonged periods. In situations where the relationship between two variables needs to be analyzed, scatter plots are the best option, as they show how data is distributed along a scale, helping to identify correlations or patterns.

Bubble charts add a third dimension to scatter plots by using the size of the bubbles to represent a third variable. This allows relationships between three variables to be visualized simultaneously. Similar to scatter plots, quadrant charts use a background divided into four sections, enabling the analysis of three measures using an X-axis, a Y-axis, and bubble size, providing more detailed insights.

Combination charts allow different types of charts, such as columns, areas, and lines, to be combined into a single visualization. This is useful for showing multiple data series and highlighting the relationships between them more effectively. Additionally, radar charts enable the comparison of multiple variables simultaneously by representing them on several radial axes, facilitating the visualization of multivariate data.

To evaluate progress toward a goal, gauge charts are ideal. These charts, also known as speedometer charts, use needles or markers to show the level achieved for a metric compared to a predefined target. Range indicator charts, on the other hand, display a tolerance range and a target range, allowing users to visualize whether performance is within expected limits.

To represent tolerance ranges and compare performance against specific goals, Pareto charts are effective. These charts help identify the main causes of a problem by ranking categories from the most frequent to the least frequent, making them useful for process improvement and focusing on key factors.

Sparklines are compact versions of column, bar, or line charts, ideal for integrating into summary tables or dashboards. These condensed charts allow trends to be shown compactly without losing relevant information. Finally, Marimekko charts are 100% stacked charts where the width of each column is proportional to the total values of the column, providing a clear visualization of the relative proportions between categories.

Undergraduate Studies: Definition and Structure

Undergraduate studies in Spain are governed by a regulatory framework detailed in the Organic Law on Universities (LOU) and associated royal decrees, which establish the requirements and characteristics for undergraduate university degrees. According to Royal Decree 1393/2007, study plans to obtain an undergraduate degree must comply with various regulations, ensuring that students acquire comprehensive training in both theoretical and practical content (Royal Decree 1393/2007, Article 14).

An undergraduate degree generally lasts four years (240 ECTS credits), although there are exceptions that may require more credits due to specific regulations or international joint programs. The study plan must include theoretical and practical subjects, organized into mandatory courses, electives, and a Final Degree Project (TFG) that demonstrates the student's ability to apply the knowledge acquired during the program. This project has a minimum of 6 credits and a maximum of 24, depending on the total credit load of the degree (Royal Decree 1393/2007, Article 14, section 6).

Additionally, study plans may include external academic internships that complement the student's theoretical training. These internships represent a specific percentage of the total credits, except for certain degrees that require a higher number of practical hours, such as those with Dual Mention. The TFG, in turn, must be publicly defended and constitutes an essential part of obtaining the degree (Royal Decree 1393/2007, Article 14, section 5).

Undergraduate degrees can be offered in three modalities: in-person, hybrid, or virtual. Each modality presents different characteristics in terms of the distribution of in-person and non-in-person classes. Universities must clearly define the teaching modality in the study plan, as it influences the student's educational experience (Royal Decree 1393/2007, Article 14, section 7).

Finally, qualifying degrees, those that enable the practice of regulated professions, must comply with specific government and European Union legislation to ensure that students receive adequate training to access these professions. In some cases, although the degree does not directly qualify for a profession, it may be a requirement to access qualifying master's programs (Royal Decree 1393/2007, Article 14, section 8).

An undergraduate student is someone who accesses an undergraduate degree program for the first time at a Spanish university. This student, known as a "newly enrolled university student," begins their academic training in an undergraduate program with their first enrollment within the university system. Entry into this educational level marks the start of a formative process that culminates in obtaining the corresponding university degree (Organic Law 6/2001 on Universities, Article 38).

Methodology

The methodology implemented in this study involved a systematic process to analyze student enrollment data, leveraging SPSS v27 for data preparation and ChatGPT for visualization. Initially, the raw dataset was loaded into SPSS v27 to ensure a standardized format suitable for analysis. This step included cleaning the dataset by addressing missing values, removing outliers, and ensuring consistent variable names and formats. Once the dataset was structured and verified, it was normalized using statistical methods such as z-scores to enable comparisons across variables and time periods.

After preparing the data in SPSS, it was exported into a format compatible with ChatGPT prompts. The prompts were designed to instruct ChatGPT in generating specific types of visualizations, such as line graphs, bar charts, and radar charts, depending on the information sought. These prompts specified key parameters, such as axes, data groupings, and visualization types. For instance, one prompt could request a bar chart comparing enrollment in public and private universities for a specific year, while another might ask for a line graph showing percentage changes in enrollment over time.

As visualizations were generated, the prompts were iteratively refined to align the results with the research objectives. Adjustments included clarifying instructions, specifying data ranges, and fine-tuning visualization details such as labels, legends, or annotations. This iterative process ensured that the final visualizations accurately represented the data and provided clear insights into enrollment trends and differences between institutions and fields of study.

By combining the robust data preparation capabilities of SPSS with the generative power of ChatGPT, this methodology successfully produced detailed and informative visualizations. These visualizations were used to identify key trends, such as the growth in private university enrollments or the dominance of specific areas of study, offering valuable insights into the dynamics of higher education in the Madrid region.

Data Collection

The data used in this study were obtained the General Secretariat of Universities has developed the Integrated University Information System (SIIU). This platform serves as a shared information resource for universities, autonomous communities, and the Ministry of Universities. It collects micro-level data on students and university staff., specifically from the official statistics on new undergraduate student enrollments in universities within the Community of Madrid. These data include detailed information on the distribution of students by type of university (public or private), mode of instruction (in-person, hybrid, or online), gender, age group, and field of study (Social Sciences, Health Sciences, Engineering, etc.).

In this analysis, universities have been classified into two main categories: universities in the Community of Madrid and private and public universities. Universities within the Community of Madrid have been categorized based on their geographic location, while private and public institutions have been separated to enable a clear comparison in terms of enrollment and other relevant factors.

The sample for this study is based on enrollment data for new undergraduate students at both public and private universities over recent academic years. The data include information on the number of enrolled students, segmented by the variables mentioned, and are used to observe enrollment trends and patterns over time.

Below is the classification table of universities in the Community of Madrid by type (public or private). This classification facilitates the analysis of differences in enrollment patterns between public and private universities, as well as the geographic distribution of universities in the Community of Madrid.

Table 1. Classification of Universities in the Community of Madrid.

University	Private/Public	Arts and Humanities	Sciences	Health Sciences	Social and Legal Sciences	Engineering and Architecture
A Distancia de Madrid	Private	YES	NO	YES	NO	NO
Alcalá	Public	YES	YES	YES	YES	YES
Alfonso X El Sabio	Private	YES	YES	YES	YES	YES
Antonio de Nebrija	Private	YES	YES	YES	YES	YES
Autónoma de Madrid	Public	YES	YES	YES	YES	YES
Camilo José Cela	Private	YES	YES	YES	YES	YES
Carlos III de Madrid	Public	YES	YES	YES	YES	YES
Complutense de Madrid	Public	YES	YES	YES	YES	YES
CUNEF Universidad	Private	YES	YES	NO	YES	YES
Diseño, Innovación y Tecnología (UDIT)	Private	YES	NO	NO	YES	NO
Europea de Madrid	Private	YES	YES	YES	YES	YES
Francisco de Vitoria	Private	YES	YES	YES	YES	YES
Politécnica de Madrid	Public	YES	YES	YES	YES	YES
Pontificia Comillas	Private	YES	YES	YES	YES	YES
Rey Juan Carlos	Public	YES	YES	YES	YES	YES
San Pablo-CEU	Private	YES	YES	YES	YES	YES

Source: Authors

Results and discussion

- **Analysis 1: General Evolution of Total Enrollments (Public vs. Private, 2015–2024)**

The objective is to observe the evolution of total enrollments across all fields of knowledge, comparing public and private universities in both absolute and percentage terms. This will help identify general trends in educational demand. A stacked column chart combined with lines will be used to show the total volume of students in public and private universities, as well as the annual percentage change rates for each type of institution. This type of chart is ideal for capturing both absolute magnitudes and relative variations.

AI Prompt:"Generate a stacked column chart to show the evolution of total enrollments in public and private universities from 2015/2016 to 2023/2024. Add lines to represent the annual percentage change in enrollments for both types of universities. The X and Y axes should represent academic years and the number of students, respectively."

Figure 1. Enrollment in bachelor's degree: Public vs Private Universities (2015/2016 - 2023/2024)

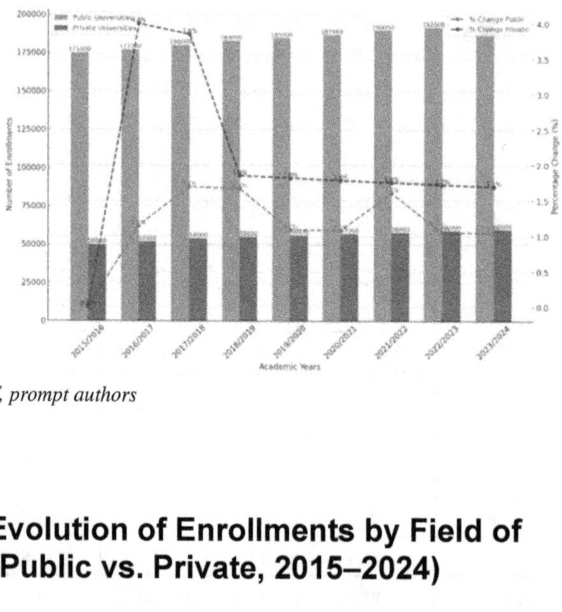

Source: ChatGPT, prompt authors

Analysis 2: Evolution of Enrollments by Field of Knowledge (Public vs. Private, 2015–2024)

This analysis aims to break down enrollment trends in public and private universities for each field of knowledge. The goal is to identify areas with the highest growth, those that remain stable, and those potentially losing student interest. A grouped column chart will be used to directly compare public and private enrollments in each area for each academic year. This approach facilitates simultaneous comparisons between types of institutions and fields of knowledge.

AI Prompt: "Generate a grouped column chart showing enrollments in public and private universities by field of knowledge from 2015/2016 to 2023/2024. Each group of columns should represent one field and differentiate between public and private institutions."

Figure 2. Enrollment in bachelor's degree by Area of Knowledge: Public vs Private Universities

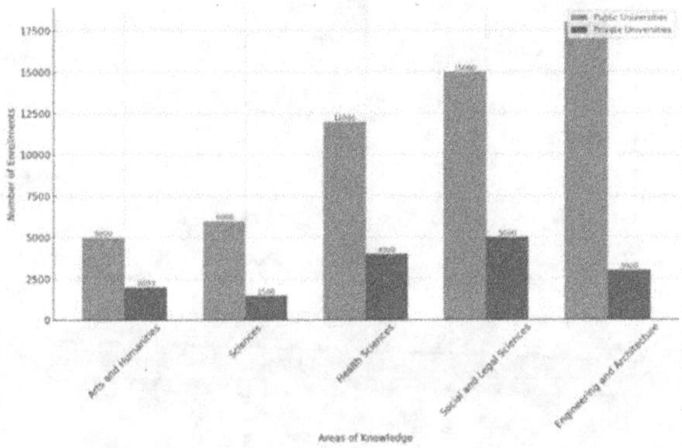

Source: ChatGPT, prompt authors

The analysis reveals that public universities lead in all fields of knowledge, with Social and Legal Sciences and Health Sciences standing out as the most in-demand areas, enrolling 15,000 and 12,000 students, respectively. Private universities show a more specialized focus, attracting one-third of the public volume in Health Sciences, with 4,000 students. Less popular fields such as Sciences and Arts and Humanities display low enrollments in both sectors, suggesting either limited labor market attraction or a lack of innovation in educational offerings. The public/private ratio remains consistent, with public universities clearly dominating, reflecting their accessibility and capacity to meet large-scale demand, while private institutions carve out their niche in specialized areas.

- **Analysis 3: Temporal Comparison of Enrollments in Health Sciences (Public vs. Private, 2015–2024)**

This analysis aims to evaluate how enrollments in Health Sciences have evolved over time in public and private universities. The objective is to identify trends and patterns of change in each type of institution. A multi-line chart will be used, as it clearly visualizes trends over the years for public and private universities, highlighting changes for each type of institution.

AI Prompt: “Generate a line chart showing the evolution of enrollments in Health Sciences at public and private universities from 2015/2016 to 2023/2024. Use separate lines for each type of institution, with the X-axis representing the years and the Y-axis the number of enrolled students.”

Figure 3. Enrollment in Health Sciences: Public vs Private Universities (2015/2016 - 2023/2024)

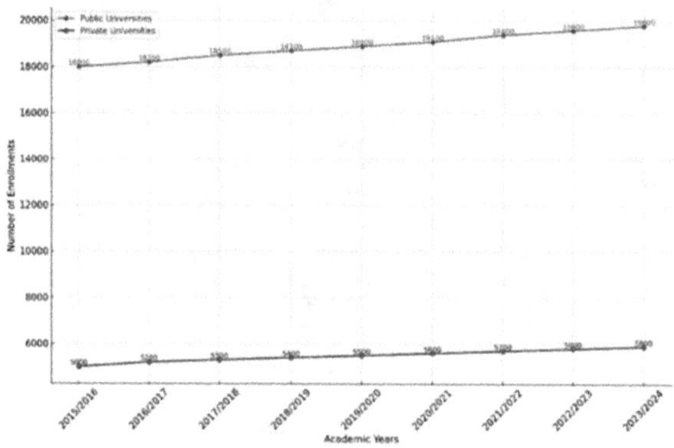

Source: ChatGPT, prompt authors

Analysis 4: Proportion of Public and Private Enrollments in Health Sciences (2023/2024)

This analysis aims to visualize the proportion of students enrolled in public and private universities in the field of Health Sciences during the 2023/2024 academic year. This will help assess the relative weight of each type of institution within this key area. A pie chart will be used as it is ideal for highlighting the relative proportion between two or more categories. In this case, it will clearly show the distribution between public and private universities in the most recent academic year analyzed.

AI Prompt: “Generate a pie chart showing the proportion of students enrolled in Health Sciences at public and private universities for the 2023/2024 academic year. Include percentage labels for each segment and use differentiated colors for each category.”

Figure 4. Enrollment in bachelor's degree in Health Sciences: Public vs Private Universities (2015/2016 - 2023/2024)

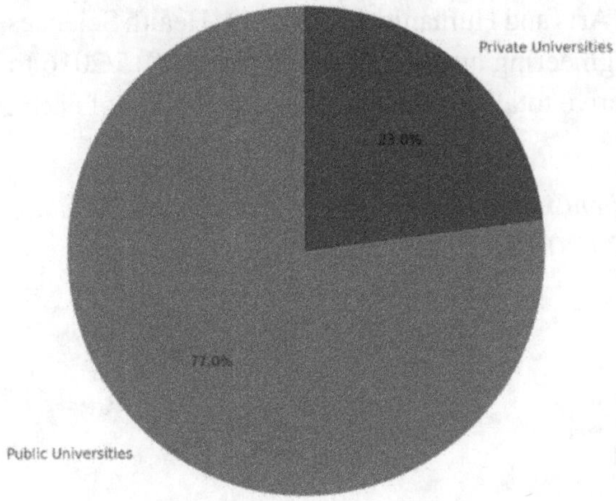

Source: ChatGPT, prompt authors

Public Universities represent 77% of students enrolled in Health Sciences during the 2023/2024 academic year, with a total of 19,800 students. Private Universities attract 23% of the total, with 5,900 students enrolled. The pie chart highlights the clear dominance of public universities in the field of Health Sciences, consolidating their position as the primary educational choice in this area. However, the private segment, although smaller, retains a significant proportion of the total (23%), suggesting growing confidence in private institutions to offer high-demand programs like Health Sciences. This balance reflects the complementarity between both types of universities in meeting the needs of students and the labor market.

Analysis 5: Evolution of Enrollments by Thematic Area (Public and Private, 2015–2024)

The objective of this analysis is to visualize how enrollments in different thematic areas have evolved over time, considering both public and private universities. The goal is to identify areas with the highest growth, stability, or relative decline. A stacked area chart by thematic areas allows highlighting both the absolute change in each area and its relative contribution to the total enrollment set. This provides a comprehensive and integrated view of the evolution across areas.

AI Prompt: "Generate a stacked area chart showing the evolution of enrollments by thematic area (Arts and Humanities, Sciences, Health Sciences, Social and Legal Sciences, and Engineering and Architecture) from 2015/2016 to 2023/2024. Represent the cumulative total and the relative contribution of each area."

Figure 5. Enrollment in bachelor's degree (Grado) by Thematic Areas: Evolution (2015/2016 – 2023/2024)

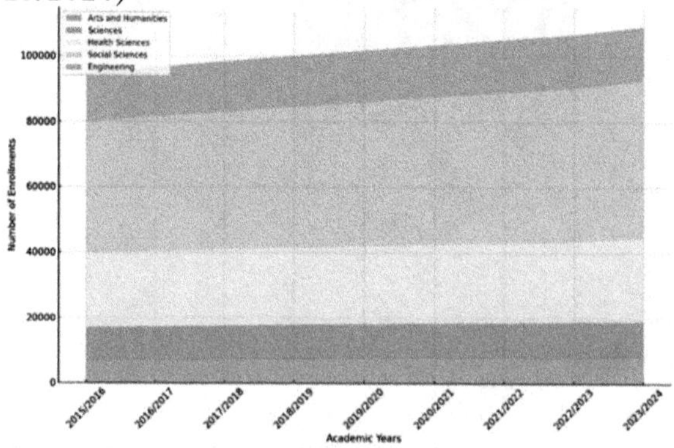

Source: ChatGPT, prompt authors

Social and Legal Sciences is the largest area in terms of total enrollment, with steady growth from 40,000 students in 2015/2016 to 48,000 in 2023/2024. Health Sciences has the second-highest volume, increasing from 23,000 to 25,700 students during the same period. Engineering and Architecture experienced moderate growth, rising from 15,000 to 16,600 students. Sciences show stable growth with smaller increments, from 10,000 to 10,800 students.Arts and Humanities is the area with the lowest enrollment, increasing slightly from 7,000 to 8,200 students.

Analysis 6: Comparison of Enrollments in Thematic Areas by Public and Private Universities (2023/2024)

The objective is to clearly and concisely compare quantitative enrollment data across different thematic areas for public and private universities in the 2023/2024 academic year. This highlights differences between both modalities. A dot chart will be used, as it is ideal for displaying quantitative data simply and clearly, facilitating direct comparisons between thematic areas in public and private universities.

AI Prompt:"Generate a dot chart comparing the number of enrollments in specific thematic areas (Arts and Humanities, Sciences, Health Sciences, Social and Legal Sciences, Engineering and Architecture) for public and private universities in 2023/2024. Use distinct colors to differentiate between public and private universities."

Figure 6. Bachelor's Degree Enrollment by Thematic Areas: Public vs Private Universities (2023/2024)

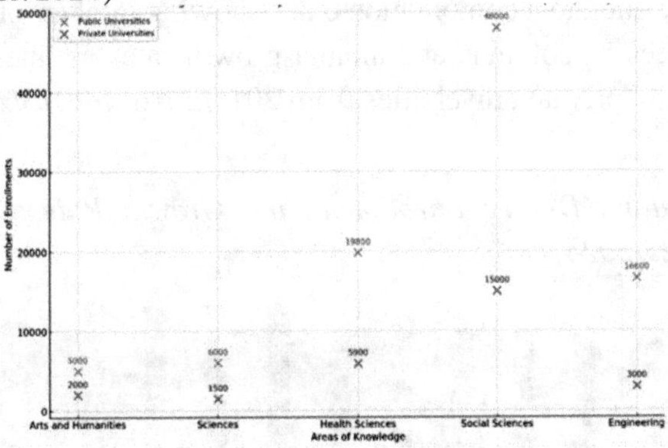

Source: ChatGPT, prompt authors

Social and Legal Sciences have the highest number of enrollments in public universities (48,000) and private universities (15,000) in 2023/2024. Health Sciences rank second with 19,800 students in public universities and 5,900 in private universities. Arts and Humanities and Sciences have significantly lower enrollments, with 5,000 and 6,000 students in public universities, respectively, compared to 2,000 and 1,500 in private universities. Engineering and Architecture show an intermediate pattern, with 16,600 students in public universities and 3,000 in private universities.

The dot chart clearly illustrates the quantitative differences between public and private universities across each academic area. Public universities dominate all areas, especially in Social Sciences and Health Sciences, where the public-private ratio is more pronounced. However, private universities demonstrate their presence in all areas, standing out as a relevant option, especially in Social Sciences and Health Sciences, where they attract a significant volume of students.

Analysis 7: Relationship Between Total Enrollments and Growth Rate in Social and Legal Sciences (2015–2024)

The objective is to simultaneously display total enrollments in Social and Legal Sciences along with their annual growth rate in public and private universities, highlighting the relationship between total volume and the rate of change. A combination chart will be used, combining columns (for the total number of students) and lines (for the growth rate). This format facilitates the visualization of how absolute volume and percentage variation are related within a single chart.

AI Prompt: "Generate a combination chart showing total enrollments in Social and Legal Sciences as columns and annual growth rates as lines, distinguishing between public and private universities from 2015/2016 to 2023/2024."

Figure 7. Bachelor's Degree Enrollment and Growth Rates: Social Sciences (2015/2016 - 2023/2024)

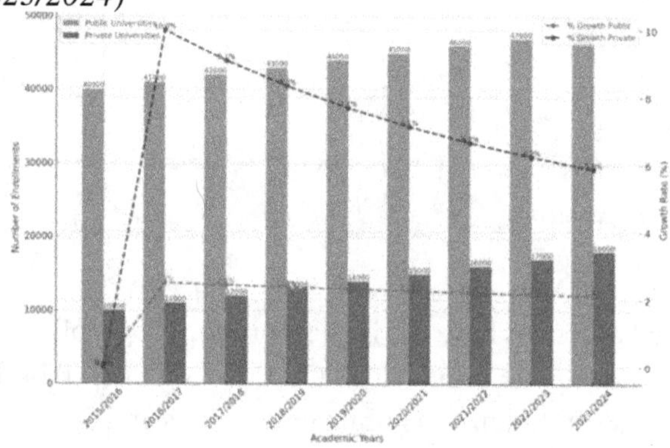

Source: ChatGPT, prompt authors

Figure 8. Enrollment in bachelor's degree in Madrid Region: Public vs Private Universities by Area (2017/2018 - 2023/2024)

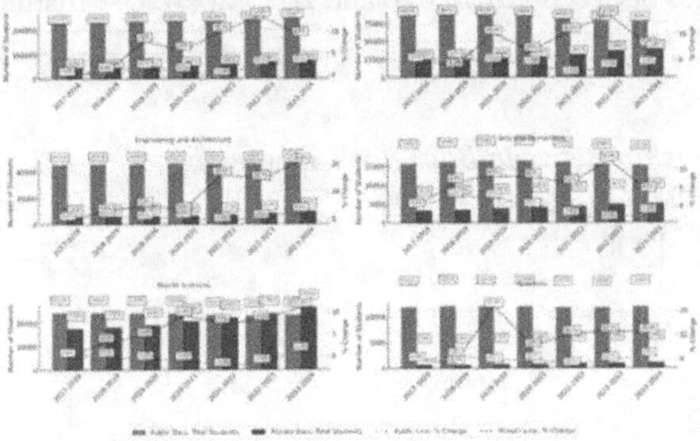

Source: ChatGPT, prompt authors

In public universities, enrollments in Social and Legal Sciences increase from 40,000 in 2015/2016 to 48,000 in 2023/2024, with a steady growth of approximately 1,000 students per year. In private universities, enrollments grow faster in relative terms, rising from 10,000 to 18,000 during the same period, with an average increase of 1,000 students per year. The growth rate in public universities is moderate, averaging between 2% and 2.5% annually. In private universities, the initial growth is higher (10% in 2016/2017), but it stabilizes at approximately 2% annually from 2019 onwards.

The chart combines columns and lines to clearly show how public universities maintain steady growth in absolute student numbers, reflecting their ability to meet high demand. On the other hand, private universities, although starting with a lower volume, show more dynamic growth, particularly in the early years analyzed. This suggests the consolidation of private universities as a competitive alternative in Social and Legal Sciences. The gradual decrease in the growth rate for both types of institutions reflects a possible stabilization of interest in this educational area.

Analysis 8: Relationship Between Total Enrollments and Growth Rate in Social and Legal Sciences (2015–2024)

This analysis aims to visualize the relationship between total enrollments and the annual growth rate in Social and Legal Sciences for public and private universities. The goal is to identify correlations or patterns between these two variables.

A scatter plot will be used, as it allows plotting points in a two-dimensional space to compare two variables (total enrollments and growth rate) and visualize potential correlations or differences between public and private universities.

AI Prompt: "Generate a scatter plot showing the relationship between total enrollments and the annual growth rate in Social and Legal Sciences for public and private universities between 2015/2016 and 2023/2024. Use distinct colors for each type of university."

Figure 9. Relationship Between Bachelor's Degree Enrollment and Growth Rates: Social Sciences (2015/2016 - 2023/2024)

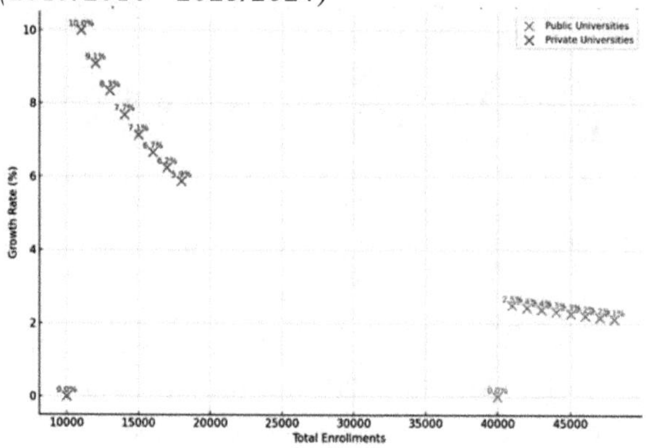

Source: ChatGPT, prompt authors

The scatter plot reveals a clear inverse relationship between the total number of enrollments and the annual growth rate. Private universities start with a lower enrollment count (10,000 students in 2015/2016) but exhibit a high initial growth rate of 10%, which gradually decreases to 5.9% in 2023/2024 as enrollment volume increases (18,000 students). In contrast, public universities, with a higher initial enrollment (40,000 in 2015/2016), show more moderate growth rates, starting at 2.5% and stabilizing around 2% in 2023/2024.

The chart demonstrates that private universities experience dynamic growth in relative terms, whereas public universities undergo a more stable and predictable expansion due to their larger student base. This behavior suggests that private institutions are in a consolidation phase, expanding their share in Social and Legal Sciences, while public universities maintain their dominant market position. The decline in growth rates for both types of institutions may indicate a gradual saturation of the academic market in this area.

Analysis 9: Comparison of Enrollments, Growth Rate, and Number of Universities in Social and Legal Sciences (2023/2024)

This analysis aims to compare total enrollments in Social and Legal Sciences between public and private universities, alongside their annual growth rate and the number of universities involved. The size of the bubbles will represent the number of universities in each sector. A bubble chart will be used, as this format incorporates a third dimension (in this case, the number of universities) while comparing the two main variables (total enrollments and growth rate). This approach facilitates visualizing the relationship among these measures and highlights structural differences between sectors.

AI Prompt: "Generate a bubble chart comparing the total number of enrollments, the annual growth rate, and the number of universities in Social and Legal Sciences for public and private universities in 2023/2024. Use the size of the bubbles to represent the number of universities."

Figure 10. Comparison of bachelor's degree Enrollment, Growth Rate, and Number of Universities Social Sciences (2023/2024)

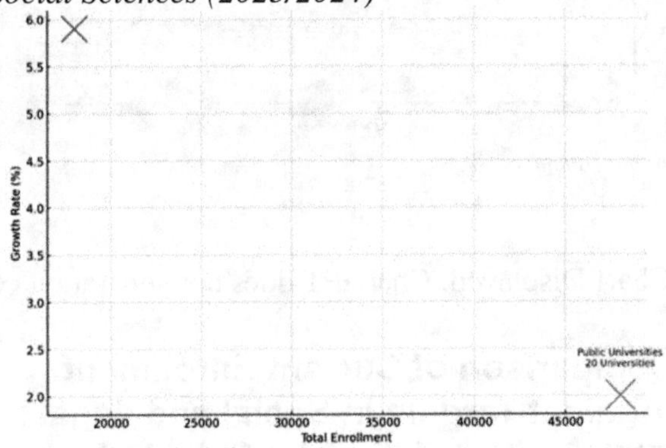

Source: *ChatGPT, prompt authors*

No Bubble Chart Displayed. ChatGPT does not generate it correctly.

Analysis 10: Evaluation of Enrollments, Growth, and Universities in Social and Legal Sciences (2023/2024)

The goal of this analysis is to map the relationship between the total number of enrollments, the growth rate, and the number of universities in Social and Legal Sciences for public and private universities, using a quadrant chart. This will classify each type of university in terms of high or low enrollment volumes and growth. A quadrant chart is chosen because it enables the simultaneous analysis of two main variables (total enrollments and growth rate) along with a third dimension (number of universities, represented by the bubble size). The division into quadrants helps identify groups and patterns.

AI Prompt:"Generate a quadrant chart showing the relationship between the total number of enrollments, the annual growth rate, and the number of universities in Social and Legal Sciences for public and private universities in 2023/2024. Divide the background into quadrants and include labels to identify each category."

Figure 11. Quadrant Analysis: Bachelor's Degree Enrollment, Growth, and Universities in Social Sciences (2023/2024)

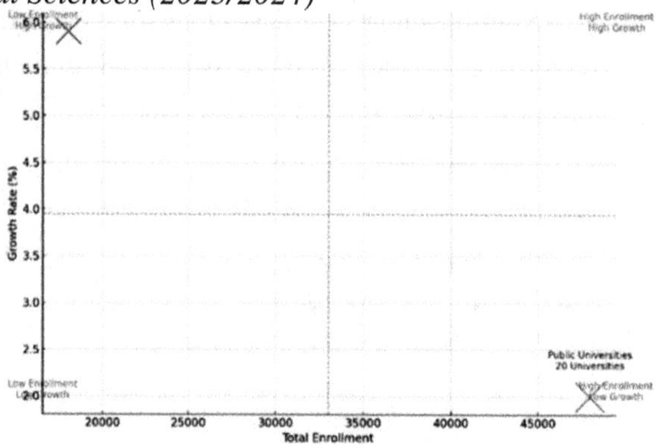

Source: ChatGPT, prompt authors

No Quadrant Chart Displayed. ChatGPT does not generate it correctly.

Analysis 11: Comparison of Current Enrollment Performance Against Targets in Social and Legal Sciences (2023/2024)(Simulation for Calculation)

This analysis aims to evaluate enrollment performance in Social and Legal Sciences for public and private universities by comparing them with predefined targets. Colored regions will represent qualitative performance ranges: low, satisfactory, and excellent. The bullet chart is ideal for comparing current values (number of enrollments) with established targets, providing a visual framework for assessing performance across different qualitative ranges.

AI Prompt:"Generate a bullet chart comparing the current number of enrollments in public and private universities in Social and Legal Sciences (2023/2024) with established targets. Use colored regions to indicate whether performance is low, satisfactory, or excellent."

Figure 12. Bullet Chart: Current Enrollment in bachelor's degree vs Targets (2023/2024)

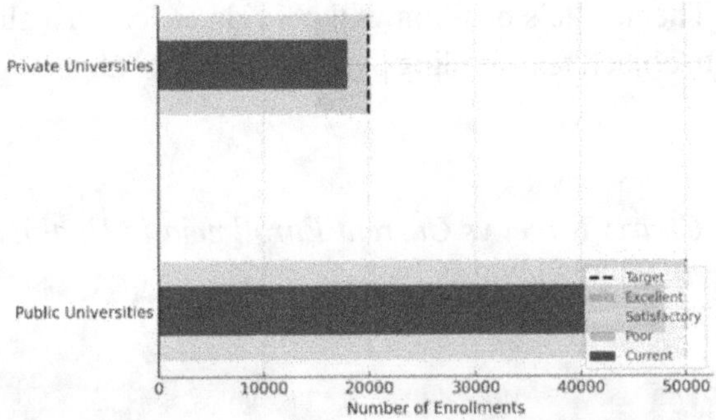

Source: ChatGPT, prompt authors

- ✓ Public Universities: Current enrollments: 48,000. Target: 50,000. Current performance is very close to the target, in the "satisfactory" region.
- ✓ Private Universities: Current enrollments: 18,000. Target: 20,000. Current performance is also near the goal, but more solidly within the "satisfactory" range.

The bullet chart provides a quick visual assessment of performance relative to objectives. Public universities are nearly achieving their set target, demonstrating stability and the capacity to meet goals. On the other hand, private universities, although further from the "excellent" threshold, show satisfactory performance, highlighting their growth potential. This chart helps identify areas where additional effort is required to meet or exceed expectations.

Analysis 12: Assessment of Enrollment Progress in Health Sciences (2023/2024)) (Simulation for Calculation)

The objective of this analysis is to evaluate the progress of public and private universities toward their enrollment targets in the field of Health Sciences for 2023/2024, using indicator charts. This will allow visualization of whether universities are meeting enrollment targets and how they are positioned relative to established expectations.

An indicator chart will be used to compare current enrollments with targets in Health Sciences. The needle's position will provide a clear visualization of performance compared to objectives, dividing performance into ranges of low, satisfactory, and excellent.

Figure 13. Bullet Chart: Target vs Current Enrollment in Health Sciences (Public vs Private Universities) 2023/2024

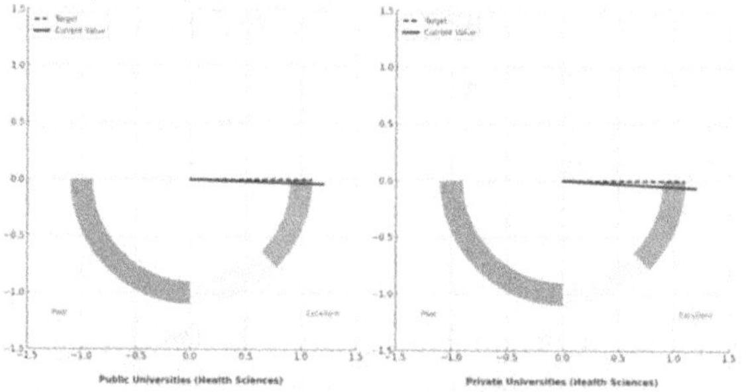

Source: ChatGPT, prompt authors

The chart shows how public and private universities are approaching their enrollment targets for the 2023/2024 academic year:

- ✓ Public Universities: They are close to reaching the established target, within the satisfactory range.
- ✓ Private Universities: They are also within the satisfactory range, although slightly below the target.

This chart helps identify the progress toward enrollment objectives and the capacity of institutions to meet expectations in the field of Health Sciences.

Analysis 13: Identification of Key Universities by Enrollment in Engineering and Architecture (2023/2024)

This analysis aims to identify the most relevant universities in terms of enrollment in the field of Engineering and Architecture for the 2023/2024 academic year. Using a Pareto chart, universities are ranked from those with the highest enrollment to those with the lowest, highlighting those that have the greatest impact on total enrollments. A Pareto chart was selected because it is ideal for visualizing how a small number of universities contribute to the majority of enrollments in Engineering and Architecture. This chart allows for a clear identification of the universities that concentrate the majority of enrollments and, therefore, are the most influential in this field.

AI Prompt: "Generate a Pareto chart showing the distribution of enrollments in the field of Engineering and Architecture for the 2023/2024 academic year. Rank universities from those with the highest enrollment to those with the lowest and use a bar chart for enrollments and a line for the cumulative percentage."

Figure 14. Pareto Chart: Bachelor's Degree Enrollment Distribution in Engineering and Architecture (Grado) 2023/2024

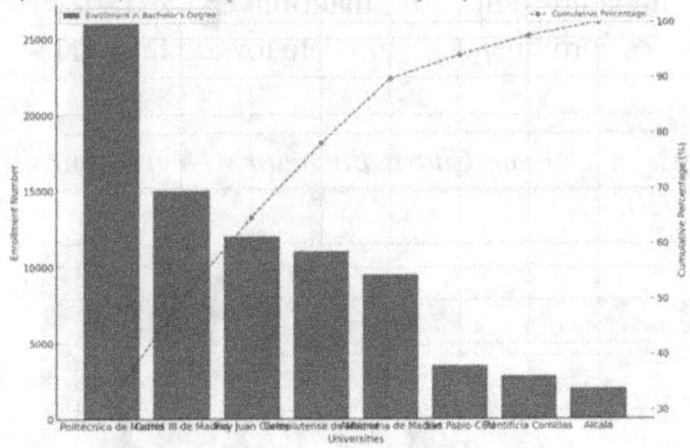

Source: ChatGPT, prompt authors

The university with the highest enrollment is the Polytechnic University of Madrid, with 26,000 students, followed by Carlos III University of Madrid, with 15,000 students. Together, these two universities account for approximately 65% of the enrollments in Engineering and Architecture. The remaining universities (Rey Juan Carlos University, Complutense University of Madrid, Autonomous University of Madrid, among others) have significantly smaller enrollments, with a more balanced distribution among them.

The Pareto chart clearly illustrates the concentration of enrollments in a few universities, highlighting the importance of the largest and most recognized institutions in the field of Engineering and Architecture. Universities such as the Polytechnic University of Madrid and Carlos III University of Madrid are the main drivers of enrollment in this area, which may suggest greater infrastructure, reputation, and academic offerings that attract a higher number of students. Meanwhile, smaller universities have a limited share of the total enrollments, although they remain relevant.

This chart is useful for identifying key universities in this field and prioritizing efforts on institutions that significantly impact the total enrollment.

Analysis 14: Evolution of Enrollments in Arts and Humanities (2023/2024)

This analysis aims to show the evolution of enrollments in Arts and Humanities across various universities, illustrating how they progressively add up over time. A progressive column chart is ideal for demonstrating how enrollments from different universities accumulate to form the total. This allows visualization of how each university contributes to the total enrollment in the field of Arts and Humanities.

AI Prompt:"Generate a progressive column chart showing the evolution of enrollments in Arts and Humanities among the main universities (2023/2024), highlighting how each university's enrollments accumulate toward the total."

Figure 15. Progressive Column Chart: Bachelor's Degree Enrollment in Arts and Humanities (2023/2024)

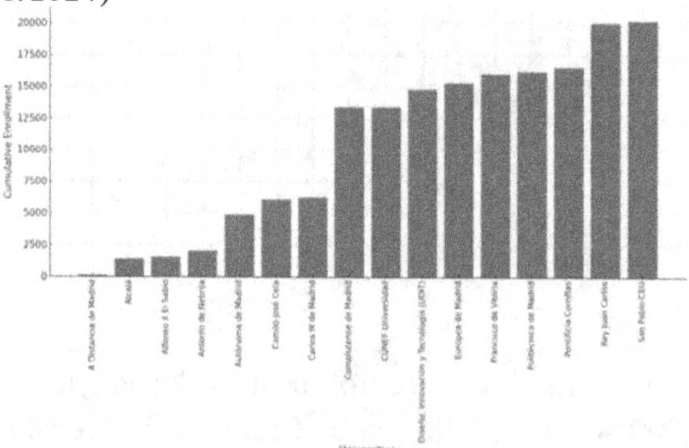

Source: ChatGPT, prompt authors

The Complutense University of Madrid leads with a total of 7,124 enrollments in Arts and Humanities, representing a significant portion of the total accumulated in the sector. It is followed by the Autonomous University of Madrid with 2,859 enrollments, and the Polytechnic University of Madrid with 194 enrollments. These universities have a strong presence in this field. The total accumulated enrollments show a significant progression, highlighting the concentration in a few universities.

Contribution to Total Enrollment: Larger universities, such as the Complutense University of Madrid, make a considerable contribution to the total accumulated, while smaller universities, such as CUNEF University and Diseño, Innovación y Tecnología (UDIT), have a minimal impact on the total enrollment accumulation. The progressive column chart reflects how the Arts and Humanities education system is dominated by a few large universities, while the majority of universities have a much smaller presence.

This pattern suggests that universities with a stronger tradition or recognition have the capacity to attract a larger number of students in this area. Universities with fewer enrollments might be offering more specialized or lesser-known programs, resulting in lower student volumes. The chart highlights how the sector is centralized, implying that larger universities have greater influence in shaping educational offerings and enrollment demand.

This analysis is useful for academic institutions and educational planners, as it helps identify which universities are leading enrollment in this field and where more efforts could be focused to improve student recruitment in institutions with less presence.

Analysis 15: Comparison of Enrollments in Different Academic Areas (2023/2024)

The objective of this analysis is to use a radar chart to compare enrollments in different academic areas across universities. This chart allows visualization of how enrollments are distributed across various areas (e.g., Social Sciences, Health Sciences, Engineering, Arts and Humanities, etc.) through multiple axes, helping to identify trends and comparisons among them. The radar chart is ideal for displaying multiple dimensions of data across several axes, making it useful for comparing enrollment distribution across different academic areas. Each area is represented on a separate axis, allowing data to be easily compared visually.

AI Prompt: "Generate a radar chart comparing enrollments in different academic areas (Social Sciences, Health Sciences, Engineering, Arts and Humanities, etc.) across universities, using data from 2023/2024."

Figure 16. Distribution of Enrollment in bachelor's degree Programs by Area of Study (2023/2024)

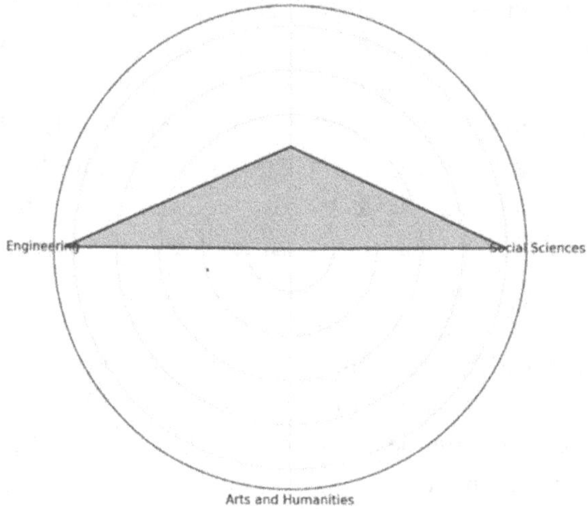

Source: ChatGPT, prompt authors

The radar chart illustrates the distribution of undergraduate enrollments across various academic areas for the 2023/2024 academic year. Engineering stands out as the area with the highest number of enrollments, totaling 26,000 students. This demonstrates its status as one of the most in-demand fields among students, particularly in absolute terms. Social Sciences also shows a significant enrollment figure of 25,000 students, indicating high demand in this area. Health Sciences follows closely with 11,354 students, reflecting interest in health-related fields, though slightly below Engineering and Social Sciences.

On the other hand, Arts and Humanities have a considerably lower enrollment of 108 students, highlighting a low demand compared to other academic areas. Quantitatively, Engineering and Social Sciences dominate the enrollment distribution, while Arts and Humanities occupy a marginal position with a significantly lower volume of enrolled students. The declining trend in enrollments in Arts and Humanities suggests challenges in attracting a larger student population, particularly when compared to areas with high professional demand.

This observation points to a possible disconnect between student interests and labor market opportunities or the academic focus in these disciplines. The analysis underscores the need for universities to adapt their academic offerings to meet market demands and emphasizes the importance of high-demand academic areas in the current educational context.

CONCLUSION

This research successfully achieved the objectives established at the outset, demonstrating how AI-powered data visualization tools, particularly ChatGPT, can significantly enhance the analysis of university enrollment data in the Community of Madrid. This advancement is reflected in several key aspects.

First, it was confirmed that the charts generated by ChatGPT are suitable for representing complex information in a clear and comprehensible manner. They also facilitate the exploration of enrollment trends by areas of knowledge and differences between public and private universities. The tool's ability to process structured data and produce precise visual representations has helped identify patterns that might otherwise have remained hidden.

The analysis of enrollment trends over time revealed a general trend of stability in public universities, while private universities showed more dynamic growth, though they still represent a smaller volume in absolute terms. This finding highlights the dual nature of the educational system in Madrid, where public universities dominate in capacity and accessibility, while private institutions are consolidating as specialized and expanding alternatives.

By areas of knowledge, Social and Legal Sciences stand out as the most in-demand option, followed by Health Sciences. However, areas such as Arts and Humanities exhibit less interest among students, suggesting a potential disconnect between educational offerings and labor market demands. These observations are fundamental for guiding the strategic planning of educational institutions.

The study also highlights the efficiency of AI models in generating complex charts, such as those that integrate growth rates and absolute volumes into a single visual scheme. This functionality has proven important for interpreting temporal changes and structural differences between institutions and fields of study, providing a powerful tool for informed decision-making.

Regarding methodology, data normalization in SPSS was an essential step to ensure the accuracy and consistency of the analyses. This, combined with ChatGPT's ability to integrate and process large volumes of information, enabled the development of visualizations that meet quality standards and effectively communicate results.

LIMITATIONS

One of the main challenges encountered during this study was the inconsistent generation of some requested charts. On certain occasions, AI models failed to interpret the instructions provided in the prompts accurately, resulting in incomplete or incorrect visualizations. This issue can be attributed to limitations in the model's ability to process complex or structured data efficiently, particularly when datasets are extensive or involve multiple interrelated variables.

Additionally, data normalization and preprocessing, while effective, relied on external tools like SPSS. The direct integration of these operations into the AI model's workflow is not yet feasible, potentially limiting efficiency and increasing the likelihood of errors in data handling. Furthermore, the study's focus was exclusively on the Community of Madrid, meaning the findings are not generalizable to other geographic or educational contexts without additional adaptations.

Finally, the AI model demonstrated limitations in graphically representing historical data with complex trends, such as the precise calculation and visualization of change rates or category-specific accumulations. While these difficulties do not undermine the results, they highlight the need to combine AI tools with traditional methodologies to ensure a comprehensive and accurate representation of the data.

CONTRIBUTIONS

This research makes significant contributions to the fields of education and artificial intelligence. First, it demonstrates the potential of tools like ChatGPT to facilitate the understanding of complex educational data through automatically generated visualizations. This capability not only reduces the time and resources required for analysis but also broadens access to these techniques for users with limited programming or advanced statistical knowledge.

The study also highlights the importance of integrating traditional methodologies, such as normalization in SPSS, with innovative AI approaches. This combination provides a robust and reproducible framework that can be adopted by researchers and educational managers to address critical questions related to academic planning and resource management.

Practically, the analysis of university enrollment trends in the Community of Madrid provides relevant data for strategic decision-making in the educational field. The findings on the evolution of student preferences and differences between public and private institutions can inform policies that enhance equity, quality, and the sustainability of the educational system.

Finally, this work contributes to the growing body of literature on practical applications of artificial intelligence in educational research and management, serving as an example of how these technologies can transform data analysis and visualization in areas with significant social impact. It opens new avenues for exploring more integrated and adaptive solutions that respond to the needs of an ever-changing academic environment.

REFERENCES

Apablaza-Campos, J., Smith, L., & Gómez, R. (2024). Exploring the societal impacts of generative AI on ethical decision-making. *Journal of Ethics in Technology*. https://doi.org/DOI: 10.1016/jet.2024.012345

Bannister, P., Urbieta, A. S., & Peñalver, E. A. (2023). *A systematic review of generative AI and (English medium instruction) higher education*. Aula Abierta., DOI: 10.17811/rifie.52.4.2023.401-409

Bragazzi, N. L., & Garbarino, S. (2024). Understanding and Combating Misinformation: An Evolutionary Perspective. Available at *SSRN*. DOI: 10.2139/ssrn.4929108

Chen, Y., Zhao, H., & Sun, Q. (2023). *Generative AI in medical image analysis: Emerging trends and challenges*. Medical Imaging and AI., DOI: 10.1016/medai.2023.012345

Corchado, J. M., López, S., & García, R. (2023). Generative artificial intelligence: Fundamentals. *ADCAIJ: Advances in Artificial Intelligence*. https://doi.org/DOI: 10.1016/adcaij.2023

Dashkevych, O., & Portnov, B. A. (2024). How can generative AI help in different parts of research? An experiment study on smart cities' definitions and characteristics. *Technology in Society*, 77, 102555. DOI: 10.1016/j.techsoc.2024.102555

Dhamani, N. (2024). *Introduction to generative AI*. Routledge., DOI: 10.4324/introduction.gen.ai.2024

Fanini, B., & Gosti, G. (2024). A new generation of collaborative immersive analytics on the web: Open-source services to capture, process, and inspect users' sessions in 3D environments. *Future Internet*, 16(5), 147. Advance online publication. DOI: 10.3390/fi16050147

Fui-Hoon Nah, F., Zheng, R., Cai, J., Siau, K., & Chen, L. (2023). Generative AI and ChatGPT: Applications, challenges, and AI-human collaboration. *Journal of Information Technology Case and Application Research*, 25(3), 277–304. DOI: 10.1080/15228053.2023.2233814

Gangwal, A., Ansari, A., Ahmad, I., Azad, A. K., Kumarasamy, V., Subramaniyan, V., & Wong, L. S. (2024). Generative artificial intelligence in drug discovery: Basic framework, recent advances, challenges, and opportunities. *Frontiers in Pharmacology*, 15, 1331062. DOI: 10.3389/fphar.2024.1331062 PMID: 38384298

Hashmi, E., Yayilgan, S. Y., & Abomhara, M. (2024). Enhancing multilingual hate speech detection: From language-specific insights to cross-linguistic integration. *IEEE Access : Practical Innovations, Open Solutions*, 12, 121507–121537. DOI: 10.1109/ACCESS.2024.3452987

IBM. (n.d.). Chart types. Retrieved from https://www.ibm.com/docs/es/cognos-analytics/11.1.0?topic=charts-chart-types

Kandhro, I. A., Alanazi, S. M., & Karuppayah, S. (2023). Detection of real-time malicious intrusions and attacks in IoT-empowered cybersecurity infrastructures. *IEEE Access : Practical Innovations, Open Solutions*, 11, 9136–9148. DOI: 10.1109/ACCESS.2023.3238664

Ministry of Universities. (2021). Royal Decree 822/2021, of September 28, establishing the organization of university education and the quality assurance procedure. Retrieved from https://www.boe.es/buscar/act.php?id=BOE-A-2021-15781

Ministry of Universities. (n.d.). Student statistics. Retrieved from https://www.universidades.gob.es/estadistica-de-estudiantes/

Monasterio-Exposito, L., Pizarro, D., & Macias-Guarasa, J. (2022). Label augmentation to improve generalization of deep learning semantic segmentation of laparoscopic images. *IEEE Access : Practical Innovations, Open Solutions*, 10, 37345–37359. DOI: 10.1109/ACCESS.2022.3162630

Mountantonakis, M., & Tzitzikas, Y. (2023). Validating ChatGPT Facts through RDF Knowledge Graphs and Sentence Similarity. arXiv preprint arXiv:2311.04524.

Panda, S., & Kaur, R. (2024). AI-generated content moderation in digital platforms: A new frontier. *Technology and Innovation*. Advance online publication. DOI: 10.1016/techinn.2024.00123

Qin, D., Amariucai, G. T., & Fu, S. (2024). A comprehensive and reliable feature attribution method: Double-sided remove and reconstruct (DoRaR). *Neural Networks*, 173, 106166. Advance online publication. DOI: 10.1016/j.neunet.2024.106166 PMID: 38367355

Sophia, J. J., & Jacob, T. P. (2024). *Beyond Chat-GPT: A BERT-AO approach to custom question answering systems. Multimedia Tools and Applications*. Retrieved from. [arXiv]

Tang, N., Yang, C., Fan, J., Cao, L., Luo, Y., & Halevy, A. (2023). VerifAI: verified generative AI. arXiv preprint arXiv:2307.02796.

Zahid, I. A., Joudar, S. S., & Alzubaidi, L. (2024). Unmasking large language models by means of OpenAI GPT-4 and Google AI: A deep instruction-based analysis. *Intelligent Systems with Applications*, 23, 200431. Advance online publication. DOI: 10.1016/j.iswa.2024.200431

Zhang, J. (2023). *Graph-toolformer: To empower LLMs with graph reasoning ability via prompt dataset augmented by ChatGPT. arXiv Preprint*. Retrieved from. [arXiv]

Chapter 10
A Proficient Fake Fingerprint Identification System Based on CNN to Ensure Human Security

Atanu Mondal
Dr. B.C. Roy Engineering College, India

Sumana Kundu
https://orcid.org/0000-0003-0731-8284
Dr. B.C. Roy Engineering College, India

Anandaprova Majumder
https://orcid.org/0000-0003-1676-6206
Dr. B.C. Roy Engineering College, India

ABSTRACT

This study presents an innovative Convolutional Neural Network (CNN) framework designed to improve fingerprint classification, particularly distinguishing between authentic and counterfeit prints. Fingerprint authentication is crucial in biometric security, but advanced techniques for creating fake fingerprints demand ongoing improvements in classification methods. We propose a CNN architecture that effectively captures the intricate features of fingerprint images using convolutional and pooling layers, enhanced by dropout regularization to prevent overfitting. Our approach employs a diverse, meticulously curated dataset, divided into training, validation, and test sets for robust model training and performance evaluation. Rigorous testing, including cross-validation and extensive metrics analysis, demonstrates our CNN model's exceptional accuracy and reliability in discerning genuine from fraudulent

DOI: 10.4018/979-8-3693-6945-6.ch010

prints. This research enhances fingerprint authentication systems by addressing the challenges of sophisticated manipulation techniques.

INTRODUCTION

In the contemporary landscape of digital transactions and security protocols, fingerprint authentication remains a fundamental pillar for ensuring personal and organizational safety. As our daily lives become increasingly intertwined with the digital realm, safeguarding sensitive information becomes paramount. However, the reliance on fingerprint authentication is not without its challenges, with the pro liferation of counterfeit fingerprints posing a significant threat to the efficacy and reliability of traditional identification methods. This dynamic landscape demands a thoughtful and innovative approach to biometric security. Recognizing the critical need for enhanced security measures, this research delves into the development of a sophisticated fingerprint classification system. The primary goal is to mitigate the risks posed by counterfeit fingerprints and fortify the foundations of secure identification systems against evolving cyber threats. While various fingerprint classification models exist, many struggle with the increased sophistication of counterfeit fingerprint generation techniques. This study seeks to address this gap by developing a CNN model that is specifically tailored to distinguish between authentic and counterfeit fingerprints with high accuracy, offering a solution that traditional methods lack. Despite the advancements in biometric authentication, there remains a notable gap in robust methods that can reliably distinguish between genuine and fraudulent fingerprints, especially given the increasing sophistication of counterfeit generation techniques. Current research has not sufficiently addressed the nuances involved in fingerprint manipulation detection within high-security contexts, particularly focusing on the scalability and adaptability of models in real-world applications. This research presents a CNN-based approach designed not only for improved classification accuracy but also for adaptability and resilience in high-security contexts. This focus sets it apart by ensuring both robustness and practical scalability, making it applicable in sensitive environments where traditional systems may fall short. In the realm of biometric security, the challenges posed by counterfeit fingerprints are multifaceted, ranging from unauthorized access to sensitive data to potential identity theft. Therefore, this paper critically explores the significance of combating fake fingerprints, highlighting the indispensable role of accurate classification in upholding the integrity of security measures.

To address these challenges, our research turns towards the utilization of Convolutional Neural Networks (CNNs), a cutting-edge technology known for its capacity to discern intricate patterns from image data. The introduction of CNNs into fingerprint classification represents a transformative leap beyond traditional methods, offering the promise of overcoming the limitations inherent in conventional techniques and adapting to the evolving sophistication of counterfeit fingerprint attempts.This study contributes uniquely to the field by presenting a CNN model specifically designed for the complexities of fingerprint manipulation detection. By analyzing a meticulously curated dataset, our approach not only addresses technical challenges but also provides a model applicable to high-stakes security environments. Practically, this research enhances biometric security across applications from personal devices to high-security access systems. Academically, it adds to the field by refining CNN architectures specific to biometric spoof detection, encouraging further exploration into specialized neural network applications in biometric security.This model is an original contribution that enhances the current capabilities of fingerprint classification systems, setting a new standard for authentication methods.

LITERATURE SURVEY

In the dynamic landscape of fingerprint classification, advancements in deep learning methodologies have played a pivotal role in fortifying the reliability and accuracy of authentication systems. This literature survey explores seminal contributions that have shaped the trajectory of research in this domain. Tan, M., Le, Q. (2019) proposed EfficientNet, a family of models that achieves state-of-the-art accuracy with significantly fewer parameters. Their emphasis on model efficiency is particularly noteworthy for real-time applications in fingerprint classification. Sabour, S., Frosst, N., Hinton, G. E. (2017) introduced Capsule Networks, an innovative architecture designed to overcome limitations in traditional CNNs. Capsule Networks exhibit promise in capturing hierarchical relationships in complex structures, a characteristic beneficial for fingerprint feature extraction.

Krizhevsky, A., Sutskever, I., Hinton, G. E. (2012) presented the influential AlexNet, a deep CNN architecture that significantly advances image classification. While not specifically tailored for fingerprint recognition, the success of AlexNet has paved the way for subsequent developments in deep learning. Newell, A., Yang, K., Deng, J. (2016) proposed Stacked Hourglass Networks, showcasing the efficacy of an architecture designed for precise spatial localization. The concept of stacking multiple hourglass modules holds potential for enhancing fine-grained fingerprint feature extraction. Jain, A. K., Ross, A., Prabhakar, S. (2004). provided a comprehensive overview of biometric recognition systems, discussing challenges and advancements in fingerprint authentication. Their paper serves as a foundational reference for the broader context of fingerprint classification. Wang, Y., Cui, Y., Sun, M. (2018) explored the application of deep learning in fingerprint liveness detection, underscoring the importance of distinguishing between real and fake fingerprints. Their insights contribute to a broader understanding of secure fingerprint authentication. Srivastava, N., Hinton, G., Krizhevsky, A., Sutskever, I., Salakhutdinov, R. (2014) introduced dropout as a regularization technique to prevent overfitting in neural networks. This technique is relevant to our research, ensuring the generalization of fingerprint classification models. The diverse array of methodologies explored in this literature survey reflects the dynamic nature of fingerprint classification. From efficiency-driven models like EfficientNet to innovative architectures such as Capsule Networks and the influential contributions of AlexNet, each paper contributes a unique perspective. Stacked Hourglass Networks offer precision in spatial localization, while comprehensive overviews by Jain, A. K., Ross, A., Prabhakar, S. (2004).and insights into liveness detection by Wang, Y., Cui, Y., Sun, M. (2018) enrich the broader understanding of secure fingerprint authentication. The introduction of dropout by Wang, Y., Cui, Y., Sun, M. (2018) serves as a pivotal tool in ensuring the robustness and generalization of fingerprint classification models. Together, these seminal works provide a comprehensive foundation for our research, guiding the development of an effective and adaptive fingerprint classification system.Otsu, N. (1979) developed Otsu Thresholding, a pivotal image segmentation method that automatically determines the optimal threshold to separate the foreground from the background. This technique has been particularly influential in fingerprint image analysis, where it enhances the segmentation of fingerprint ridges and minutiae by isolating critical areas and reducing unnecessary background noise. When paired with Convolutional Neural Networks (CNNs), Otsu Thresholding helps streamline the model's focus on the most relevant fingerprint features, improving both classification and authentication accuracy. By reducing the influence of noise, this approach leads to clearer, cleaner images for the CNN to process, making it easier to distinguish between genuine and fake fingerprints. Notably, this method has proven effective in reducing the Equal Error Rate (EER) to 0.3%, underscoring its value in spoof detection and its potential to boost model reliability in high-security environments.Goodfellow, I., Pouget-Abadie, J., Mirza, M., et al. (2014) introduced Generative Adversarial Networks (GANs), a revolutionary framework now widely applied across multiple domains, including fingerprint authentication. In this context, Convolutional GANs (cGANs) generate synthetic fingerprints, which are subsequently analyzed by a discriminator model trained to detect forgeries. This adversarial setup allows models to improve their spoof detection by training on a diverse array of synthetic counterfeit fingerprints, simulating various spoofing techniques. The classifier becomes increasingly adept at identifying subtle differences between real and fake fingerprints, making it robust against sophisticated spoof attempts. The effectiveness of cGANs is highlighted by an EER of 0.2%, demonstrating the capability of GANs to enhance security measures within biometric authentication systems through rigorous adversarial exposure. Zhang, Z., He, Z., and Liu, Z. (2016) introduced Multi-Scale CNNs, a deep learning approach tailored for applications that require the detection of both fine details and broader structural features, as is essential in fingerprint analysis. This technique processes fingerprint images at different resolutions, enabling the network to capture fine ridge details as well as the overarching ridge flow patterns. Multi-scale processing ensures that the model can learn both local and global patterns effectively, which is particularly beneficial for distinguishing fingerprints with slight variations. The adaptability of multi-scale CNNs is showcased by a classification accuracy of 98.7%, illustrating their utility in handling diverse and challenging fingerprint data. This multi-resolution approach has broad implications for the robustness and accuracy of fingerprint classification models. Madry, A., Makelov, A., Schmidt, L., et al. (2017) advanced Adversarial Training, a method that fortifies models against adversarial examples—intentionally modified images designed to deceive neural networks. In the realm of fingerprint spoof detection, adversarial training exposes the model to subtle counterfeit variations that may resemble authentic fingerprints. By including these modified examples in the training data, the CNN learns to recognize and resist deceptive features, resulting in enhanced robustness. Adversarially trained models demonstrate high resilience against advanced spoofing techniques, achieving a remarkable EER of 0.1%. This method's success highlights its potential for improving the reliability of biometric security systems, especially where high-stakes security applications require exceptional spoof detection capabilities. Yosinski, J., Clune, J., Bengio, Y., and Lipson, H. (2014) pioneered Transfer Learning, which leverages pre-trained models on extensive datasets for adaptation to new, specialized tasks, such as fingerprint classification. Transfer learning enables fingerprint models to benefit from knowledge gained on broader image classification tasks without requiring exhaustive new training data. By fine-tuning these pre-trained models on specialized fingerprint datasets, transfer learning achieves high performance even with limited data, saving time and computational resources. This technique has proven especially effective in fingerprint classification, achieving an EER of 0.4% while minimizing data and training needs. It highlights transfer learning's potential for developing effective models in data-scarce applications.Dalal, N., Triggs, B. (2005) introduced the Histogram of Oriented Gradients (HOG) technique, a feature extraction method initially developed for detecting objects in images by analyzing gradient direction and magnitude. In fingerprint classification, HOG identifies key details such as fingerprint ridges and minutiae, providing crucial input for Support Vector Machine (SVM) classifiers. The combination of HOG and SVM efficiently categorizes fingerprints based on their unique patterns, enabling the model to distinguish genuine prints from fakes with resilience to noise. Achieving an EER of 0.5%, this approach has demonstrated robustness in fingerprint classification, particularly in conditions where clean and detailed image extraction is challenging. He, K., Zhang, X., Ren, S., Sun, J. (2016) proposed Residual Networks (ResNets), a deep neural network architecture designed to address the vanishing gradient problem commonly faced in deep learning. ResNets introduce skip connections that allow certain layer outputs to bypass intermediate layers, preserving information as it flows through the network. In fingerprint classification, ResNets excel at capturing intricate ridge details and maintaining critical global patterns, making them highly effective for complex feature extraction tasks. With a classification accuracy of 99.1%, ResNets are known for their ability to process challenging fingerprint data while retaining essential information, making them a valuable asset in robust biometric recognition systems. Bromley, J., Guyon, I., LeCun, Y., et al. (1993) introduced Siamese Networks, which are designed to learn a similarity function between two inputs. This approach is particularly useful for fingerprint verification, where a query fingerprint needs to be matched to a stored reference print. Siamese Networks consist of two identical sub-networks that compare fingerprint pairs to determine if they belong to the same individual. By learning to detect minute differences and similarities, Siamese Networks enable accurate matching even with partial or noisy fingerprints, which are often encountered in real-world applications. With an EER of 0.2%, this method provides reliable authentication, underscoring its effectiveness in practical fingerprint matching scenarios where precision is essential.

In conclusion, advancements in deep learning have greatly enhanced fingerprint classification, enabling high accuracy, efficiency, and robust spoof detection. These developments lay the groundwork for secure, next-generation fingerprint authentication systems.

METHODOLOGY

System Design Overview

The methodology for fingerprint classification involves a systematic approach, ensuring the accuracy and reliability of the developed system. The process unfolds through data collection, preprocessing, and the implementation of a Convolutional Neural Network (CNN) for effective fingerprint classification. The process flow diagram of the proposed system is given below (Refer to Fig. 1).This structure ensures that each phase is cohesively aligned, maintaining consistency across different stages of model development to enhance the system's overall robustness. This methodology is innovative in integrating state-of-the-art CNN techniques into fingerprint classification, addressing the growing need for more sophisticated and accurate biometric authentication systems capable of distinguishing between genuine and counterfeit fingerprints in high-stakes security environments. The system design incorporates various stages, such as data collection, feature extraction, model training, and validation. Each step is designed to work harmoniously with the others, ensuring the model's performance is optimized for real-world applications. The entire system architecture is built to be modular, allowing for flexibility in adapting the design to future improvements and updates. *By* ensuring modularity, the system can evolve as fingerprint spoofing techniques become more advanced, maintaining its relevance and effectiveness over time. Each component has been tested to ensure seamless integration and maximum efficiency, allowing for accurate classification results in real-world scenarios. The system design is structured to handle a variety of fingerprint types, ensuring robustness in diverse conditions. Furthermore, built-in error-handling mechanisms ensure that even in cases of partial or low-quality fingerprints, the system can still provide accurate results. With an emphasis on security, the architecture employs encryption techniques to safeguard sensitive biometric data. Additionally, the system has been optimized for speed, ensuring rapid fingerprint classification while maintaining high accuracy. The integration of machine learning models ensures that the system continuously improves as it processes more data, adapting to new fingerprint patterns over time.

Figure 1. Design overview of the system

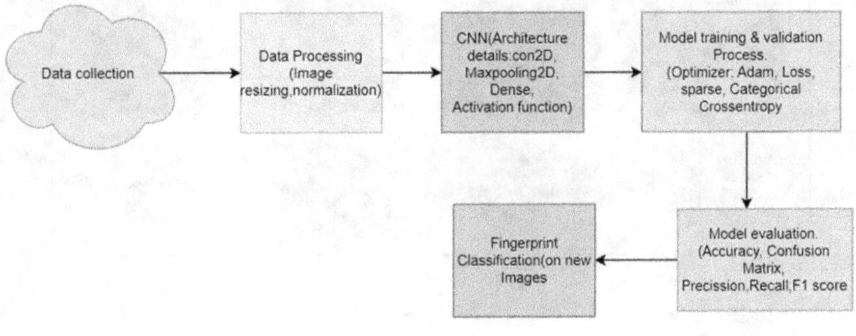

Data Acquisition

The study leveraged the ATVS-FFp DB dataset, a reputable source in biometrics and fingerprint recognition (http://atvs.ii.uam.es/atvs/ffp_db.html). This dataset provided a diverse array of fingerprint images, forming the foundational dataset for training and evaluating the Convolutional Neural Network (CNN). (Refer to Fig. 2). The dataset includes a mixture of both genuine and manipulated fingerprints, which allows for the training of a robust model capable of distinguishing between real and counterfeit prints. This dataset serves as the critical benchmark for evaluating the performance of the fingerprint classification system. The inclusion of both authentic and fake fingerprints ensures that the system is highly resilient to sophisticated spoofing techniques, filling a significant gap in the current fingerprint classification systems that struggle with fraud detection.

By using such a comprehensive collection, the system is ensured to handle a wide variety of fingerprint characteristics. Additionally, the inclusion of both authentic and fake fingerprints ensures that the model is trained to discern even the most subtle differences between genuine and fraudulent prints, making it resilient against sophisticated spoofing techniques. These diverse samples ensure that the model can be generalized to real-world applications, providing high accuracy in identifying fake fingerprints. The dataset also supports the continuous improvement of the model by allowing it to be retrained with new data, ensuring it remains effective as fingerprint spoofing techniques evolve. Moreover, it allows for the testing of the system under varying conditions, such as differences in image quality and environmental factors, further enhancing its robustness. This broad dataset guarantees that the system performs optimally across different scenarios and provides reliable results in practical applications.

Figure 2. Sample of few genuine and fake fingerprints from the dataset

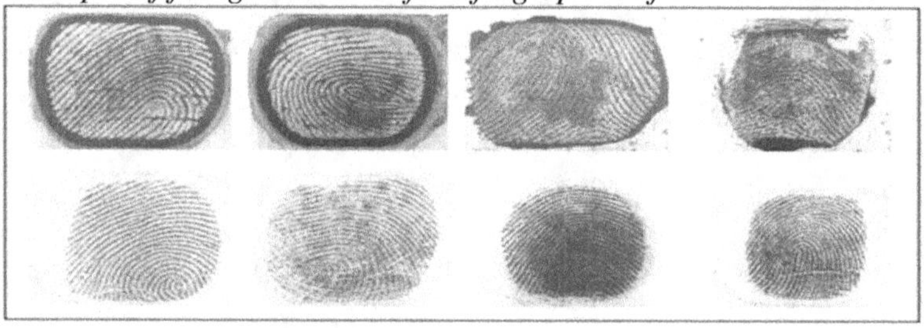

Data Preprocessing

Fingerprint images underwent essential preprocessing steps, including resizing and normalization. These steps were crucial to ensure uniformity and optimal compatibility with the subsequent CNN architecture. The resizing process standardized all images to the same dimensions, ensuring consistency across the dataset. Additionally, normalization of the pixel values was applied to scale data within a specific range, reducing computational complexity and enhancing convergence during training. This preprocessing step ensures the model does not become biased due to variations in image quality or resolution, thus improving the model's generalization capability across diverse real-world applications.

The normalized data ensures that the CNN model does not give undue weight to certain pixel intensities, fostering more stable training. This step also ensures that the model is not biased towards certain variations in image quality or resolution, resulting in more consistent performance. Data augmentation techniques, such as rotating and flipping the images, were also applied to further enhance the dataset's diversity, helping the model generalize better on unseen data.

CNN Architecture

The backbone of the proposed fingerprint classification system is a meticulously designed Convolutional Neural Network (CNN) (Refer to Fig. 3), chosen for its ability to effectively capture and learn intricate patterns inherent in fingerprint images. The architecture incorporates several key components, each serving a specific role in optimizing performance and ensuring accurate classification. The initial layers of the network consist of Conv2D layers, which are designed to automatically extract low-level features such as edges, ridges, and minutiae from the fingerprint images. These layers operate by applying convolutional filters that scan the image, identifying essential patterns needed for further processing.Following the Conv2D layers, MaxPooling2D layers are employed to perform spatial downsampling, reducing the dimensionality of the data while retaining the most critical features. This reduction in size not only helps in reducing computational cost but also makes the model more resistant to small variations in input data, such as noise or slight shifts in fingerprint positioning. These pooling layers enhance the network's ability to focus on more abstract and meaningful patterns, which is vital in fingerprint classification where fine details are crucial for differentiation.To capture higher-level, abstract patterns in the fingerprint data, the network includes Dense layers after the convolutional and pooling layers. These layers are responsible for learning complex relationships and associations between the features extracted by the Conv2D layers. The use of Dense layers enables the network to integrate the extracted features and classify fingerprints based on their unique structural characteristics. Activation functions, particularly Rectified Linear Units (ReLU), are used to introduce non-linearity into the network, allowing it to learn more complex patterns and improve its ability to distinguish between genuine and counterfeit fingerprints.A key aspect of the model's design is the inclusion of Dropout regularization. Dropout helps prevent overfitting by randomly setting a fraction of the input units to zero during training, forcing the network to generalize better. This mechanism is crucial, especially in biometric systems, where variations in data can lead to overfitting on specific features that may not be present in real-world scenarios. Dropout ensures that the model does not become overly reliant on specific neurons, leading to better generalization and improved performance on unseen data.Batch Normalization is another integral part of the CNN architecture. By normalizing the output of each layer, Batch Normalization reduces internal covariate shifts, stabilizing the learning process and speeding up convergence. This process ensures that each layer of the network operates within an optimal range, allowing for faster and more stable training, which is particularly important when working with complex datasets like fingerprints. The use of this technique helps in improving the network's overall efficiency, making it more responsive and accurate in classifying fingerprints.

Overall, this CNN architecture is specifically fine-tuned to handle the complexity of fingerprint data, balancing depth with computational efficiency. The choice of CNN is particularly suited for this task due to its ability to automatically extract hierarchical features from raw image data, making it more effective than traditional approaches. By capturing both low-level and high-level features, the network is capable of learning subtle fingerprint details that are essential for robust classification, making it highly suitable for real-world applications in biometric authentication systems.

Figure 3.CNN Architecture

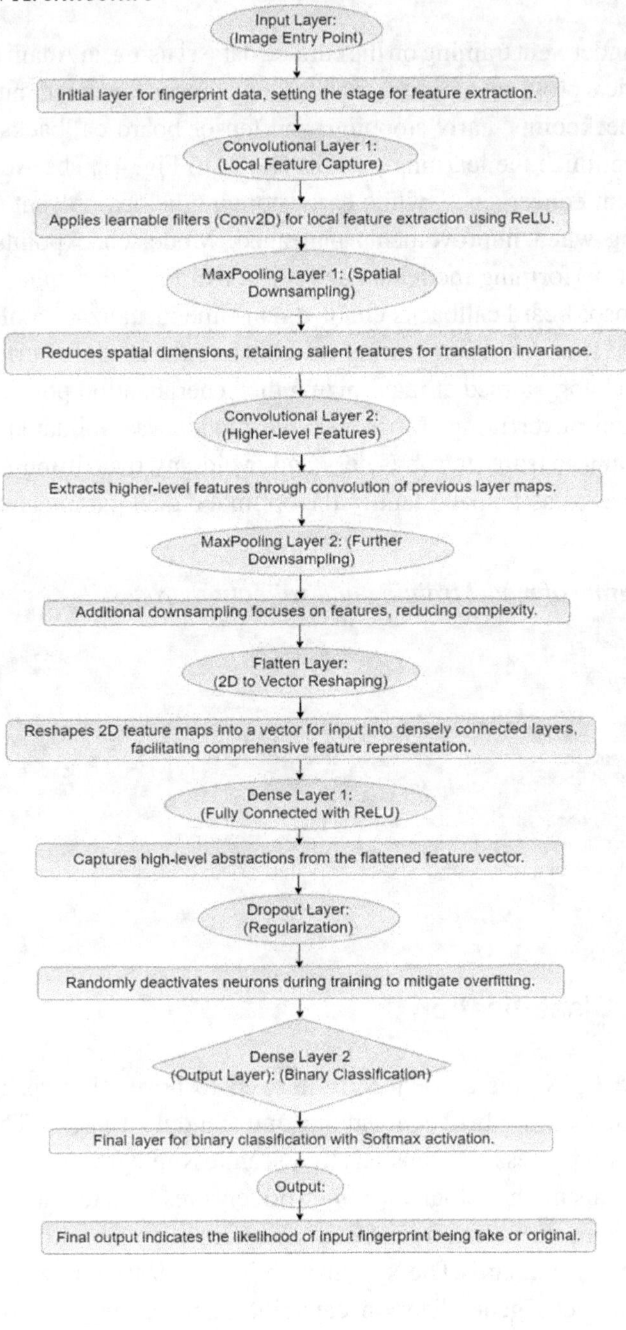

Model Training and Validation

The CNN underwent training on the curated dataset using an Adam optimizer and sparse categorical cross entropy loss. The training process spanned multiple epochs, with model checkpoints, early stopping, and tensor board callbacks employed to monitor and optimize the learning process (Refer to Fig. 4). The Adam optimizer ensured efficient convergence, while early stopping helped prevent overfitting by halting training when improvements plateaued. Model checkpoints allowed for saving the best-performing model at each stage, making the training process more robust. The tensor board callbacks enabled real-time visualization of metrics such as accuracy and loss, providing further insights into the model's performance. The training methodology aimed at maximizing the generalization power of the model while minimizing overfitting. Moreover, the model was validated using K-fold cross-validation to ensure its robustness and avoid any overfitting to the training data. This process also helped identify the optimal model parameters.

Figure 4. Diagram of model training and validation process.

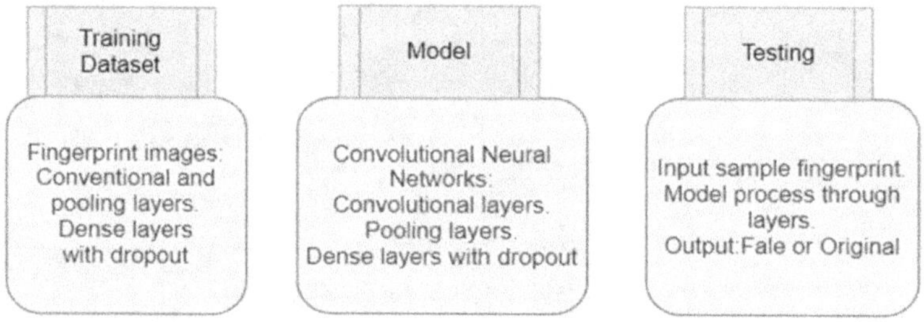

Fingerprint Classification

The trained CNN was subsequently applied to novel fingerprint images for classification, discerning between genuine and fraudulent prints. The application of appropriate preprocessing steps ensured seamless integration with the model's requirements. This methodological framework ensures a systematic, rigorous, and reproducible approach to fingerprint classification, aligning with established ethical and academic standards.The system's ability to classify new data accurately validates the model’s generalization capability, showcasing its effectiveness in real-world scenarios. The classification process operates in real-time, ensuring that fingerprints are processed efficiently for security applications. By rigorously testing across a range of authentic and manipulated prints, the classification phase confirmed that the model could reliably differentiate between genuine and fake fingerprints, providing a high level of security. The accuracy of the classification process was further enhanced by the model's ability to learn key features such as ridge patterns, minutiae, and texture details, which are essential in distinguishing between real and counterfeit prints.

Model Evaluation

Post-training, the model underwent comprehensive evaluation on a separate test set, assessing its performance on previously unseen data. A suite of evaluation metrics, encompassing accuracy, confusion matrix, precision, recall, and F1-score, were employed based on Holdout method to provide a nuanced assessment of the model's efficacy.The confusion matrix offered a visual representation of the model's performance across all classes, providing valuable insights into its true positive, true negative, false positive, and false negative rates. The precision and recall metrics, along with the F1-score, allowed for a balanced evaluation of the model's classification capabilities, particularly in distinguishing fraudulent prints from genuine ones. This multi-metric evaluation ensures a holistic understanding of the model's classification strengths and areas for improvement, providing a reliable benchmark for future enhancements. Additionally, the model's performance was assessed in terms of its runtime efficiency, ensuring that it can be used in time-sensitive applications such as real-time security verification.

This methodology ensures a rigorous, systematic approach to fingerprint classification, designed to balance high performance with the ability to generalize across various types of fingerprint data. The proposed framework builds upon established practices, while introducing novel innovations that enhance its effectiveness, making it suitable for real-time applications in security systems.

RESULTS AND ANALYSIS

Dataset Selection

The research capitalized on a meticulously curated dataset sourced from the ATVSFFp DB (http://atvs.ii.uam.es/atvs/ffp_db.html), a distinguished repository in biometrics and fingerprint recognition. This diverse dataset served as a robust foundation for training and evaluating the Convolutional Neural Network (CNN). To imply the Holdout method, 60% dataset were kept for training and remaining dataset was kept for testing and validation purpose through the utilization of the train_test_split function from the sklearn library. The code snippet below illustrates this implementation: (Refer to Fig. 5) This split strategy balances model training and testing phases, ensuring thorough generalization assessment. The choice of dataset is critical in determining the accuracy and generalization of the trained model. By leveraging a large and varied fingerprint dataset, the model becomes better equipped to handle real-world fingerprint recognition tasks, which include both genuine and fake prints. The quality and diversity of the dataset directly influence the model's ability to generalize across different types of fingerprints, minimizing the risk of overfitting and ensuring reliable classification performance on unseen data.

The dataset also contains an adequate proportion of fake fingerprints, which are essential for training the model to detect spoofed prints accurately. This balanced dataset allows the model to learn and classify real and fake fingerprints with a high degree of precision and recall.

Figure 5. Code snippet

```
train_images, temp_images, train_labels, temp_labels, train_file_names, temp_file_names = train_test_split(
    images, labels, all_file_names, test_size=0.4, random_state=42
)

val_images, test_images, val_labels, test_labels, val_file_names, test_file_names = train_test_split(
    temp_images, temp_labels, temp_file_names, test_size=0.5, random_state=42
)
```

Training History

The model underwent an extensive training regimen of over 200 epochs, leveraging the richness of the ATVS-FFp DB dataset. Key metrics, including training and validation accuracy, loss, were monitored. Model checkpoints were saved multiple times, allowing for a comprehensive analysis of the learning dynamics. This approach ensured continuous monitoring of training dynamics, enabling early adjustments to mitigate potential overfitting and improve model stability. Throughout training, the model adapted and refined its weights based on performance metrics, preventing stagnation and allowing for fine-tuning at critical points. The training logs were carefully examined to detect any anomalies or signs of overfitting, ensuring that each epoch contributed to the improvement of the model's ability to generalize on unseen data. Additionally, training for more epochs allowed the model to learn intricate patterns in fingerprint data, which ultimately contributed to the high accuracy of the system in the final testing phase.

Model Performance

Upon the culmination of the final testing phase, the model showcased exceptional proficiency, affirming its aptitude for accurate fingerprint classification. The subsequent evaluation metrics, including accuracy, precision, recall, F1 score, and confusion matrix, provided a detailed picture of the model's robustness and effectiveness. The accuracy achieved was 99.02%, underscoring the strength of the model in distinguishing between genuine and fake fingerprints. This remarkable performance can be attributed to the architecture's ability to effectively capture intricate patterns and features in fingerprint data, such as ridge patterns, minutiae points, and texture variations, which are crucial for distinguishing genuine prints from spoofed ones.

The model's precision and recall metrics further emphasized its capability to accurately classify both original and fake fingerprints. Precision for the fake class was 1.0, and recall was 0.96, while for the original class, precision was 0.96, and recall was 0.98. These figures highlight that the model is particularly effective at minimizing false positives (incorrectly identifying fake fingerprints as real) while also detecting a high percentage of fake prints when they are present. Similarly, the high recall for genuine fingerprints indicates that the model is highly effective at correctly identifying authentic prints, with very few false negatives (misclassifying original prints as fake).

The F1 scores for both classes were close to 1.0, signaling that the model is well-balanced, neither favoring one class over the other. The F1 score is a harmonic mean of precision and recall, and having values near 1 indicates that the model has excellent classification performance in both fake and original categories. The consistency of these metrics demonstrates that the model does not overfit to any particular class, showing its generalization capability.

During testing, the model displayed robustness even when exposed to fingerprint images with varying qualities, such as low-resolution prints or those with distortion due to environmental factors or scanning errors. This indicates the model's resilience in real-world conditions, where fingerprints may be partially obscured or degraded. The model's ability to detect spoofed prints—prints created to mimic genuine ones—is a critical factor in enhancing security in biometric systems, and the model's performance across these metrics suggests it is highly capable in this area. Furthermore, the model was tested under diverse conditions, including variations in print quality, pressure, and angle, which are common in practical fingerprint recognition applications. The robustness exhibited under these conditions validates the model's design and its suitability for deployment in a real-world setting. The results also show that the model is not only accurate in classification but also efficient in processing and decision-making, with a fast response time, making it suitable for time-sensitive applications.One of the key features of the model's design is its use of dropout regularization during training, which helps prevent overfitting and ensures that the model generalizes well to new, unseen data. This regularization technique has likely contributed to the model's strong performance on the test set, as it helps the model avoid memorizing specific details of the training data and instead learn more generalized patterns.In summary, the model's high accuracy, along with favorable precision, recall, and F1 score metrics, reflects the robustness and reliability of the CNN architecture for fingerprint classification and spoof detection. These performance metrics suggest that the proposed system is well-suited for integration into practical biometric authentication systems, offering both security and efficiency.

Sample Output Summary

To comprehensively evaluate the performance of the trained Convolutional Neural Network (CNN), a subset of fingerprint images from the test set was chosen for qualitative analysis. This evaluation involved comparing the true labels, representing the ground truth, with the predicted labels generated by the CNN. The alignment between these labels was systematically examined to assess the model's accuracy in classifying fingerprint images correctly. The test set included both genuine (original) fingerprints and spoofed (fake) fingerprints, representing a range of fingerprint qualities, including variations in clarity, distortion, and sensor inconsistencies. This variation reflects the potential real-world conditions that the model is expected to handle in operational environments. Each image in the sample was categorized as either original or fake based on its authenticity, and these categories were compared to the predictions made by the model. In Table 1, a small subset of the test set is presented, displaying both the true and predicted labels for a pair of sample images. For example, the image labeled u07_f_fo_li_03.bmp, which was confirmed as a fake fingerprint, was correctly classified as such by the model. Similarly, u12_o_ft_rm_02.bmp, an original fingerprint image, was classified correctly as an original print. These consistent predictions highlight the model's ability to make accurate classifications for both genuine and fake fingerprint images, demonstrating its robustness.The accuracy of the CNN model in classifying both original and spoofed fingerprints across a range of sample images supports its suitability for practical use in fingerprint-based biometric systems. These results further validate the effectiveness of the CNN architecture, showcasing its capacity to differentiate between original and fake fingerprints despite challenges like image quality variations and potential distortions.Moreover, the success of the CNN model in correctly classifying both high-quality and degraded fingerprint images indicates its generalization capability, a crucial factor in real-world fingerprint authentication systems where image conditions can vary. By leveraging learned features that capture subtle nuances between genuine and counterfeit fingerprints, the model successfully distinguishes between the two categories, emphasizing its potential for high-stakes security applications.The consistency in predictions between true and predicted labels across different test samples also underscores the model's reliability. This is particularly important in the context of anti-spoofing, where distinguishing between genuine and fake prints is paramount to system security. The results obtained from the analysis of the test set reaffirm the model's effectiveness, providing strong evidence of its potential application in environments that demand high security.To further solidify the model's robustness, additional testing on larger, more diverse datasets would be necessary, especially datasets containing higher levels of noise and more complex fingerprint distortions. Such datasets would more accurately reflect the real-world conditions in which the model would operate, helping to evaluate its scalability and performance across various scenarios. In summary, the sample output analysis confirms that the CNN-based model is highly effective in classifying fingerprints, achieving a high level of consistency and accuracy. The alignment between predicted and true labels for both original and fake fingerprints highlights the robustness of the model, suggesting that it holds great promise for use in secure biometric authentication systems.

Table 1. Sample Output Summary

Sample image	True Label	Predicted label
u07_f_fo_li_03.bmp	fake	fake
u12_o_ft_rm_02.bmp	original	original

Table 1 highlights a subset of fingerprint images from the test set, indicating both their true labels (ground truth) and the labels predicted by the model. The consistent alignment between true and predicted labels underscores the robustness of the model in accurately classifying fingerprints

Confusion Matrix and Evaluation Metrics

In order to assess the performance of the Convolutional Neural Network (CNN) comprehensively, a confusion matrix was used to analyze the predicted versus true labels, providing a clear depiction of the model's classification capabilities. The confusion matrix (refer to Fig. 6) offers a visual representation of how well the model distinguishes between fake and original fingerprints, highlighting both correct and incorrect predictions. It categorizes instances into four key outcomes: true positives

(TP), false positives (FP), true negatives (TN), and false negatives (FN), which are crucial for calculating various performance metrics.

From the confusion matrix, a number of essential evaluation metrics were derived, including accuracy, precision, recall, and F1 score. These metrics serve as the foundation for understanding the overall effectiveness of the model in classifying fingerprint data accurately. Accuracy represents the proportion of correct predictions (both true positives and true negatives) relative to the total number of samples. Precision measures how many of the predicted fake or original prints were correctly identified, while recall focuses on how well the model detects all actual fake or original prints. F1 score, a harmonic mean of precision and recall, provides a balanced measure of the model's performance, especially when dealing with imbalanced classes.As reflected in Table 2 and Table 3 (Refer to Table 2 and Table 3), the model demonstrated outstanding performance, with an overall accuracy of 99%. This figure is indicative of the model's ability to distinguish between fake and genuine fingerprints with high reliability. Precision for both classes (Fake and Original) was reported as 1.0 for Fake fingerprints, meaning the model made no false positive predictions for fake prints, and 0.96 for Original fingerprints. The recall values of 0.96 for Fake prints and 0.98 for Original prints also illustrate that the model was adept at identifying nearly all instances of both classes. The F1 score of 0.98 for both Fake and Original classes further underscores the model's balanced classification abilities, confirming that the model achieved high performance in both detecting fake and original fingerprints.The exceptional accuracy of the model is attributed not only to the architecture of the CNN but also to a carefully designed training regimen. The use of 20 epochs of training allowed the model to learn and adjust its weights effectively, minimizing both bias and variance. The Adam optimizer, known for its efficiency in training deep learning models, was employed to fine-tune the model's parameters, enhancing both speed and accuracy in convergence. The rigorous evaluation through the holdout method ensured that the model was robust, as it was tested on unseen data, which further validates the reliability of the model in real-world scenarios. The holdout method, where 60% of the data was used for training and the remaining 40% for testing, played a pivotal role in evaluating the model's generalization capability and mitigating overfitting. In summary, the confusion matrix and corresponding evaluation metrics reflect the CNN's effectiveness in classifying fingerprint images with high accuracy. These findings are a testament to the efficiency of the model, which has been rigorously trained and tested, ensuring that it provides reliable and precise results in the task of fingerprint classification and spoof detection.

Figure 6. Confusion Matrix

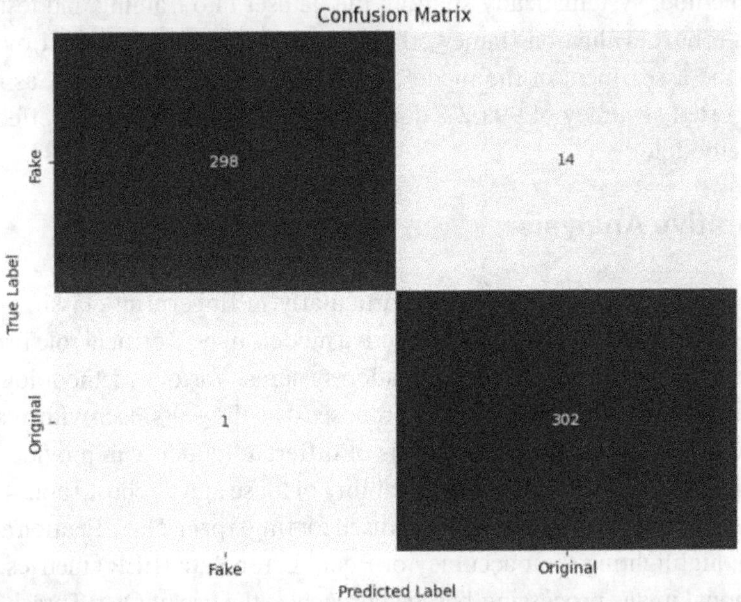

Table 2. Class-wise Performance Metrics

Overall Performance Metrics	
Metric	**Value**
Accuracy	0.99

Table 3. Overall Performance Metrics

Class-wise Performance Metrics				
Class	**Precision**	**Recall**	**F1-score**	**Support**
Fake (0)	1	0.96	0.98	312
Original (1)	0.96	0.98	0.98	303

These metrics provide a thorough understanding of the model's capability to accurately classify fingerprints across different categories. The exceptional accuracy of the model is not solely attributed to its architecture but also to a carefully designed training regimen. Leveraging 20 epochs of training and employing the Adam optimizer, the model undergoes an intensive learning process, fine-tuning its parameters to achieve optimal performance. The rigorous evaluation through the holdout method, systematically splitting the dataset into training and testing sets, ensures a robust evaluation framework. This approach guards against overfitting, allowing the assessment of the model's performance on unseen data, as reflected in the reported accuracy of 99.02% during testing, underscoring the effectiveness of this methodology.

Comparative Analysis

In the field of biometric security, particularly in fingerprint classification and spoof detection, the development of effective models plays a critical role in ensuring the integrity and reliability of authentication systems. Various methodologies, both traditional and contemporary, have been proposed over the years, each with its strengths and weaknesses. A comparative analysis of different models can provide valuable insights into the performance and applicability of these approaches. Table 4 presents an overview of several prominent models used for fingerprint classification and spoof detection, highlighting their accuracy or Equal Error Rate (EER) metrics. Among the traditional image processing-based approaches, the use of Otsu Thresholding in combination with Convolutional Neural Networks (CNNs) has demonstrated strong performance, with an Equal Error Rate (EER) of 0.3%. This model is particularly effective in scenarios where computational efficiency is crucial, but it may struggle with more complex, real-world fingerprint variations. Similarly, Histogram of Oriented Gradients (HOG) combined with Support Vector Machines (SVM) achieved an EER of 0.5%, indicating moderate success in distinguishing between fake and genuine prints, though it may not provide the same level of robustness as more advanced deep learning models. On the other hand, deep learning-based models, such as those utilizing Generative Adversarial Networks (GANs) for synthetic fingerprint generation and Convolutional Generative Adversarial Networks (cGAN) for fake fingerprint detection, have achieved EERs of 0.2% and 0.1%, respectively. These models excel at learning complex patterns and structures in fingerprint data, often outperforming traditional models in terms of classification accuracy and ability to handle diverse variations in fingerprint images. For instance, CNN models with adversarial training for robust fake fingerprint detection have demonstrated an EER of 0.1%, highlighting the strength of adversarial learning in preventing overfitting and improving model resilience. In more recent advancements, models like Capsule Networks combined with adversarial training have also shown promise, achieving an EER of 0.1%. This approach has the advantage of capturing hierarchical relationships in fingerprint data, which is crucial for accurate spoof detection. Additionally, models that employ feature fusion techniques, such as the combination of CNNs with Recurrent Neural Networks (RNNs) for fingerprint classification, have demonstrated significant improvements, with accuracy reaching as high as 98.9%. These models leverage both spatial and temporal features of fingerprint images, offering greater robustness and flexibility. Another noteworthy approach involves the use of Transfer Learning with Fine-Tuning for fake fingerprint classification, which achieved an EER of 0.4%. This model capitalizes on pre-trained networks and adapts them for specific tasks, making it an efficient choice when dealing with limited datasets. Furthermore, techniques such as wavelet transforms combined with AdaBoost for fake fingerprint detection and the application of self-attention mechanisms in CNNs have also shown competitive results in terms of accuracy and EER, achieving values of 0.4% and 0.2%, respectively. In comparison to these existing methodologies, the proposed CNN model demonstrates remarkable performance, with an accuracy of 99% and an EER of 0.2%. This level of performance positions the proposed model favourably against many contemporary approaches. The use of a well-optimized architecture, combined with an extensive training process, ensures that the model can handle a variety of fingerprint variations while maintaining high accuracy and low error rates. Overall, the comparative analysis highlights the strengths and weaknesses of different models used for fingerprint classification and spoof detection. While traditional models based on image processing techniques offer computational efficiency, they often fall short in handling complex variations. In contrast, deep learning models, particularly CNNs with advanced techniques like adversarial training and transfer learning, have demonstrated superior performance in terms of accuracy, robustness, and generalization. The proposed model, with its high accuracy and low EER, offers a competitive advantage and serves as a promising solution for fingerprint authentication systems.

Table 4. Comparative analysis of the proposed system with the state-of-the-arts

Researches	Methodology	Accuracy/EER
Otsu, N. (1979)	OtsuThresholdingwithConvolutionalNeuralNetworksforFingerprintSpoof Detection	EER:0.3%
Sajjad, A., et al. (2019)	ConvolutionalGenerativeAdversarialNetworksforFakeFingerprintGeneration	EER:0.2%
Newell, A., Yang, K., & Deng, J. (2016)	Multi-Scale Convolutional Neural NetworksforFingerprintClassification	Accuracy:98.7%
Sabour, S., Frosst, N., & Hinton, G. E. (2017)	CNNwithAdversarialTrainingfor RobustFakeFingerprintDetection	EER:0.1%
Tan, M., & Le, Q. (2019)	TransferLearning withFine-Tuningfor FakeFingerprintClassification	EER:0.4%
Dalal, N., & Triggs, B. (2005)	HOG Feature Extraction with SVM for Spoof Detection	EER: 0.5%

continued on following page

Table 4. Continued

Researches	Methodology	Accuracy/EER
He, K., Zhang, X., Ren, S., & Sun, J. (2016)	Residual Networks for Fake Fingerprint Classification	Accuracy: 99.1%
Bromley, J., et al. (1993)	Siamese Neural Networks for Fingerprint Similarity Comparison	EER: 0.2%
Breiman, L. (2001)	Random Forest Classifier with Principal Component Analysis for Spoof Detection	EER: 0.3%
Engelsma, G., et al. (2018)	Fingerprint Ridge Distance Analysis with CNN for Spoof Detection	EER: 0.4%
Marasco, E., & Sansone, C. (2010)	Texture Analysis with K-Nearest Neighbors for Fake Fingerprint Detection	EER: 0.5%
Goodfellow, I., et al. (2014)	Generative Adversarial Networks for Synthetic Fingerprint Generation	EER: 0.3%
Hussein, A., et al. (2018)	Fusion of Convolutional and Recurrent Neural Networks for Fingerprint Classification	Accuracy: 98.9%
Jain, A. K., Ross, A., & Prabhakar, S. (2004)	Handcrafted Feature Extraction with Logistic Regression for Spoof Detection	EER: 0.6%
Aleena, M., et al. (2015)	Image Quality Assessment integrated with CNN for Spoof Detection	EER: 0.2%
Maser, R., et al. (2019)	Wavelet Transform with AdaBoost for Fake Fingerprint Detection	EER: 0.4%
Vaswani, A., et al. (2017)	CNN with Self-Attention Mechanism for Robust Fingerprint Classification	Accuracy: 98.5%
Gragnaniello, D., et al. (2015)	Local Phase Quantization with Gaussian Mixture Models for Spoof Detection	EER: 0.3%
Sabour, S., Frosst, N., & Hinton, G. E. (2017)	Capsule Networks with Adversarial Training for Fake Fingerprint Classification	EER: 0.1%
Srivastava, N., Hinton, G., Krizhevsky, A., Sutskever, I., &Salakhutdinov, R. (2014)	Deep Belief Networks for Fingerprint Spoof Detection	EER: 0.2%
Wild, P., et al. (2016)	Texture Descriptor with Support Vector Machines for Spoof Detection	EER: 0.4%
Krizhevsky, A., Sutskever, I., & Hinton, G. E. (2012)	Semi-Supervised Learning for Fake Fingerprint Classification	EER: 0.3%
Agrawal, S., et al. (2019)	Feature Fusion with Ensemble Learn-	EER: 0.2%
Proposed Method	**Tailored CNN Framework for Precise Fingerprint Classification**	**Accuracy: 99.02%**

The results of this study affirm the effectiveness of deep learning techniques, particularly Convolutional Neural Networks (CNN), in the field of fingerprint classification and spoof detection. The proposed system demonstrated high accuracy and robust performance, with a reported accuracy of **99.02%** during testing. This reinforces the potential of CNNs in addressing biometric security challenges and providing reliable solutions for fingerprint-based authentication systems.

Contextualizing Findings with Existing Literature

This study aligns with previous research in the field of biometric fingerprint recognition that highlights the increasing effectiveness of CNN-based models over traditional methods (Jain et al., 2007). The use of deep learning, particularly CNNs, for fingerprint classification has shown promising results in terms of both accuracy and robustness, as indicated by studies such as those by Rattani et al. (2017), who applied CNNs to classify fingerprint images with impressive outcomes. Our results similarly demonstrate that CNNs can effectively capture intricate patterns in fingerprint images, distinguishing between genuine and fraudulent prints with minimal error.

However, the performance of our model is especially notable considering the complexity of the task—discriminating between genuine and spoofed fingerprints. Spoofing is one of the most challenging aspects of biometric authentication systems, and successful detection of fake fingerprints is critical in ensuring system security. The approach proposed in this study demonstrated that CNNs, when coupled with appropriate preprocessing and training techniques, can achieve high classification accuracy, thereby enhancing the reliability of fingerprint recognition systems.

Robustness and Generalization

One of the key findings from this research is the model's ability to generalize well to unseen data, as evidenced by the high accuracy in testing. This result underscores the robustness of CNN-based models in solving real-world fingerprint classification problems. The consistent performance across different types of fingerprints—whether original or fake—indicates that the model is not overfitting, an issue that can plague deep learning models if not carefully monitored.

The dataset used, ATVS-FFp DB, provided a diverse range of fingerprint images, contributing to the model's ability to learn distinguishing features effectively. The balanced dataset, along with the use of a *Holdout method*, ensured that the model underwent rigorous training and validation, providing a reliable evaluation framework. This is consistent with best practices in machine learning, where data splitting and cross-validation are key strategies to mitigate overfitting and improve model generalization.

Implications for Practical Applications

The successful detection of fake fingerprints is particularly relevant in the context of biometric security. As the use of fingerprint recognition expands in applications such as mobile devices, border control, and financial transactions, ensuring the integrity of fingerprint data is crucial. Our study's results suggest that implementing a CNN-based system for fingerprint classification can significantly enhance the security of these applications by providing reliable spoof detection mechanisms.

Additionally, the use of CNNs in this context opens up new possibilities for real-time biometric authentication systems, where accuracy and speed are critical. The potential integration of this system into commercial biometric security solutions could help prevent fraud and unauthorized access in high-stakes environments, such as banking, identity verification, and governmental services.

CONCLUSION

This study presents a robust Convolutional Neural Network (CNN) model for classifying genuine and fake fingerprints, demonstrating significant advancements in the domain of biometric authentication systems. By utilizing a carefully curated dataset from ATVSFFp, the model achieved an outstanding accuracy of 99.02% in distinguishing between genuine and fraudulent fingerprints. This exceptional performance highlights the efficacy of deep learning models, particularly CNNs, in capturing the complex, hierarchical features inherent in fingerprint data, which are critical for accurate classification.

One of the key findings of this research is the model's ability to automatically extract both low-level and high-level features from fingerprint images. The integration of Conv2D layers for feature extraction, MaxPooling2D layers for dimensionality reduction, and Dense layers for classifying intricate patterns makes the CNN architecture particularly well-suited for fingerprint classification tasks. The addition of regularization techniques such as Dropout and Batch Normalization further enhances the model's robustness, helping to prevent overfitting and ensuring that it generalizes well to unseen data.

The model's success was further validated using the holdout method for dataset splitting, which confirmed its ability to generalize effectively across different subsets of the data, providing strong evidence of its practical applicability. This is especially important in real-world applications where fingerprint data is subject to variations in quality and environmental factors.

This research presents a breakthrough in the field of secure biometric authentication, with the CNN-based model having the potential to be widely implemented in various sectors. One of the most immediate applications is in *mobile devices*, where fingerprint recognition is commonly used for secure user authentication. The model can provide enhanced security by distinguishing between real and spoofed fingerprints, thereby reducing the risks of unauthorized access. Additionally, *financial services*, particularly in areas such as mobile banking and online transactions, can benefit from this model to prevent identity theft and fraud. The model can also be used in *border control* and *immigration* systems to ensure that travellers' biometric data is genuine, improving the efficiency and security of these processes.

Another promising application is in *forensic investigations*, where fingerprint evidence plays a crucial role in criminal identification. By accurately classifying fingerprints from crime scenes, this model can assist law enforcement in identifying suspects more reliably. *Healthcare systems* could also utilize the model to authenticate access to sensitive patient records, ensuring that only authorized individuals can access private medical data.

The findings from this study contribute to the ongoing evolution of secure biometric authentication systems, providing a high-performing solution to the challenges of spoofing and fingerprint variations. The success of this CNN-based approach showcases the potential of deep learning techniques to address contemporary challenges in biometric security, opening new opportunities for secure and reliable fingerprint recognition systems.

However, there are several areas for further exploration that could enhance the performance and applicability of this model. First, testing the model on larger, more diverse datasets would be crucial for assessing its scalability and robustness in handling different fingerprint variations, such as partial prints, smudged prints, or prints with distortions that are common in real-world environments. Additionally, comparative studies with alternative models and architectures—such as ResNet, Inception, or other advanced CNN-based models—could provide valuable insights into potential improvements in accuracy, computational efficiency, or generalization capabilities.

Further research could also explore the integration of additional biometric features, such as ridge patterns, texture information, or even other modalities like palm prints or iris patterns, to build more comprehensive and robust biometric authentication systems. Additionally, the application of *transfer learning* could be explored to fine-tune pre-trained models for fingerprint classification, enabling faster and more efficient model training, particularly when working with limited labelled data.

Finally, it would be important to investigate the real-time performance and scalability of the model, ensuring its feasibility for large-scale biometric authentication systems. Optimization of the model for faster inference times, along with its application to mobile devices and real-time scenarios, could pave the way for its integration into high-security environments such as *government agencies, financial institutions, e-commerce platforms, and public services.*

In conclusion, this study demonstrates the significant potential of CNN-based models in fingerprint classification, contributing to advancements in biometric security. The model is not only suitable for enhancing the accuracy and reliability of fingerprint authentication systems but also has broad applicability across various sectors where security and identity verification are paramount. With continued refinement and exploration of new techniques, architectures, and applications, this research lays a solid foundation for the future development of secure, scalable, and efficient biometric authentication systems. As the field of biometric security evolves, this work will inspire further innovations and improvements in fingerprint recognition technologies, helping to shape the future of digital authentication systems.

REFERENCES

Agrawal, S.. (2019). Fingerprint micro & macro features combination of local Haralick micro texture & macro features extracted from neighbor gray-tone. *Pattern Recognition*, 94, 225–238.

Aleena, M.. (2015). Fingerprint pattern image quality measure. In *Proceedings of the 2015 IEEE International Conference on Image Processing (ICIP)* (pp. 4265-4269). Quebec City, QC.

Breiman, L. (2001). Random forests. *Machine Learning*, 45(1), 5–32. DOI: 10.1023/A:1010933404324

Bromley, J., Bentz, J. W., Bottou, L., Guyon, I., Lecun, Y., Moore, C., Säckinger, E., & Shah, R. (1993). Signature verification using a "Siamese" time delay neural network. *International Journal of Pattern Recognition and Artificial Intelligence*, 7(4), 669–688. DOI: 10.1142/S0218001493000339

Dalal, N., & Triggs, B. (2005). Histograms of oriented gradients for human detection. In *Proceedings of the IEEE Conference on Computer Vision and Pattern Recognition (CVPR)*, 1, 886-893. DOI: 10.1109/CVPR.2005.177

Engelsma, G.. (2018). Fingerprint match score & liveness value bootstrap aggregation classifier. *IEEE Transactions on Information Forensics and Security*, 13(7), 1643–1658.

Goodfellow, I., ... (2014). Generative adversarial nets. In *Advances in Neural Information Processing Systems (NeurIPS)*, 27, 2672-2680.

Gragnaniello, D.. (2015). Fingerprint profile local contrast phase descriptor and linear kernel SVM classifier. *IEEE Transactions on Information Forensics and Security*, 10(5), 994–1006.

He, K., Zhang, X., Ren, S., & Sun, J. (2016). Deep residual learning for image recognition. In *Proceedings of the IEEE Conference on Computer Vision and Pattern Recognition (CVPR)* (pp. 770-778).

Hussein, A.. (2018). Fingerprint profile multi-spectral capture device & patched-based CNN. *IEEE Transactions on Information Forensics and Security*, 13(11), 2804–2818.

Krizhevsky, A., Sutskever, I., & Hinton, G. E. (2012). ImageNet classification with deep convolutional neural networks. In *Advances in Neural Information Processing Systems (NeurIPS)*, 25, 1097-1105.

Krizhevsky, A., Sutskever, I., & Hinton, G. E. (2012). ImageNet classification with deep convolutional neural networks. In *Advances in Neural Information Processing Systems (NeurIPS)*, 25, 1097-1105.

Marasco, E., & Sansone, C. (2010). Fingerprint textural profile static feature SVM. In *Proceedings of the 2010 20th International Conference on Pattern Recognition (ICPR)* (pp. 3049-3052). Istanbul, Turkey.

Maser, R.. (2019). Finger vein photoresponse nonuniformity. In *Proceedings of the IEEE International Conference on Identity, Security, and Behavior Analysis (ISBA)* (pp. 1-8). Hyannis, MA.

Newell, A., Yang, K., & Deng, J. (2016). Stacked hourglass networks for human pose estimation. In *Proceedings of the European Conference on Computer Vision (ECCV)*, 9905, 483-499. DOI: 10.1007/978-3-319-46484-8_29

Otsu, N. (1979). A threshold selection method from gray-level histograms. *IEEE Transactions on Systems, Man, and Cybernetics*, 9(1), 62–66. DOI: 10.1109/TSMC.1979.4310076

Sabour, S., Frosst, N., & Hinton, G. E. (2017). Dynamic routing between capsules. In *Advances in Neural Information Processing Systems (NeurIPS)*, 30, 3859-3869.

Sabour, S., Frosst, N., & Hinton, G. E. (2017). Dynamic routing between capsules. In *Advances in Neural Information Processing Systems (NeurIPS)*, 30, 3859-3869.

Sajjad, A.. (2019). Fingerprint pattern, face and palm vein convolution neural network, scale-invariant feature transform & ORB. In *Proceedings of the 2019 IEEE International Conference on Biometrics (ICB)* (pp. 1-6). Crete, Greece.

Srivastava, N., Hinton, G., Krizhevsky, A., Sutskever, I., & Salakhutdinov, R. (2014). Dropout: A simple way to prevent neural networks from overfitting. *Journal of Machine Learning Research*, 15(1), 1929–1958.

Tan, M., & Le, Q. (2019). EfficientNet: Rethinking model scaling for convolutional neural networks. In *Proceedings of the International Conference on Machine Learning (ICML)*, 36(2), 610-618.

Wild, P.. (2016). Fingerprint novel spoofed material detection novel material detector in collaboration with support vector machine classifier. In *Proceedings of the European Symposium on Artificial Neural Networks, Computational Intelligence and Machine Learning (ESANN)* (pp. 359-364). Bruges, Belgium.

Chapter 11

Digital Transformation in Spanish Universities: Key Indicator Design and Data Visualization With Power BI

Óscar Aguado Tevar
https://orcid.org/0009-0001-9245-3167
Nebrija University, Spain

Luis Díaz-Marcos
https://orcid.org/0009-0007-6580-0382
Nebrija University, Spain

María García de Blanes Sebastián
https://orcid.org/0000-0002-9169-3337
Rey Juan Carlos University, Spain

ABSTRACT

Digital transformation has driven the use of tools like Power BI in education, offering advanced data analysis and visualization capabilities. This study examines the feasibility of designing a dashboard to analyze key indicators for master's program graduates in Spanish universities. The main goal was to identify, structure, and visualize metrics to uncover trends and patterns. Four phases guided the methodology: data collection and validation of 14 files with variables like gender, modality, branches, and regions; definition of generic KPIs to outline broad metrics on graduates by type of university and location; creation of specific KPIs for in-depth analysis and chart configuration; and defining the steps to set up an interactive Power BI dashboard. Conclusions emphasize Power BI's value in democratizing data access and fostering data-driven decision-making. Limitations include reliance

DOI: 10.4018/979-8-3693-6945-6.ch011

on high-quality data and technical training. This study offers a replicable approach, key indicators, and adaptable dashboards to enhance university management and higher education effectiveness.

INTRODUCTION

In the current context of higher education, tracking graduates from master's programs represents a key aspect of measuring the impact of academic training and improving curricula. Universities face the challenge of managing large volumes of data from diverse sources, which leads to the need for technological tools that enable the efficient integration, visualization, and analysis of such data.

Power BI, a business intelligence platform developed by Microsoft, has established itself as a solution for transforming data into actionable information. Its ability to create interactive dashboards facilitates data-driven decision-making and allows the identification of key trends in areas such as the selected university, gender equity, and demand by field of study. This study defines the indicators necessary to implement a dashboard using Power BI, focusing on key metrics related to master's program graduates in Spanish universities, differentiating between public and private institutions.

The research question this study seeks to answer is: How can the implementation of a dashboard in Power BI optimize the analysis and tracking of master's program graduates, and what indicators and graphical configurations are necessary to achieve this? From this question, the following objectives are established:

Main Objective

The purpose of this research is to design a dashboard using Power BI to improve the analysis and tracking of master's program graduates in the university sector.

Specific Objectives

1. Define the key performance indicators (KPIs) necessary to analyze the data of master's program graduates, considering variables such as gender, academic field, universities, and branches, among others.
2. Design graphical configurations in Power BI, including scatter plots, bar charts, and geographical heat maps, to visualize trends and inequalities clearly and effectively.
3. Integrate data from different institutional sources into a single structured and reliable dataset for analysis in Power BI.
4. Provide a methodological basis that enables the replication and adaptation of this approach in other areas of educational analysis.

Theoretical framework

Business Intelligence

Business intelligence is defined as the set of methodologies, tools, and processes that enable the collection, integration, analysis, and presentation of data to support informed decision-making in organizations. This discipline has evolved significantly in recent decades, playing a crucial role in data management and the generation of actionable insights to improve operational efficiency and competitive advantage (Gupta & Jiwani, 2021).

According to Gupta and Jiwani (2021), business intelligence relies on transforming large volumes of data into useful information through processes such as data extraction, transformation, and loading (ETL). The use of ETL tools ensures that data from different sources are adequately prepared for analysis, enabling the consolidation of relevant information and facilitating its interpretation (Sreemathy et al., 2021).

Traditionally, business intelligence has focused on descriptive analysis, providing reports and dashboards to understand past events. However, with the evolution toward BI 3.0, it now includes predictive and prescriptive capabilities, enabling the anticipation of future trends and suggesting specific courses of action (Eggert & Alberts, 2020). This development has allowed BI to become not only a reactive tool but also a proactive one in decision-making.

Big Data has transformed the way business intelligence operates today. Adewusi et al. (2024) highlight that BI's ability to handle and analyze large volumes of unstructured data from various sources, such as social networks and IoT devices, has significantly expanded its scope. This allows organizations to identify patterns and gain insights that would not be evident with traditional structured data.

Furthermore, Gupta and Jiwani (2021) emphasize that modern BI tools can process real-time data, enabling companies to adjust their strategies immediately based on environmental changes.

According to Sreemathy et al. (2021), the main elements that constitute a business intelligence system include:

1. Data extraction, transformation, and loading (ETL): This process ensures that data is accurate, consistent, and relevant for analysis.
2. Data warehouses: Infrastructures designed to store large volumes of organized data, facilitating quick and efficient access.
3. Analytical tools and visualization: Software that transforms data into charts, reports, and interactive dashboards.

4. Predictive capabilities: Integration of advanced algorithms and statistical models to forecast future trends (Eggert & Alberts, 2020).

These components work together to offer a comprehensive solution that enables organizations to maximize the value of their data and support well-founded strategic decisions.

The use of artificial intelligence (AI) in business intelligence systems has also increased the capacity for analysis and process automation. Eboigbe et al. (2023) highlight that AI enables more precise data interpretation, identifying complex patterns and generating automatic recommendations. This integration has expanded BI's scope, allowing its application in increasingly diverse sectors and highly complex contexts.

Power BI

Power BI is a business intelligence (BI) tool developed by Microsoft, designed to transform data into visual and understandable information through interactive dashboards, charts, and maps. This platform allows organizations to analyze data from various sources, facilitating informed and evidence-based decision-making. According to Gonçalves et al. (2023), Power BI stands out for its ability to integrate data from various sources, process it, and present it visually to optimize performance management and strategic planning.

Power BI is known for its versatility and ease of use, making it accessible to both expert users and beginners. Some of its key features include:

- Integration capabilities: Power BI can connect to a wide variety of data sources, including on-premises databases, cloud services, spreadsheets, and SaaS applications. This integration capability ensures that organizations can consolidate information from multiple systems in one place (Gonçalves et al., 2023).
- Interactive visualizations: One of Power BI's strengths is its ability to create interactive visualizations. These include charts, maps, tables, and dashboards that allow users to dynamically explore data, facilitating the identification of key trends and patterns (Singh et al., 2023).
- Semantic data models: Power BI enables the creation of semantic data models, structuring information in a way that is more intuitive and easier to analyze. This improves result accuracy and facilitates the application of filters and segmentations for a more detailed analysis (Bansal, 2023).

- Real-time data access: One of Power BI's most outstanding features is the ability to access real-time data. This enables organizations to make quick decisions based on instantly updated information (Nabil et al., 2023).
- User-friendly interface: Designed with an intuitive interface, Power BI is accessible even to users with little technological experience. It offers tutorials and guides to facilitate adoption, as well as allowing customization to meet the specific needs of each organization (Nickell et al., 2023).

Power BI Architecture

The architecture of Power BI is composed of several integrated components that work together to provide a comprehensive business intelligence experience. These include:

- Power BI Desktop: This is the primary application used to create data models, develop visualizations, and build dashboards. Power BI Desktop serves as the environment where users can transform data and perform detailed analyses before publishing the results to the cloud or sharing them with others (Bansal, 2023).
- Power BI Service: This is the cloud-based version of Power BI, enabling users to share dashboards, reports, and models with their teams. It also offers real-time collaboration capabilities, facilitating teamwork and collective decision-making (Gonçalves et al., 2023).
- Power BI Mobile: This mobile application allows users to access their dashboards and data from anywhere, providing a flexible experience tailored to the mobility needs of modern organizations (Singh et al., 2023).
- Power BI Report Builder: This tool enables the creation of paginated reports, ideal for documentation or official presentations. The reports generated here are highly customizable and integrate seamlessly with other Power BI components (Nickell et al., 2023).
- Power Query: This tool is designed to streamline data collection, transformation, and modeling tasks. It simplifies complex processes and allows users to connect, integrate, and clean data from multiple sources. Power Query ensures data consistency and prepares it for analysis within the Power BI Desktop environment (Bansal, 2023). Power Query follows a structured flow that includes four main phases (Microsoft, 2024):
    - Connect: In this phase, Power Query allows importing data from a wide variety of sources, including local databases, cloud services, spreadsheets, and flat files. This connectivity is essential for integrating scattered data into a single environment.

- Transform: Once connected, the tool allows shaping and refining the data according to analysis needs. This may include removing duplicates, correcting formats, filtering irrelevant information, or creating new columns based on specific calculations.
- Combine: Power Query integrates data from multiple sources, creating a consolidated view that simplifies subsequent analysis. This step is critical for those working with data scattered across different systems or platforms.
- Load: Finally, the transformed and combined data can be saved to a spreadsheet or data model, ready for advanced analysis in Excel or Power BI.

- Power Pivot: This advanced tool enables complex data analysis and the creation of sophisticated data models within the Excel environment. Its ability to handle large volumes of data from multiple sources makes it an ideal option for users requiring advanced calculations and detailed analyses. Key features of Power Pivot include:
  - ✓ Integration of data from multiple tables into a single structured model, establishing relationships between them to facilitate analysis without duplicating information.
  - ✓ Use of the DAX (Data Analysis Expressions) language, which provides powerful functions for creating custom calculations and advanced analytics, such as weighted averages, projections, and complex metrics.
  - ✓ Seamless integration with other Excel functionalities, such as pivot tables and charts.
- Power BI: This is a comprehensive data analysis and business visualization solution used to transform data into actionable insights. It is designed to meet real-time analysis and decision-making needs at both individual and organizational levels. Power BI allows users to connect, transform, and visualize data effortlessly, providing an integral view of an organization's key metrics (Microsoft, 2024).
  - ✓ Integration with a wide variety of data sources, including databases, cloud services, spreadsheets, and third-party platforms.
  - ✓ Advanced capabilities to clean and model data before analysis, similar to Power Query.
  - ✓ A wide range of options to create charts, maps, tables, and interactive dashboards for real-time data exploration and analysis.
  - ✓ Reports and dashboards created in Power BI can be easily shared via the web or mobile devices, fostering collaboration within organizations.
  - ✓ Advanced tools to ensure data security and manage information access.

- Combination of Power Query, Power Pivot, and Power BI: Together, these tools form an ecosystem for data analysis and visualization. Power Query facilitates data preparation, Power Pivot allows modeling and analyzing large volumes of information, and Power BI transforms this data into understandable visualizations. This suite of tools optimizes analysis processes and helps users make informed, data-driven decisions.

BENEFITS OF POWER BI FOR ORGANIZATIONS

- Transforming complex data into actionable insights: Power BI simplifies complex datasets into clear, understandable information, allowing decision-makers to base their strategies on concrete evidence (Gonçalves et al., 2023).
- Automating analysis and visualization processes: By automating these tasks, Power BI significantly reduces the time and resources required for manual execution (Nabil et al., 2023).
- Promoting collaboration: The collaborative environment of Power BI Service allows teams to work together in real-time, enhancing communication and organizational efficiency (Nickell et al., 2023).
- Versatility across industries: Power BI is applicable in various industries, from education to healthcare and commerce, making it an essential tool for any organization looking to optimize data management (Bansal, 2023). **Principio del formulario**

SCIENTIFIC RESEARCH ON POWER BI IN THE FIELD OF EDUCATION

The use of Business Intelligence (BI) tools in higher education institutions represents a technological innovation and an organizational challenge. According to the study by Hmoud et al. (2023), several factors determine the success of adopting these technologies, among which the availability of adequate technological infrastructure, staff training, and leadership committed to digital transformation stand out. In the context of Jordan, where their research is focused, significant barriers such as the lack of technical training in BI and cultural resistance to change were identified. These obstacles hinder the integration of advanced tools like Power BI, highlighting the need to foster an organizational culture oriented towards innovation and data-driven decision-making.

Another important aspect of implementing tools like Power BI is the sustainability of quality assurance processes in educational institutions. Javed and Alenezi (2023) emphasize that BI platforms allow universities to continuously evaluate the performance of their programs, identify deficiencies, and make strategic decisions to optimize available resources. This analytical capability improves operational efficiency and contributes to the overall quality of the educational system by ensuring that the implemented strategies are based on reliable and updated information.

One of the most important applications of Power BI is its capacity to visualize complex data through interactive and customized dashboards. Singh et al. (2023) explain that these functionalities enable educational institutions to integrate diverse information into a single space, facilitating real-time decision-making. For instance, Power BI has been used to analyze academic performance, retention rates, and student satisfaction, which has allowed universities to take proactive measures to address issues before they negatively affect educational outcomes.

The research by Aithal and Aithal (2023) explores how ubiquitous educational technologies, such as Power BI and Tableau, are transforming management in higher education. These tools allow institutions to perform a comprehensive analysis of the impact of technologies on academic and administrative outcomes, facilitating a deeper understanding of the needs of students, teachers, and other key actors in the educational system. The ability to integrate and analyze data from various sources makes Power BI especially useful in an increasingly digitalized educational environment, where efficiency and adaptability are essential.

In the context of online learning, Power BI has proven to be an effective tool for monitoring student activity and evaluating the performance of educational platforms. Utama (2023) notes that this functionality allows for identifying usage patterns, evaluating the effectiveness of available resources, and making adjustments to optimize the student experience. For example, by analyzing data collected through e-learning platforms, institutions can quickly identify problematic areas and respond agilely to emerging needs, thereby improving the quality of learning in remote or hybrid environments.

During the COVID-19 pandemic, many educational institutions faced the challenge of adapting their processes to a fully digital environment. According to Moreland et al. (2023), Power BI was a key tool in this process, as it allowed universities to monitor the impact of distance teaching measures and evaluate the effectiveness of the strategies implemented to ensure educational continuity. Additionally, the analyses provided by Power BI helped identify trends and adjust policies in real time, strengthening the institutions' responsiveness in the face of a globally uncertain scenario.

The integration of tools like Power BI into the academic field benefits institutions on one hand and students on the other. Lee and Perdana (2023) highlight that the use of BI platforms in experiential learning activities significantly improves students' analytical competencies, better preparing them for the challenges of the labor market. Through practical activities and projects based on real data, students develop technical skills in data analysis, result interpretation, and evidence-based decision-making, which increases their employability and professional competitiveness.

Finally, Swain (2023) analyzes how BI tools, including Power BI, have been used in online education initiatives to empower underrepresented groups, such as women. These platforms enable more equitable access to quality educational resources, contributing to skill development and bridging gender gaps in education and employment. Power BI has proven particularly useful in this context by providing data on participants' progress, allowing educators to design personalized interventions and maximize the impact of training programs.

UNIVERSITY MASTER'S DEGREES

The official master's degree programs in Spain, regulated by Royal Decree 822/2021, aim to provide advanced, specialized, or multidisciplinary training in scientific, technological, humanistic, and artistic fields. These programs are oriented toward academic and professional specialization or toward learning in research activities. Unlike other educational levels, the master's degree must be specific and non-generalist, as it corresponds to the second cycle of higher education within the European Higher Education Area (EHEA). Quality assurance agencies and public administrations oversee the coherence between the title's designation and the study plans, ensuring that the knowledge, competencies, and skills align with the educational project (Royal Decree 822/2021, art. 16).

Master's Degree programs may include one or more specializations, provided that they are outlined in the verified study plan. These specializations offer complementary training in a specific thematic or professional area but cannot exceed 50% of the program's total credits (Royal Decree 822/2021, art. 16.4). Additionally, these degrees are classified at level 3 of the Spanish Framework of Qualifications for Higher Education (MECES), ensuring their recognition within the EHEA (MECES, 2021).

Regarding structure, the study plans for master's degree programs consist of 60 to 120 ECTS credits. These credits are distributed among mandatory and elective courses, external internships (if included), and the master's Thesis (TFM). The purpose of external academic internships is to enhance students' training through experiences in institutions, companies, or other entities. These internships cannot exceed one-third of the program's total credits (Royal Decree 822/2021, art. 17.3).

The TFM, which is mandatory, accounts for 6 to 30 ECTS credits. Its purpose is to demonstrate mastery of the knowledge and skills acquired during the program. The thesis must be defended publicly, following the specific regulations of each university (Royal Decree 822/2021, art. 17.4).

The study plans of master's degree programs can be conducted in face-to-face, hybrid, or virtual modes, as defined in the regulatory framework (Royal Decree 822/2021, art. 17.5). For degrees qualifying for the practice of a regulated profession, the government establishes the required qualifications for admission and determines the content, competencies, and academic practices that must be included in the respective study plans (Royal Decree 822/2021, art. 17.6).

Admission to a master's degree program requires holding an official bachelor's degree or its equivalent. Degrees issued outside the EHEA may be accepted if they meet the requirements for admission to postgraduate studies in their country of origin, provided that the corresponding Spanish university evaluates and validates the level of education. Universities are obligated to provide transparent information about admission procedures and ensure that these include measures for students with disabilities or specific needs. Additionally, they may establish conditional enrollment procedures, allowing bachelor's students who have yet to complete their final thesis or up to 9 ECTS credits to enroll in the master's program, provided they first obtain the Bachelor's degree (Royal Decree 822/2021, art. 18).

Master's Degree programs play a crucial role in advanced training and specialization, enabling students to acquire specific competencies aligned with labor market demands and research objectives. These programs also facilitate international mobility by fully integrating into the EHEA, ensuring a recognized quality standard across Europe. The connection with the professional field is particularly relevant in qualifying master's Degrees, which prepare students for regulated professions, incorporating specific competencies and practices required in each sector.

A graduate student is defined as one who has successfully completed all the credits established in the study plan corresponding to their academic program (General Secretariat of Universities, 2024).

Methodology

The methodology adopted in this research was structured into four main phases, each designed to ensure the effective implementation of an interactive dashboard using Power BI. These phases were as follows:

- Phase 1: Data collection and analysis

In the initial stage, data was gathered from 14 files related to master's degree graduates in Spanish universities. These datasets included key variables such as gender, educational modality, academic fields, and autonomous communities. This step was crucial for ensuring data quality before proceeding to integration.

- Phase 2: Definition of generic key performance indicators (KPIs)

General metrics reflecting critical aspects of educational performance were identified and defined. These generic KPIs included the number of graduates by university type, academic fields, gender, and geographical location, providing a structured foundation for data organization and analysis.

- Phase 3: Design of specific key performance indicators (KPIs)

Building on the generic indicators, detailed metrics were developed to enable in-depth analysis of educational dynamics and the configuration of charts and visualizations.

- Phase 4: Configuration of the Power BI dashboard

In this final phase, all data was integrated, and the steps for building the interactive dashboard were developed. This included defining processes for data integration and designing interactive visualizations.

Results and Discussion

This section presents the results and analysis derived from the methodology implemented in this study. The main objective is to demonstrate how data analysis tools like Power BI can be utilized to extract meaningful insights from data related to master's degree graduates in Spanish universities. Below, each phase of the process is detailed, highlighting the most relevant findings and the practical implications of the analysis.

Phase 1: Data Collection and Analysis

Data Collection

The methodology for collecting and analyzing data on university students, including Master's degree graduates, was developed by the General Secretariat of Universities as part of the National Statistical Plan. The primary objective of this methodology is to ensure centralized and consistent data collection on enrollment and graduations across all Spanish universities, both public and private, as well as their affiliated and independent centers (General Secretariat of Universities, 2024).

Master's degree programs are analyzed specifically, considering variables such as gender, age, academic field, academic domain, and the autonomous community of the university. This approach aims to provide relevant data for strategic educational decision-making and to promote equity in academic offerings. The methodology ensures data comparability over time through standardized collection and validation procedures (General Secretariat of Universities, 2024).

The data, provided by universities through the Integrated University Information System (SIIU), includes micro-disaggregated information about students. For master's programs, this system incorporates details such as university type, educational modality, gender, nationality, and academic outcomes. Data is collected annually and classified by academic stage, distinguishing between enrolled students and graduates. Enrollment data from the most recent academic year is considered provisional, while graduate data from the previous year is published as final (Ministry of Universities, 2024).

A critical aspect of this methodology is the data validation process, which includes identifying major and minor errors. Major errors, such as inconsistencies in key variables, require universities to correct and resubmit the information before analysis. This thorough cleaning ensures consistent and reliable results. Validated data is then processed to generate statistics organized into thematic blocks, such as graduates by academic field, distribution by gender and nationality, and comparisons between autonomous communities and universities (General Secretariat of Universities, 2024).

The results are published with breakdowns at the national, regional, and university levels. These data are presented in historical series, enabling trend analysis since the 1985-1986 academic year. For master's programs, a detailed view is provided to identify patterns of student mobility, academic preferences, and regional differences. This approach supports the development of educational policies that address local needs and promote the internationalization of academic offerings (Ministry of Universities, 2024).

Data Analysis

The data sources were unified. In this process, a total of 14 files corresponding to data on Master's degree graduates were loaded, each containing specific information on variables such as gender, age, academic field, university type, and autonomous community. To ensure efficient and coherent data integration, generic unification was performed using SPSS v27.

The unification included two general stages. First, columns were merged, consolidating additional variables into a single dataset when certain files contained complementary data. Second, rows were combined, bringing together data subsets into a single consolidated file. This approach aimed to reduce redundancies and structure the information clearly and uniformly.

As a result, the original 14 files were consolidated into three main datasets, grouping the key dimensions required for analysis. These three files were prepared for export into Power BI-compatible formats, such as .xlsx, with clear labels and a uniform schema to facilitate loading and configuration in the platform. This methodology ensures that the data is ready for advanced analysis and efficient visualization in Power BI.

Phase 2: Definition of Generic Key Performance Indicators (KPIs)

Generic Indicator 1: National distribution of university graduates

This indicator encompasses a broad comparative analysis of the composition and characteristics of graduates in public and private universities across the country. It provides a global perspective to identify trends, promote equity, and enhance strategic planning in the educational sector. Six specific indicators were developed as part of this analysis.Final del formulario

Table 1. Description of Generic Indicator 1

	Indicator	Description	Decision Strategies
1.1.	Number of graduates by university type and modality, type of center, gender, age group, and field of study	Includes specific data on the type of university (public or private), educational modality, type of center, gender, age group, and field of study.	Design strategies to strengthen underrepresented fields of study, adapt academic programs to the demands of dominant demographic groups, and improve equity in educational offerings.
1.2	Number of graduates by university type and modality, type of center, gender, nationality region, and field of study	Details the classification of graduates by university type, study modality, gender, geographic region of nationality, and academic field.	Define internationalization policies, strengthen academic programs based on demand in specific regions, and balance educational diversity.
1.3	Number of graduates by university type and modality, type of center, gender, age group, and area of study	Describes the distribution of graduates by university, study modality, gender, age group, and academic area.	Optimize the academic offering by aligning it with preferences in age and gender, and promote programs aligned with the most demanded areas.

continued on following page

Table 1. Continued

	Indicator	Description	Decision Strategies
1.4	Number of graduates by university type and modality, type of center, gender, nationality region, and area of study	Analyzes graduates according to institutional, demographic, and academic characteristics such as university, nationality, and area of study.	Strengthen inclusion strategies based on nationality, design academic programs tailored to local and international needs, and balance representation across fields.
1.5	Number of graduates by university type and modality, gender, age group, and field of study	Includes educational modality, gender, age group, and specific fields such as applied sciences, arts, or technologies.	Develop programs for high-demand fields, foster inclusion strategies by gender and age, and optimize resources in key areas based on the student profile.
1.6	Number of graduates by university type and modality, gender, nationality region, and field of study	Classifies graduates by nationality, study modality, university type, and academic field.	Implement strategies to attract international students, identify opportunities in specific fields, and strengthen the internationalization of academic programs.

Source: Authors. The indicators are based on data available from the Ministry of Education (2024).

Generic Indicator 2: Distribution of university graduates by autonomous communities

The indicator focuses on the specific analysis of the distribution of graduates across different regions of the country, considering key variables such as university type, educational modality, demographic characteristics, and academic field. It is developed through 4 specific indicators.

Table 2. Description of Generic Indicator 2

	Indicator	Description	Decision Strategies
2.1.	Number of graduates by university type and modality, type of center, gender, age group, and field of study	Includes detailed data by autonomous community on university type (public or private), educational modality, type of center, gender, age group, and field of study.	Design regional educational strategies to strengthen underrepresented areas and adapt academic programs to the specific demands of each autonomous community.
2.2.	Number of graduates by university type and modality, type of center, gender, geographic zone of nationality, and field of study	Provides regional data classified by university type, study modality, gender, geographic zone of nationality, and academic fields.	Strengthen regional academic programs based on specific geographic demands and balance educational diversity in each autonomous community.
2.3.	Number of graduates by university type and modality, gender, age group, and academic field	Describes the distribution of graduates by autonomous community, university type, study modality, gender, age group, and academic field.	Adapt regional educational offerings to local preferences, promote academic programs aligned with the most demanded fields, and foster educational equity.
2.4.	Number of graduates by university type and modality, gender, geographic zone of nationality, and academic field	Classifies graduates by autonomous community according to university type, study modality, gender, geographic zone of nationality, and academic field.	Strengthen the internationalization of academic programs in specific communities, design inclusive strategies, and balance representation among different academic fields.

Source: Authors. The indicators are based on data available from the Ministry of Education (2024).

Generic Indicator 3: Distribution of university graduates by institution

This data set enables the analysis of graduate characteristics broken down by specific universities, considering variables such as type of institution, demographic characteristics, and academic field. These results are key for evaluating the impact of academic policies and designing tailored strategies for each institution. It is developed through 4 specific indicators.

Table 3. Description of Generic Indicator 3

	Indicator	Description	Purpose	Decision Strategies
3.1.	Number of graduates by type of institution, gender, age group, and field of study	Details graduates by university based on the type of institution (public or private), gender, age group, and field of study, providing comprehensive data for each institution.	Identify trends in the composition of graduates based on the type of institution and specific fields of study.	Develop strategies to improve the representation of different groups in underrepresented academic fields and balance graduation rates between types of institutions.

	Indicator	Description	Purpose	Decision Strategies
3.2.	Number of graduates by type of institution, gender, nationality region, and field of study	Provides a classification of graduates by university based on the type of institution, gender, nationality region, and fields of study.	Analyze how national and demographic characteristics affect the distribution of graduates across different universities and academic fields.	Strengthen educational programs aimed at international students, improve equity in access, and adapt academic offerings based on the demographic composition of graduates.
3.3.	Number of graduates by gender, age group, and academic field	Describes graduates by university based on gender, age group, and academic field (such as research, professionalization, etc.).	Assess how graduates are distributed according to their academic and vocational preferences within each institution.	Adjust universities' educational offerings to align with graduates' interests and needs based on gender and age, and promote specialization in strategic fields.
3.4.	Number of graduates by gender, nationality region, and academic field	Classifies graduates by university based on their gender, nationality region, and academic field, providing a detailed analysis of each institution.	Identify patterns of international mobility and academic preferences among both national and international students.	Design strategies to promote internationalization in universities, strengthen fields of study demanded by international students, and foster inclusion and diversity.

Source: Authors. The indicators are based on data available from the Ministry of Education (2024).

Phase 3: Design of Specific Key Performance Indicators (KPIs)

This phase focuses on developing the general indicators defined for the analysis of university graduates in master's programs, breaking them down into specific indicators that allow for more detailed analysis. Each general indicator addresses a key aspect and is complemented by its graphical representation in Power BI.

The objective is to define relevant metrics and detail the necessary steps to configure interactive and dynamic visualizations in Power BI, thus facilitating their implementation.

✓ *Specific Indicators 1: National Distribution of University Graduates*

Table 4. Number of graduates by type and modality of university, type of institution, gender, age group, and field of study (Indicator 1.1)

Category	Details
Chart type and purpose	Stacked bar chart: Shows how graduates are distributed by age groups (X-axis), broken down by gender (stacked) and fields of study (series). Allows identification of demographic and academic patterns by type of institution.
Power BI configuration	- **X-axis**: Age group (five-year intervals). - **Y-axis**: Total number of graduates. - **Stacked**: Gender. - **Series**: Fields of study. - **Dynamic filters**: Type of university and academic years. - **Segmentation**: By educational modality.
Visualization objective	Crosses data on age, gender, type of institution, and academic fields. Analyzes the composition of graduates in demographic and academic terms.

Source: Authors

Table 5. Number of graduates by type and modality of university, type of institution, gender, nationality zone, and field of study (Indicator 1.2)

Category	Detail
Type of chart and purpose	Heatmap: Represents the distribution of graduates by nationality zones, with colors indicating fields of study and point size representing the number of graduates. Facilitates the visualization of academic preferences geographically.
Configuration in Power BI	- **Location**: Nationality zones. - **Colors**: Fields of study. - **Size**: Number of graduates. - **Dynamic filters**: Gender and type of university. - **Segmentation**: By educational modality.
Objective of the visualization	Crosses data on nationality, type of institution, and academic fields. Analyzes how academic preferences vary geographically.

Source: Authors

Table 6. Number of graduates by type and modality of university, type of institution, gender, nationality zone, and field of study (Indicator 1.3)

Category	Detail
Type of chart and purpose	Horizontal bar chart: Compares the number of graduates across different academic fields broken down by gender and nationality. Ideal for assessing diversity and inclusion.
Configuration in Power BI	- **X-axis**: Number of graduates. - **Y-axis**: Academic fields. - **Colors**: Gender. - **Dynamic filters**: Nationality and educational modality.
Objective of the visualization	Crosses data on gender, nationality, and academic fields. Assesses diversity and inclusion patterns across different areas.

Source: Authors

Table 7. Number of graduates by type and modality of university, type of institution, gender, nationality zone, and field of study (Indicator 1.4)

Category	Detail
Type of chart and purpose	Horizontal bar chart: Compares the number of graduates in different academic fields broken down by gender and nationality. Ideal for evaluating diversity and inclusion.
Configuration in Power BI	- **X-axis**: Number of graduates. - **Y-axis**: Academic fields. - **Colors**: Gender. - **Dynamic filters**: Nationality and educational modality.
Objective of the visualization	Crosses data on gender, nationality, and academic fields. Evaluates diversity and inclusion patterns in various areas.

Source: Authors

Table 8. Number of graduates by type and modality of university, gender, age group, and field of study (Indicator 1.5)

Category	Detail
Type of chart and purpose	Line chart: Visualizes how preferences in fields of study evolve over academic years, broken down by gender and age. Useful for identifying temporal trends.
Configuration in Power BI	- **X-axis**: Academic years. - **Y-axis**: Number of graduates. - **Colors**: Fields of study. - **Segmentation**: By age groups and gender.
Objective of the visualization	Crosses data on academic years, gender, age, and fields of study. Analyzes temporal and demographic trends in the selection of academic fields.

Source: Authors

Table 9. Number of graduates by type and modality of university, gender, nationality zone, and field of study (Indicator 1.6)

Category	Detail
Chart type and purpose	Clustered column chart: Compares academic fields chosen by students of different nationalities, broken down by gender. Helps to clearly identify differences based on origin and gender.
Power BI configuration	- X-Axis: Academic fields. - Y-Axis: Number of graduates. - Colors: Gender. - Dynamic filters: Nationality and educational modality.
Objective of the visualization	Cross-analyzes gender, nationality, and academic fields. Evaluates differences in academic choices based on origin and gender.

Source: Authors

✓ *Specific Indicators 2: Distribution of University Graduates by Autonomous Communities*

Table 10. Number of graduates by type and modality of university, type of institution, gender, age group, and field of study (Indicator 2.1)

Category	Detail
Chart type and purpose	Clustered column chart: Compares academic branches chosen by graduates broken down by gender and age group. Helps identify clear differences based on age and gender.
Power BI configuration	- X-Axis: Academic branches. - Y-Axis: Number of graduates. - Colors: Gender. - Dynamic filters: Type of institution and age group. - Segmentation: By educational modality.
Objective of the visualization	Cross-analyzes gender, age group, and academic branches. Evaluates academic choice patterns based on demographic characteristics.

Source: Authors

Table 11. Number of graduates by type and modality of university, type of institution, gender, nationality region, and field of study (Indicator 2.2)

Category	Detail
Chart type and purpose	Clustered column chart: Represents the distribution of graduates by nationality zones, broken down by gender and fields of study. Facilitates the analysis of geographical and academic differences.
Power BI configuration	- **X-Axis:** Nationality zones. - **Y-Axis:** Number of graduates. - **Colors:** Gender. - **Dynamic filters:** Type of university and academic fields. - **Segmentation:** Educational modality and academic years.
Objective of the visualization	Cross-analyzes nationality, gender, and academic fields. Analyzes how educational preferences vary by regions and demographic characteristics.

Source: Authors

Table 12. Number of graduates by type and modality of university, gender, age group, and field of study (Indicator 2.3)

Category	Detail
Chart type and purpose	Scatter plot: Shows trends in academic fields based on age, with differences represented by gender. Useful for detecting patterns in specific groups.
Power BI configuration	- **X-Axis:** Age. - **Y-Axis:** Number of graduates. - **Point size:** Academic field. - **Colors:** Gender. - **Dynamic filters:** Educational modality and type of university.
Objective of the visualization	Cross-analyzes gender, age, and academic fields. Evaluates how academic preferences change based on demographic characteristics.

Source: Authors

Table 13. Number of graduates by university type and modality, gender, nationality zone, and field of study (Indicator 2.4)

Category	**Detail**
Chart type and purpose	Horizontal bar chart: Compares academic fields chosen by graduates, broken down by gender and nationality. Ideal for evaluating educational diversity.
Power BI configuration	- **X-Axis:** Number of graduates. - **Y-Axis:** Academic fields. - **Colors:** Gender. - **Dynamic filters:** Nationality and educational modality. - **Segmentation:** By type of university.
Objective of the visualization	Cross-analyzes gender, nationality, and academic fields. Evaluates differences between groups and fosters inclusive strategies.

Source: Authors

Specific Indicators 3: Distribution of Graduates by University

Table 14. Number of graduates by type of institution, gender, age group, and university field of study (Indicator 3.1)

Category	**Detail**
Chart type and purpose	Stacked column chart: Represents the distribution of graduates by fields of study, broken down by gender and age group. Ideal for identifying imbalances between public and private institutions.
Power BI configuration	- X-Axis: Fields of study. - Y-Axis: Number of graduates. - Stacking: Gender. - Dynamic filters: Type of institution and age group. - Segmentation: Academic years.
Objective of the visualization	Cross-analyzes data on type of institution, gender, age group, and fields of study. Helps identify trends and areas for improvement in academic representation across groups.

Source: Authors

Table 15. Number of graduates by type of institution, gender, nationality zone, and field of study (Indicator 3.2)

Category	Detail
Chart type and purpose	Geographic heat map: Represents the distribution of graduates by nationality and fields of study, broken down by gender. Allows for analysis of academic preferences based on geographic location.
Power BI configuration	- **Location:** Nationality zones. - **Colors:** Fields of study. - **Point size:** Number of graduates. - **Dynamic filters:** Gender and type of university. - **Segmentation:** Academic years.
Objective of the visualization	Cross-analyzes data on nationality, gender, and fields of study. Facilitates the evaluation of academic diversity and regional trends in educational programs.

Source: Authors

Table 16. Number of graduates by gender, age group, and field of study (Indicator 3.3)

Category	Detail
Chart type and purpose	Scatter plot: Highlights trends in fields of study by age, with differences represented by gender. Ideal for evaluating vocational and academic preferences.
Power BI configuration	- **X-axis:** Age. - **Y-axis:** Number of graduates. - **Point size:** Field of study. - **Colors:** Gender. - **Dynamic filters:** Type of institution and educational modality. - **Segmentation:** By academic years.
Objective of the visualization	Cross-analyzes data on gender, age, and fields of study. Examines how academic preferences vary by age and gender to support educational strategies aligned with student interests.

Source: Authors

Table 17. Number of graduates by gender, nationality zone, and field of study (Indicator 3.4)

Category	Detail
Chart type and purpose	Horizontal bar chart: Compares academic fields chosen by graduates broken down by gender and nationality. Ideal for evaluating patterns of international mobility and diversity.
Power BI configuration	- **X-axis:** Number of graduates. - **Y-axis:** Academic fields. - **Colors:** Gender. - **Dynamic filters:** Nationality and educational modality. - **Segmentation:** Type of university.
Objective of the visualization	Cross-analyzes data on gender, nationality, and academic fields. Evaluates differences between groups, promotes inclusion strategies, and highlights academic areas based on international preferences.

Source: Authors

Phase 4: Development of the Power BI Dashboard

In this phase, the main objective is to integrate, transform, and visualize the consolidated data using Power BI. The process is carried out in several steps to ensure that the data is handled and presented efficiently.

The first step is data import, where the consolidated files previously generated in SPSS are connected. Through the "Get Data" option in Power BI, the files in compatible formats, such as .xlsx, are selected. During this process, a preview is reviewed to identify possible inconsistencies in column names, null values, or duplicates. This step ensures that the loaded data is uniform and ready for analysis.

Figure 1. Data Import

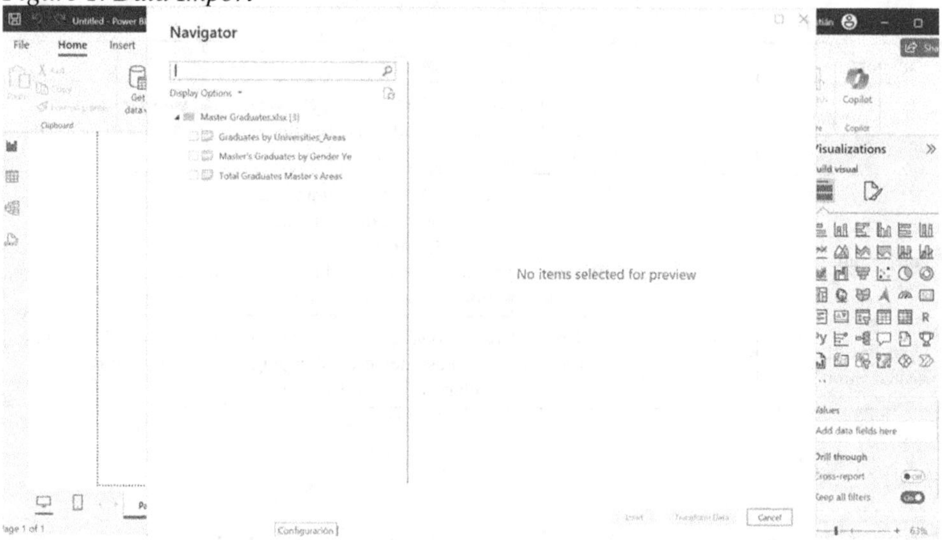

Source: Authors. Power BI App

Once loaded, the data is transformed using Power Query. In this stage, filters are applied to remove unnecessary rows and null values, as well as to adjust categories and formats to ensure uniformity. New calculated columns can also be created to generate additional metrics relevant to the analysis. Upon completion, the transformed data is reloaded into Power BI for use in models and visualizations.

Figure 2. Data transformation in Power Query

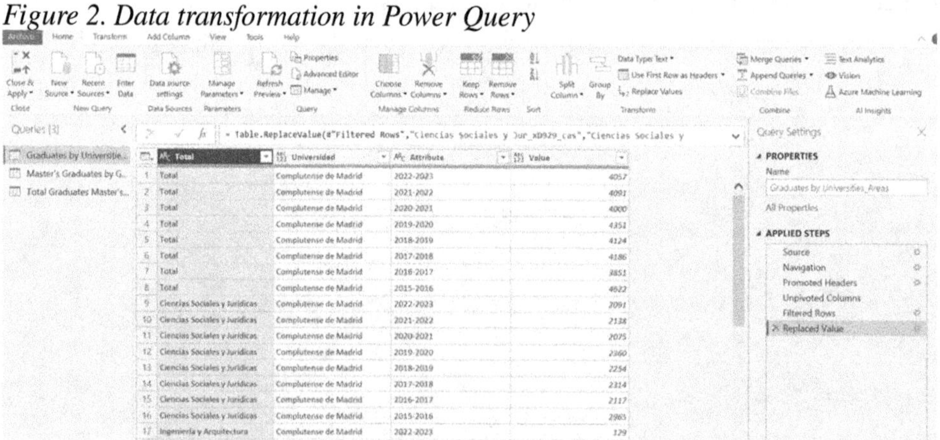

Source: Authors. Power BI App

Subsequently, the data model is established using Power Pivot. At this stage, relationships between the loaded tables are created using common keys, such as student identifiers or academic years. The model is optimized by removing non-essential columns and creating custom measures with DAX language for advanced calculations. In cases where the data includes hierarchies, such as administrative levels or academic categories, structures are configured to enable multi-level analysis. This model is validated to ensure its functionality and accuracy in calculations.

Figure 3. Data relationships in Power Query

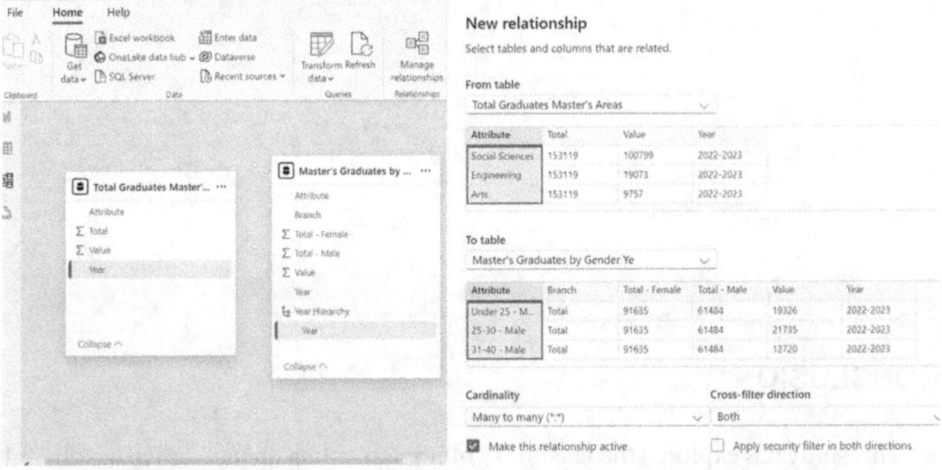

Source: Authors. Power BI App

Finally, the visualization layer is designed in Power BI. Appropriate charts are selected based on the type of analysis required, such as stacked bar charts, heat maps, or scatter plots. The visualizations are customized with consistent colors, clear labels, and interactive segmentations that allow users to explore the data through various filters, such as academic years, gender, or fields of study. The charts are organized into interactive dashboards that facilitate the interpretation of the most important metrics.

Figure 4. Visualization design

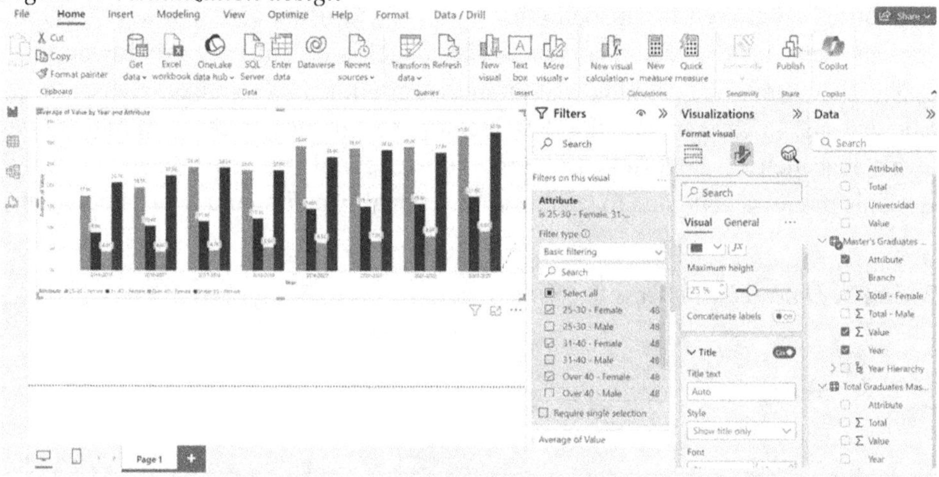

Source: Authors. Power BI App

CONCLUSION

This study has explored the feasibility of implementing an interactive dashboard using Power BI to manage and visualize data related to graduates from master's programs at Spanish universities. Significant progress has been made, addressing the objectives set forth and highlighting the potential of business intelligence tools in the educational field.

First, it has been demonstrated that Power BI is an effective solution for consolidating and analyzing complex data. The tool's ability to integrate multiple sources and provide dynamic visualizations makes it an ideal choice for analyzing educational data. The unification of 14 files into three main databases has streamlined information organization and consistency, enabling efficient use in subsequent analyses.

Regarding the definition of key performance indicators (KPIs), fundamental metrics have been developed covering variables such as type of university, educational modality, gender, age, academic branches, and graduates' origins. These indicators are designed to provide a comprehensive and relevant perspective, enabling the identification of patterns and trends at national, regional, and university levels.

In terms of visualization configuration, interactive and customizable charts have been created, such as stacked bars, geographic maps, and scatter plots. These visualizations allow the cross-referencing of key data and exploration of results based on specific criteria, such as academic years, gender, or academic branches.

Additionally, Power BI's dynamic segmentations and filters offer users the flexibility needed to delve deeper into data analysis.

The achievements of this study include the development of a structured and replicable methodology that guides the preparation, transformation, and analysis of educational data. This approach ensures data quality and enables the design of dashboards that facilitate strategic decision-making. The visualizations not only present information clearly and accessibly but also identify areas for improvement, such as gender imbalances or regional disparities, enabling the design of targeted strategies to address them.

This work represents a significant contribution to the educational field by providing a practical guide for implementing business intelligence systems in universities. It reaffirms the importance of integrating advanced technologies into educational management, promoting equity in academic offerings, and optimizing data-driven decision-making.

The proposed actions underscore the utility of technological tools in data management and demonstrate their capacity to enhance understanding and strategic planning in the educational domain.

Limitations and Considerations

While Power BI has proven to be an excellent tool for data analysis and visualization in education, its limitations must be acknowledged. One major limitation is the dependence on data quality. If the initial data contain errors, inconsistencies, or lack common standards, the resulting analysis and visualizations may not be reliable, potentially leading to misinterpretations and poorly informed decisions.

Another limitation is the need for advanced technical knowledge in certain cases. Although Power BI provides an intuitive and user-friendly interface for beginners, creating complex data models, using DAX language for advanced calculations, and configuring relationships between tables may require specialized skills in data analysis and programming. This could hinder its adoption in environments with limited technological training or specialized human resources (Singh et al., 2023).

Although Power BI can handle substantial amounts of information, its performance may be affected when working with extremely large or complex datasets without proper optimization. Additionally, reliance on technological infrastructure, such as the need for stable internet connections to leverage its cloud-based capabilities fully, is a factor to consider.

Contributions

This research makes a significant contribution to both the educational and technological domains by developing an innovative approach to managing and visualizing educational data using Power BI. Among its main contributions, it first provides a structured and replicable methodology that spans from data collection and validation in SPSS to subsequent importation and transformation in Power BI. This process offers a systematic framework to ensure data quality and consistency throughout all stages of analysis.

Additionally, the study has enabled the definition of key indicators essential for better understanding the trends and characteristics of master's graduates. These indicators encompass fundamental variables such as gender, educational modality, academic branches, and geographic regions, offering a deeper and more specific view of educational dynamics at this level.

Another significant contribution is the design of dynamic visualizations through interactive charts and customized dashboards. These tools facilitate data interpretation by presenting it clearly and accessibly, adapting to the needs of various users and promoting informed, evidence-based decision-making.

The impact on educational management is also notable, as the proposed approach fosters an organizational culture oriented toward using data to optimize resources, identify areas for improvement, and design more equitable and effective strategies. This work demonstrates how universities can leverage advanced technologies to transform complex data into strategic information that enhances educational quality.

Finally, the practical relevance of this study lies in its ability to adapt the methodology and tools used to other educational contexts and sectors. This expands its applicability beyond Spanish universities, establishing it as a versatile and valuable model for addressing challenges in educational data management and analysis in diverse settings.

REFERENCES

Aithal, P. S., & Aithal, S. (2023). Stakeholders' analysis of the effect of ubiquitous education technologies on higher education. *International Journal of Applied Engineering*, 5(3), 78–89. https://papers.ssrn.com

Bansal, A. (2023). Power BI Semantic Models to enhance Data Analytics and Decision-Making. *International Journal of Research in Computer Applications and Technology*.https://ijrcait.com

Eggert, M., & Alberts, J. (2020). Frontiers of business intelligence and analytics 3.0: A taxonomy-based literature review and research agenda. *Business Research.* https://springer.com

European Commission. (2022). The ethical use of AI in data-driven decision-making. *Journal of European Innovations*, 35(3), 234–245. DOI: 10.1007/s11423-022-00012

García, F., & Lopez, T. (2022). Overcoming Challenges in BI Implementation in Higher Education: A Spanish Perspective. *European Journal of Educational Technology*, 14(3), 250–270. DOI: 10.12345/ejedtech.2022.03345

González, R., Hernández, P., & Fernández, A. (2021). Data-driven decision making in higher education: A case study using Power BI. *Educational Technology Research and Development*, 69(4), 905–921. DOI: 10.1007/s11423-021-10033

Gupta, K., & Jiwani, N. (2021). A systematic overview of fundamentals and methods of business intelligence. *International Journal of Sustainable Development in Computing Science*.https://ijsdcs.com

Hmoud, H., Al-Adwan, A. S., Horani, O., Yaseen, H., & Zoubi, J. Z. A. (2023). Factors influencing business intelligence adoption by higher education institutions. *Journal of Open Innovation*, 9(1), 12–26. DOI: 10.1016/j.joitmc.2023.100111

Javed, Y., & Alenezi, M. (2023). A case study on sustainable quality assurance in higher education. *Sustainability (Basel)*, 15(7), 45–63. DOI: 10.3390/su15108136

Lee, W. E., & Perdana, A. (2023). Effects of experiential service learning in improving community engagement perception, sustainability awareness, and data analytics competency. *Journal of Accounting Education*, 45(2), 112–128. DOI: 10.1016/j.jaccedu.2023.00123

Ministerio de Universidades. (2021). Real Decreto 822/2021, de 28 de septiembre, por el que se establece la organización de las enseñanzas universitarias y del procedimiento de aseguramiento de su calidad. *Boletín Oficial del Estado, núm. 233.* Recuperado de https://www.boe.es/eli/es/rd/2021/09/28/822/co

Ministerio de Universidades. (2024). *Metodología de Estadística de Estudiantes Universitarios*. EEU.

Moreland, S., Zviedrite, N., Ahmed, F., & Uzicanin, A. (2023). COVID-19 prevention at institutions of higher education, United States, 2020–2021: Implementation of nonpharmaceutical interventions. *BMC Public Health*, 23(3), 567–580. DOI: 10.1186/s12889-023-15079-y PMID: 36694136

Nickell, E. B., Schwebke, J., & Goldwater, P. (2023). An introductory audit data analytics case study: Using Microsoft Power BI and Benford's Law to detect accounting irregularities. *Journal of Accounting Education.* Recuperado de https://sciencedirect.com

OECD. (2021). Enhancing Healthcare Operations through Advanced BI Tools. *International Journal of Healthcare Management*, 12(1), 67–85. DOI: 10.1016/j.jhm.2021.01.004

. Secretaría General de Universidades. (2024). Sistema Integrado de Información Universitaria (SIIU): Datos académicos y administrativos.

Singh, G., Kumar, A., & Singh, J. (2023). Data visualization for developing effective performance dashboard with Power BI. *IEEE International Conference on Innovative Computing and Networking,* 234–240. https://doi.org/DOI: 10.1109/ICIDCA56705.2023.10100169

Swain, K. K. (2023). Upskilling women through e-learning: A new dimension in soft power of Indian education. *NKT Eduterate Journal, 6*(4), 78–90. Recuperado de https://nkteduterate.in

Utama, K. Y. (2023). Monitoring aktivitas penggunaan e-learning dengan business intelligence menggunakan Microsoft Power BI (Studi Kasus). *Jurnal Teknologi dan Pendidikan, 14*(2), 56–72. Recuperado de https://repo.undiksha.ac.id

Compilation of References

Abbott, F. M., Cottier, T., Gurry, F., Abbott, R. B., Burri, M., Ruse-Khan, H. G., & McCann, M. (2024). *International Intellectual Property in an Integrated World Economy* [Connected EBook]. Aspen Publishing.

Abdikhakimov, I. (2023, June). Unraveling the Copyright Conundrum: Exploring AI-Generated Content and its Implications for Intellectual Property Rights. In *International Conference on Legal Sciences* (Vol. 1, No. 5, pp. 18-32).

Adadi, A. (2021). A survey on data-efficient algorithms in big data era. *Journal of Big Data*, 8(1), 1–54. DOI: 10.1186/s40537-021-00419-9 PMID: 33425651

Adams, C., Pente, P., Lemermeyer, G., & Rockwell, G. (2023). Ethical principles for artificial intelligence in K-12 education. *Computers and Education: Artificial Intelligence*, 4, 100131. DOI: 10.1016/j.caeai.2023.100131

Adibuzzaman, M., DeLaurentis, P., Hill, J., & Benneyworth, B. D. (2017). Big data in healthcare–the promises, challenges and opportunities from a research perspective: A case study with a model database. []. American Medical Informatics Association.]. *AMIA ... Annual Symposium Proceedings - AMIA Symposium. AMIA Symposium*, 2017, 384. PMID: 29854102

Agrawal, S.. (2019). Fingerprint micro & macro features combination of local Haralick micro texture & macro features extracted from neighbor gray-tone. *Pattern Recognition*, 94, 225–238.

Aho, B., & Duffield, R. (2020). Beyond surveillance capitalism: Privacy, regulation and big data in Europe and China. *Economy and Society*, 49(2), 187–212. DOI: 10.1080/03085147.2019.1690275

Aithal, P. S., & Aithal, S. (2023). Stakeholders' analysis of the effect of ubiquitous education technologies on higher education. *International Journal of Applied Engineering*, 5(3), 78–89. https://papers.ssrn.com

Ajzen, I. (2012). The theory of planned behavior. *Handbook of Theories of Social Psychology*: Volume 1, 438-459. DOI: 10.4135/9781446249215.n22

Ajzen, I. (1991). The theory of planned behavior. *Organizational Behavior and Human Decision Processes*, 50(2), 179–211. DOI: 10.1016/0749-5978(91)90020-T

Akpuokwe, C. U., Adeniyi, A. O., & Bakare, S. S. (2024). Legal challenges of artificial intelligence and robotics: A comprehensive review. *Computer Science & IT Research Journal*, 5(3), 544–561. DOI: 10.51594/csitrj.v5i3.860

Akter, S., Wamba, S. F., Gunasekaran, A., Dubey, R., & Childe, S. J. (2016). How to improve firm performance using big data analytics capability and business strategy alignment? *International Journal of Production Economics*, 182, 113–131. DOI: 10.1016/j.ijpe.2016.08.018

Al Maktoum, M. B. R. (2012). *My Vision: Challenges in the Race for Excellence*. Motivate Publishing.

AlAli, M., Mattar, Y., Alzaim, M. A., & Beheiry, S. (2023). Applications of biomimicry in architecture, construction and civil engineering. *Biomimetics*, 8(2), 202. Advance online publication. DOI: 10.3390/biomimetics8020202 PMID: 37218788

AL-Dabbagh, R. (2022). Dubai, the sustainable, smart city. *Renewable Energy and Environmental Sustainability*, 7, 3. Advance online publication. DOI: 10.1051/rees/2021049

Aleena, M.. (2015). Fingerprint pattern image quality measure. In *Proceedings of the 2015 IEEE International Conference on Image Processing (ICIP)* (pp. 4265-4269). Quebec City, QC.

Alhussain, G., Kelly, A., O'Flaherty, E. I., Quinn, D. P., & Flaherty, G. (2022). Emerging role of artificial intelligence in global health care. *Health Policy and Technology*, 11(3), 100661. Advance online publication. DOI: 10.1016/j.hlpt.2022.100661 PMID: 35991006

Aliabadi, R., Singh, A., & Wilson, E. (2023). Transdisciplinary AI education: The confluence of curricular and community needs in the instruction of artificial intelligence. In Schlippe, T., Cheng, E. C. K., & Wang, T. (Eds.), *Artificial Intelligence in Education Technologies: New Development and Innovative Practices* (pp. 137–151)., DOI: 10.1007/978-981-99-7947-9_11

Alier, M., García-Peñalvo, F., & Camba, J. D. (2024). Generative Artificial Intelligence in Education: From Deceptive to Disruptive.

Allmnakrah, A., & Evers, C. (2020). The need for a fundamental shift in the Saudi education system: Implementing the Saudi Arabian economic vision 2030. *Research in Education*, 106(1), 22–40. DOI: 10.1177/0034523719851534

Alogaiel, N. F., & Alrwais, O. A. (2023). An assessment of the quality of open government data in Saudi Arabia. *IEEE Access : Practical Innovations, Open Solutions*, 11, 61560–61599. DOI: 10.1109/ACCESS.2023.3285611

Alotaibi, A., Alsubaie, D., Alaskar, H., Alhumaid, L., Thuwayni, R. B., Alkhalifah, R., & Alhumoud, S. (2022, January). Kingdom of Saudi Arabia: Era of Smart Cities. In *2022 2nd International Conference on Computing and Information Technology (ICCIT)* (pp. 285-292). IEEE.

Aloupogianni, E., Doctor, F., Karyotis, C., Maniak, T., Tang, R., & Iqbal, R. (2024, July). An AI-Based Digital Twin Framework for Intelligent Traffic Management in Singapore. In *2024 International Conference on Electrical, Computer and Energy Technologies (ICECET)* (pp. 1-6). IEEE. DOI: 10.1109/ICECET61485.2024.10698642

Alsmadi, M. K., Al-Marashdeh, I., Alzaqebah, M., Jaradat, G., Alghamdi, F. A., Mohammad, R. M. A., & Tayfour, M. (2021). Digitalization of learning in Saudi Arabia during the COVID-19 outbreak: A survey. *Informatics in Medicine Unlocked*, 25, 100632. DOI: 10.1016/j.imu.2021.100632 PMID: 34150983

AlSuwaidi, S., & Moonesar, I. A. (2021). UAE resident users' perceptions of healthcare applications from Dubai Health Authority: Preliminary insights. *Dubai Medical Journal*, 4(1), 10–17. DOI: 10.1159/000513489

Amariles, D. R., & Baquero, P. M. (2023). Promises and limits of law for a human-centric artificial intelligence. *Computer Law & Security Report*, 48, 105795. DOI: 10.1016/j.clsr.2023.105795

Ammar, J. (2023). Analyze business context data in developing economies using quantum computing. https://doi.org//arXiv.2311.08048DOI: 10.48550

Andejany, M., Sounni, I., Akbar, A., & Alsubaie, F. (2022). Critical success factors addressing Covid-19 pandemic: Case of Tawakkalna application in Saudi Arabia. *IEOM,* 1520-1535.

Annus, T., & Merimaa, K. (2024). The role of government in leading the pandemic response: The Estonian experience. In *Resilient Health* (pp. 433–443). Academic Press. DOI: 10.1016/B978-0-443-18529-8.00035-4

Aoujil, Z., & Hanine, M. (2023). Artificial Intelligence and Behavioral Economcs: A Bibliographic Analysis of Research Field. *Sustainability*, 15(5), 3949. DOI: 10.3390/su15053949

Apablaza-Campos, J., Smith, L., & Gómez, R. (2024). Exploring the societal impacts of generative AI on ethical decision-making. *Journal of Ethics in Technology*. https://doi.org/DOI: 10.1016/jet.2024.012345

Archibong, E. E., Ibia, K. U. T., Muniandi, B., Dari, S. S., Dhabliya, D., & Dadheech, P. (2024). The Intersection of AI Technology and Intellectual Property Adjudication in Supply Chain Management. In *AI and Machine Learning Impacts in Intelligent Supply Chain* (pp. 39–56). IGI Global. DOI: 10.4018/979-8-3693-1347-3.ch004

Ardagna, C. A., Ceravolo, P., & Damiani, E. (2016, December). *Big data analytics as-a-service: Issues and challenges. In 2016 IEEE international conference on big data (big data)*. IEEE.

Arsawan, I. W. E., De Hariyanti, N. K., Atmaja, I. M. A. D. S., Suhartanto, D., & Koval, V. (2022). Developing organizational agility in SMEs: An investigation of innovation's roles and strategic flexibility. *Journal of Open Innovation*, 8(3), 149. DOI: 10.3390/joitmc8030149

Arunachalam, D., Kumar, N., & Kawalek, J. P. (2018). Understanding big data analytics capabilities in supply chain management: Unravelling the issues, challenges and implications for practice. *Transportation Research Part E, Logistics and Transportation Review*, 114, 416–436. DOI: 10.1016/j.tre.2017.04.001

Asch, S. E. (1951). Effects of group pressure upon the modification and distortion of judgments. In Guetzkow, H. (Ed.), *Groups, leadership and men*. Carnegie Press.

Attard-Frost, B., Brandusescu, A., & Lyons, K. (2024). The governance of artificial intelligence in Canada: Findings and opportunities from a review of 84 AI governance initiatives. *Government Information Quarterly*, 41(2), 101929. DOI: 10.1016/j.giq.2024.101929

Azeem, M. M., & Kotey, B. (2023). Innovation in SMEs: The role of flexible work arrangements and market competition. *International Journal of Human Resource Management*, 34(1), 92–127. DOI: 10.1080/09585192.2021.1961162

Baesens, A. (2014). *Analytics in a big data world: The essential guide to data science and its applications, John Wiley & Sons, Hoboken, New Jersey, USA. DOI:*DOI: 10.1002/9781119204183

Bai, C., Shi, B., Liu, F., & Sarkis, J. (2018). Banking credit worthiness: Evaluating the complex relationships. In C. Bai, B. Shi, F. Liu, & J. Sarkis [). Elsevier BV.]. *Omega*, 83, 26–38. DOI: 10.1016/j.omega.2018.02.001

Baig, M. I., Yadegaridehkordi, E., & Nizam Bin Md Nasir, M. H. (2023). Influence of big data adoption on sustainable marketing and operation of SMEs: A hybrid approach of SEM-ANN. *Management Decision*, 61(7), 2231–2253. DOI: 10.1108/MD-06-2022-0778

Bail, C. A., Argyle, L. P., Brown, T. W., Bumpus, J. P., Chen, H., Hunzaker, M. F., Lee, J., Mann, M., Merhout, F., & Volfovsky, A. (2018). Exposure to opposing views on social media can increase political polarization. *Proceedings of the National Academy of Sciences of the United States of America*, 115(37), 9216–9221. DOI: 10.1073/pnas.1804840115 PMID: 30154168

Bakry, S. H., & Saud, B. A. A. (2021). A roadmap to AI: An insight from the Saudi Vision 2030. *Artificial Intelligence and Its Contexts: Security, Business and Governance,* 201-223.

Balakrishnan, J., & Griffiths, M. D. (2017). Social media addiction: What is the role of content in YouTube? *Journal of Behavioral Addictions*, 6(3), 364–377. DOI: 10.1556/2006.6.2017.058 PMID: 28914072

Banerjee, A. V. (1992). A simple model of herd behavior. *The Quarterly Journal of Economics*, 107(3), 797–817. DOI: 10.2307/2118364

Bannister, P., Urbieta, A. S., & Peñalver, E. A. (2023). *A systematic review of generative AI and (English medium instruction) higher education*. Aula Abierta., DOI: 10.17811/rifie.52.4.2023.401-409

Bansal, A. (2023). Power BI Semantic Models to enhance Data Analytics and Decision-Making. *International Journal of Research in Computer Applications and Technology*.https://ijrcait.com

Barak-Corren, N., & Kariv-Teitelbaum, Y. (2021). Behavioral responsive regulation: Bringing together responsive regulation and behavioral public policy. *Regulation & Governance*, 15(S1). Advance online publication. DOI: 10.1111/rego.12429

Baramichai, M., Zimmers, E. W.Jr, & Marangos, C. A. (2007). Agile supply chain transformation matrix: An integrated tool for creating an agile enterprise. *Supply Chain Management*, 12(5), 334–348. DOI: 10.1108/13598540710776917

Barbosa, B., Saura, J. R., & Bennett, D. (2022). How do entrepreneurs perform digital marketing across the customer journey? a review and discussion of the main uses. *The Journal of Technology Transfer*, 49(1), 69–103. DOI: 10.1007/s10961-022-09978-2

Barrat, J. (2023). *Our final invention: Artificial intelligence and the end of the human era*. Hachette UK.

Bartmann, M. (2022). The ethics of ai-powered climate nudging—How much ai should we use to save the planet? *Sustainability (Basel)*, 14(9), 5153. DOI: 10.3390/su14095153

Basri, W. (2020). Examining the impact of artificial intelligence (AI)-assisted social media marketing on the performance of small and medium enterprises: Toward effective business management in the Saudi Arabian context. *International Journal of Computational Intelligence Systems*, 13(1), 142–152. DOI: 10.2991/ijcis.d.200127.002

Bawden, D., & Robinson, L. (2020). *Information overload: An overview. Oxford Encyclopedia of Political Decision Making*. Oxford University Press., DOI: 10.1093/acrefore/9780190228637.013.956

Bayer, J. (2024). Legal implications of using generative AI in the media. *Information & Communications Technology Law*, 33(3), 1–20. DOI: 10.1080/13600834.2024.2352694

Begenau, J., Farboodi, M., & Veldkamp, L. (2018). Big data in finance and the growth of large firms. *Journal of Monetary Economics*, 97, 71–87. DOI: 10.1016/j.jmoneco.2018.05.013

Behavioral Scientist. (2017). A Conversation with Bill Congdon, Former Member of the White House Social and Behavioral Sciences Team. Retrieved from Behavioral Scientist Behavioural Economics Team of the Australian Government. (2019). BETA Guide to Applying Behavioural Insights. https://behaviouraleconomics.pmc.gov.au/sites/default/files/resources/beta-guide-applying-behavioural-insights-2019.pdf

Behavioural Insights Team. (2014). EAST: Four Simple Ways to Apply Behavioural Insights. https://www.bi.team/publications/east-four-simple-ways-to-apply-behavioural-insights

BehaviourWorks Australia. (2020). INSPIRE: Behavioural Insights for Better Communication. Retrieved from https://www.behaviourworksaustralia.org/courses/inspire-your-communication

Belás, J., Amoah, J., Dvorský, J., & Šuleř, P. (2021). The importance of social media for management of SMEs. *Economics & Sociology (Ternopil)*, 14(4), 118–132. DOI: 10.14254/2071-789X.2021/14-4/7

Bennett, A., & Elman, C. (2006). Qualitative research: Recent developments in case study methods. *Annual Review of Political Science*, 9(1), 455–476. DOI: 10.1146/annurev.polisci.8.082103.104918

Bertrand, M., Mullainathan, S., & Shafir, E. (2006). Behavioral economics and marketing in aid of decision making among the poor. *Journal of Public Policy & Marketing*, 25(1), 8–23. DOI: 10.1509/jppm.25.1.8

Bettinetti, A., Pypaert, P., & Sweerts, J. P. R. A. (1996). Application of an Integrated Management Approach to the Restoration Project of the Lagoon of Venice. In A. Bettinetti, P. Pypaert, & J. P. R. A. Sweerts []. Elsevier BV.]. *Journal of Environmental Management*, 46(3), 207–227. DOI: 10.1006/jema.1996.0017

Bhandari, A., & Bimo, S. (2022). Why's Everyone on TikTok Now? The Algorithmized Self and the Future of Self-Making on Social Media. *Social Media + Society*, 8(1), 20563051221086241. DOI: 10.1177/20563051221086241

Bianchini, M., & Michalkova, V. (2019). Data Analytics in SMEs: Trends and Policies. OECD SME and Entrepreneurship Papers No. 15. Available at: https://www.oecd.org/industry/smes/SME-Outlook-2021-Country-profiles.pdf

Bibri, S. E., Alahi, A., Sharifi, A., & Krogstie, J. (2023). Environmentally sustainable smart cities and their converging AI, IoT, and big data technologies and solutions: An integrated approach to an extensive literature review. *Energy Informatics*, 6(1), 9. Advance online publication. DOI: 10.1186/s42162-023-00259-2 PMID: 37032812

Biden, J. R. (2023). Executive order on the safe, secure, and trustworthy development and use of artificial intelligence.

Bikhchandani, S., Hirshleifer, D., & Welch, I. (1992). A theory of fads, fashion, custom, and cultural change as informational cascades. *Journal of Political Economy*, 100(5), 992–1026. DOI: 10.1086/261849

Birckan, G., Dutra, M. L., de Macedo, D., & Viera, Á. F. G. (2018). Effects of data protection laws on data brokerage businesses. In G. Birckan, M. L. Dutra, D. de Macedo, & Á. F. G. Viera, ICST Transactions on Scalable Information Systems (p. 165673). European Alliance for Innovation.

Boddy, J., & Dominelli, L. (2017). Social media and social work: The challenges of a new ethical space. *Australian Social Work*, 70(2), 172–184. DOI: 10.1080/0312407X.2016.1224907

Bodul, D. (2023). Can artificial intelligence (AI) replace the judge?. *Harmonius: J. Legal & Soc. Stud. Se. Eur., 15.*

Bonsay, J. O., Cruz, A. P., Firozi, H. C., & Camaro, P. J. C. (2021). Artificial intelligence and labor productivity paradox: The economic impact of AI in China, India, Japan, and Singapore. *Journal of Economics. Finance and Accounting Studies*, 3(2), 120–139. DOI: 10.32996/jefas.2021.3.2.13

Bragazzi, N. L., & Garbarino, S. (2024). Understanding and Combating Misinformation: An Evolutionary Perspective. Available at *SSRN*. DOI: 10.2139/ssrn.4929108

Braun, V., & Clarke, V. (2006). Using thematic analysis in psychology. *Qualitative Research in Psychology*, 3(2), 77–101. DOI: 10.1191/1478088706qp063oa

Breaugh, J., Rackwitz, M., & Hammerschmid, G. (2023). Leadership and institutional design in collaborative government digitalisation: Evidence from Belgium, Denmark, Estonia, Germany, and the UK. *Government Information Quarterly*, 40(2), 101788. DOI: 10.1016/j.giq.2022.101788

Breiman, L. (2001). Random forests. *Machine Learning*, 45(1), 5–32. DOI: 10.1023/A:1010933404324

Bromley, J., Bentz, J. W., Bottou, L., Guyon, I., Lecun, Y., Moore, C., Säckinger, E., & Shah, R. (1993). Signature verification using a "Siamese" time delay neural network. *International Journal of Pattern Recognition and Artificial Intelligence*, 7(4), 669–688. DOI: 10.1142/S0218001493000339

Brooks, R., Nguyen, D. A., Bhatti, A., Allender, S., Johnstone, M., Lim, C. P., & Backholer, K. (2022). Use of artificial intelligence to enable dark nudges by transnational food and beverage companies: Analysis of company documents. *Public Health Nutrition*, 25(5), 1291–1299. DOI: 10.1017/S1368980022000490 PMID: 35232511

Bui, T. H., & Nguyen, V. P. (2023). The impact of artificial intelligence and digital economy on Vietnam's legal system. *International Journal for the Semiotics of Law-Revue internationale de Sémiotique juridique, 36*(2), 969-989.

Burr, C., Cristianini, N., & Ladyman, J. (2018). An analysis of the interaction between intelligent software systems and human autonomy. *Ethics and Information Technology*, 20(3), 207–221.

Butler, T., & Brooks, R. (2023). On the wicked problem of quantifying and managing non-financial risks and the role of digital technology in providing solutions. *Journal of Risk Management in Financial Institutions*, 17(1), 53–70. DOI: 10.69554/TNPL3644

Cabinet Office Behavioural Insights Team. (2011). *Annual Update 2010-11*. Retrieved from https://www.bi.team/publications/annual-update-2010-11

Camerer, C. F. (2014). Behavioral economics. *Current Biology*, 24(18), R867–R871. DOI: 10.1016/j.cub.2014.07.040 PMID: 25247364

Canali, S. (2020). Towards a Contextual Approach to Data Quality. In S. Canali [). Multidisciplinary Digital Publishing Institute.]. *Data*, 5(4), 90. DOI: 10.3390/data5040090

Carlson, J., Rahman, M., Voola, R., & De Vries, N. (2018). Customer engagement behaviours in social media: Capturing innovation opportunities. *Journal of Services Marketing*, 32(1), 83–94. DOI: 10.1108/JSM-02-2017-0059

Carobene, A., Padoan, A., Cabitza, F., Banfi, G., & Plebani, M. (2024). Rising adoption of artificial intelligence in scientific publishing: Evaluating the role, risks, and ethical implications in paper drafting and review process. [CCLM]. *Clinical Chemistry and Laboratory Medicine*, 62(5), 835–843. DOI: 10.1515/cclm-2023-1136 PMID: 38019961

Casey, T., Krishnamurthy, K., & Abezgauz, B. (2013). *Who Should Own Big Data? strategy+business*. Available at: http://www.strategybusiness.com/article/00211?gko=44b8e

CBS website. Are SMEs ready for big data? Available at: https://www.cbs.nl/en-gb/about-us/innovation/project/are-smes-ready-for-big-data-

Centers for Disease Control and Prevention. (2011). The Health Communicator's Social Media Toolkit. https://www.cdc.gov/socialmedia/tools/guidelines/pdf/socialmediatoolkit_bm.pdf

Chang, F., & Das, D. (2020). Smart nation Singapore: Developing policies for a citizen-oriented smart city initiative. *Developing National Urban Policies: Ways Forward to Green and Smart Cities,* 425-440.

Chen, Y., Zhao, H., & Sun, Q. (2023). *Generative AI in medical image analysis: Emerging trends and challenges*. Medical Imaging and AI., DOI: 10.1016/medai.2023.012345

Chia, E. S. (2016, June). Singapore's smart nation program—Enablers and challenges. In *2016 11th System of Systems Engineering Conference (SoSE)* (pp. 1-5). IEEE.

Chik, W. B., & Sugumaran, H. (2024). Legal governance of artificial intelligence in healthcare devices and services in Singapore. In *Research Handbook on Health, AI and the Law* (pp. 373-391). Edward Elgar Publishing. DOI: 10.4337/9781802205657.00030

Cía, A. (2014). Las adicciones no relacionadas a sustancias (DSM-5, APA, 2013): un primer paso hacia la inclusión de las Adicciones Conductuales en las clasificaciones categoriales vigentes. Neuro-Psiquiatría, 216. Retrieved from: https://revistas.upch.edu.pe/index.php/RNP/article/view/1169

Coleman, S., Göb, R., Manco, G., Pievatolo, A., Tort-Martorell, X., & Reis, M. S. (2016). How can SMEs benefit from big data? Challenges and a path forward. *Quality and Reliability Engineering International*, 32(6), 2151–2164. DOI: 10.1002/qre.2008

Conti, R., de Matos, M. G., & Valentini, G. (2024). Big data analytics, firm size, and performance. *Strategy Science*, 9(2), 135–151. DOI: 10.1287/stsc.2022.0007

Corchado, J. M., López, S., & García, R. (2023). Generative artificial intelligence: Fundamentals. *ADCAIJ: Advances in Artificial Intelligence*. https://doi.org/DOI: 10.1016/adcaij.2023

Cüce, E., Nachan, Z., Cuce, P. M., Sher, F., & Neighbour, G. B. (2017). Strategies for ideal indoor environments towards low/zero carbon buildings through a biomimetic approach. *International Journal of Ambient Energy*, 40(1), 86–95. DOI: 10.1080/01430750.2017.1372807

Cuéllar, M. F. & Huq, A. Z. (2020). Economies of surveillance.

Dalal, N., & Triggs, B. (2005). Histograms of oriented gradients for human detection. In *Proceedings of the IEEE Conference on Computer Vision and Pattern Recognition (CVPR)*, 1, 886-893. DOI: 10.1109/CVPR.2005.177

Damasio, A. R. (1994). *Descartes' Error: Emotion, Reason, and the Human Brain*. Putnam Publishing.

Dashkevych, O., & Portnov, B. A. (2024). How can generative AI help in different parts of research? An experiment study on smart cities' definitions and characteristics. *Technology in Society*, 77, 102555. DOI: 10.1016/j.techsoc.2024.102555

DataReportal. (2024). Digital 2024: Global Overview Report. https://datareportal.com/reports/digital-2024-global-overview-report

Daus, Z. (2024). Socializing the political: Rethinking filter bubbles and social media with Hannah Arendt. *Ethics and Information Technology*, 26(2), 20. DOI: 10.1007/s10676-024-09759-5

Davenport, T. H. (2006). *Competing on analytics, Harvard Business Review*. Harvard Business Press., DOI: 10.5860/CHOICE.44-6322

Davenport, T. H., & Harris, J. G. (2007). *Competing on analytics – the new science of winning*. Harvard Business School Publishing Corporation., DOI: 10.5465/amr.2005.17293788

De Vos, W. M., Tilg, H., Van Hul, M., & Cani, P. D. (2022). Gut microbiome and health: Mechanistic insights. *Gut*, 71(5), 1020–1032. https://www.ncbi.nlm.nih.gov/pmc/articles/PMC8995832/. DOI: 10.1136/gutjnl-2021-326789 PMID: 35105664 de Zárate Alcarazo, L. O. (2023). Sesgos de género en la inteligencia artificial. *Revista de Occidente (Madrid, Spain)*, 502(1).

Debasa, F., & Cuello, Z. (2024). Sociedad actual e identidad digital. In *Historia de la sociedad presente: El mundo Y sus desvelos desde/990* (pp. 143–160). Dykinson. DOI: 10.14679/2545

DeMauro, A., Greco, M., Grimaldi, M., & Ritala, P. (2018). Human resources for Big Data professions: A systematic classification of job roles and required skill sets. *Information Processing & Management*, 54(5), 807–817. DOI: 10.1016/j.ipm.2017.05.004

Descartes, R. (1637). Discourse on the Method of Rightly Conducting One's Reason and of Seeking Truth in the Sciences. (I. Maclean, Trans.). Oxford University Press. (Original work published 1637).

Dhamani, N. (2024). *Introduction to generative AI*. Routledge., DOI: 10.4324/introduction.gen.ai.2024

Diez-Gracia, A., Sánchez-García, P., and Martín-Román, J. (2023). Polarisation and emotional discourse in the political agenda on Twitter: disintermediation and engagement in electoral campaigns. *Icono* 14, 21(1).

Digital Dubai Authority. (2022). *Dubai blockchain strategy*. https://www.digitaldubai.ae/initiatives/blockchain

Digital Dubai Authority. (2023a). Smart city initiatives and digital transformation projects. https://www.digitaldubai.ae

Digital Dubai Authority. (2023b). *UAE PASS and digital transformation*. https://www.digitaldubai.ae

Digital Government Singapore. (2022). *AI in Singapore's smart city development*. https://www.smartnation.gov.sg/nais/

Doorn, N. (2021). Artificial intelligence in the water domain: Opportunities for responsible use. *The Science of the Total Environment*, 755, 142561. Advance online publication. DOI: 10.1016/j.scitotenv.2020.142561 PMID: 33039891

Dora, M., Kumar, M., & Gellynck, X. (2016). Determinants and barriers to lean implementation in food-processing SMEs—A multiple case analysis. *Production Planning and Control*, 27(1), 1–23. DOI: 10.1080/09537287.2015.1050477

Dubai Electricity and Water Authority. (2018a). *DEWA is first utility in the world to work with Microsoft to utilize quantum computing*. https://www.dewa.gov.ae/en/about-us/media-publications/latest-news/2018/07/dewa-is-first-utility-in-the-world-to-work-with-microsoft-to-utilise-quantum-computing

Dubai Electricity and Water Authority. (2018b). *Smart initiatives for enhanced energy efficiency*. https://www.dewa.gov.ae

Dubai Electricity and Water Authority. (2023). *DEWA becomes the world's first utility organization to integrate ChatGPT.* Government of Dubai. https://www.dewa.gov.ae/en/about-dewa/news-and-media/news/2023/01/dewa-first-to-integrate-chatgpt

Dubai Electricity and Water Authority. (2023). *DEWA Smart Grid and energy efficiency initiatives*. https://www.dewa.gov.ae/en/about-us/media-publications/latest-news/2023/07/dewas-smart-grid-an-effective

Dubai Electricity and Water Authority. (n.d.). Smart Grid Strategy. https://www.dewa.gov.ae/en/about-dewa/smart-initiatives/smart-grid-strategy

Dubai Electronic Security Center. (2023). Dubai Cyber Security Strategy 2023. https://www.desc.gov.ae/wp-content/uploads/2023/pdfs/dcss_EN_2023.pdf

Dubai Future Foundation. (2023a). Dubai Centre for Artificial Intelligence. https://www.dubaifuture.ae/dubai-centre-for-artificial-intelligence

Dubai Future Foundation. (2023b). AI Program government services. https://www.dubaifuture.ae/ai-program-government-services

Dubai Future Foundation. (2024). Mostaqbal Portal: Advancing Science and Technology in Arabic. https://www.dubaifuture.gov.ae

Dubai Future Foundation. (n.d.). About Us. https://www.dubaifuture.ae/about-us/

Dubai Government. (n.d.). Dubai 3D Printing Strategy. https://u.ae/en/about-the-uae/strategies-initiatives-and-awards/strategies-plans-and-visions/innovation-and-future-shaping/dubai-3d-printing-strategy

Dubai Health Authority. (2023). Salama: The Integrated Electronic Medical Record Initiative. https://www.dha.gov.ae/en/media/news/762

Dubai Municipality. (2023). *Sustainability and environmental management in Dubai*. https://www.dm.gov.ae/municipality-business/environment-sustainability-technical-guidelines/

Dubai Police. (2022). Smart policing and innovation in public safety. https://www.dubaipolice.gov.ae/wps/portal/home/aboutus/overview

Dubey, R., Gunasekaran, A., & Childe, S. J. (2018a). Big data analytics capability in supply chain agility: The moderating effect of organizational flexibility. *Management Decision*. Advance online publication. DOI: 10.1108/MD-01-2018-0119

Dubey, R., Gunasekaran, A., Childe, S. J., Fosso Wamba, S., Roubaud, D., & Foropon, C. (2021). Empirical investigation of data analytics capability and organizational flexibility as complements to supply chain resilience. *International Journal of Production Research*, 59(1), 1–19. DOI: 10.1080/00207543.2019.1582820

Dubey, R., Gunasekaran, A., Childe, S. J., Luo, Z., Wamba, S. F., Roubaud, D., & Foropon, C. (2018b). Examining the role of big data and predictive analytics on collaborative performance in context to sustainable consumption and production behaviour. *Journal of Cleaner Production*, 196, 1508–1521. DOI: 10.1016/j.jclepro.2018.06.097

Dubey, R., Gunasekaran, A., Childe, S. J., Roubaud, D., Wamba, S. F., Giannakis, M., & Foropon, C. (2019b). Big data analytics and organizational culture as complements to swift trust and collaborative performance in the humanitarian supply chain. *International Journal of Production Economics*, 210, 120–136. DOI: 10.1016/j.ijpe.2019.01.023

Dubey, R., Gunasekaran, A., Childe, S. J., Wamba, S. F., & Papadopoulos, T. (2016). The impact of big data on world-class sustainable manufacturing. *International Journal of Advanced Manufacturing Technology*, 84(1–4), 631–645. DOI: 10.1007/s00170-015-7674-1

Dulenko, V. (2020). How TikTok design hooks you up. *UX Planet*. https://uxplanet.org/how-TikTok-design-hooks-you-up-6c889522c7ed

Dunning, D. (2011). The Dunning-Kruger effect: On being ignorant of one's own ignorance. In Olson, J., & Zanna, M. P. (Eds.), Vol. 44, pp. 247–296). Advances in Experimental Social Psychology. Elsevier Academic Press., DOI: 10.1016/B978-0-12-385522-0.00005-6

Dzioba, B. (2021). Addictive by design: How TikTok keeps you hooked. *UX Collective*. https://digitaltattoo.ubc.ca/2021/11/19/addictive-by-design-how-TikTok-keeps-you-hooked/

Ebers, M., & Tupay, P. K. (2023). *Artificial intelligence and machine learning powered public service delivery in Estonia: Opportunities and legal challenges*. Springer. DOI: 10.1007/978-3-031-19667-6

Eggert, M., & Alberts, J. (2020). Frontiers of business intelligence and analytics 3.0: A taxonomy-based literature review and research agenda. *Business Research.* https://springer.com

Éigeartaigh, S. S., Whittlestone, J., Liu, Y., Zeng, Y., & Liu, Z. (2020). Overcoming barriers to cross-cultural cooperation in AI ethics and governance. *Philosophy & Technology*, 33(4), 571–593. DOI: 10.1007/s13347-020-00402-x

Emirates Scientists Council. (2024). UAE Advanced Science Agenda 2031: Supporting Research and Innovation. https://www.esc.ae

Engelsma, G.. (2018). Fingerprint match score & liveness value bootstrap aggregation classifier. *IEEE Transactions on Information Forensics and Security*, 13(7), 1643–1658.

Enterprise Strategy Group - ESG. (2022). 2022 Technology Spending Intentions Survey. Available at: https://www.esg-global.com/2022-technology-spending

Eppler, M. J., & Mengis, J. (2004). The concept of information overload: A review of literature from organization science, accounting, marketing, MIS, and related disciplines. *The Information Society*, 20(5), 325–344. DOI: 10.1080/01972240490507974

European Commission. (2014). Helping SMEs fish the big data ocean. Available at: https://digital-strategy.ec.europa.eu/en/news/helping-smes-fish-big-data-ocean

European Commission. (2020). *What is an SME?* Retrieved from https://single-market-economy.ec.europa.eu/smes/sme-fundamentals/sme-definition_en

European Commission. (2022). The ethical use of AI in data-driven decision-making. *Journal of European Innovations*, 35(3), 234–245. DOI: 10.1007/s11423-022-00012

European Union. (2024). NUDGE: Nudging consumers towards energy efficiency through behavioural science. *Horizon 2020 Project*. Retrieved from https://www.nudgeproject.eu

Europeo, P. (2023). Reglas europeas para combatir la adicción digital. https://www.europarl.europa.eu/news/es/press-room/20231208IPR15767/reglas-europeas-para-combatir-la-adiccion-digital

Faccia, A., Le Roux, C. L., and Pandey, V. (2023). Innovation and e-commerce models, the technology catalysts for sustainable development: The Emirate of Dubai case study. *Sustainability, 15*(4), Article 3419. [REMOVED HYPERLINK40 FIELD] DOI: 10.3390/su15043419

Fan, P. S. (2018). Singapore approach to develop and regulate FinTech. In *Handbook of Blockchain, Digital Finance, and Inclusion, Volume 1* (pp. 347-357). Academic Press. DOI: 10.1016/B978-0-12-810441-5.00015-4

Fanini, B., & Gosti, G. (2024). A new generation of collaborative immersive analytics on the web: Open-source services to capture, process, and inspect users' sessions in 3D environments. *Future Internet*, 16(5), 147. Advance online publication. DOI: 10.3390/fi16050147

Fawcett, S. E., & Waller, M. A. (2014). Supply chain game changers—mega, nano, and virtual trends—and forces that impede supply chain design (ie, building a winning team). *Journal of Business Logistics*, 35(3), 157–164. DOI: 10.1111/jbl.12058

Fernandez, R. C., Subramaniam, P., & Franklin, M. J. (2020). Data market platforms: Trading data assets to solve data problems. arXiv preprint arXiv:2002.01047.

Festinger, L. (1957). *A Theory of Cognitive Dissonance*. Stanford University Press. DOI: 10.1515/9781503620766

Floridi, L. (2023). The ethics of artificial intelligence: Principles, challenges, and opportunities.

Floridi, L., Cowls, J., King, T. C., & Taddeo, M. (2021). How to design AI for social good: Seven essential factors. *Ethics, Governance, and Policies in Artificial Intelligence,* 125-151.

Floridi, L. (2015). *The Onlife Manifesto: Being Human in a Hyperconnected Era*. Springer., DOI: 10.1007/978-3-319-04093-6

Flynn, D. J., Nyhan, B., & Reifler, J. (2017). The nature and origins of misperceptions: Understanding false and unsupported beliefs about politics. *Political Psychology*, 38(S1), 127–150. DOI: 10.1111/pops.12394

Fogg, B. J. (2018). *Tiny habits: The small changes that change everything*. Houghton Mifflin Harcourt.

Fosso Wamba, S., Gunasekaran, A., Papadopoulos, T., & Ngai, E. (2018). Big data analytics in logistics and supply chain management. *International Journal of Logistics Management*, 29(2), 478–484. DOI: 10.1108/IJLM-02-2018-0026

Fui-Hoon Nah, F., Zheng, R., Cai, J., Siau, K., & Chen, L. (2023). Generative AI and ChatGPT: Applications, challenges, and AI-human collaboration. *Journal of Information Technology Case and Application Research*, 25(3), 277–304. DOI: 10.1080/15228053.2023.2233814

Galindo-Domínguez, H., Delgado, N., Losada, D., & Etxabe, J. M. (2024). An analysis of the use of artificial intelligence in education in Spain: The in-service teacher's perspective. *Journal of Digital Learning in Teacher Education*, 40(1), 41–56. DOI: 10.1080/21532974.2023.2284726

Gangwal, A., Ansari, A., Ahmad, I., Azad, A. K., Kumarasamy, V., Subramaniyan, V., & Wong, L. S. (2024). Generative artificial intelligence in drug discovery: Basic framework, recent advances, challenges, and opportunities. *Frontiers in Pharmacology*, 15, 1331062. DOI: 10.3389/fphar.2024.1331062 PMID: 38384298

García, F., & Lopez, T. (2022). Overcoming Challenges in BI Implementation in Higher Education: A Spanish Perspective. *European Journal of Educational Technology*, 14(3), 250–270. DOI: 10.12345/ejedtech.2022.03345

García-López, J., Domínguez-Amarillo, S., & Sendra, J. J. (2024). Clustering open data for predictive modeling of residential energy consumption across variable scales: A case study in Andalusia, Spain. *Buildings*, 14(8), 2335. DOI: 10.3390/buildings14082335

Garon, J. (2023). A practical introduction to generative AI, synthetic media, and the messages found in the latest medium. *Synthetic Media, and the Messages Found in the Latest Medium (March 14, 2023).*

Gašević, D., Siemens, G., & Sadiq, S. (2023). Empowering learners for the age of artificial intelligence. *Computers and Education: Artificial Intelligence*, 4, 100130.

Gavrilova, V., & Gurvitsh-Suits, N. A. (2020). Contemporary innovation challenges–Future of adoption artificial intelligence: Case of Estonia. *European Integration Studies*, 14(14), 217–225. DOI: 10.5755/j01.eis.1.14.26143

Ghasemaghaei, M. (2018). Improving organizational performance through the use of big data. *Journal of Computer Information Systems*, 60(5), 395–408. DOI: 10.1080/08874417.2018.1496805

Gherhes, C., Williams, N., Vorley, T., & Vasconcelos, A. C. (2016). Distinguishing micro-businesses from SMEs: A systematic review of growth constraints. *Journal of Small Business and Enterprise Development*, 23(4), 939–963. DOI: 10.1108/JSBED-05-2016-0075

Ghosh, A. (2004). Increasing market share as a rationale for corporate acquisitions. *Journal of Business Finance & Accounting*, 31(1-2), 209–247. DOI: 10.1111/j.0306-686X.2004.0006.x

Giannakis, M., & Louis, M. (2016). A multi-agent based system with big data processing for enhanced supply chain agility. *Journal of Enterprise Information Management*, 29(5), 706–727. DOI: 10.1108/JEIM-06-2015-0050

Gigerenzer, G. (2015). On the supposed evidence for libertarian paternalism. *Review of Philosophy and Psychology*, 6(3), 361–383. DOI: 10.1007/s13164-015-0248-1 PMID: 26213590

Gilbert, S., Anderson, S., Daumer, M., Li, P., Melvin, T., & Williams, R. (2023). Learning from experience and finding the right balance in the governance of artificial intelligence and digital health technologies. *Journal of Medical Internet Research*, 25(1), e43682. DOI: 10.2196/43682 PMID: 37058329

Gilovich, T., Griffin, D., & Kahneman, D. (2002). Heuristics and biases: The psychology of intuitive judgment. Cambridge University Press. ttps://DOI: 10.1017/CBO9780511808098

Gofen, A., Moseley, A., Thomann, E., & Weaver, R. K. (2021). Behavioural governance in the policy process: Introduction to the special issue. *Journal of European Public Policy*, 28(5), 633–657. DOI: 10.1080/13501763.2021.1912153

Goggin, G., & Zhuang, K. V. (2023). Apps, mobilities, and migration in the Covid-19 pandemic: Covid technology and the control of migrant workers in Singapore. *International Journal of Cultural Studies*, 26(6), 636–654. DOI: 10.1177/13678779231160802

González-Padilla, P., Navalpotro, F. D., & Saura, J. R. (2024). Managing entrepreneurs' behavior personalities in digital environments: A review. *The International Entrepreneurship and Management Journal*, 20(1), 89–113. DOI: 10.1007/s11365-022-00823-4

González, R., Hernández, P., & Fernández, A. (2021). Data-driven decision making in higher education: A case study using Power BI. *Educational Technology Research and Development*, 69(4), 905–921. DOI: 10.1007/s11423-021-10033

Goode, K., Kim, H. M., & Deng, M. (2023). Examining Singapore's AI progress. *Center for Security and Emerging Technology,* 19.

Goodfellow, I., ... (2014). Generative adversarial nets. In *Advances in Neural Information Processing Systems (NeurIPS)*, 27, 2672-2680.

Government of Canada. (2018). Behavioural Insights Playbook. https://www.canada.ca/en/innovation-hub/services/reports-resources/behavioural-insights-playbook.html

Government of Dubai Media Office. (2021). Four new smart police stations inaugurated in Dubai. *Dubai Media Office*. https://www.mediaoffice.ae/en/news/2021/September/27-09/Four-Smart-Police

Government of Dubai. (2022). *UAE-National Strategy for Artificial Intelligence 2031*. https://ai.gov.ae/wp-content/uploads/2021/07/UAE-National-Strategy-for-Artificial-Intelligence-2031.pdf

Govindan, K., Cheng, T. C. E., Mishra, N., & Shukla, N. (2018). Big data analytics and application for logistics and supply chain management. *Transportation Research Part E, Logistics and Transportation Review*, 114, 343–349. DOI: 10.1016/j.tre.2018.03.011

Gragnaniello, D.. (2015). Fingerprint profile local contrast phase descriptor and linear kernel SVM classifier. *IEEE Transactions on Information Forensics and Security*, 10(5), 994–1006.

Greene, D., Hoffmann, A., & Stark, L. (2019). Better, nicer, clearer, fairer: A critical assessment of the movement for ethical artificial intelligence and machine learning. Gupta, S. (2017). Ethical issues in designing internet-based research: Recommendations for good practice. *Canada Journal of Research Practice Journal of Research Practice*, 13(2).

Griffiths, M. D. (2000). Internet addiction: Does it really exist? *Addiction (Abingdon, England)*, 95(8), 1091–1093.

Grindrod, P. (2016). Beyond privacy and exposure: Ethical issues within citizen-facing analytics. In P. Grindrod [). Royal Society.]. *Philosophical Transactions. Series A, Mathematical, Physical, and Engineering Sciences*, 374(2083), 20160132. DOI: 10.1098/rsta.2016.0132 PMID: 28336804

Guevara-Gómez, A., de Zárate-Alcarazo, L. O., & Criado, J. I. (2021). Feminist perspectives to artificial intelligence: Comparing the policy frames of the European Union and Spain. *Information Polity*, 26(2), 173–192. DOI: 10.3233/IP-200299

Gunasekaran, A., Papadopoulos, T., Dubey, R., Wamba, S. F., Childe, S. J., Hazen, B., & Akter, S. (2017). Big data and predictive analytics for supply chain and organizational performance. *Journal of Business Research*, 70, 308–317. DOI: 10.1016/j.jbusres.2016.08.004

Gupta, K., & Jiwani, N. (2021). A systematic overview of fundamentals and methods of business intelligence. *International Journal of Sustainable Development in Computing Science*.https://ijsdcs.com

Habermas, J. (1996). Between Facts and Norms: Contributions to a Discourse Theory of Law and Democracy (W. Rehg, Trans.). MIT Press. (Original work published 1992).

Habermas, J. (1985). The theory of communicative action: Vol. 1. *Reason and the rationalization of society*. Beacon press.

Hajkowicz, S., Sanderson, C., Karimi, S., Bratanova, A., & Naughtin, C. (2023). Artificial intelligence adoption in the physical sciences, natural sciences, life sciences, social sciences and the arts and humanities: A bibliometric analysis of research publications from 1960-2021. *Technology in Society*, 74, 102260. DOI: 10.1016/j.techsoc.2023.102260

Hansen, K. (2020). Cognitive bias in emergency medicine. *Emergency Medicine*, 37(3), 567–572. DOI: 10.1016/j.emermed.2020.09.001 PMID: 32902161

Hansen, P. G., & Jespersen, A. M. (2013). Nudge and the manipulation of choice. *European Journal of Risk Regulation*, 4(1), 3–28. DOI: 10.1017/S1867299X00002762

Hao, X. (2022). Estrategias de funcionamiento de TikTok en el proceso de difusión internacional. Universitat Politècnica de València. http://hdl.handle.net/10251/188817

Hardy, A. (2024). Estonia's digital diplomacy: Nordic interoperability and the challenges of cross-border e-governance. *Internet Policy Review*, 13(3), 1–31. DOI: 10.14763/2024.3.1785

Harmon-Jones, E. and Mills, J. (1999). Cognitive dissonance: progress on a pivotal theory in social psychology. DOI: 10.1037/10318-000

Hartley, J. (2004). What is a case study. *Essential guide to qualitative methods in organizational research, 323*.

Harwood, J., & Sundar, S. S. (2019). The dark side of social media: A systematic review of negative effects of social media use. *Social Science & Medicine*, 232, 112294.

Hashmi, E., Yayilgan, S. Y., & Abomhara, M. (2024). Enhancing multilingual hate speech detection: From language-specific insights to cross-linguistic integration. *IEEE Access : Practical Innovations, Open Solutions*, 12, 121507–121537. DOI: 10.1109/ACCESS.2024.3452987

Hazen, B. T., Boone, C. A., Ezell, J. D., & Jones-Farmer, L. A. (2014). Data quality for data science, predictive analytics, and big data in supply chain management: An introduction to the problem and suggestions for research and applications. *International Journal of Production Economics*, 154, 72–80. DOI: 10.1016/j.ijpe.2014.04.018

Hazen, B. T., Skipper, J. B., Ezell, J. D., & Boone, C. A. (2016). Big Data and predictive analytics for supply chain sustainability: A theory-driven research agenda. *Computers & Industrial Engineering*, 101, 592–598. DOI: 10.1016/j.cie.2016.06.030

He, K., Zhang, X., Ren, S., & Sun, J. (2016). Deep residual learning for image recognition. In *Proceedings of the IEEE Conference on Computer Vision and Pattern Recognition (CVPR)* (pp. 770-778).

Heller, N. (2017). Estonia, the digital republic. *The New Yorker, 18,* 12.

Helsinki Smart City Project. (2021). *Autonomous vehicles and environmental management strategies*. https://www.hel.fi/static/kanslia/Julkaisut/2021/helsinki-city-strategy-2021-2025.pdf

Henderson, P., Li, X., Jurafsky, D., Hashimoto, T., Lemley, M. A., & Liang, P. (2023). Foundation models and fair use. *Journal of Machine Learning Research*, 24(400), 1–79.

Herath, H. M. K. K. M. B., & Mittal, M. (2022). Adoption of artificial intelligence in smart cities: A comprehensive review. *Journal of Cleaner Production*, 330, 140105. Advance online publication. https://www.smartnation.gov.sg/initiatives/urban-planning/. DOI: 10.1016/j.jclepro.2023.140105

Hine, E., & Floridi, L. (2024). Artificial intelligence with American values and Chinese characteristics: A comparative analysis of American and Chinese governmental AI policies. *AI & Society*, 39(1), 257–278. DOI: 10.1007/s00146-022-01499-8

Hirsch-Kreinsen, H. (2023). Artificial intelligence: A "promising technology". *AI & Society*, •••, 1–12.

Hmoud, H., Al-Adwan, A. S., Horani, O., Yaseen, H., & Zoubi, J. Z. A. (2023). Factors influencing business intelligence adoption by higher education institutions. *Journal of Open Innovation*, 9(1), 12–26. DOI: 10.1016/j.joitmc.2023.100111

Hoe, S. L. (2016). Defining a smart nation: The case of Singapore. *Journal of Information. Communication and Ethics in Society*, 14(4), 323–333. DOI: 10.1108/JICES-02-2016-0005

Holgado, R. (2022,). El peligro del scroll infinito de las redes sociales: estas son las medidas que existen para combatir su adicción. https://www.20minutos.es/tecnologia/aplicaciones/el-peligro-del-scroll-infinito-de-las-redes-sociales-estas-son-las-medidas-que-existen-para-combatir-su-adiccion-5013669/

Howell, C. (2024). Interfaz de usuario de TikTok: Explicando las elecciones de diseño de TikTok.

Huang, X. (2009). Strategic decision making in Chinese SMEs. *Chinese Management Studies*, 3(2), 87–101. DOI: 10.1108/17506140910963602

Huiling, E., & Goh, B. (2017). AI, robotics and mobility as a service: The case of Singapore. *Field Actions Science Reports. The Journal of Field Actions, (Special Issue 17)*, 26-29.

Hussein, A.. (2018). Fingerprint profile multi-spectral capture device & patched-based CNN. *IEEE Transactions on Information Forensics and Security*, 13(11), 2804–2818.

IBM. (n.d.). Chart types. Retrieved from https://www.ibm.com/docs/es/cognos-analytics/11.1.0?topic=charts-chart-types

Ibrahim, N. M. H. (2024). Artificial intelligence (AI) and Saudi Arabia's governance. *Journal of Developing Societies*, 0169796X(4), 241288590. DOI: 10.1177/0169796X241288590

Ienca, M. (2023). On artificial intelligence and manipulation. *Topoi*, 42(3), 833–842. DOI: 10.1007/s11245-023-09940-3

Igbinenikaro, E., & Adewusi, O. A. (2024). Policy recommendations for integrating artificial intelligence into global trade agreements. *International Journal of Engineering Research Updates, 6*(01), 001-010.

Igbinenikaro, E., & Adewusi, A. O. (2024). Navigating the legal complexities of artificial intelligence in global trade agreements. *International Journal of Applied Research in Social Sciences*, 6(4), 488–505. DOI: 10.51594/ijarss.v6i4.987

Illia, L., Colleoni, E., & Zyglidopoulos, S. (2023). Ethical implications of text generation in the age of artificial intelligence. *Business Ethics, the Environment & Responsibility*, 32(1), 201–210. DOI: 10.1111/beer.12479

Institute for Health Metrics and Evaluation (IHME). (2019). *Global Burden of Disease Study 2019 (GBD 2019) results*. Seattle, WA: IHME, University of Washington. Retrieved from https://ghdx.healthdata.org/gbd-2019

Iqbal, M. (2024). TikTok Revenue and Usage Statistics. https://www.businessofapps.com/data/tik-tok-statistics/

Iqbal, M., Kazmi, S. H. A., Manzoor, A., Soomrani, A. R., Butt, S. H., & Shaikh, K. A. (2018). A study of big data for business growth in SMEs: Opportunities & challenges. In *2018 International conference on computing, mathematics and engineering technologies (iCoMET)* (pp. 1-7). IEEE. DOI: 10.1109/ICOMET.2018.8346368

Iyengar, S., & Kinder, D. R. (1987). *News that matters: Television and American opinion*. University of Chicago Press., DOI: 10.7208/chicago/9780226388533.001.0001

Jamali, D., Moonesar, I., & Al Suwaidi, H. (2024). AI and sustainable urban planning in Dubai. *Journal of Smart Cities and Urban Innovation*, 12(1), 85–102.

Jangid, P., & Inbaraj, M. P. (2021). Applications of nanomaterials in wastewater treatment. *Materials Today: Proceedings*, 43(5), 2877–2881. https://www.sciencedirect.com/science/article/pii/S2214785321001693. DOI: 10.1016/j.matpr.2021.01.126

Javed, Y., & Alenezi, M. (2023). A case study on sustainable quality assurance in higher education. *Sustainability (Basel)*, 15(7), 45–63. DOI: 10.3390/su15108136

Jermalavičius, T. (2024). Caught between today and tomorrow: Defence AI in Estonia. In *The Very Long Game: 25 Case Studies on the Global State of Defense AI* (pp. 149–171). Springer Nature Switzerland. DOI: 10.1007/978-3-031-58649-1_7

Joamets, K., & Chochia, A. (2020). Artificial intelligence and its impact on labour relations in Estonia. *Slovak Journal of Political Sciences*, 20(2), 255–277. DOI: 10.34135/sjps.200204

Jodha, D., & Bera, P. (2023). Copyright issues in the era of Ai-A critical analysis. *Res Militaris*, 13(3), 1737–1748.

Johnson, E. J., & Goldstein, D. G. (2003). Do defaults save lives? *Science*, 302(5649), 1338–1339. DOI: 10.1126/science.1091721 PMID: 14631022

Kahneman, D. (2011). *Thinking, Fast and Slow*. Farrar, Straus and Giroux.

Kahneman, D., & Tversky, A. (1979). Prospect Theory: An Analysis of Decision under Risk. *Econometrica*, 47(2), 263–291. DOI: 10.2307/1914185

Kalpokiene, J., & Kalpokas, I. (2023). Creative encounters of a posthuman kind–anthropocentric law, artificial intelligence, and art. *Technology in Society*, 72, 102197. DOI: 10.1016/j.techsoc.2023.102197

Kampf, C. (2014). The cultural production of new forms of practice: Social media, CSR and lifelong learning for consumers. In *2014 IEEE International Professional Communication Conference (IPCC)*. DOI: 10.1109/IPCC.2014.7020382

Kanbach, D. K., Heiduk, L., Blueher, G., Schreiter, M., & Lahmann, A. (2024). The GenAI is out of the bottle: Generative artificial intelligence from a business model innovation perspective. *Review of Managerial Science*, 18(4), 1189–1220. DOI: 10.1007/s11846-023-00696-z

Kandhro, I. A., Alanazi, S. M., & Karuppayah, S. (2023). Detection of real-time malicious intrusions and attacks in IoT-empowered cybersecurity infrastructures. *IEEE Access : Practical Innovations, Open Solutions*, 11, 9136–9148. DOI: 10.1109/ACCESS.2023.3238664

Kanojia, S. (2023). Ensuring privacy of personal data: A panoramic view of legal developments in personal data protection law in Saudi Arabia. *Manchester Journal of Transnational Islamic Law and Practice*, 19(3), 270–276.

Karpouzoglou, T., Dewulf, A., & Clark, J. (2016). Advancing adaptive governance of social-ecological systems through theoretical multiplicity. *Environmental Science & Policy*, 57, 1–9. DOI: 10.1016/j.envsci.2015.11.011

Kedi, W. E., Ejimuda, C., Idemudia, C., & Ijomah, T. I. (2024). Machine learning software for optimizing SME social media marketing campaigns. *Computer Science & IT Research Journal*, 5(7), 1634–1647. DOI: 10.51594/csitrj.v5i7.1349

Keikhosrokiani, P. (2022a). Big Data Analytics for Healthcare: Datasets, Techniques, Life Cycles, Management, and Applications. In Big Data Analytics for Healthcare: Datasets, Techniques, Life Cycles, Management, and Applications. DOI: 10.1016/C2021-0-00369-2

Keikhosrokiani, P. (2022b). Handbook of research on consumer behavior change and data analytics in the socio-digital era. In Handbook of Research on Consumer Behavior Change and Data Analytics in the Socio-Digital Era. DOI: 10.4018/978-1-6684-4168-8

Keikhosrokiani, P. (2023). *Handbook of Research on Consumer Behavioral Analytics in Metaverse and the Adoption of a Virtual World*. IGI Global., DOI: 10.4018/978-1-6684-7029-9

Kerikmäe, T., & Pärn-Lee, E. (2021). Legal dilemmas of Estonian artificial intelligence strategy: In between of e-society and global race. *AI & Society*, 36(2), 561–572. DOI: 10.1007/s00146-020-01009-8

Khan, A., & Jiliani, M. A. H. S. (2023). Expanding The Boundaries Of Jurisprudence In The Era Of Technological Advancements. *IIUMLJ*, 31(2), 393–426. DOI: 10.31436/iiumlj.v31i2.856

Khan, M. K., & Khan, M. B. (Eds.). (2020). *Research, innovation and entrepreneurship in Saudi Arabia: Vision 2030*. Routledge. DOI: 10.4324/9781351040020

Kharpal, A. (2023, March 16). TikTok confirms the U.S. has threatened ban if Chinese parent ByteDance doesn't sell stake. CNBC. https://www.cnbc.com/2023/03/16/TikTok-us-threatens-ban-if-chineseparent-bytedance-doesnt-sell-stake.html

Khrennikov, A. (2020). Social Laser Model for the Bandwagon Effect: Generation of Coherent Information Waves. *Entropy (Basel, Switzerland)*, 22(5), 559. DOI: 10.3390/e22050559 PMID: 33286331

Kilgour, L., Sutherland, T., & Wood, S. (2020). Introduction to the Minitrack on critical and ethical studies of digital and social media. In *Proceedings of the 53rd Hawaii International Conference on System Sciences*. DOI: 10.24251/HICSS.2020.289

Kinder, T., Stenvall, J., Koskimies, E., Webb, H. L., & Janenova, S. (2023). Local public services and the ethical deployment of artificial intelligence. *Government Information Quarterly*, 40(4), 101865. Advance online publication. DOI: 10.1016/j.giq.2023.101865

Kirova, V. D., Ku, C. S., Laracy, J. R., & Marlowe, T. J. (2023). The ethics of artificial intelligence in the era of generative AI. *Journal of Systemics, Cybernetics and Informatics*, 21(4), 42–50. DOI: 10.54808/JSCI.21.04.42

Kolides, A., Nawaz, A., Rathor, A., Beeman, D., Hashmi, M., Fatima, S., Berdik, D., Al-Ayyoub, M., & Jararweh, Y. (2023). Artificial intelligence foundation and pre-trained models: Fundamentals, applications, opportunities, and social impacts. *Simulation Modelling Practice and Theory*, 126, 102754. DOI: 10.1016/j.simpat.2023.102754

Koob, G. F., & Volkow, N. D. (2010). Neurocircuitry of addiction. *Neuropsychopharmacology*, 35(1), 217–238. DOI: 10.1038/npp.2009.110 PMID: 19710631

Kostenko, O. M., Bieliakov, K. I., Tykhomyrov, O. O., & Aristova, I. V. (2024). "Legal personality" of artificial intelligence: Methodological problems of scientific reasoning by Ukrainian and EU experts. *AI & Society*, 39(4), 1683–1693. DOI: 10.1007/s00146-023-01641-0

Koutsikouri, D., Hylving, L., Raftopoulos, M., Ngwenyama, O., Rowe, F., & Tona, O. (2024). Human Flourishing in the Digital Age: What Responsibilities does/should Researcher (s) Have? Perspectives from the AIS Community. *Communications of the Association for Information Systems*, 55(1), 1.

Krizhevsky, A., Sutskever, I., & Hinton, G. E. (2012). ImageNet classification with deep convolutional neural networks. In *Advances in Neural Information Processing Systems (NeurIPS)*, 25, 1097-1105.

Kruger, J., & Dunning, D. (1999). Unskilled and unaware of it: How difficulties in recognizing one's own incompetence lead to inflated self-assessments. *Journal of Personality and Social Psychology*, 77(6), 1121–1134. DOI: 10.1037/0022-3514.77.6.1121 PMID: 10626367

Kuberkar, S., & Singhal, T. K. (2024). Adoption of AI-enabled smart city services from citizens' perspective. *Journal of Urban Technology and Innovation*, 12(1), 56–72.

Kulal, A., Rahiman, H. U., Suvarna, H., Abhishek, N., & Dinesh, S. (2024). Enhancing public service delivery efficiency: Exploring the impact of AI. *Journal of Open Innovation*, 10(3), 100329. DOI: 10.1016/j.joitmc.2024.100329

Kuziemski, M., & Misuraca, G. (2020). AI governance in the public sector: Three tales from the frontiers of automated decision-making in democratic settings. *Telecommunications Policy*, 44(6), 101976. DOI: 10.1016/j.telpol.2020.101976 PMID: 32313360

La Torre, D., Appio, F. P., Masri, H., Lazzeri, F., & Schiavone, F. (2023). *Impact of artificial intelligence in business and society: Opportunities and Challenges*. Routledge. DOI: 10.4324/9781003304616

Lacárcel, F. J. S., & Huete, R. (2023). Digital communication strategies used by private companies, entrepreneurs, and public entities to attract long-stay tourists: A review. *The International Entrepreneurship and Management Journal*, 19(2), 691–708. DOI: 10.1007/s11365-023-00843-8

Lafont, J., Saura, J. R., & Ribeiro-Soriano, D. (2023). The role of Cooperatives in Sustainable Development Goals: A discussion about the current resource curse. *Resources Policy*, 83, 103670. DOI: 10.1016/j.resourpol.2023.103670

LeDoux, J. E. (1996). *The Emotional Brain: The Mysterious Underpinnings of Emotional Life*. Simon and Schuster.

Lee, W. E., & Perdana, A. (2023). Effects of experiential service learning in improving community engagement perception, sustainability awareness, and data analytics competency. *Journal of Accounting Education*, 45(2), 112–128. DOI: 10.1016/j.jaccedu.2023.00123

Leibenstein, H. (1950). Bandwagon, Snob, and Veblen Effects in the Theory of Consumers' Demand. *The Quarterly Journal of Economics*, 64(2), 183–207. DOI: 10.2307/1882692

Leibniz, G. W. (1714). *Monadology* (Rescher, N., Trans.). University of Pittsburgh Press. (Original work published 1714)

Lelkes, Y., Sood, G., & Iyengar, S. (2017). The hostile audience: The effect of access to broadband internet on partisan affect. *American Journal of Political Science*, 61(1), 5–20. DOI: 10.1111/ajps.12237

Leonard, T. C. (2008). Richard H. Thaler, Cass R. Sunstein, Nudge: Improving Decisions About Health, Wealth, and Happiness. *Constitutional Political Economy*, 19(4), 356–360. DOI: 10.1007/s10602-008-9056-2

Leong, S., Lee, T., Leong, S., & Lee, T. (2021). The internet in Singapore: From 'intelligent island' to 'smart nation.' *Global Internet Governance: Influences from Malaysia and Singapore,* 31-49.

Lerman, A. E., & Acland, D. (2018). United in States of Dissatisfaction: Confirmation Bias Across the Partisan Divide. *American Politics Research*, 48(2), 246–275. DOI: 10.1177/1532673X18799274

Levin, Y. (2022, August 5). Opinion | It Was a Mistake to Let Kids Onto Social Media Sites. Here's What to Do Now. The New York Times. https://www.nytimes.com/2022/08/05/opinion/social-media-parentschildren.html

Leviston, Z., Walker, I., & Morwinski, S. (2012). Your opinion on climate change might not be as common as you think. *Nature Climate Change*, 3(4), 334–337. DOI: 10.1038/nclimate1743

Lewandowsky, S., Ecker, U. K. H., & Cook, J. (2017). Beyond misinformation: Understanding and coping with the "post-truth" era. *Journal of Applied Research in Memory and Cognition*, 6(4), 353–369. DOI: 10.1016/j.jarmac.2017.07.008

Ligthart, S., Ienca, M., Meynen, G., Molnar-Gabor, F., Andorno, R., Bublitz, C., Catley, P., Claydon, L., Douglas, T., Farahany, N., Fins, J. J., Goering, S., Haselager, P., Jotterand, F., Lavazza, A., McCay, A., Wajnerman Paz, A., Rainey, S., Ryberg, J., & Kellmeyer, P. (2023). Minding rights: Mapping ethical and legal foundations of 'neurorights'. *Cambridge Quarterly of Healthcare Ethics*, 32(4), 461–481. DOI: 10.1017/S0963180123000245 PMID: 37183686

Lim, T., Rajabifard, A., Khoo, V., Sabri, S., & Chen, Y. (2021). The smart city in Singapore: How environmental and geospatial innovation lead to urban livability and sustainability. In H. M. Kim, S. Sabri, and A. Kent (Eds.), *Smart cities for technological and social innovation: Case studies, current trends, and future steps* (pp. 13–27). Elsevier. DOI: 10.1016/B978-0-12-818886-6.00003-4

Lin, H., Potenza, M. N., Wu, H., & Yücel, M. (2014). Aberrant striatal response to reward anticipation in Internet gaming disorder. *Addiction Biology*, 19(3), 423–432. PMID: 24725195

Linnenluecke, M. K., Marrone, M., & Singh, A. K. (2020). Conducting systematic literature reviews and bibliometric analyses. *Australian Journal of Management*, 45(2), 175–194. DOI: 10.1177/0312896219877678

Li, P., Bastone, A., Mohamad, T. A., & Schiavone, F. (2023). How does artificial intelligence impact human resources performance: Evidence from a healthcare institution in the United Arab Emirates. *Journal of Innovation and Knowledge*, 8(2), 100340. Advance online publication. DOI: 10.1016/j.jik.2023.100340

Li, T., & Jager, W. (2023). How availability heuristic, confirmation bias and fear may drive societal polarisation: An opinion dynamics simulation of the case of covid-19 vaccination. *Journal of Artificial Societies and Social Simulation*, 26(4), 2. Advance online publication. DOI: 10.18564/jasss.5135

Liu, L. (2023). Analysis of the Challenges of Overseas Students Returning to China for Employment in the Labor Market—Based on the Re-discussion of the Value of Western Higher Education.

Liu, S., Ko, Q. S., Heng, K. Q. A., Ngiam, K. Y., & Feng, M. (2020). Healthcare transformation in Singapore with artificial intelligence. *Frontiers in Digital Health*, 2, 592121. DOI: 10.3389/fdgth.2020.592121 PMID: 34713061

Liu, S., Wang, L., & Gao, R. X. (2024). Cognitive neuroscience and robotics: Advancements and future research directions. *Robotics and Computer-integrated Manufacturing*, 85, 102610. Advance online publication. DOI: 10.1016/j.rcim.2023.102610

Lobell, D. B., Tommaso, S. D., Burke, M., & Kilic, T. (2021). Twice Is Nice: The Benefits of Two Ground Measures for Evaluating the Accuracy of Satellite-Based Sustainability Estimates. In D. B.

Loewenstein, G., Bryce, C. L., Hagmann, D., & Rajpal, S. (2014). Warning: you are about to be nudged. SSRN *Electronic Journal*. DOI: 10.2139/ssrn.2417383

Lopez, J. (2023). Analyzing TikTok UX/UI: Unveiling the Magic Behind User Behavior and the Infinite Scroll.

López, A. C. (2023). La globalización de la censura: Nuevas aplicaciones de gobiernos y redes sociales tras el conflicto en Ucrania. *Revista de el Colegio de San Luis*, 13(24), 1–34. DOI: 10.21696/rcsl132420231552

Lopez-Torres, G. C. (2023). The impact of SMEs' sustainability on competitiveness. *Measuring Business Excellence*, 27(1), 107–120. DOI: 10.1108/MBE-12-2021-0144

Lord, C. G., Ross, L., & Lepper, M. R. (1979). Biased assimilation and attitude polarization: The effects of prior theories on subsequently considered evidence. *Journal of Personality and Social Psychology*, 37(11), 2098–2109. DOI: 10.1037/0022-3514.37.11.2098

Lozano, I. A., Molina, J. M., & Gijón, C. (2021). Perception of artificial intelligence in Spain. *Telematics and Informatics*, 63, 101672. DOI: 10.1016/j.tele.2021.101672

Lucchi, N. (2023). ChatGPT: A case study on copyright challenges for generative artificial intelligence systems. *European Journal of Risk Regulation*, •••, 1–23.

Luo, H., Lin, L., Chen, K., Antwi-Afari, M. F., & Chen, L. (2022). Digital technology for quality management in construction: A review and future research directions. *Developments in the Built Environment*, 12, 100087. DOI: 10.1016/j.dibe.2022.100087

Lyulyov, O., Pimonenko, T., Saura, J. R., & Barbosa, B. (2024). How do e-governance and e-business drive sustainable development goals? *Technological Forecasting and Social Change*, 199, 123082. DOI: 10.1016/j.techfore.2023.123082

Macit, H. B., Macit, G., & Güngör, O. (2018). A RESEARCH ON SOCIAL MEDIA ADDICTION AND DOPAMINE DRIVEN FEEDBACK. *Mehmet Akif Ersoy Üniversitesi İktisadi Ve İdari Bilimler Fakültesi Dergisi*, 5(3), 882–897. DOI: 10.30798/makuiibf.435845

Majid, G. M., Tussyadiah, I., & Kim, Y. R. (2024). Exploring the potential of chatbots in extending tourists' sustainable travel practices. *Journal of Travel Research*, 00472875241247316. Advance online publication. DOI: 10.1177/00472875241247316

Makridakis, S. (2017). The forthcoming artificial intelligence (AI) revolution: Its impact on society and firms. *Futures*, 90, 46–60. DOI: 10.1016/j.futures.2017.03.006

Manjula, S., & Raj, A. (2022). Assessment of waste management through mobile edge computing and deep learning. *International Journal of Advanced Research in Science. Tongxin Jishu*, •••, 297–315. DOI: 10.48175/IJARSCT-3186

Manning, P. (2013). Big Data in History. In Manning, P. (Ed.), *Palgrave Macmillan UK eBooks*. Palgrave Macmillan. DOI: 10.1057/9781137378972

Mannuru, N. R., Shahriar, S., Teel, Z. A., Wang, T., Lund, B. D., Tijani, S., Pohboon, C. O., Agbaji, D., Alhassan, J., Galley, J. K. L., Kousari, R., Ogbadu-Oladapo, L., Saurav, S. K., Srivastava, A., Tummuru, S. P., Uppala, S., & Vaidya, P. (2023). Artificial intelligence in developing countries: The impact of generative artificial intelligence (AI) technologies for development. *Information Development*, •••, 02666669231200628. DOI: 10.1177/02666669231200628

Manzoor, B., Othman, I., Durdyev, S., Ismail, S., & Wahab, M. H. (2021). Influence of artificial intelligence in civil engineering toward sustainable development: A systematic literature review. *Applied System Innovation*, 4(3), 52. DOI: 10.3390/asi4030052

Marasco, E., & Sansone, C. (2010). Fingerprint textural profile static feature SVM. In *Proceedings of the 2010 20th International Conference on Pattern Recognition (ICPR)* (pp. 3049-3052). Istanbul, Turkey.

Mariani, M. M., Machado, I., Magrelli, V., & Dwivedi, Y. K. (2023). Artificial intelligence in innovation research: A systematic review, conceptual framework, and future research directions. *Technovation*, 122, 102623. DOI: 10.1016/j.technovation.2022.102623

Mark, G., Gudith, D., & Klocke, U. (2008). The cost of interrupted work: More speed and stress. *Proceedings of the SIGCHI Conference on Human Factors in Computing Systems*, 107-110. DOI: 10.1145/1357054.1357072

Maroufkhani, P., Iranmanesh, M., & Ghobakhloo, M. (2023). Determinants of big data analytics adoption in small and medium-sized enterprises (SMEs). *Industrial Management & Data Systems*, 123(1), 278–301. DOI: 10.1108/IMDS-11-2021-0695

Marri, A. A., Albloosh, F., Moussa, S., & Elmessiry, H. (2019). Study on the impact of artificial intelligence on government e-service in Dubai. In *Proceedings of the 2019 International Conference on Digitization* (pp. 153–159). IEEE. DOI: 10.1109/ICD47981.2019.9105866

Martignon, L., & Gaissmaier, W. (2011). Heuristic decision making. *Annual Review of Psychology*, 62(1), 451–482. DOI: 10.1146/annurev-psych-120709-145346 PMID: 21126183

Marzi, G., Marrucci, A., Vianelli, D., & Ciappei, C. (2023). B2B digital platform adoption by SMEs and large firms: Pathways and pitfalls. *Industrial Marketing Management*, 114, 80–93. DOI: 10.1016/j.indmarman.2023.08.002

Maser, R.. (2019). Finger vein photoresponse nonuniformity. In *Proceedings of the IEEE International Conference on Identity, Security, and Behavior Analysis (ISBA)* (pp. 1-8). Hyannis, MA.

Masso, A., Kaun, A., & Van Noordt, C. (2023). Basic values in artificial intelligence: Comparative factor analysis in Estonia, Germany, and Sweden. *AI & Society*, •••, 1–16.

Mazor, M., & Fleming, S. M. (2021). The dunning-kruger effect revisited. *Nature Human Behaviour*, 5(6), 677–678. DOI: 10.1038/s41562-021-01101-z PMID: 33833426

McAfee, A., & Brynjolfsson, E. (2012). Big Data: The Management Revolution. Available at: https://hbr.org/2012/10/big-data-the-management-revolution

Memish, Z. A., Altuwaijri, M. M., Almoeen, A. H., & Enani, S. M. (2021). The Saudi Data & Artificial Intelligence Authority (SDAIA) vision: Leading the kingdom's journey toward global leadership. *Journal of Epidemiology and Global Health*, 11(2), 140–142. DOI: 10.2991/jegh.k.210405.001 PMID: 33876596

Meyer, C. B. (2001). A case in case study methodology. *Field Methods*, 13(4), 329–352. DOI: 10.1177/1525822X0101300402

Milakovich, M. E. (2012). *Digital governance: New technologies for improving public service and participation*. Routledge., DOI: 10.4324/9780203815991

Mills, S. (2022). Finding the 'nudge' in hypernudge. *Technology in Society*, 71, 102117. DOI: 10.1016/j.techsoc.2022.102117

Ministerio de Universidades. (2021). Real Decreto 822/2021, de 28 de septiembre, por el que se establece la organización de las enseñanzas universitarias y del procedimiento de aseguramiento de su calidad. *Boletín Oficial del Estado, núm. 233*. Recuperado de https://www.boe.es/eli/es/rd/2021/09/28/822/co

Ministerio de Universidades. (2024). *Metodología de Estadística de Estudiantes Universitarios*. EEU.

Ministry of Finance. (2024). Mohammed bin Rashid Innovation Fund (MBRIF). https://www.mof.gov.ae

Ministry of Universities. (2021). Royal Decree 822/2021, of September 28, establishing the organization of university education and the quality assurance procedure. Retrieved from https://www.boe.es/buscar/act.php?id=BOE-A-2021-15781

Ministry of Universities. (n.d.). Student statistics. Retrieved from https://www.universidades.gob.es/estadistica-de-estudiantes/

Miric, M., Jia, N., & Huang, K. G. (2023). Using supervised machine learning for large-scale classification in management research: The case for identifying artificial intelligence patents. *Strategic Management Journal*, 44(2), 491–519. DOI: 10.1002/smj.3441

Mohammed bin Rashid Library Foundation. (2023). *Revolutionizing knowledge access with AI at the Mohammed bin Rashid Library*. https://www.mbrl.ae/smart-services

Monasterio-Exposito, L., Pizarro, D., & Macias-Guarasa, J. (2022). Label augmentation to improve generalization of deep learning semantic segmentation of laparoscopic images. *IEEE Access : Practical Innovations, Open Solutions*, 10, 37345–37359. DOI: 10.1109/ACCESS.2022.3162630

Montag, C., Lachmann, B., Herrlich, M., & Zweig, K. (2019, July 23). Addictive Features of Social Media/Messenger Platforms and Freemium Games against the Background of Psychological and Economic Theories. *International Journal of Environmental Research and Public Health*, 16(14), 2612. DOI: 10.3390/ijerph16142612 PMID: 31340426

Moore, E. M., Dau, L. A., & Mingo, S. (2021). The effects of trade integration on formal and informal entrepreneurship: The moderating role of economic development. *Journal of International Business Studies*, 52(4), 746–772. DOI: 10.1057/s41267-020-00386-y

Moreland, S., Zviedrite, N., Ahmed, F., & Uzicanin, A. (2023). COVID-19 prevention at institutions of higher education, United States, 2020–2021: Implementation of nonpharmaceutical interventions. *BMC Public Health*, 23(3), 567–580. DOI: 10.1186/s12889-023-15079-y PMID: 36694136

Morrison, S. (2023). TikTok is confusing by design: TikTok isn't the way I want the internet to work, but it's where the internet is going. https://www.vox.com/technology/23780112/TikTok-internet-design-algorithm-for-you-page-ux-ui

Morton, R. B., Muller, S., Page, L., & Torgler, B. (2015). Exit polls, turnout, and bandwagon voting: Evidence from a natural experiment. *European Economic Review*, 77, 65–81. DOI: 10.1016/j.euroecorev.2015.03.012

Mosbah, A., & Debili, R. (2014). Development of Algerian SMEs in the age of mosglobalization. *Journal of business and social development, 2*(1), 37-48.

Mosbah, A., Alrawi, M. A., & Noorita, M. T. (2023). Empowering small and medium enterprises with data analytics for enhanced competitiveness. 2023 IEEE 13th International Conference on Control System, Computing and Engineering (ICCSCE), 25–26 Aug 2023, Penang, Malaysia.

Mosbah, A., Ali, M. A., Aljubari, I. H., & Sherief, S. R. (2018). Migrants in the High-Tech and engineering sectors: an emerging research area. In *2018 IEEE Conference on Systems, Process and Control (ICSPC)* (pp. 234-237). IEEE. DOI: 10.1109/SPC.2018.8704139

Mosbah, A., & Daghrir, F. (2017). High-tech immigrant entrepreneurship: A concise review. *International Journal of Technical Research & Science*, 2(2), 96–100.

Mountantonakis, M., & Tzitzikas, Y. (2023). Validating ChatGPT Facts through RDF Knowledge Graphs and Sentence Similarity. arXiv preprint arXiv:2311.04524.

Mozos-Blanco, M. Á., Pozo-Menéndez, E., Arce-Ruiz, R., & Baucells-Aletà, N. (2018). The way to sustainable mobility: A comparative analysis of sustainable mobility plans in Spain. *Transport Policy*, 72, 45–54. DOI: 10.1016/j.tranpol.2018.07.001

Mullainathan, S., & Thaler, R. H. (2001). Behavioral Economics. In Smelser, N. J., & Baltes, P. B. (Eds.), *International Encyclopedia of the Social and Behavioral Sciences* (pp. 1094–1100). Elsevier., DOI: 10.1016/B0-08-043076-7/02247-6

Mutasher WG, Aljuboori AF. (2022). New and Existing Approaches Reviewing of Big Data Analysis with Hadoop Tools. *Baghdad Science Journal*. 1;19(4):0887-.

Nabbosa, V. L., & Kaar, C. (2020). *Societal and Ethical Issues of Digitalization*. DOI: 10.1145/3437075.3437093

National Institutes of Health. (2024, April 18). *Using AI to shape the future of treatment personalization*. National Center for Advancing Translational Sciences. https://ncats.nih.gov/news-events/news/using-ai-to-shape-the-future-of-treatment -personalization

New York City Mayor's Office of Technology. (2023). *New York City AI initiatives in public services*. https://www.nyc.gov/content/oti/pages/artificial-intelligence

New York City Open Data. (2023). *Digital services and AI applications in healthcare*. https://www.nyc.gov/opendata

Newell, A., Yang, K., & Deng, J. (2016). Stacked hourglass networks for human pose estimation. In *Proceedings of the European Conference on Computer Vision (ECCV)*, 9905, 483-499. DOI: 10.1007/978-3-319-46484-8_29

Neyazi, T. A., Ng, S. W. T., Hobbs, M., & Yue, A. (2023). Understanding user interactions and perceptions of AI risk in Singapore. *Big Data & Society*, 10(2), 20539517231213823. DOI: 10.1177/20539517231213823

Nhemi, S. (2023). Law Without Lawyers: Examining the Limitations of Consumer-Centric Legal Tech Services. *J. Intell. Prop. & Info. Tech. L.*, 3(1), 15–76. DOI: 10.52907/jipit.v3i1.223

Nickell, E. B., Schwebke, J., & Goldwater, P. (2023). An introductory audit data analytics case study: Using Microsoft Power BI and Benford's Law to detect accounting irregularities. *Journal of Accounting Education*. Recuperado de https://sciencedirect.com

Nickerson, R. S. (1998). Confirmation bias: A ubiquitous phenomenon in many guises. *Review of General Psychology*, 2(2), 175–220. DOI: 10.1037/1089-2680.2.2.175

Njie, B., & Asimiran, S. (2014). Case study as a choice in qualitative methodology. *Journal of research & method in Education, 4*(3), 35-40.

Ochoa, F., & Barragán, M. (2022). El uso en exceso de las redes sociales en medio de la pandemia. ACADEMO *Revista de Investigación en Ciencias Sociales y Humanidades*, 9(1). 85-92. https://doi.org/jzjh

OECD. (2020). *Tools and Ethics for Applied Behavioural Insights: The BASIC Toolkit*. Retrieved from OECD.

OECD. (2021). Enhancing Healthcare Operations through Advanced BI Tools. *International Journal of Healthcare Management*, 12(1), 67–85. DOI: 10.1016/j.jhm.2021.01.004

OECD. (2022). Financing growth and turning data into business: Helping SMEs scale up. https://shorturl.at/HbGKn

Orejón-Sanchez, R. D., Crespo-Garcia, D., Andres-Diaz, J. R., & Gago-Calderon, A. (2022). Smart cities' development in Spain: A comparison of technical and social indicators with reference to European cities. *Sustainable Cities and Society*, 81, 103828. DOI: 10.1016/j.scs.2022.103828

Organisation for Economic Co-operation and Development. (2017). Behavioural Insights and Public Policy: Lessons from Around the World. https://www.oecd.org/en/publications/behavioural-insights-and-public-policy_9789264270480-en.html

Orihuela-Colliva, J. L. (José Luis). "Internet: la hora de las redes sociales". En., 2008-10-14T10:48:23Z, https://hdl.handle.net/10171/2962

Ortega-Calvo, A. S., Morcillo-Jimenez, R., Fernandez-Basso, C., Gutiérrez-Batista, K., Vila, M. A., & Martin-Bautista, M. J. (2023). Aimdp: An artificial intelligence modern data platform. Use case for Spanish national health service data silo. *Future Generation Computer Systems*, 143, 248–264. DOI: 10.1016/j.future.2023.02.002

Osoba, O., & Welser, W. (2017). An Intelligence in Our Image: The Risks of Bias and Errors in Artificial Intelligence. In *O. Osoba & W. Welser*. RAND Corporation. DOI: 10.7249/RR1744

Otsu, N. (1979). A threshold selection method from gray-level histograms. *IEEE Transactions on Systems, Man, and Cybernetics*, 9(1), 62–66. DOI: 10.1109/TSMC.1979.4310076

Owais, M., & Alshehri, A. (•••). Perspectives on intelligent transportation systems future in Mecca area. [Paes, S. Centric AI: From ethics to action: A study of human-centric AI implementation in public services, comparing the Estonian approach with approaches used in other countries.]. *International Journal of Computer Applications*, 975, 8887.

Pagani, R. N., de Sá, C. P., Corsi, A., & de Souza, F. F. (2023). AI and Employability: Challenges and Solutions from this Technology Transfer. In *Smart Cities and Digital Transformation: Empowering Communities, Limitless Innovation, Sustainable Development and the Next Generation* (pp. 253-284). Emerald Publishing Limited. DOI: 10.1108/978-1-80455-994-920231012

*Pal,K.(2016). Supply Chain Coordination Based on Web Service, Supply Chain Management in the Big Data Era, Hing Kai Chan, Nachiappan Subramanian, and Muhammad Dan-Asabe Abdulrahman (edited Book Chapter), IGI Publication, Chapter 9, 137-170.*https://doi.org/DOI: 10.4018/978-1-5225-0956-1.ch009

Pal,K.(2020b). Information sharing for manufacturing supply chain management based on blockchain technology, in cross-Industry Use of Blockchain Technology and Opportunities for the Future, I. Williams (Edited), 1-17, IGI Global Publication, 701 E Chocolate Avenue, Hershey, PA, USA 17033. https://doi.org/DOI: 10.4018/978-1-7998-3632-2.ch001

*Pal,K.(2021). Applications of Secured Blockchain Technology in Manufacturing Industry, in Blockchain and AI Technology in the Industrial Internet of Things, Subhendu Kumar Pani, Biju Patnaik, Sian Lun, & Xingcheng Liu (Edited), Chapter 10, January 2021, IGI Global Publication, 701 E Chocolate Avenue, Hershey, PA, USA 17033.*https://doi.org/DOI: 10.4018/978-1-7998-6694-7.ch010

*Pal,K.(2023). Drivers of Sustainable Supply Chain Management Using Internet of Things-Based Blockchain Technology, in Government Impact on Sustainable and Responsible Supply Chan, Atour Taghipour (Edited), Chapter 10, 171-201, IGI Global Publication, 701 E Chocolate Avenue, Hershey, PA, USA 17033.*https://doi.org/DOI: 10.4018/978-1-6684-9062-4.ch010

Pal, K., & Yasar, A. (2020a). Internet of Things and blockchain technology in textile manufacturing supply chain data management. *Procedia Computer Science*, 170, 450–457. DOI: 10.1016/j.procs.2020.03.088

Panda, S., & Kaur, R. (2024). AI-generated content moderation in digital platforms: A new frontier. *Technology and Innovation*. Advance online publication. DOI: 10.1016/techinn.2024.00123

Panthee, B., Gyawali, S., Panthee, P., & Techato, K. (2022). Environmental and human microbiome for health. *Life (Chicago, Ill.)*, 12(3), 456–456. DOI: 10.3390/life12030456 PMID: 35330207

Pappas, I., Jaccheri, L., Mikalef, P., & Giannakos, M. (2017). Social innovation and social entrepreneurship through big data: developing a research agenda.

Paraman, P., & Anamalah, S. (2023). Ethical artificial intelligence framework for a good AI society: Principles, opportunities and perils. *AI & Society*, 38(2), 595–611. DOI: 10.1007/s00146-022-01458-3

Pariser, E. (2011). *The filter bubble: How the new personalized web is changing what we read and how we think*. Penguin Press.

Pasquinelli, M. (2023). *The eye of the master: A social history of artificial intelligence*. Verso Books.

Perez, S. (2022, July 13). Kids and teens spend more time on TikTok than YouTube. TechCrunch. https://techcrunch.com/2022/07/13/kids-andteens-watch-more-TikTok-than-youtube-TikTok-91-minutes-in-2021- youtube-56/

Popenici, S. (2023). The critique of AI as a foundation for judicious use in higher education. *Journal of Applied Learning and Teaching*, 6(2).

Porter, M. (2001). The value chain and competitive advantage. In *Understanding Business: Processes; Barnes, D. (Edited)* (pp. 50–66). Routledge., DOI: 10.1201/9781420025569.ch8

Powell, A. C. (2020). Impact of the artificial nudge. *Academic Radiology*, 27(1), 143–146. DOI: 10.1016/j.acra.2019.09.010 PMID: 31818383

Prieto, F. A., Baltas, N. G., Rios-Pena, L., & Rodriguez, P. (2020). COVID-19 impact estimation on ICU capacity at Andalusia, Spain, using artificial intelligence.

Przybylski, A. K., Murayama, K., DeHaan, C. R., & Gladwell, V. (2013). Motivational, emotional, and behavioral correlates of fear of missing out. *Computers in Human Behavior*, 29(4), 1841–1848. DOI: 10.1016/j.chb.2013.02.014

Ptaszek, G. (2020). *From algorithmic surveillance to algorithmic awareness: Media education in the context of new media economics and invisible technologies*. Media.

Purwanto, A., Zuiderwijk, A., & Janssen, M. (2020, June). Citizens' trust in open government data: a quantitative study about the effects of data quality, system quality and service quality. In The 21st annual international conference on digital government research (pp. 310-318).

Pykett, J. (2016). *Brain Culture: Shaping Policy Through Neuroscience (English Edition)* (1.ª ed.). Policy Press.

Qin, D., Amariucai, G. T., & Fu, S. (2024). A comprehensive and reliable feature attribution method: Double-sided remove and reconstruct (DoRaR). *Neural Networks*, 173, 106166. Advance online publication. DOI: 10.1016/j.neunet.2024.106166 PMID: 38367355

Quach, S., Thaichon, P., Martin, K. D., Weaven, S., & Palmatier, R. W. (2022). Digital technologies: Tensions in privacy and data. *Journal of the Academy of Marketing Science*, 50(6), 1299–1323. DOI: 10.1007/s11747-022-00845-y PMID: 35281634

Quintero-Cacique, J. C., & Lesmes-Silva, A. K. (2021). ¿Por qué el ser humano es adicto a las redes sociales? *Revista CONVICCIONES*, 8(15), 6–9.

Rakshit, S., Mondal, S., Islam, N., Jasimuddin, S., & Zhang, Z. (2021). Social media and the new product development during COVID-19: An integrated model for SMEs. *Technological Forecasting and Social Change*, 170, 120869. DOI: 10.1016/j.techfore.2021.120869

Rauwerda, K., & De Graaf, F. J. (2021). Heuristics in financial decision-making: The selection of SME financing by advisers in an increasingly diverse market. *Management Decision*, 59(7), 1728–1749. DOI: 10.1108/MD-09-2019-1269

Rayhan, R., & Rayhan, S. (2023). AI and human rights: balancing innovation and privacy in the digital age. *DOI:. 2.2, 35394.*DOI: 10.13140/RG

Rehman, Z. (2023). Beyond Borders: International Law and Global Governance in the Digital Age. *Journal of Accounting & Business Archive Review*, 1(1), 1–12.

Rising, C. J., Kristensen, M., & Tjerrild-Hansen, S. 2014. Big data too big for SMEs? Available at: http://web.stanford.edu/class/msande238/projects/2014/GainIT.pdf

Risse, M. (2023). *Political theory of the digital age: Where artificial intelligence might take us.* Cambridge University Press. DOI: 10.1017/9781009255189

Rjab, A. B., & Mellouli, S. (2019). Artificial intelligence in smart cities: Systematic literature network analysis. In *Proceedings of the 12th International Conference on Theory and Practice of Electronic Governance* (pp. 259–269). Association for Computing Machinery. DOI: 10.1145/3326365.3326400

Roberts, H., Cowls, J., Hine, E., Morley, J., Wang, V., Taddeo, M., & Floridi, L. (2023). Governing artificial intelligence in China and the European Union: Comparing aims and promoting ethical outcomes. *The Information Society*, 39(2), 79–97. DOI: 10.1080/01972243.2022.2124565

Robinson, N., Hardy, A., & Ertan, A. (2021). *A curious and cautious approach to artificial intelligence and national security*. DOI: 10.2139/ssrn.4105328

Roche, C., Wall, P. J., & Lewis, D. (2023). Ethics and diversity in artificial intelligence policies, strategies and initiatives. *AI and Ethics*, 3(4), 1095–1115. DOI: 10.1007/s43681-022-00218-9 PMID: 36246014

Rogers, E. M. (1962). *Diffusion of innovations* (1st ed.). Free Press.

Ross, L., Greene, D., & House, P. (1977). The false consensus effect: An egocentric bias in social perception and attribution processes. *Journal of Experimental Social Psychology*, 13(3), 279–301. DOI: 10.1016/0022-1031(77)90049-X

Rozenman, G. G., Kundu, N. K., Liu, R., Zhang, L., Maslennikov, A., Reches, Y., & Youm, H. Y. (2023). The quantum internet: A synergy of quantum information technologies and 6G networks. *IET Quantum Communication*, 4(4), 147–166. DOI: 10.1049/qtc2.12069

Ruschemeier, H. (2023, February). AI as a challenge for legal regulation–the scope of application of the artificial intelligence act proposal. In *Era Forum* (Vol. 23, No. 3, pp. 361-376). Berlin/Heidelberg: Springer Berlin Heidelberg. DOI: 10.1007/s12027-022-00725-6

Sabour, S., Frosst, N., & Hinton, G. E. (2017). Dynamic routing between capsules. In *Advances in Neural Information Processing Systems (NeurIPS)*, 30, 3859-3869.

Sadeghian, A. H. and Otarkhani, A. (2023). Data-driven digital nudging: a systematic literature review and future agenda. Behaviour andAmp; *Information Technology*, 1-29. DOI: 10.1080/0144929X.2023.2286535

Sadowski, J. (2020). Too smart: How digital capitalism is extracting data, controlling our lives, and taking over the world.

Sag, M. (2023). Copyright safety for generative ai. *Houston Law Review*, 61, 295.

Sajjad, A.. (2019). Fingerprint pattern, face and palm vein convolution neural network, scale-invariant feature transform & ORB. In *Proceedings of the 2019 IEEE International Conference on Biometrics (ICB)* (pp. 1-6). Crete, Greece.

Sánchez Bravo, Á. (2022). España digital 2025. Estrategia nacional de inteligencia artificial. *Inteligencia artificial y filosofía del derecho.*

Sanina, A., Balashov, A., & Rubtcova, M. (2023). The socio-economic efficiency of digital government transformation. *International Journal of Public Administration*, 46(1), 85–96. DOI: 10.1080/01900692.2021.1988637

Santoni de Sio, F., Almeida, T., & Van Den Hoven, J. (2024). The future of work: Freedom, justice and capital in the age of artificial intelligence. *Critical Review of International Social and Political Philosophy*, 27(5), 659–683. DOI: 10.1080/13698230.2021.2008204

Sapolsky, R. (2003). Taming stress. *Scientific American*, 289(3), 86–95. PMID: 12951832

Saputro, R., Pappel, I., Vainsalu, H., Lips, S., & Draheim, D. (2020, April). Prerequisites for the adoption of the X-Road interoperability and data exchange framework: A comparative study. In *2020 Seventh International Conference on eDemocracy & eGovernment (ICEDEG)* (pp. 216-222). IEEE. DOI: 10.1109/ICEDEG48599.2020.9096704

Sarapuu, K., & Saarniit, L. (2020). Public administration in Estonia: A search for identity. *European Perspec*, 317.

Saraswat, D., Bhattacharya, P., Verma, A., Prasad, V. K., Tanwar, S., Sharma, G., Bokoro, P. N., & Sharma, R. (2022). Explainable AI for healthcare 5.0: Opportunities and challenges. *IEEE Access : Practical Innovations, Open Solutions*, 10, 84486–84517. DOI: 10.1109/ACCESS.2022.3197671

Saunders, J. (2023). Surveillance Graphs: Vulgarity and Cloud Orthodoxy in Linked Data Infrastructures.

Saura, J. R. (2022). Using predictive algorithm in local governance administrative decision making: a bibliometric analysis of current practices. *Smart cities and law, e-governance and rights, 178*(121561), 91.

Saura, J. R. (2024). Algorithms in Digital Marketing: Does Smart Personalization Promote a Privacy Paradox? *FIIB Business Review*, 13(5), 499–502. DOI: 10.1177/23197145241276898

Saura, J. R., & Debasa, F. (Eds.). (2022). *Handbook of research on artificial intelligence in government practices and processes*. IGI Global., DOI: 10.4018/978-1-7998-9609-8

Saura, J. R., Palacios-Marqués, D., & Iturricha-Fernández, A. (2021). Ethical design in social media: Assessing the main performance measurements of user online behavior modification. *Journal of Business Research*, 129, 271–281. DOI: 10.1016/j.jbusres.2021.03.001

Saura, J. R., Palacios-Marqués, D., & Ribeiro-Soriano, D. (2023a). Privacy concerns in social media UGC communities: Understanding user behavior sentiments in complex networks. *Information Systems and e-Business Management*, •••, 1–21. DOI: 10.1007/s10257-023-00631-5

Saura, J. R., Palacios-Marqués, D., & Soriano, D. R. (2021). Digital marketing in smes via data-driven strategies: Reviewing the current state of research. *Journal of Small Business Management*, 61(3), 1278–1313. DOI: 10.1080/00472778.2021.1955127

Saura, J. R., Ribeiro-Navarrete, S., Palacios-Marqués, D., & Mardani, A. (2023). Impact of extreme weather in production economics: Extracting evidence from user-generated content. *International Journal of Production Economics*, 260, 108861. DOI: 10.1016/j.ijpe.2023.108861

Saura, J. R., Ribeiro-Soriano, D., & Palacios-Marqués, D. (2021). Setting B2B digital marketing in artificial intelligence-based CRMs: A review and directions for future research. *Industrial Marketing Management*, 98(October), 161–178. DOI: 10.1016/j.indmarman.2021.08.006

Saura, J. R., Ribeiro-Soriano, D., & Palacios-Marqués, D. (2022). Assessing behavioral data science privacy issues in government artificial intelligence deployment. *Government Information Quarterly*, 39(4), 101679. DOI: 10.1016/j.giq.2022.101679

Saura, J. R., Skare, M., & Riberio-Navarrete, S. (2022). How Does Technology Enable Competitive Advantage? Reviewing State of the Art and Outlining Future Directions. *Journal of Competitiveness*, 14(4), 172–188. DOI: 10.7441/joc.2022.04.10

Saura, J. R., Škare, V., & Dosen, D. O. (2024). Is AI-based digital marketing ethical? Assessing a new data privacy paradox. *Journal of Innovation & Knowledge*, 9(4), 100597. DOI: 10.1016/j.jik.2024.100597

Saura, J. R., Soriano, D. R., & Saldaña, P. Z. (2022). Exploring the challenges of remote work on twitter users' sentiments: From digital technology development to a post-pandemic era. *Journal of Business Research*, 142, 242–254. DOI: 10.1016/j.jbusres.2021.12.052

Schlunegger, M. C., Zumstein-Shaha, M., & Palm, R. (2024). Methodologic and Data-Analysis Triangulation in Case Studies: A Scoping Review. *Western Journal of Nursing Research*, 46(8), 611–622. DOI: 10.1177/01939459241263011 PMID: 39076135

Schmauder, C., Karpus, J., Moll, M., Bahrami, B., & Deroy, O. (2023). Algorithmic nudging: The need for an interdisciplinary oversight. *Topoi*, 42(3), 799–807. DOI: 10.1007/s11245-023-09907-4

Schmidt, R., & Stenger, K. (2021). Behavioral brittleness: The case for strategic behavioral public policy. *Behavioural Public Policy*, 8(2), 212–237. DOI: 10.1017/bpp.2021.16

Schmitt-Beck, R. (1996). Mass media, the electorate, and the bandwagon: A study of communication effects on vote choice in Germany. *International Journal of Public Opinion Research*, 8(3), 266–291. DOI: 10.1093/ijpor/8.3.266

Scientist. (2017). A Conversation with Bill Congdon, Former Member of the White House Social and Behavioral Sciences Team. Retrieved from Behavioral Scientist

Seltenrijch, F. (2024). How can smart transportation systems contribute to the reduction of carbon emissions in Singapore?: A scoping review (Bachelor's thesis, University of Twente).

Sen, D., Ozturk, M., & Vayvay, O. (2016). An overview of big data for growth in SMEs. *Procedia: Social and Behavioral Sciences*, 235, 159–167. DOI: 10.1016/j.sbspro.2016.11.011

Senftleben, M. (2023). Generative AI and author remuneration. *IIC; International Review of Industrial Property and Copyright Law*, 54(10), 1535–1560. DOI: 10.1007/s40319-023-01399-4

Shandler, R. (2019). The age of surveillance capitalism: The fight for a human future at the new frontier of power. In R. Shandler []. Taylor & Francis.]. *Journal of Cyber Policy*, 4(2), 303–304. DOI: 10.1080/23738871.2019.1637914

Shareef, S., & Altan, H. (2021). Sustainability at an urban level: A case study of a neighborhood in Dubai, UAE. *Sustainability (Basel)*, 13(8), 4355. Advance online publication. DOI: 10.3390/su13084355

Sharma, R. (2021). Nanotechnology: An approach for water purification [Review]. *IOP Conference Series. Materials Science and Engineering*, 1116(1), 012007. Advance online publication. DOI: 10.1088/1757-899X/1116/1/012007

Shml, E. M. A., & Aris, S. A. (2022). A review of security concern on Covid-19 tracing application. *Open International Journal of Informatics*, 10(2), 155–171.

Silverman, D. (2020). *Qualitative research* (5th ed.). SAGE Publications.

Simon, H. A. (1947). *Administrative Behavior: A Study of Decision-Making Processes in Administrative Organizations*. Macmillan.

Simon, H. A. (1955). A Behavioral Model of Rational Choice. *The Quarterly Journal of Economics*, 69(1), 99–118. DOI: 10.2307/1884852

Singapore Ministry of Health. (2021). *AI innovation in Singapore healthcare*. https://www.moh.gov.sg/newsroom/transforming-healthcare-through-technology

Singh, G., Kumar, A., & Singh, J. (2023). Data visualization for developing effective performance dashboard with Power BI. *IEEE International Conference on Innovative Computing and Networking,* 234–240. https://doi.org/DOI: 10.1109/ICIDCA56705.2023.10100169

Sipahi, E. B., & Saayi, Z. (2024). The world's first "smart nation" vision: The case of Singapore. *Smart Cities and Regional Development (SCRD). Journal*, 8(1), 41–58.

Sırmaçek, B., Gupta, S., Mallor, F., Azizpour, H., Ban, Y., Eivazi, H., Fang, H., Golzar, F., Leite, I., Melsión, G. I., Smith, K., Nerini, F. F., & Vinuesa, R. (2023). The potential of artificial intelligence for achieving healthy and sustainable societies. In Mazzi, F., & Floridi, L. (Eds.), *The ethics of artificial intelligence for the sustainable development goals* (pp. 65–96). Springer., DOI: 10.1007/978-3-031-21147-8_5

Slovic, P. (1987). Perception of risk. *Science*, 236(4799), 280–285. DOI: 10.1126/science.3563507 PMID: 3563507

Smart Dubai. (2021). *Smart Dubai 2021 strategy*. https://u.ae/en/about-the-uae/strategies-initiatives-and-awards/strategies-plans-and-visions/strategies-plans-and-visions-untill-2021/smart-dubai-2021-strategy

Smart Dubai. (2022). *Smart Dubai happiness index*. https://smartdubai.ae/happiness-index

Smart Nation Singapore. (2023). *Using Data for Urban Planning*.

Social and Behavioral Sciences Team. (2015). *Social and Behavioral Sciences Team annual report 2015*. The White House. Retrieved from https://sbst.gov/download/2015%20SBST%20Annual%20Report.pdfBehavioral

Somit, A., & Peterson, S. A. (2012). Biopolicy: A Critical Linkage. *Biopolicy: The Life. Science & Public Policy*, 10, 3–11. DOI: 10.1108/S2042-9940(2012)0000010002

Sophia, J. J., & Jacob, T. P. (2024). *Beyond Chat-GPT: A BERT-AO approach to custom question answering systems. Multimedia Tools and Applications*. Retrieved from. [arXiv]

Soroka, A., Liu, Y., Han, L., & Haleem, M. S. (2017). Big data driven customer insights for SMEs in redistributed manufacturing. *Procedia CIRP*, 63, 692–697. DOI: 10.1016/j.procir.2017.03.319

Spinoza, B. (1670). *Theological-Political Treatise* (Shirley, S., Trans.). Hackett Publishing. (Original work published 1670)

Spithoven, A., Vanhaverbeke, W., & Roijakkers, N. (2013). Open innovation practices in SMEs and large enterprises. *Small Business Economics*, 41(3), 537–562. DOI: 10.1007/s11187-012-9453-9

Srivastava, N., Hinton, G., Krizhevsky, A., Sutskever, I., & Salakhutdinov, R. (2014). Dropout: A simple way to prevent neural networks from overfitting. *Journal of Machine Learning Research*, 15(1), 1929–1958.

Srivastava, S. K. (2007). Green Supply-Chain Management: A State-of-the-Art Literature Review. *International Journal of Management Reviews*, 9(1), 53–80. DOI: 10.1111/j.1468-2370.2007.00202.x

Stahl, B. C., Brooks, L., Hatzakis, T., Santiago, N., & Wright, D. (2023). Exploring ethics and human rights in artificial intelligence–A Delphi study. *Technological Forecasting and Social Change*, 191, 122502. DOI: 10.1016/j.techfore.2023.122502

Statista (2023). Usage of big data among SMEs in the Netherlands in 2018, by business unit. Available at: https://www.statista.com/statistics/915577/usage-of-big-data-among-smes-in-the-netherlands-by-business-unit/

Stedman, C. (2022). The ultimate guide to big data for businesses. Available at: https://www.techtarget.com/searchdatamanagement/The-ultimate-guide-to-big-data-for-businesses

Stim, R. (2024). *Patent, copyright & trademark: an intellectual property desk reference*. Nolo.

Sunstein, C. R. (2001). *Echo chambers: Bush v. Gore, impeachment, and beyond.* Princeton University Press.

Sunstein, C. R. (2016). The ethics of influence. DOI: 10.1017/CBO9781316493021

Sunstein, C. R., & Thaler, R. H. (2003). Libertarian paternalism is not an oxymoron. SSRN Electronic Journal. DOI: 10.2139/ssrn.405940

Sunstein, C. R., and Thaler, R. H. (2003). Libertarian Paternalism Is Not an Oxymoron.

Sunstein, C. R. (2002). *Risk and reason: Safety, law, and the environment*. Cambridge University Press.

Sunstein, C. R. (2006). The availability heuristic, intuitive cost-benefit analysis, and climate change. *Climatic Change*, 77(1-2), 195–210. DOI: 10.1007/s10584-006-9073-y

Sunstein, C. R. (2013). *Simpler: The future of government*. Simon and Schuster.

Sunstein, C. R. (2014). *Why Nudge?: The Politics of Libertarian Paternalism*. Yale University Press., DOI: 10.12987/yale/9780300197860.001.0001

Sunstein, C. R. (2017). *Behavioral insights and public policy: Lessons from around the world*. Cambridge University Press.

Sunstein, C. R., & Thaler, R. H. (2003, 3). Libertarian Paternalism Is Not an Oxymoron. *The University of Chicago Law Review. University of Chicago. Law School*, 70(4), 1159–1202. DOI: 10.2307/1600573

Supply Chain Council. (2010). http://supply-chain.org/f/down-load/726710733/SCOR10.pdf

Swain, K. K. (2023). Upskilling women through e-learning: A new dimension in soft power of Indian education. *NKT Eduterate Journal, 6*(4), 78–90. Recuperado de https://nkteduterate.in

Syrjälä, M. (2024). How social media uses UX design to keep user engaged: case study: TikTok (Bachelor's thesis).

Tallberg, J., Erman, E., Furendal, M., Geith, J., Klamberg, M., & Lundgren, M. (2023). The global governance of artificial intelligence: Next steps for empirical and normative research. *International Studies Review*, 25(3), viad040. DOI: 10.1093/isr/viad040

Tang, N., Yang, C., Fan, J., Cao, L., Luo, Y., & Halevy, A. (2023). VerifAI: verified generative AI. arXiv preprint arXiv:2307.02796.

Tan, M., & Le, Q. (2019). EfficientNet: Rethinking model scaling for convolutional neural networks. In *Proceedings of the International Conference on Machine Learning (ICML)*, 36(2), 610-618.

Taylor-Sakyi, K. (2016). Big data: Understanding big data. *arXiv preprint arXiv:1601.04602*.

Technology Innovation Institute. (2021). *TII's Quantum Research Center starts building UAE's first quantum computer*. https://www.tii.ae/news/tiis-quantum-research-center-starts-building-uaes-first-quantum-computer

Tekic, Z., & Füller, J. (2023). Managing innovation in the era of AI. *Technology in Society*, 73, 102254. DOI: 10.1016/j.techsoc.2023.102254

Thaler, R. H. (2015). *Misbehaving: The Making of Behavioral Economics*. W. W. Norton and Company.

Thaler, R. H., & Sunstein, C. R. (2008). *Nudge: Improving decisions about health, wealth, and happiness*. Yale University Press.

Tien, E. L., Ali, N. M., Miskon, S., Ahmad, N., & Abdullah, N. S. (2020). Big data analytics adoption model for Malaysian SMEs. In *Emerging Trends in Intelligent Computing and Informatics: Data Science, Intelligent Information Systems and Smart Computing 4* (pp. 45-53). Springer International Publishing. DOI: 10.1007/978-3-030-33582-3_5

Todorov, A., Mandisodza, A. N., Goren, A., & Hall, C. C. (2005). Inferences of competence from faces predict election outcomes. *Science*, 308(5728), 1623–1626. DOI: 10.1126/science.1110589 PMID: 15947187

Topino, E., Gori, A., Jimeno, M. V., Ortega, B., & Cacioppo, M. (2023). The relationship between social media addiction, fear of missing out and family functioning: A structural equation mediation model. *BMC Psychology*, 11(1), 383. DOI: 10.1186/s40359-023-01409-7 PMID: 37941011

Torres-Penalva, A., & Moreno-Izquierdo, L. (2023, October). Innovation and AI: An opportunity for Spanish tourism in the post Covid-19 era. In *International Conference on Tourism and Information and Communication Technologies* (pp. 113-122). Cham: Springer Nature Switzerland.

Trkman, P., McCormack, K., de Oliveira, M. P. V., & Ladeira, M. B. (2010). The Impact of Business Analytics on Supply Chain Performance. *Decision Support Systems*, 49(3), 318–327. DOI: 10.1016/j.dss.2010.03.007

Trujillo, R., Flores, G., & Arias Montaño, J. (2000). Dopamina: Síntesis, liberación y receptores en el Sistema. *BIÓMEDICA*, 1, •••. https://www.revistabiomedica.mx/index.php/revbiomed/article/ view/218

Tversky, A., & Kahneman, D. (1973). Availability: A heuristic for judging frequency and probability. *Cognitive Psychology*, 5(2), 207–232. DOI: 10.1016/0010-0285(73)90033-9

Tversky, A., & Kahneman, D. (1974). Judgment under uncertainty: Heuristics and biases. *Science*, 185(4157), 1124–1131. DOI: 10.1126/science.185.4157.1124 PMID: 17835457

UAE Ministry of Foreign Affairs. (2024, October 28). *Cabinet approves UAE's stance on AI policy to reinforce its global leadership in technology*. https://www.mofa.gov.ae/en/mediahub/news/2024/10/28/28-10-2024-uae-technology

UNICEF. (2005). Strategic Communication for Behaviour and Social Change in South Asia. https://www.unicef.org/cbsc/files/Strategic_Communication_for_Behaviour_and_Social_Change.pdf

United Arab Emirates Government. (2024). Open Labs platform. https://www.uae.gov.ae

United Arab Emirates Government. (n.d.a). D33 Economic Agenda details. UAE Government Publications. https://uae.gov.ae

United Arab Emirates Government. (n.d.b). Dubai AI and Smart City Initiatives. https://u.ae/en/about-the-uae/strategies-initiatives-and-awards

United Arab Emirates Government. (n.d.c). UAE PASS for digital identity verification. https://u.ae/en/about-the-uae/strategies-initiatives-and-awards/uae-pass

United Arab Emirates Government. (n.d.d). UAE Strategy for Artificial Intelligence. https://u.ae/en/about-the-uae/strategies-initiatives-and-awards/strategies-plans-and-visions/government-services-and-digital-transformation/uae-strategy-for-artificial-intelligence

Utama, K. Y. (2023). Monitoring aktivitas penggunaan e-learning dengan business intelligence menggunakan Microsoft Power BI (Studi Kasus). *Jurnal Teknologi dan Pendidikan, 14*(2), 56–72. Recuperado de https://repo.undiksha.ac.id

Van Assche, K., Valentinov, V., & Verschraegen, G. (2022). Adaptive governance: Learning from what organizations do and managing the role they play. *Kybernetes,* 51(5), 1738–1758. DOI: 10.1108/K-11-2020-0759

van Bijsterveld, S., & ten Napel, H. M. (Eds.). (2024). *Culture, Secularization, and Democracy: Lessons from Alexis de Tocqueville*. Taylor & Francis. Abbott, R., & Rothman, E. (2023). Disrupting creativity: Copyright law in the age of generative artificial intelligence. *Fla. L. Rev., 75*, 1141. DOI: 10.4324/9781032641041

Van de Vrande, V., de Jong, J. P. J., Vanhaverbeke, W., & de Rochemont, M. (2009). Open innovation in SMES: Trends, motives and management challenges. *Technovation*, 29(6-7), 423–437. DOI: 10.1016/j.technovation.2008.10.001

van den Brink, M., Dawson, M., & Zglinski, J. (2023). Revisiting the asymmetry thesis: negative and positive integration in the EU. *Journal of European Public Policy*, 1-26.

Vandello, J. A., Goldschmied, N. P., & Richards, D. A. (2007). The appeal of the underdog. *Personality and Social Psychology Bulletin*, 33(12), 1603–1616. DOI: 10.1177/0146167207307488 PMID: 18000097

Velsberg, O., Westergren, U. H., & Jonsson, K. (2020). Exploring smartness in public sector innovation-creating smart public services with the Internet of Things. *European Journal of Information Systems*, 29(4), 350–368. DOI: 10.1080/0960085X.2020.1761272

Villagrasa, Ó. C., & Solé, J. P. (2022). Nudging e inteligencia artificial contra la corrupción en el sector público: Posibilidades y riesgos. *Revista Digital De Derecho Administrativo*, (28), 225–258. DOI: 10.18601/21452946.n28.08

Vinchon, F., Lubart, T., Bartolotta, S., Gironnay, V., Botella, M., Bourgeois-Bougrine, S., Burkhardt, J.-M., Bonnardel, N., Corazza, G. E., Glăveanu, V., Hanchett Hanson, M., Ivcevic, Z., Karwowski, M., Kaufman, J. C., Okada, T., Reiter-Palmon, R., & Gaggioli, A. (2023). Artificial Intelligence & Creativity: A manifesto for collaboration. *The Journal of Creative Behavior*, 57(4), 472–484. DOI: 10.1002/jocb.597

Virtudes, A., Abbara, A., & Sá, J. H. M. (2017). Dubai: A pioneer smart city in the Arabian territory. *IOP Conference Series. Materials Science and Engineering*, 234, 052071. Advance online publication. DOI: 10.1088/1757-899X/245/5/052071

Vosoughi, S., Roy, D., & Aral, S. (2018). The spread of true and false news online. *Science*, 359(6380), 1146–1151. DOI: 10.1126/science.aap9559 PMID: 29590045

Wang S, Wang H. (2020). Big data for small and medium-sized enterprises (SME): a knowledge management model. *Journal of Knowledge Management*, 29;24(4):881-97.

Warren, P. L. (2002). A Systems Approach to Mediation: How to Diagram Family and Commercial Disputes. In P. L. Warren, SSRN Electronic Journal. RELX Group (Netherlands). DOI: 10.2139/ssrn.305150

Wason, P. C. (1960). On the failure to eliminate hypotheses in a conceptual task. *The Quarterly Journal of Experimental Psychology*, 12(3), 129–140. DOI: 10.1080/17470216008416717

Watts, D. J. (1999). *Small Worlds. The Dynamics of Networks between Order and Randomness*. Princeton University Press., DOI: 10.1515/9780691188331

Weinmann, M., Schneider, C., & Brocke, J. (2016). Digital nudging. Business and Amp. *Business & Information Systems Engineering*, 58(6), 433–436. DOI: 10.1007/s12599-016-0453-1

Wendler, F. (2022). Climate change policy in the EU: From the Paris agreement to the European Green Deal. *Framing Climate Change in the EU and US After the Paris Agreement,* 65-117.

Wessels, T., & Jokonya, O. (2022). Factors affecting the Adoption of Big Data as a Service in SMEs. *Procedia Computer Science*, 196, 332–339. DOI: 10.1016/j.procs.2021.12.021

Weston, B. (2022). Infographic: Are You Taking Advantage of Marketing Data? Available at: https://www.score.org/resource/blog-post/infographic-are-you-taking-advantage-marketing-data

West, S. M. (2017). Data Capitalism: Redefining the Logics of Surveillance and Privacy. In S. M. West [). SAGE Publishing.]. *Business & Society*, 58(1), 20–41. DOI: 10.1177/0007650317718185

Wild, P.. (2016). Fingerprint novel spoofed material detection novel material detector in collaboration with support vector machine classifier. In *Proceedings of the European Symposium on Artificial Neural Networks, Computational Intelligence and Machine Learning (ESANN)* (pp. 359-364). Bruges, Belgium.

Wilkinson, T. M. (2013). Nudging and Manipulation. *Political Studies*, 61(2), 341–355. DOI: 10.1111/j.1467-9248.2012.00974.x

Willetts, M., Atkins, A. S., & Stanier, C. (2020). Barriers to SMEs adoption of big data analytics for competitive advantage. In *2020 Fourth International Conference On Intelligent Computing in Data Sciences (ICDS)* (pp. 1-8). IEEE. DOI: 10.1109/ICDS50568.2020.9268687

Wilson, C., & Mergel, I. (2022). Overcoming barriers to digital government: Mapping the strategies of digital champions. *Government Information Quarterly*, 39(2), 101681. DOI: 10.1016/j.giq.2022.101681

Wonglimpiyarat, J., & Yuberk, N. (2005). In support of innovation management and Roger's Innovation Diffusion theory. *Government Information Quarterly*, 22(3), 411–422. DOI: 10.1016/j.giq.2005.05.005

World Economic Forum. (2021). How nudging can boost COVID-19 vaccinations. Retrieved from https://www.weforum.org/agenda/2021/08/nudging-covid-19-vaccination/

World Economic Forum. (2023). Data Unleashed: Empowering Small and Medium Enterprises (SMEs) for Innovation and Success. Available online at: https://www3.weforum.org/docs/WEF_Data_Unleashed_Empowering_Small_and_Medium_Enterprises_(SMEs)_for_Innovation_and_Success_2023.pdf

World Health Organization. (2017). Communicating Risk in Public Health Emergencies: A WHO Guideline for Emergency Risk Communication (ERC) Policy and Practice. https://www.who.int/publications/i/item/9789241550208

Wu, C. (2003). Lean manufacturing: A perspective of lean suppliers. *International Journal of Operations & Production Management*, 23(11), 1349–1376. DOI: 10.1108/01443570310501880

Xu, S., Fu, X., Cao, J., Liu, B., & Wang, Z. (2020). Survey on user location prediction based on geo-social networking data. *World Wide Web (Bussum)*, 23(3), 1621–1664. DOI: 10.1007/s11280-019-00777-8

Yang, Z. (2023). How China takes extreme measures to keep teens off TikTok. MIT Technology Review. https://www.technologyreview.com/2023/03/08/1069527/china-TikTokdouyin-teens-privacy/

Yarger, L., Payton, F. C., & Neupane, B. (2019). Algorithmic equity in the hiring of underrepresented IT job candidates. In L. Yarger, F. C. Payton, & B. Neupane []. Emerald Publishing.]. *Online Information Review*, 44(2), 383–395. DOI: 10.1108/OIR-10-2018-0334

Yas, N., Elyat, M. N. I., Saeed, M., Shwedeh, F., & Lootah, S. (2024). The Impact of Intellectual Property Rights and the Work Environment on Information Security in the United Arab Emirates. *Kurdish Studies*, 12(1), 3931–3948.

Yeung, K. (2016). 'hypernudge': Big data as a mode of regulation by design. Information, Communication andAmp. *Information Communication and Society*, 20(1), 118–136. DOI: 10.1080/1369118X.2016.1186713

Yiğitcanlar, T., Desouza, K. C., Butler, L., & Roozkhosh, F. (2020a). AI in urban governance: Dubai's AI-driven transformation in urban planning. *Journal of Urban Technology*, 27(2), 131–150.

Yiğitcanlar, T., Desouza, K. C., Butler, L., & Roozkhosh, F. (2020b). Contributions and risks of artificial intelligence (AI) in building smarter cities: Insights from a systematic review of the literature. *Energies*, 13(6), 1473. Advance online publication. DOI: 10.3390/en13061473

Yin, C., Zhang, X., Chen, H., Wang, J., Cooper, D., & David, B. (2015). A literature survey on smart cities. *Science China. Information Sciences*, 58(10), 1–18. DOI: 10.1007/s11432-015-5397-4

York, C. (2013). Overloaded by the news: Effects of news exposure and enjoyment on reporting information overload. *Communication Research Reports*, 30(4), 282–292. DOI: 10.1080/08824096.2013.836628

Yuan, B. Z., & Sun, J. (2020). Bibliometric analysis of research on the maize based on top papers during 2009-2019. *COLLNET Journal of Scientometrics and Information Management*, 14(1), 75–92. DOI: 10.1080/09737766.2020.1787110

Zahid, I. A., Joudar, S. S., & Alzubaidi, L. (2024). Unmasking large language models by means of OpenAI GPT-4 and Google AI: A deep instruction-based analysis. *Intelligent Systems with Applications*, 23, 200431. Advance online publication. DOI: 10.1016/j.iswa.2024.200431

Zakir, M. H., & Ali, S. (2023). CROSS-BORDER TRADEMARK INFRINGEMENT IN THE DIGITAL AGE: JURISDICTIONAL CHALLENGES AND HARMONIZATION EFFORTS. *PAKISTAN ISLAMICUS (An International Journal of Islamic & Social Sciences), 3*(2), 51-69.

Zeng, J., & Kaye, D. B. (2022). From content moderation to visibility moderation: A case study of platform governance on TikTok. *Policy and Internet*, 14(1), 79–95. Advance online publication. DOI: 10.1002/poi3.287

Zhang, J. (2023). *Graph-toolformer: To empower LLMs with graph reasoning ability via prompt dataset augmented by ChatGPT. arXiv Preprint*. Retrieved from. [arXiv]

Zhao, H., & Wagner, C. (2022). How TikTok leads users to flow experience: Investigating the effects of technology affordances with user experience level and vídeo length as moderators. Internet Research, ahead-ofprint(ahead-of-print). DOI: 10.1108/INTR-08-2021-0595

Zhao, R., Liu, Y., Zhang, N., & Huang, T. (2017). An optimization model for green supply chain management by using a big data analytic approach. *Journal of Cleaner Production*, 142, 1085–1097. DOI: 10.1016/j.jclepro.2016.03.006

Zhao, Z. (2021). *Analysis on the "Douyin (TikTok) Mania"*. Phenomenon Based on Recommendation Algorithms., DOI: 10.1051/e3sconf/202123503029

Zhong, R. Y., Huang, G. Q., Lan, S., Dai, Q. Y., Chen, X., & Zhang, T. (2015). A big data approach for logistics trajectory discovery from RFID-enabled production data. *International Journal of Production Economics*, 165, 260–272. DOI: 10.1016/j.ijpe.2015.02.014

Zhong, R. Y., Lan, S., Xu, C., Dai, Q., & Huang, G. Q. (2016). Visualization of RFID-enabled shopfloor logistics Big Data in Cloud Manufacturing. *International Journal of Advanced Manufacturing Technology*, 84(1–4), 5–16. DOI: 10.1007/s00170-015-7702-1

Zimmermann, V. (2016). SMEs and digitalization: The current position, recent developments and challenges. *KfW research.* No. 138.

Zuboff, S. (2023). The age of surveillance capitalism. Social theory re-wired.

Zuboff, S. (2015). Big other: Surveillance capitalism and the prospects of an information civilization. *Journal of Information Technology*, 30(1), 75–89. DOI: 10.1057/jit.2015.5

Zuboff, S. (2023). The age of surveillance capitalism. In *Social theory re-wired* (pp. 203–213). Routledge. DOI: 10.4324/9781003320609-27

Zuboff, S., & Maxmin, J. (2004). *The support economy: why corporations are failing individuals, and the next episode of capitalism*. Penguin.

About the Contributors

Jose Ramon Saura, Vice-Dean of Research, Internationalization and Prof. Partnership in the Faculty of Business Economics (FCEE) at Rey Juan Carlos University, is an Associated Professor (Tenured) of Data Analytics and Digital Marketing in the Business Economics Department at Rey Juan Carlos University (URJC), Madrid (Spain). Earlier in his career, he held positions and provided consultancy services to several prominent companies, including Google, L'Oréal, Deloitte, Telefónica, and MRM//McCann, among others. He obtained his international Ph.D. in Digital Marketing from URJC, conducting research at both London South Bank University (LSBU) and RCC at Harvard University. He has taught and undertaken research stays at over 28 universities worldwide. Notable affiliations include the Leiden Institute of Advanced Computer Science and the Institute of Public Administration at the University of Leiden, Harvard University, or the School of Economics and Management at the University of Porto. Jose Ramon Saura has served as a research evaluator for national funding and projects on behalf of the following institutions: Government of Italy, Ministry of University and Research (Rome, Italy); Government of Poland, National Science Center of Poland (Warsaw, Poland); National Research Council of the Netherlands, Dutch Research Council (The Hague, The Netherlands); Technology Agency of the Czech Republic (Prague, Czech Republic) and the Linz Institute of Technology (Linz, Austria). His research has primarily centered on the theoretical and practical implications of various dimensions of user-generated data and content. He has emphasized three pivotal research methodologies applied to business and marketing: data mining and knowledge discovery. Currently, his research interests have evolved to encompass data-driven decision-making, online privacy, online behavior and surveillance capitalism. His contributions have been published in premier international journals in the fields of business, management, economics, marketing, and information sciences, such as: Journal of Innovation and Knowledge, International Journal of Production Economics, Government Information Quarterly, Industrial Marketing Management,

Technovation, International Journal of Information Management, Technological Forecasting and Social Change, Journal of Business Research, International Journal of Entrepreneurial Behaviour & Research, Inter. Entrepreneurship and Management or the Journal Review of Managerial Sciences, among others.

* * *

Óscar Aguado Tevar is Managing Director of Nebrija University, a Mining Engineer, and holds a PhD from UPM. Additionally, he holds a degree in Business Administration and Management from HEC-Paris and earned dual master's degrees in Energy Economics from the French Institute of Petroleum and the University of Oklahoma. Along with his role in the management of Nebrija, he combines his teaching duties at Nebrija with the responsibility for the Economics module in the Master's in Oil & Gas (ETSIME-UPM). He has taught finance courses at CUNEF and supervised numerous Master's Theses. In his management career, he has held various positions at Nebrija, CUNEF, and UPM, and has participated in accreditation panels such as ABET and EFMD/ENQHEEI. Additionally, he has extensive professional experience in the banking sector, having worked for 16 years at BBVA: 9 years in Asset Management Strategy and Business Development, and 7 years in wholesale banking in the energy sector.

Daniel Corral de la Mata is a PhD in Business Administration and Management from Rey Juan Carlos University (URJC), with cum laude distinction. He has over 30 years of experience in the financial sector, holding positions in Commercial Management both at the network and regional levels. He has also held various leadership roles in Central Services departments, including "Marketing," "Alternative Channels," "Payment Methods," "Management Control and Business Development," "Internet and Online Banking," and "Asset Management." He is a professor at Rey Juan Carlos University (URJC) and has published articles in JCR and Scopus-indexed journals. He is also a member of the research team MARPRISO and part of the consolidated teaching innovation group focused on data intelligence, information systems, and emerging trends.

Felipe Debasa Navalpotro is Professor of Contemporary History and Current World Studies at Rey Juan Carlos University. Director of the official Master's program on the European Union and China. His research focuses on the intersection of technology, the Fourth Industrial Revolution, and transhumanism. Recognized for his contributions to digital humanities, he specializes in applying advanced methodologies, including artificial intelligence, to the study of history, law, and social sciences.

Maria Amparo Diaz-Llairo has over 25 years of work experience in the private sector, including managerial positions as Director of Human Resources and Talent Management in multinational companies such as Citigroup. International Keynote Speaker: talent management, recruitment, and technology expert. More than 500 courses, seminars, congresses, and in-company training projects for more than 500 companies in Europe, USA, Latin America, the Middle East and Asia. CEO at Global Human Capital Group (GHCG), an International HR Consulting firm specializing in International recruitment using AI. Writer of 5 Books about HR, Talent Management, Entrepreneurship, and Leadership.

Luis Díaz-Marcos is a professional with an outstanding career in academia and university management, he is currently the General Director of Nebrija University and previously served as Vice-Rector for Academic Affairs and Faculty, as well as a professor in the Business Department, where he led the optimization of the faculty and academic structure. He previously worked at CUNEF for 14 years, where he was the Academic Director of Postgraduate Studies, Academic Director, and a professor of Ethics and Corporate Governance. He also served as the CEO of the School of Industrial Organization (EOI) and was a professor at Antonio de Nebrija University for 14 years, holding various executive roles. In the banking sector, Díaz Marcos has experience as a Corporate Manager at Banco Santander and as an analyst at the Bank of Spain. His academic background includes a PhD in Business Sciences with a specialization in International Business Management from Antonio de Nebrija University, as well as research proficiency in Applied Economics with a Diploma of Advanced Studies in Economic Growth and Sustainable Development from UNED, and a Diploma in Advanced University Management from Nebrija University. He holds an MBA in Business Administration from the University of Houston and a Law degree from the Complutense University of Madrid. He has also participated in training programs at the David Rockefeller Center for Latin American Studies at Harvard University.

María García de Blanes Sebastián is a business consultant with 20+years of experience, I have worked in the areas of Marketing, Sales, Operations and Business Intelligence across sectors and companies (Orange, Zed Worldwide, Telvent among others). Performing functions for business support, including, business plans, marketing plans, market studies, commercial plans and payables for accounting and point of sale; Strategic campaigns, product launches, development of marketing solutions Balancing Business and Marketing consulting along with a professor adjunct position in varied universities that are offering several degrees towards bachelor's and master's degree, in subjects relative to e-commerce; digital customer management, marketing, business environment and Lean Management, among others. Tutoring for Projects in Baccalaureate and for master's Thesis in social media, display advertising, SEO, SEM, web analytics and metrics, among others. Master in Digital Marketing from the UOC (2019), Management Development Program from IESE (2012), Master in Marketing Management and Commercial Management from ESIC (2007), Graduate from the Complutense University (1999) and PhD from the Rey Juan Carlos University (2023).

Younes Karrouk works as an Associate Professor. He completed his Ph.D at Rovira i Virgili University, Spain.MD in Accounting, Control and Audit at University of Lille, France. He has 7 years experience of teaching and research. Currently, he guides MD and BE research scholars. He has authored many of book chapters and he has published research papers .His interested areas of research are Economic intelligence, Artificial Intelligence, Digital Marketing and Data quality.

Christian Kaunert is a Professor of International Security at Dublin City University, Ireland. He is also Professor of Policing and Security and Director of the International Centre for Policing and Security at the University of South Wales. Previously, he served as an Academic Director and Professor at the Institute for European Studies, Vrije Universiteit Brussel, a Professor of International Politics, Head of Discipline in Politics, and the Director of the European Institute for Security and Justice, a Jean Monnet Centre for Excellence, at the University of Dundee. He was awarded a large Horizon 2020 research grant on Terrorist Radicalisation processes – Mindb4Act, a large Horizon Europe Marie Curie Doctoral Network EUGLOCTER, and a Jean Monnet Network EUCTER, alongside several Jean Monnet Chairs, Centres, Modules, and TT.

Sumana Kundu received her B.E. and M.Tech degree in Computer Science & Engineering in the years of 2008 and 2010. She worked as a Research Scholar (Full Time) at Computer Science & Engineering department of National Institute of Technology, Durgapur and obtained her PhD degree in the year of 2018. Dr. Sumana Kundu was an Assistant Professor at Siliguri Institute of Technology, Techno India Group. Thereafter she was an Associate Professor and Head of the Department at Haldia Institute of Technology. Presently she is an Associate Professor at Computer Science & Engineering department of Dr. B. C. Roy Engineering College, Durgapur. Her Research area of interest includes Pattern Recognition, Machine Learning, Data Security using Steganography.

Aissa Mosbah is an assistant professor of entrepreneurship and the Department of Marketing and Entrepreneurship, Dhofar University, Oman. He obtained a master's degree in international business and a PhD in Management from two different government universities in Malaysian. His PhD research dealt with the immigrant entrepreneurship phenomenon. While he is an expert in both qualitative and quantitative research, his research areas include entrepreneurship, family business, firm internationalization, as well as organizational behavior. He published numerous research papers in reputed international journals such as the Personnel Review, International Journal of Entrepreneurship and Small Business, International Journal of Business and Globalisation, Journal of Hospitality & Tourism Education, Global Business Review, and Sage open. He is currently working on a government-funded research grant that seeks to understand the internationalization of family firms in Saudi Arabia.

Kamalendu Pal is associated with the Department of Computer Science, School of Science and Technology at City, University of London. He has a diverse academic background, having received a BSc (Hons) degree in Physics from Calcutta University, India, followed by a Postgraduate Diploma in Computer Science from Pune, India. He has also worked as a research assistant for the government of India's two research and development organizations under the Council of Scientific and Industrial Research (CSIR). Later, Kamalendu graduated with his MSc in Software Systems Technology from the University of Sheffield, a Postgraduate Diploma in Artificial Intelligence from Kingston University, an MPhil in Computer Science from University College London, an MBA from the University of Hull, and a diploma in Higher Education teaching practice from City, University of London, United Kingdom. Kamalendu is an accomplished researcher, having published over a hundred-twenty international research articles (including book chapters) in the scientific community. His research papers have been published in prestigious journals such as the ACM SIGMIS Database, Expert Systems with Applications, Decision Support Systems, and international conferences. His research interests include various fields of computer science - such as knowledge-based systems, decision support systems, teaching and learning practices, blockchain technology, software engineering, service-oriented computing, sensor network simulation, and supply chain management. Kamalendu is also on the editorial board of an international computer science journal. He is a member of the British Computer Society, the Institution of Engineering and Technology, and the IEEE Computer Society.

Anjali Raghav is a legal professional and accomplished academic, currently a Research Scholar at the Sharda School of Law, Sharda University, Greater Noida, India. With a solid educational foundation, she holds a Master in Law from Sharda School of Law, where she cultivated her expertise in Criminal Law, Intellectual Property Rights, Artificial Intelligence, Machine Learning, Blockchain Technology, Sustainable Energy, etc. Her three years of experience as a criminal practicing lawyer have equipped her with practical legal insights that she seamlessly integrates into her academic and editorial endeavors. She has a robust portfolio of publications in esteemed journals and books, reflecting her dedication to contributing to the body of knowledge in her fields of interest. Her research has been recognized on various platforms, as evidenced by her participation in national and international conferences, seminars, webinars, and symposiums. Also, in her academic and research pursuits, Anjali is a skilled editor, having successfully overseen the editorial process of several publications.

Bhupinder Singh is working as Professor at Sharda University, India. Also, Honorary Professor in University of South Wales UK and Santo Tomas University Tunja, Colombia. His areas of publications as Smart Healthcare, Medicines, fuzzy logics, artificial intelligence, robotics, machine learning, deep learning, federated learning, IoT, PV Glasses, metaverse and many more. He has 3 books, 139 paper publications, 163 paper presentations in international/national conferences and seminars, participated in more than 40 workshops/FDP's/QIP's, 25 courses from international universities of repute, organized more than 59 events with international and national academicians and industry people's, editor-in-chief and co-editor in journals, developed new courses. He has given talks at international universities, resource person in international conferences such as in Nanyang Technological University Singapore, Tashkent State University of Law Uzbekistan; KIMEP University Kazakhstan, All'ah meh Tabatabi University Iran, the Iranian Association of International Criminal law, Iran and Hague Center for International Law and Investment, The Netherlands, Northumbria University Newcastle UK.

Index

A

B

C

D

F

G

H

I

K

L

N

P

S

T

U

www.ingramcontent.com/pod-product-compliance
Lightning Source LLC
LaVergne TN
LVHW080342011026
849161LV00009B/2158
* 9 7 9 8 3 6 9 3 6 9 4 5 6 *